By Me, William Shakespeare

By Me, William Shakespeare

by

Robert Payne

EVEREST HOUSE

Publishers   New York

For the Principal Players:

Analita Alexander
Patricia Ellsworth
Anne Fremantle
Jillian Lindig
John Michalski
Katherine Rao
Alex Sokoloff

Contents

By me William Shakspeare

Introduction

ON THE LAST PAGE OF HIS WILL, written shortly before his death, Shakespeare wrote the clearest of all the signatures that have come down to us. In an astonishingly firm hand he wrote: "By me William Shakespeare," employing his pen vigorously until just before the end, when, writing the last syllable of his name, his strength begins to fail, the pen quivers, and the letters melt and fuse into one another. It was as though every ounce of his energy had been directed toward composing the words precisely and elegantly, and suddenly, when he had almost completed it, there was a failure of nervous energy, and he found himself incapable of doing it properly. One imagines an enormous willpower which collapsed in the midst of writing his name for the last time.

What is chiefly moving about the document is not the failure but the achievement. The letters are beautifully formed and possess great dignity. It is not the secretary hand favored by the officials and educated men of his time, but an older English script akin to modern German with a Gothic *B* and *S* and a decorative *W*, where a dot, which may be the dot over the first *i* of William, is enclosed within the final loop of the *W*. This *W* has a long descender and gives an effect of grace and a certain imperiousness. The *B* is as monumental as a Chinese ideogram and is well-balanced by the *y* with a sweeping tail. Everything about the handwriting suggests refinement and studied ease, as of a man who took care with his handwriting and enjoyed his skill in forming letters, until we come to the letter *k*, where there occurs the first sign of disintegration. Thereafter there is little more than a scratchy blur, although he is still attempting with a failing hand to form the remaining letters of his name.

There are some other things which should be noted in this signature. Quite evidently Shakespeare had intended to write the four words clearly and neatly. He maintained a steady rhythm throughout the writing of the first three words. The rhythm is broken when he comes to "Shakespeare," for the *S*, although grandly conceived in the Gothic manner, lacks the clear definition of the *W*: there is already a hint of the catastrophe to come. Usually when a man's handwriting weakens, it tends to droop, to go downhill. Shakespeare's handwriting moves upward as he still doggedly attempts to form the name which is the most important part of his signature.

One can make too much of handwriting, but these four words have a special significance. They are the only four words written by him in his most careful handwriting that have survived. There are five other authentic signatures, and all of them have been written quickly, carelessly, and impatiently; there are two in the will, one on a deposition, another on a conveyance, and still another on a mortgage. In addition, there are the pages of his handwriting in the uncompleted play *Sir Thomas More*, which he wrote in collaboration with at least four other playwrights, but these pages were written hurriedly, with no concern for penmanship, as the inspiration took hold of him. It is only on the last page of the will that we see him taking his own time to write legibly, knowing that his words will be examined by those who come after him.

Today the will lies in a glass case in the museum of the Public Record Office in Chancery Lane, London. It is crumpled with age and bears the marks of many folds and many stains. It is one of the most venerated documents in England, and people come to it to see if they can find, amid the tangle of a law clerk's handwriting streaming across the whole page, the famous bequest of the second-best bed. In the dimly lit room, which looks as though it was once a dungeon, the words stand out, "By me William Shakespeare," dark and luminous, possessing a hallucinatory quality. Suddenly we feel that we are in his presence.

What do they tell us about Shakespeare? They tell us, I believe, of his sense of style, his fortitude, his imperiousness and authority. It is the handwriting of a man completely in charge of whatever he undertakes, who gives orders and expects them to be obeyed. In his own time he was known as "gentle Shakespeare," but there is nothing gentle in the handwriting. Gentle he may have been among his friends, but I suspect that his gentleness concealed an angelic ruthlessness. He was a man without diffidence who asserted himself whenever it suited him. I detect a certain fierceness and inner violence, a man capable of lashing out in fury as ghosts and enemies, vivid and alert even when he was dying. He possessed the Tudor ferocity, which tends to have been forgotten by scholars, and he would have looked at a hanging, disemboweling, and quartering at Tyburn without flinching.

He towers over English literature, so mountainous and craggy that we are all in awe of him, as he may have been in awe of his own gifts. In New York's Central Park his statue fittingly confronts the statue of Columbus: they were both discoverers of new worlds. We are still exploring those worlds and he is therefore our contemporary. Since he is the friendliest of guides, there are some advantages in knowing the living man.

Shakespeare reveals himself continually. Like Montaigne, he is too proud to play with subterfuges; and while every character in every play is a disguise worn by him, the disguise is palpably transparent. The plays are the records of his spiritual adventures written in a manner wonderfully suited to display the spirit's trajectories, the landscapes of his dreams, abysses and avalanches and lonely journeys into unknown territories. He is surefooted and always knows when to step back at the cliff's edge.

We know the outward man almost as well as we know any man of the Elizabethan age. The Droeshout portrait and the Stratford bust between them present a clear image of him. One might wish that Hilliard had painted him in one of those bright enameled miniatures or that Holbein had lived long enough to include him in his portraits of Tudor worthies. The auburn hair, the hazel eyes, the heavy lids, the flush of excitement on the cheeks, the moustache trimmed cunningly, the huge domed forehead bald as an apple—we know him well and would recognize him if he entered the room. He has the soaring forehead of a man who thinks too much for his own comfort, but the sensual nose and chin show that he had many remedies against the oppressive weight of thought. We have only to look at the Droeshout portrait to know that he has fine manners and is fastidious to a fault. He is a natural aristocrat fully aware of his responsibilities. He met kings and queens, and was at ease with them, and he was on terms of intimacy with many members of the nobility and felt equal to them. Knowing that he was himself descended from ancient Saxon kings, he felt no need to humble himself before anyone.

We know a good deal about his daily habits, his likes and dislikes, his hatreds, his loves, and his fears. We know, for example, that he talked quickly with a Warwickshire accent which he retained throughout his life, that he suffered from insomnia, that in his later years he suffered from sciatica. We know that he detested the dogs that often crowded round an Elizabethan table. He had never been a soldier; he knew no more about seafaring than a man might learn by sailing in a ship down the Thames to Gravesend. He knew brawls, and his excitement is present whenever he describes them. He liked bowling, which is a suitable pastime for a meditative man who enjoys having company around him, and detested fishing, which is a solitary occupation. He was happily married to Anne Hathaway, who bore his children; we can be certain that if the marriage had been unhappy some gossipmonger would have recorded that she was a shrew. He adored his two daughters; and his grief over the death of his only son haunted him through all the remaining years of his life. He was obsessively afraid of death by drowning, and some of his greatest poetry is an attempt to exorcise his fear. He attended church regularly, but in his works there is scarcely a trace anywhere of Christian sentiment. He believed in the fall of the sparrow. He believed even more strongly in the need to explore the boundaries of the human spirit, and to do this single-handedly, nakedly, at whatever cost to his reason and his spiritual health. He would have agreed with Dostoyevsky, who wrote: "Man is a mystery. This mystery must be solved, and even if you pass your entire life solving it, do not say you have wasted your time. I occupy myself with this mystery, because I want to be a man."

He was not well read, and it is likely that there were very few books in his library; Holinshed's *Chronicles of England* and North's *Plutarch* between them provided him with the subject matter for about a third of his plays. For the rest he garnered among Italian novellas, the works of Chaucer, Belleforest, and Bandello, the plots of many of his comedies. He must have possessed Holinshed and North, for he uses them frequently, but he could have picked up what he wanted for the other plays by browsing in the bookshops in St. Paul's churchyard or in the library of the Earl of Southampton. To Ben Jonson's regret he was not a learned man; nor did he hold learned men in honor, for in his plays he makes mock of them.

Above all he was a producer, stage manager, and actor. To a quite extraordinary degree he possessed a sense of the stage. He knew stage space, entrances and exits, the way to achieve dramatic focus, confrontation following swiftly on confrontation in order to maintain theatrical excitement. There are few stage directions; the poetry includes them. The stage, for him, was like a lake, mirroring whatever colors the playwright poured into it, changing its shape according to his fancy, so fluid that he should shape it at will and so solid that it took on the appearance of woodlands, rocks, palaces, and battlements.

Everything in the plays suggests that he was a player who enjoyed acting and was at ease on the boards. We think of him as a poet and dramatist first and an actor second, but it is much more likely that he spent more time acting than he ever spent writing at his desk. He acted often and played many roles, not only the Ghost in *Hamlet*.

The miracle is that he could be all the things he was—poet, playwright, actor, stage manager, producer, landowner, buyer of houses, occasional moneylender, friend of noblemen, family man, and all these simultaneously, and for so short a time. He died at fifty-two, with a quarter of a century of work still in front of him. *The Tempest* was not his farewell to the stage, for he wrote at least two plays subsequently.

I have written this book because I wanted to know what manner of man he was. It was necessary to stretch him, to shake him out, to break him up and then put the pieces together again in order to see him afresh. I found him more violent and more authoritarian than I had expected, and closer to intrigues and conspiracies than I had thought possible. I have relied on what Coleridge, Blake, and Keats said of Shakespeare more often than I have relied on academic scholars. I have attempted to seek him out in his own works rather than in the footnotes provided by his innumerable editors. I have paid special attention to the Shoreditch years, which are usually glossed over, although he spent more than half of his working life in Shoreditch. *The Two Noble Kinsmen* and *Edward III* are now commonly accepted into the canon, and I believe with Professor E. B. Everitt that he wrote *War Hath Made All Friends* and have discussed the play at some length. I wanted to see him in the flesh and to walk by his side through the streets of Stratford and London, and so there is a good deal about his landlord, Christopher Mount-joy, and about Bankside, and the Theatre and the Curtain, the two theatres where most of his early plays were performed. I have sometimes tried to catch him unawares as he built the mythologies that still haunt us.

Ben Jonson spoke of his "rage and influence," and those three words haunted me through the writing of the book. Violent, imperious, wonderfully learned in the ways of the world and determined to penetrate the heavenly mysteries, he comes to us like a blaze of pure intellectual energy and human sympathy, and we can still warm ourselves beside his fire.

Shakespeare of Stratford

The Elms
of Stratford

T HE SMALL MARKET TOWN of Stratford-upon-Avon in Warwickshire had in Shakespeare's time a population of 2,000, which is less than the population of a New York City block. It is scarcely more than a village, a place where everyone knew one another, where few secrets could be kept, and where the rich lived next door to the poor, and there was much envy and bickering. Incendiaries from among the poor townspeople set an unusually large number of fires. The town consisted of six streets, three parallel to the river, three crossing them, with names like Swine Street, Sheep Street, Tinker's Lane, and Chapel Lane. Moderately prosperous, with many small industries, it included a small enclave of Welsh-speaking citizens with names like Fluellen, Thomas, Williams, Powell, Griffin, and Welch, for Wales was not far away. These Welshmen had once been hired as common laborers and they were still among the poorest members of the community. Shakespeare knew some Welsh, for he included a Welsh greeting in *The Merry Wives of Windsor*.

The river Avon flows past the town; so gentle a river that it sometimes seems to be a lake. It is not one of England's great rivers; it has no pride. Very quiet, very feminine, it meanders through a peaceful countryside of woodlands, orchards, farms, small villages, stately mansions, and large estates, with castles perched on its banks. In Shakespeare's time fruit and vegetables came up to Stratford by boat from the rich Vale of Evesham, but the locks that permitted their passage have long ago decayed. Cows stand knee-deep in the water meadows, and the fat grasses on the riverbank have the luminous green that can only be seen in the English midlands.

The river shaped the town and was reason for its existence. From the river the town receives its character, which is somnolent, dreamy, lost in its ancient past. It is a venerable past, going back at least to A.D. 691, when King Ethelred granted to the Bishop of Worcester the right to build a monastery on the site now occupied by the Church of the Holy Trinity. The town is mentioned in Domesday Book, and at some time in the thirteenth century it began to be ruled by the Gild of the Holy Cross, which only meant that it continued to be ruled by the ecclesiastical authorities. When Henry VIII assumed all the powers previously in the possession of the Church, Stratford began to be ruled by its own citizens, the ruling body being known as a Corporation. They still met in the Gild House. Shakespeare's father became a member of the Corporation and ultimately he was elected bailiff, or mayor, of Stratford.

Stratford produced more than its fair share of notables, for this obscure little town gave England an Archbishop of Canterbury, two Lord Chancellors, and a Lord Mayor of London. Ambitions flourished amid a dreaming landscape. The citizens were well schooled and worked hard, and though most of them were content to remain there, a surprisingly large number of them made their way to London.

In the Tudor age, as in the Middle Ages, every town had its full complement of skills. There was no specialization in the sense that one town would manufacture plows while another would manufacture beer, and each town would exchange its products. In Stratford there was beer making by maltsters, plows were made in a foundry or a smithy, ropes in a ropery, cloth on looms, dyeing at the dye works, leather at the tannery, wool stapling in the wool shop, and so on. The town was nearly self-sufficient; and to save money a man living in one of those half-timbered, thatch-roofed houses might grow his own vegetables, make his own rope, keep his own kiln house for brewing and his own yeling house for cooling the beer, shoe his own horses, salt his own meat, build his own cabinets with his own carpentry tools, and think nothing of it. Men practiced many trades, and so we find July Shaw, a friend of the Shake-speares, practicing the trade of maltster and wool merchant, and John Shakespeare, the father of William, was a glover and a wool merchant; throughout Stratford were men practicing two or three trades.

They were an industrious people who kept themselves busy from morning to night. In the town the Protestants were in the saddle, while the neighboring villages were largely Catholic. The Protes-tants had few pleasures. There were sumptuary laws dictating what people should wear and what they should eat; card playing was forbidden; profanity was punished with a fine; and there were fines for allowing animals to stray and for leaving dogs unmuzzled and for leaving piles of rubbish outside the house. John Shakespeare was ordered to pay one shilling—a considerable sum of money in those days—for leaving a *sterquinarium*, or muckheap, outside his house. There were fines for not attending church and for drunken-ness. The sumptuary laws bred informers, who were usually rewarded with part of the fines. In this way lifelong enmities were created and the gossipmongers were encouraged to invent more gossip.

On the whole, life in Stratford was austere: not in the New England way, but in the characteristic Warwickshire way, where cheerfulness was allowed to break in. On Sundays the parishioners were warned against sinning and permitted to contemplate the horrors of Doomsday, but for the rest of the week Doomsday was conveniently forgotten. The Stratfordians were realists: they had no illusions about the impermanence of life and about the need to placate the Creator. The Catholics were not prepared to go to war against the Protestants, and the Protestants were holding their breath, waiting for Queen Mary to die. Conspiracies abounded: the decision to put Elizabeth on the throne put an end to the burning of Protestants. Under Elizabeth the Catholics went to the stake.

While the Protestants derived satisfaction from the fact that Elizabeth was a Protestant queen determined to uphold the sovereignty of England against the Pope and Philip II of Spain, who from being King of England became England's most implacable enemy, the religious life of Stratford was very little altered. The Mass was no longer celebrated in the Church of the Holy Trinity, the communion plate was melted down, and gaudy vestments were sold to become bedcovers and wall hangings, but a deep religious feeling, touched with memories of centuries of Catholic domination, remained. We would be mistaking the temper of the times if we thought that religion played a small role in daily life. The people were God-fearing, and they feared God only a little less than they feared Elizabeth, His earthly representative.

Stratford lay outside the main currents of English thought and enterprise. It was sequestered and self-contained, and news from London arrived slowly by way of Warwick, the capital of the county, where many of the crucial decisions affecting the town were made. Warwick had its castle and its power. In Stratford the only large building was the Church of the Holy Trinity, which stood on the river's edge south of the town and therefore a little remote from it. Ecclesiastical power over the people of Stratford was exercised by the Bishop of Worcester from his throne in Worcester Cathedral, far away and in another county.

When we walk through Stratford today, observing that the street plan has changed little over the centuries and that black-and-white-timbered Elizabethan houses can still be seen in the High Street, we are sometimes under the illusion that little has changed since Shakespeare's day. There was, however, one enormous difference. In Shakespeare's day there were elm trees everywhere. There were elms lining the streets, in gardens, and on both sides of the long avenue leading to the church. In 1582 someone counted the elms and found more than a thousand. In summer a man might walk from one end of Stratford to the other in deep shade and feel himself still in the Forest of Arden. Those stately and noble trees penetrated men's characters, and they were loud with birdsong. Nearer the river the elms gave place to weeping willows, light green and feathery, trembling with every shift of the wind. So we may imagine a man walking through Stratford seeing almost nothing but trees and the patterns of branches on plastered walls. Most of the houses were rather lower and smaller than the ones we see now, and the town therefore had something of the appearance of cottages set in the woodlands.

The winter rains transformed the town into a lake, and when the waters receded, quagmires remained. Cartwheels spun in the mud, and a passerby would find himself soaked with mud while trying to lift up a horse that had fallen to its knees. There was no drainage system, no sewage system, no paved roads. In winter, too, came the heavy drenching fogs which hung on the elm trees: at such times the town looked ghostly. Then the snows came and Stratford might be cut off from the rest of England for a week. In winter men kept close to their homes, huddled over their wood fires, the elm smoke burning their eyes.

Spring was the best season, but it was treacherous. A few days of warm, cloudless skies would bring out the flowers in the fields, and soon a sharp frost would wither them on their stems. The elms would begin to put on their leaves: "the bare ruin'd choirs where late the sweet birds sang" would turn green again, and then a snowstorm would cripple them and the branches would be bare again. Then toward the end of March and the beginning of April there would come a day when all the flowers came alive and the world was carpeted with daffodils, violets, primroses, celandines, marigolds, strawberry-leaved cinquefoil, and anemones, and the elms were misty blue and putting forth small purple tufts, and the birds sang all day long. Then came the long days of summer and the heat of July when men and animals took comfort in the shade.

Stratford was a country town, and the flowers grew wild in the gardens. There were plowed fields within the town limits. Only on market days, when the villagers streamed in from miles around, did it have the appearance of being crowded. On such days it knew its importance, its reticence vanished, it was swollen to twice its size, and could afford to trumpet its claim to be one of the leading towns of England. Then the villagers streamed away in their horse carts and there was only the small lost town listening to the wind in the elm trees and the quiet river.

In this town William Shakespeare was born and spent his youth, being the son of John Shakespeare, a glover, and Mary Arden, from the nearby village of Wilmcote, who brought her husband a small dowry. John Shakespeare owned a shop on Henley Street and another house on Greenhill Street. To become a glover it was necessary for him to be apprenticed for seven years; he must therefore have been about ten years old when he came to Stratford from the village of Snitterfield, where he was born, and at seventeen or eighteen he was ready to set himself up a business. He cured and dressed the skins of oxen, horses, deer, sheep, goats, and dogs, and superintended the work of his laborers, who were mostly young men and boys. In those days a glover did not sell gloves only. He made leather hose, leather jerkins, leather aprons, belts, pouches, wallets, and purses. He did not make leather caps or shoes, but he made everything of leather that was worn between the head and the feet. He dealt in wool, barley, and timber as a sideline.

He was a busy man, industrious and well respected, with a deep sense of obligation and service to the community. He was elected one by one to all the offices of the Corporation of Stratford. First he became the official taster of ale, then burgess, then chamberlain, then alderman, and finally head alderman or bailiff, which corresponds to mayor of the town. He was chamberlain for four successive years, from 1561 to 1565, and he was bailiff from October 1568 to October 1569. In these higher offices he wore a special pancake-shaped cap and a black gown with fur trimmings indicating his rank.

Of his appearance we know very little, and of his wife's appearance we know nothing at all. We have, however, one glimpse of him recorded fifty years after his death in a collection of manuscripts compiled by Thomas Plume, who wrote about Shakespeare: "He was a glover's son. Sir John Mennis saw once his old father in his shop—a merry cheeked old man that said Will was a good honest fellow, but he durst have cracked a jest with him at any time."

In those words John Shakespeare comes to life. If the recording angel permits only a single sentence to describe a man, Shakespeare's father was well served. We see him in his mellow old age, happy with the world and with his son, cracking jokes to the end.

The
Ancestors

WILLIAM SHAKESPEARE WAS BAPTIZED on April 26, 1564, on the feast day of St. Cletus, the third Pope, at the font in Holy Trinity Church in Stratford upon Avon, and the event was recorded in the parish register. The exact place and date of his birth were not recorded, and the house generally known as the birthplace on Henley Street may not be where he was born. According to the rule of the Prayer Book of 1559, baptism should take place on the Sunday following the birth of the child or on the next holy day "unless upon a great or reasonable cause to be declared to the curate and by him approved." This rule was simple and final; it was obeyed throughout the kingdom because it was felt to be in accordance with divine law. April 26, 1564, was a Wednesday, and by no means can it be regarded as a holy day. Since Shakespeare was not baptized on a Sunday or on a holy day, it must be assumed that "great and reasonable cause" had been declared on the curate. The most satisfactory explanation would be that there was a difficult birth, and the mother took a long time to recover, and that the baptism took place as soon as the mother was well enough to attend the church. The tradition that he was born on April 23, three days before the baptism, first appears in 1773, more than two hundred years later.

It was a bad year to be born in, for in the summer of 1564 the plague struck Stratford and carried away more than a tenth of the population before the end of the year. Never before and never again would the plague strike so massively. Two hundred and thirty-eight people died between June 30 and December 31; whole families were wiped out, and for years afterward the people of Stratford were in deadly fear of the plague. They lost in six months the same number of people who died during the previous five years.

John Shakespeare was in Stratford throughout the year, but there was no reason why his infant son should remain amid the unpredictable mercies of the plague. If he had any sense—and we know he was a cautious and calculating man—he would have sent his wife and son to live with relatives at Snitterfield. It was the custom during plague time to run to the villages. John Shakespeare had to stay behind because he was one of the chief burgesses, or members of the town council. An entry in the town records shows that on August 30 of this year the burgesses met in the garden of the Gild Chapel to make an assessment for the relief of the poor. It was thought that the garden was a safer place than the chapel itself. John Shakespeare was assessed a shilling. Fourteen others subscribed a greater, and six a lesser amount. These assessments give some indication of his financial standing in the community. He was not among the rich but was fairly well off and could afford the expense of spending a good deal of his time working for the Corporation.

When William Shakespeare was born, John Shakespeare was already, according to Elizabethan calculations, a middle-aged man, for he was about thirty-four years old. He must have been about twenty-seven years old and already well established in trade when he married Mary Arden, an heiress from the village of Wilmcote. The records of the marriage are lost, but it is believed that it took place in the village of Aston Cantlow near Wilmcote. John Shakespeare was marrying above his station, for he was the son of Richard Shakespeare, sometimes known as Shakstaff, a husbandman who tilled land and kept cattle around Snitterfield, and Mary

Arden belonged to the cadet branch of a well-known and influential family.

A Spanish king ruled over England when John Shakespeare married Mary Arden in or about 1557. Philip II was King of Spain, England, the Netherlands, Naples, Sicily and Milan, the Franche-Comté, and vast areas of conquered territory in America, and his name appeared together with the name of his wife, Mary, Queen of England, Ireland, and France, or so she styled herself. She was the daughter of Henry VIII by Catherine of Aragon. She would die in the following year, and her half sister Elizabeth would come to the throne.

They were extraordinary times, for with the coming of Mary to the throne England was restored to the good graces of the Papacy and all Protestants were in danger. Stratford was outside the main field of conflict and gave the world no martyrs. They were small tradesmen and farmers. The first record of Shakespeare's name has been found in the Great Rolls of Normandy, where a William Sakeespee of Bayeux is listed as being in debt to King Richard I for the sum of four marks, eight shillings, and fourpence. This was recorded in 1195. Sakeespee means "shake sword," and there is some evidence that this was the original form of the name, the knight's sword giving place by linguistic attrition to the infantry-man's spear. The first record of an Englishmen called Shakespeare appeared in 1248, when a certain William Shakespeare was hanged for robbery at Clopton, which is only seven miles from Stratford upon Avon. By the sixteenth century there were Shakespeares over most of England, and there was a large concentration of them in Warwickshire and the neighboring counties.

"Breakspear, Shakspear and the like have been surnames imposed upon the first bearers of them for valour and feats of arms," wrote Richard Verstegan in 1603 in a book called *Of the Surnames of our Ancient Families*. It is a tempting theory but unfortunately it has no basis in fact. In the records of English history no valorous Shakespeare has been discovered. John Shakespeare claimed that his ancestors had been rewarded for their valiant service by "the most prudent prince, King Henry the Seventh" but he did not name these ancestors and no trace of them has been found. The Shake-speares were ordinary, humdrum, lower-middle-class people without power or influence.

While Shakespeare's father's family amounted to very little in terms of property or station in life, it was altogether another matter with the Ardens, from whom his mother descended. There was a time before the Conquest when the Ardens were great lords with vast estates and benefices, ruling over many towns and villages in Warwickshire and the neighboring counties. The pedigree of the Ardens was well established by the learned antiquary Sir William Dugdale in his *Visitation of Warwickshire*, published in 1656. He traced the family back to Rohand, Earl of Warwick, who lived in the time of Alfred the Great, and whose only daughter, Felicia, married Guy, Lord of Wallingford, who became Earl of Warwick, inheriting the title through his wife.

Guy of Warwick was one of those half-legendary heroes about whom epics were written. He was a man of immense courage and resourcefulness, a champion of the oppressed, a soldier, and a recluse. He set out on a pilgrimage to the Holy Land, returning in A.D. 926 during the reign of King Athelstan, at a time when the Danes were besieging Winchester. The adversaries were prepared to settle the issues of war by single combat, each side choosing a champion. The Danes presented their champion, a giant called Colbrand. King Athelstan looked for a champion to represent the English, but none came forward except a poor palmer, who was the Earl of Warwick in disguise. Reluctantly King Athelstan permitted him to be the champion of the English. In armor the two champions rode against each other. The earl broke his spear on the giant's shield, and the giant cut off the head of the earl's horse. Then they fought on foot through the long afternoon, now one gaining the advantage, now the other. The earl finally beat the club out of the giant's hand and cut off his arm. The fighting continued until it grew dark. At last the giant grew faint from loss of blood, and with a mighty blow the earl cut off the giant's head. Winchester was saved from the Danes and a solemn mass was performed to celebrate the victory. The earl, however, refused all rewards; he also refused even to tell anyone except the King his real name. He returned to Warwick, built himself a hermitage beside the river Avon, and spent the rest of his life in meditation, only revealing himself in his last hours to his countess. There was a time when all over Europe people listened to the exploits of Guy, Earl of Warwick, as he fought his way through Italy and the Holy Land and returned to save Winchester for the English.

Guy's son Rayborn married Leonetta, the daughter of King Athelstan, who was the grandson of Alfred the Great, and in this way royal blood entered the family of the earls of Warwick.

Rayborn's son and grandson were both warriors. His great-grandson Wulfgeat quarreled with King Ethelred, known to history as Ethelred the Unready, and in A.D. 1006 he lost all his estates. His son Wigod recovered the estates after his marriage to Ermenhild, the sister of Leofric, Earl of Coventry and Leicester, who is chiefly remembered because his wife Godiva rode naked on horseback through Coventry in a display of courage intended to soften her husband's heart after he had imposed heavy taxes on the people of the town. Wigod's son Ailwin, who lived in the time of King Edward the Confessor, was regarded by Dugdale as the "lineal ancestor to that worthy and long-lasting family of Arden, that hath flourished ever since in this County." Ailwin's son Turchill was the first to use the Arden name.

Turchill had the good fortune to be one of the few Saxon earls who did not incur the displeasure of William the Conqueror when he invaded England in A.D. 1066. His neutrality in the war between William and King Harold was rewarded by the grant of his estates he possessed before the Conquest. In the Doomsday Book his lands fill four columns; they included forty-nine manorial demesnes in Warwickshire and many others in the surrounding counties. In the Norman fashion he called himself Turchill de Eaderne, meaning "of the Woodlands." He owned the Forest of Arden and ruled from his castle in Warwick. In the eyes of the defeated English he was a traitor.

In the days before William finally settled the fate of England, Turchill had been a political force. There was a time when he favored the right of Canute, King of Norway and Denmark, to the English throne. He sailed to Denmark with nine ships in an effort to persuade Canute to come to England; and he seems to have sent out his ships in troubled waters, lending them to whoever would pay for them, and engaging in piracy. Canute recognized his importance. In a proclamation delivered in A.D. 1020 we read: "Canute the King greeteth in friendly fashion his archbishops and bishops, and Earl Turchill, and all his earls, and subjects noble and common in England." If Turchill was not the premier earl of England, he was the one whose name was most familiar to the King of Denmark.

Under William the Conqueror Turchill, Earl of Warwick, retained his power and influence and all his estates. His eldest son, Siward, was less lucky, for the Conqueror's successor as King of England was the bullnecked, stuttering William Rufus, who had no love for the English earls. Siward lost his title and his estates, which were granted to one of the King's cronies, Henry de Newburgh, who became the first Norman Earl of Warwick. Henry married Turchill's daughter Margaret, and Siward entered the service of the new earl, while his eldest son, known as Sir Hugh de Arden, became the steward in the earl's household. Another son, Sir Henry de Arden, inherited the title of knighthood, for Sir Hugh died without issue. For four generations every head of the Arden family was known as "Lord of Rodbourn." They had titles and small estates, but were scarcely more than gentry. The great days when Turchill de Eaderne had ruled over all of Warwickshire were no more than a memory. The Ardens melted into the countryside, married well or badly, produced many children, and played no further part in history until Robert Arden became sheriff of the counties of Leicester and Warwick in 1438. Sheriff meant more than it does today. He was the representative of the royal authority in the two counties, the supreme arbiter, chief judge and court of appeal, the man through whom the King's law was administered. He was enjoying a position which in the normal course of events would enable him to acquire great wealth and influence. It was as though Turchill had come back again.

Robert Arden had been a younger son, without title. He became Sir Robert Arden by virtue of his high office, which he held for fourteen years. During the Wars of the Roses he sided with Richard, Duke of York, raised an army in Shropshire, and was about to lead it against the Lancastrians when he was captured, put on trial, and summarily executed. The chroniclers say that he was "cruelly executed," which meant that he was tortured to death. His estates were sequestered. In the reign of Edward IV the estates that had belonged to his wife, Alice de Bishopton, were restored to his son

Walter, who lived quietly in a large moated country house called Park Hall near Birmingham. Walter married Eleanor Hampden, the second daughter of John Hampden of Great Hampden in Buckinghamshire, who was the ancestor of the John Hampden who was one of those chiefly responsible for organizing the people of England against Charles I. Walter Arden had six sons and four daughters. His second son, Thomas, settled in Aston Cantlow, six miles northwest of Stratford, in 1501. In the same year he purchased lands at nearby Snitterfield. He was a gentleman farmer and left little mark on the community. He died in 1547, and his son Robert inherited his estates.

Robert Arden chose to live at Wilmcote in the parish of Aston Cantlow. At his death he owned a farmhouse and land at Wilmcote and two farmhouses and about one hundred acres at Snitterfield. He married twice, and by his first wife had eight daughters: Margaret, Joan, Alice, Joyce, Katherine, Elizabeth, Agnes, and Mary, who was the youngest. The first name of his wife was Ann, and we know no more about her. His second wife, Agnes, was the widow of a certain John Hill. In November 1556 he drew up his will, making Alice and Mary his executors. To Mary, who was evidently his favorite, he left "all my land in Wilmcote called Asbies and the crop upon the ground sown and tilled as it is." To Alice went a third part of his goods and possessions. He left only ten pounds to his wife and he asked that the remainder of his estate be divided equally between the six remaining daughters.

An inventory of his goods was drawn up on December 9, 1556, shortly after his death. The inventory lists pots and pans, basins, candlesticks, an ax, a hatchet and an adze, a kneading trough, a handsaw, eight oxen, two bullocks, four horses, nine pigs, some poultry, and the bees in the hive. There was a cart and a plow, and some timber in the yard. All together his goods were valued at seventy-seven pounds, eleven shillings, and tenpence. This was not, of course, the total value of his estate, for it did not include the value of his houses and lands.

Among the items included in the inventory were nine "painted cloths," which rarely appeared in the inventories of farmhouses. Five hung in the main hall and there were four more in the bedroom. These hangings usually depicted brightly colored biblical scenes such as the story of Tobit and the Angel and were painted by local artists. According to the inventory, one painted cloth was valued at twenty-eight shillings and eightpence.

A short while after Robert Arden's death Mary Arden married John Shakespeare. She gave him four sons and four daughters. The first of her sons was William Shakespeare, born in 1564, and the last was Edmund Shakespeare, born in 1580, who also became a player.

The story of the Ardens has been told at some length because it throws some light on Shakespeare's feeling for royalty and for history. His ancestors had sometimes played a part in English history, and not an insignificant part. They were woven into the historical fabric of the land, had reached high positions, suffered disgrace, and after many years of obscurity another Arden would arise to power and royal favor. Shakespeare lived at a time when people were deeply concerned with their lineage. He could claim, if it pleased him, that he was twenty-fifth in descent from King Athelstan and eighteenth from Turchill of Eardene. While today it might do a man very little good to know that he is twenty-fifth in a line of descent from a king, it was different in Shakespeare's time. Like Othello, he was descended from "men of royal liege." The deposition of kings, their changing fortunes, the losing and regaining of their crowns were matters which he had deeply pondered and which lay very close to his heart. His imagination played on kingship with extraordinary effect: he saw kings in the round, as though they were very close to him, as though they were his own flesh.

A little more than a hundred years before Shakespeare's birth, Sir Robert Arden, sheriff of Leicester and Warwick, had raised the family name out of obscurity and reached dizzying heights before being arrested, tortured, and executed. In the time of Henry III another ancestor, Sir Thomas Arden, took part with the barons who rose against the King under Simon de Montfort, was taken prisoner, and lost all his possessions. The Ardens were rebels who played for high stakes, arising in times of war and civil commotion, nearly always on the losing side. Their lineage was longer than that of any of the Norman nobles who came over with William the Conqueror: it went back to the ancient nobility surrounding the Anglo-Saxon kings and to the greatest of them all, King Alfred. Consciously or unconsciously they were fighting to restore their ancient possessions, their power and prestige. Richard Shakespeare, the tenant farmer who lived on the Arden estate at Snitterfield, was only one step ahead of a farm laborer. His son did better, for he amassed some wealth, became high bailiff of Stratford, and was entitled to wear a coat of arms. His grandson did better still, for he alone of those descended from the Ardens realized that the real conquests and the real power do not arise from royal courts but exist in the royal realm of the imagination.

It was as though over the centuries the ancient pre-Norman England, so long contained and imprisoned, the England of Alfred and Athelstan and Turchill, had suddenly arisen in the person of Shakespeare. The wave crested and then died, and nothing like that wave was ever seen again.

Shakespeare Sees His First Play

THE AFFAIRS OF JOHN SHAKESPEARE prospered modestly. He lived in the large house with a shop and storerooms on Henley Street and in addition he possessed the house on Greenhill Street with a garden and a barn, which he bought as an investment. He was a merchant, very money-minded, spending long hours sitting over his accounts. He was trusted and well liked. His wife was raised a Catholic; he too appears to have been a Catholic, retaining his faith in secret, and once his name appears on a list of recusants. This was the term given to those who adamantly rejected Queen Elizabeth's claim to be head of the Church of England. Remaining a Catholic in secret, he was aware of being at the mercy of informers and spies. He must spend his life acting a role: the role of a man who in all his public appearances plays the good Protestant while in his secret heart he regards Protestantism as the work of the devil. The memoirs and chronicles written by Catholics in Elizabethan England testify to their dedication to the Church, their extraordinary talent for engaging in desperate and ill-conceived conspiracies. To be an active Catholic in Elizabethan England was to court danger and despair. Many Catholics were left alone, but those who offended the Queen in any way risked torture, imprisonment, and death by the ax.

John Shakespeare, glover and general merchant, wrote a religious testament of great fervor which was discovered by a master bricklayer called Joseph Moseley who was repairing the roof of the house on Henley Street. The testament was found hidden between the rafters and the tiles at some time in the latter part of the eighteenth century and a copy of it came into the possession of Edmund Malone, a resourceful scholar, who studied and pondered it at great length and came to the conclusion that it was a genuine document. The testament consisted of five leaves stitched together. Joseph Moseley had an impeccable reputation, and he gained nothing from his discovery. Malone printed the document for the first time in a long chapter called "An Historical Account of the Rise and Progress of the English Stage" in his ten-volume edition of the works of Shakespeare published in 1790.

The testament consists of fourteen numbered paragraphs, each one vigorously affirming John Shakespeare's faith in the Catholic religion. He begins:

> In the name of God, the father, son, and holy ghost, the most holy and blessed Virgin Mary, mother of God, the holy host of archangels, patriarchs, prophets, evangelists, apostles, saints, martyrs, and all the celestial court and company of heaven, I John Shakespeare, an unworthy member of the holy Catholic religion, being at this my present writing in perfect health of body, and sound mind, memory, and understanding, but calling to mind the uncertainty of life and certainty of death, and that I may be possibly cut off in the blossom of my sins, and called to render an account of all my transgressions externally and internally, and that I may be unprepared for the dreadful trial . . .

So he continues through all the fourteen paragraphs, writing in fear and trembling, promising never to despair of the divine goodness and of the Church, which alone is the possessor and guardian of the faith. The profession of faith is superbly organized. Long after Edmund Malone studied this document, it was discovered that the text of the testament was originally composed by St. Charles Borromeo in Italian and translated by the Jesuits in all the languages of the countries where they had followers. John Shakespeare had not composed it; he had carefully written it out on the instructions of his priest and concealed it when he expected the house might be raided by the commissioners who from time to time swooped down on suspected Catholics.

Properly understood, John Shakespeare's testament is an important document for understanding the development of his son. The testament shows that William Shakespeare was brought up in a Catholic household, and during his boyhood he knew the fears, the tensions, and the exaltations of those active Catholics whom the state was trying to destroy. This is not to say that William Shakespeare was himself a believing Catholic or that he could ever have subscribed to St. Charles Borromeo's stern and implacable doctrine. The testament was a weapon of the Counter-Reformation and Borromeo was the commander in chief of that great counterthrust in the resurgence of Catholic power.

The tranquil life of John Shakespeare was shadowed by two tragedies. Two daughters were born to him: Joan, who was baptized on September 15, 1558, and Margareta, who was baptized on December 2, 1562. They lived for only a few months. William, the third child and the first son, was the pampered darling whose coming exorcised the ghosts of two dead sisters. His earliest memories may have been of accompanying his mother and father to lay flowers on their graves.

Life for a middle-class Elizabethan child was calm and ceremonial. There were wet nurses and women servants to take care of him. When the boy was four his station in life altered, for his father became a person of importance.

On September 4, 1568, John Shakespeare was elected high bailiff of Stratford, taking office on the first day of October. He was now the mayor of the town, but he was also much more, for in Elizabethan times the mayor was the chief magistrate, coroner, almoner, justice of the peace, responsible for all problems concerned with property and particularly with problems connected with the reversion of land when no heirs could be found or when there were disputes among the heirs. As mayor he represented the Crown, and he also represented the Corporation of Stratford in its dealings with the local lords of the manor. As clerk of the market he had the task of setting the weekly price of corn, which in turn set the prices of bread and ale. Thus on Thursdays, which were market days, the bakers and brewers danced around him, offering their arguments for higher prices, while the common people attempted to reason with him for the lowest possible prices. In addition to all these duties, which kept him busy for half the day, he had many ceremonial functions to perform. In public he was always escorted by an official bearing the mace, and he always wore his furred gown. In this panoply he attended council meetings, went to church on Sundays, and occupied his seat at the Gild Chapel. In the same panoply he handed down judgments at the Court of Record, which was the Queen's court, and he was her representative. He was the final arbiter in all matters of land, property, the poor laws, the disposal of the dead, prices, taxes, and justice. He was the law.

All his powers stemmed from one indisputable fact: he alone could issue and sign warrants. In this way he held the lives and happiness of everyone in Stratford in his hands.

Strangely, this man who possessed such vast and indisputable power never, so far as we know, signed his name. Instead he signed with his mark, which usually took the form of a pair of compasses or a curious squiggle said to represent a clamp used for fixing the position of a strip of leather on a board. It has been assumed that he was illiterate but this seems unlikely. Many members of the Corporation also signed with their marks. It appears to have been a matter of personal choice: a man might sign with his mark or his signature as he pleased. Nevertheless, it is disconcerting to discover that among all the documents which record his dealings with the Corporation of Stratford and with the law—for he was always suing or being sued for something or other—not one signature survives.

During his term of office two groups of players visited Stratford. One was the Queen's Players, the other the Earl of Worcester's Players. Both gave special performances before the Council, to which the people of Stratford were invited without payment. The performances probably took place in the Gild Chapel, and the fees paid to the Players—nine shillings for the Queen's and twelvepence for Worcester's—were regarded as a proper charge on the town's funds.

At the time of these performances William Shakespeare was four or five years old, still attending petty school and learning the alphabet from an abecedarius, a teacher attached to the Gild School to take care of very young children. It is possible that the coming of these players was the decisive event of his life, the one event above all others which kindled his imagination.

What was it like to be a four- or five-year-old child seeing a play for the first time in Stratford?

Since John Shakespeare was the high bailiff, he would be given the seat of honor at the Gild Chapel. He would arrive with his wife, Mary, and his son, William, and they would be given seats beside him or just behind him. It was finely built. Formerly the Gild Chapel was the chapel of the Gild of the Holy Cross. Formerly there were paintings on the walls showing the visit of the Queen of Sheba to Solomon, the Invention of the Holy Cross, the Whore of Babylon, St. George and the Dragon, and the Dance of Death. They were brightly colored, but the figures were somewhat wooden, which is not surprising, since they were painted by a not very talented local artist. When he was appointed constable of Stratford, John Shakespeare had been ordered to "deface" them, which meant covering them with whitewash. In 1804 the whitewash was removed and the paintings were discovered to be in excellent condition. Today little is left of them except for some figures above the chancel arch. In John Shakespeare's day the walls were covered were covered with tapestries, and the secular chapel with its large windows still commanded an appearance of power and luxury.

We may imagine the young Shakespeare sitting there, very close to the players, captivated by them, lifted up into a world of magic and fantasy beyond anything he expected, and standing up very solemnly when the time came for the high bailiff to thank the players and hand them the little purple velvet bag which contained their fee. Afterward there would be more speeches, food would be spread on the table, and the boy would walk about among the players, talking to them, examining their costumes, sometimes imitating those sweeping gestures and abrupt, magnificent postures. What is important is that the young Shakespeare, as the bailiff's son, would sit very close to the players with an unrestricted view of the stage, and the players would go out of their way to be kind to him. He would be received among them like a young lord. He would lose himself in the magical world of the theatre and return to it continually in his daydreams.

The crusty old Shakespearian scholar James Orchard Halliwell-Phillipps spent the greater part of his life in a sustained effort to track down as many documents connected with the life of Shakespeare as he could. He found legal documents by the score and black letter Elizabethan books by the hundreds. Among other books in his vast library was *Mount Tabor, or Private Exercises* by a certain R.W., published in 1639. R.W. proved to be R. Willis, his first name unknown. His book was an autobiography concerned largely with his moral and religious life, written down in old age and addressed to his wife and children. He was a Gloucester man, seventy-five years old when the book was printed, and therefore born in the same year as Shakespeare. He describes the circumstances of the players' arrival in the city of Gloucester and how they waited upon the mayor and Corporation and first gave a free performance, which was called "the Mayor's play," and then went on to give more performances at which the public paid for admittance. Willis could remember clearly an event that excited him beyond measure which happened seventy years earlier:

> In the city of Gloucester the manner is, as I think it is in any other like corporations, that, when players of interludes come to town, they first attend the Mayor to inform him what noblemen's servants they are, and so to get licence for their public playing; and if the Mayor like the actors, or would show respect to their lord and master, he appoints them to play their first play before himself and the Aldermen and Common Council of the city; and that is called the Mayor's play, where everyone that will comes in without money, the Mayor giving the players a reward as he thinks fit to show respect unto them.
>
> At such a play my father took me with him, and made me stand between his legs as he sat upon one of the benches, where we saw and heard very well.
>
> The play was called *The Cradle of Security*, wherein was personated a King or some great Prince, with his courtiers

of several kinds, among which three ladies were in special grace with him; and they, keeping him in delights and pleasures, drew him from his graver counsellors, hearing of sermons and listening to good counsel and admonitions, that in the end they got him to lie down in a cradle upon the stage, where these three ladies joining in a sweet song, rocked him asleep that he snorted again; and in the meantime closely conveyed under the clothes wherewithall he was covered a vizard, like a swine's snout, upon his face, with three wire chains fastened thereunto, the other end whereof being holden severally by those three ladies who fall to singing again, and then discovered his face that the spectators might see how they had transformed him, going on with their singing.

Whilst all this was acting, there came forth of another door at the farthest end of the stage two old men, the one in blue with a sergeant-at-arms' his mace on his shoulder, the other in red with a drawn sword in his hand and leaning with the other hand upon the other's shoulder; and so they two went along in a soft pace round about by the skirt of the stage, till at last they came to the cradle, when all the court was in greatest jollity; and then the foremost old man with his mace stroke a fearful blow upon the cradle, whereat all the courtiers, with the three ladies and the vizard, all vanished; and the desolate Prince starting up barefaced, and finding himself thus sent for to judgment, made a lamentable complaint of his miserable case, and so was carried away by wicked spirits.

This Prince did personate in the moral the Wicked of the World; the three ladies, Pride, Covetousness and Luxury; the two old men, the End of the World and the Last Judgment. This sight took such impression on me that when I came towards man's estate, it was as fresh in my memory as if I had seen it newly acted.*

---

*Halliwell-Phillipps makes great play of his discovery of *Mount Tabor*, as though he had been the first to set eyes on it. Edmund Malone had already published it in his edition of the complete works of Shakespeare published in 1790. Malone also observed that *The Cradle of Security* was mentioned in the play *Sir Thomas More*, which became famous only

What Willis saw was slapstick comedy in the service of religion. It was an old morality play, so hoary with age that it seems to be coated with the thick dust of the Middle Ages. Yet, as Willis recounts it, it was undeniably exciting. The prince being rocked to sleep in a cradle was the purest farce; the wearing of the swine's snout, intended to demonstrate the animality of mankind, was for a child the happiest of improvisations; the sergeant-at-arms in red, bearing his mace like a club, was deliciously terrifying; while the sudden attack on the prince in the cradle by two prowling men would keep the boy in a state of delighted panic. In these ancient morality plays the wicked spirits were usually played by boys dressed up in revolting costumes, wearing blood-curdling masks and the long tails of giant rats, and for the boy their coming may have been the crowning glory of the play.

These old morality plays were full of racy dialogue, much of it improvised on the spot. The devils, who went down to hell, had the best of it. From the tremendous threats uttered by Lucifer and King Herod came the "mighty line" of Christopher Marlowe, and sometimes the devils became clowns who winked knowingly at the audience as they praised themselves:

In comes I, Beelzebub:
In my hands I carries club,
On my head a dripping pan.
Don't you think I'm a funny old man?

Of course we do, but one of the reasons why we think he is funny is because he is shoveling souls into hell, and another reason is because the dripping pan makes him look preposterous. Nick Bottom, the Athenian weaver, wearing the ass's head, is of the same company as the prince who wears the swine's snout in his cradle.

---

in this century with the discovery that the manuscript was partly written in Shakespeare's hand. More discusses with his son Roper whether they shall put on a play before the Lord Mayor's banquet. Roper agrees and More turns to a player:

More.   I prithee, tell me, what plays have ye?
Player.   Divers, my lord. *The Cradle of Security, Hit nail o' the Head, Impatient Poverty, The Play of Four Pees, Dives and Lazarus, Lusty Juventus,* and *The Marriage of Wit and Wisdom.*

The fact that *The Cradle of Security* was placed first suggests that it was a well-known and popular play of the time.

There is much history and mythology in a boy's eyes as he looks for the first time at a play.

The Cradle of Security was played in Gloucester, which was no more than a long day's journey from Stratford, and very likely it was the play that set the young Shakespeare's imagination working in the direction of the theatre. The Queen's Players were not in any sense "strolling players." They were under the official protection of the court and went from town to town according to a fixed itinerary, staying about a week in each town before going on to the next, spending the winter in London when court festivities were at their height. The theatre was already firmly established; there were plenty of actors, but there were as yet no dramatists capable of writing plays with the passion demanded of those passionate times.

The
Schoolboy

LIFE IN STRATFORD IN 1568 had not changed very much since the fourteenth century or indeed since the time of William the Conqueror. The quiet market town lay outside the main road of history. Its ecclesiastical affairs were ordered by the Bishop of Worcester from his seat in Worcester Cathedral, and its civil affairs were ordered by the Queen's representative in Warwick, where the Earl of Warwick still maintained immense prestige and power. Robert Dudley, Earl of Leicester, had recently been presented with the Castle of Kenilworth, which stood only a few miles from Stratford. He was the Queen's favorite and sometimes felt he was destined to become her consort. The aristocracy and the gentry ruled the land, while the high bailiff and the burgesses ruled over Stratford.

The gentry spent a good part of their time hunting. They hunted the red deer and the fallow deer. With hooded hawks and falcons on their wrists they hunted pheasants, partridges, and herons, or roamed after the fox and the badger, or disported themselves in a round of expensive social engagements which demanded more and more revenue from their tenants. Outside the towns life remained feudal. The towns, conscious of their power, were beginning to fight back. The town folk had weapons, for every English boy was a trained bowman. Although tennis was coming into fashion, especially in London, it had not yet reached Stratford. The butts for the archers were set up in the common land around Stratford, and cups filled with good ale were presented to those who scored best.

While the gentry hunted the deer, usually in their own parks, chasing the deer round and round an enclosure, killing them at leisure, the common people skilled in archery hunted them in the open or in woods and forests, and often secretly, for there were laws against the hunting of the deer. The gentry hunted in style, wearing appropriate uniforms and training their dogs with the help of dog keepers and choosing them for their voices, for the Elizabethans enjoyed the barking almost as much as they enjoyed the hunt. "If you would have your kennel for sweetness of cry," wrote Gervase Markham "then you must compound it of some large dogs that have deep, solemn mouths," and goes on to explain how the orchestra is made up of roaring, loud ringing mouths forming the countertenor, and some sweeter mouths for the middle part, and a few beagles to provide the treble. In *A Midsummer Night's Dream* Shakespeare speaks of hounds "matched in mouth like bells each under each," and he evidently enjoyed the orchestral cry of hounds. Sir Thomas Cockaine in his *Discourse of Hunting* advises the hunter to procure hounds that are "durable, well mouthed, cold nosed, round footed, open bulked, and well let down there, with fine sterns and small tails."

Men hunted hares in winter, bucks in summer, stags in autumn; and they also went after otters and martens, which Cockaine regarded as "the sweetest vermin that is hunted." Hunting was not simply the sport of the gentry, for everyone took part in it, on foot or on horseback. Poaching of deer was common, not only at Charlecote; young gentlemen at Oxford were continually poaching at Radley Park, until the owner of the park wondered why he went to the trouble of maintaining his fences.

We sometimes think of the Elizabethans as living fecklessly, quaffing ale and dancing round maypoles, amusing themselves with piratical assaults on Spanish galleons and given to licentious sports and frolics. In fact, they were rather somber men who took life seriously and were brought up to accept severe discipline. This discipline began in the family and continued until the end of their school days. "Magotie-headed" John Aubrey, a wise and credulous man, and the best of reporters, described how the Elizabethans suffered under the harsh formalities of the time:

The Gentry and the Citizens had little learning of any kind, and their way of breeding up their children was suitable to the rest: for wheras one's child should be one's nearest Friend, and the time of growing-up should be most indulged, they were as severe to their children as their schoolmaster; and their Schoolmasters, as masters of the House of correction. The child perfectly loathed the sight of his parents, as the slave his Torturer. Gentlemen of 30 or 40 years old, fit for any employment in the common wealth, were to stand like great mutes and fools bare-headed before their Parents; and the Daughters (grown women) were to stand at the Cupboard's side during the whole time of the proud mother's visit, unless (as the fashion was) 'twas desired that leave (forsooth) should be given to kneel upon cushions brought them by the serving man, after they had done sufficient Penance standing. The boys (grown young fellows) had their foreheads turned up and stiffened with spittle; they were to stand mannerly forsooth, thus, the foretop ordered as before, one hand at the handstring, the other on the breech or cod-piece.

It is a comic portrait, as Aubrey writes it, but it was not comic to the long-suffering children who stood at attention in their parents' presence and continued to stand at attention when they were grown up. The Elizabethans had the old Roman quality of *gravitas*, and indeed they fashioned themselves after the ancient Romans. In school they read more Latin literature than English literature; Latin was a second language used not only by doctors and lawyers but also by town clerks writing up the minutes of the council meetings and by farm bailiffs reporting on the crops. Sir Thomas More wrote his *Utopia* in Latin and William Camden wrote his *History of England in the Reign of Elizabeth* in the

same language. Sir Walter Scott in his *Lay of the Last Minstrel*
tells of a Border nobleman, Lord William Howard, known as
Belted Will, who after leading his army against the Scots would
return to his own castle full of books in Latin which he read
avidly and annotated eagerly.

Young Shakespeare studied at the King's Free School at Stratford, housed in the overloft of the Gild of the Holy Cross. After
learning his ABCs with an abecedarius, he entered the school at the
age of seven and was at once plunged into an unremitting study of
Latin under Master Simon Hunt, who had successfully concealed
the fact that he was a Catholic, for he left the school four years later
and went to study at the University of Douai in France, became a
Jesuit, and then an English confessor at St. Peter's in Rome, where
he died quite young. Simon Hunt was followed by Thomas Jenkins,
who taught at the Free School from 1575 to 1579. It was often said
that he was a Welshman and that Shakespeare later burlesqued him
in the character of Sir Hugh Evans, who took upon himself to
humiliate Falstaff and to set him on fire with a candle. "He made
fritters of English," Falstaff said of him. Thomas Jenkins may have
been Welsh by origin, but he was in fact a Londoner, born of poor
parents, his father being a servant in the house of Sir Thomas
White, the founder of St. John's College, Oxford. Jenkins went up
to Oxford, proved to be a good student, received his M.A. in 1570,
and remained as a Fellow of St. John's College until 1572. A
fellowship could only be obtained by a man of considerable intellectual achievement. Jenkins was the master of the Free School when
Shakespeare was eleven years old, and he left Stratford when
Shakespeare was fifteen. It is therefore likely that he had more to do
with the young man's intellectual development than anyone else.

In retrospect Elizabethan school days must have seemed harsh
and wearisome. But the pupils working studiously under the roof
beams of the overloft were engaged in a work of discovery: they
were discovering an ancient and long-dead empire, its history,
literature, social customs, morality, and love poetry. They spoke
among themselves in Latin, as though it was their native tongue,
and Roman heroes were more familiar to them than Hereward the
Wake or Guy of Warwick. Cicero, Vergil, Sallust, Terence, and
Ovid became their mentors. Horace taught them about the mutabil-

ity of time, and about love's despairs. They learned from Horace
that is was perfectly possible to write poems about beautiful boys.
From Horace and Ovid they learned a new cosmology totally
different from the cosmology of the Bible: a heaven and earth
peopled by gods, nymphs, and naiads, who rarely suffered and
whose deaths were merely metamorphoses into other lives. Ovid's
Metamorphoses attempts to describe all the changing forms of the
divinities of the Roman pantheon, which was only the Greek
pantheon with Latin names. There was excitement in Sallust's
battle scenes and in Cicero's diatribes, and a boy would read
Vergil's *Eclogues* with the feeling that the poet was writing about
the Warwickshire countryside. A later generation of English schoolboys would begin to learn Latin with Caesar's ice-cold *Commentar-
ies*; Elizabethan schoolboys were spared the trouble. Erasmus and
John Collet, Dean of St. Paul's, had selected the curriculum with a
humanistic yearning for decency and sobriety, not excluding high
intelligence and daring. A boy who studied in an Elizabethan free
school could not be anything except learned. He would know whole
books of Vergil by heart, and he would be able to argue a case in
court as vehemently as Cicero. When Ben Jonson said that Shakespeare knew little Latin and less Greek, he was right on one count
and wrong on the other. Shakespeare knew no Greek at all, but he
knew Latin well and could, if necessary, have written his plays in
Latin. Later he would learn French and Italian.

Schools were strict, and schooling took up most of the day. At six
in summer and seven in winter the schoolboys arrived at school,
saluted the master at the entrance, listened to the day's text from the
Bible, sang a psalm, and said their prayers. Lessons continued for
two hours and there was a break for breakfast. Then the lessons
continued uninterruptedly until eleven, when boys made for home,
had their lunch, and they were at school again at one o'clock. They
worked until five with a brief period for play at three o'clock.
During the play periods they were permitted nothing much more
exciting than leapfrog. Wrestling was forbidden; all "clownish
sports," by which were meant the playing of cards and the throwing
of dice, were severely punished. On Thursdays and Saturdays there
were half holidays. There were about two weeks holiday at Christmas, two more weeks at Easter, two more weeks in the summer.

As a result of this hard work an English schoolboy became a young Roman. When he was eleven years old, Richard Quiney of Stratford wrote a letter to his father asking him to buy two notebooks. Paper was expensive, and he explained that he needed them very much and would put them to good use. The letter concluded with many endearments and compliments such as a boy might enjoy writing to a father he dearly loved. The letter, which survives, was written in fluent Latin of remarkable delicacy and refinement. Richard Quiney was about seven years older than the young Shakespeare, and they became close friends. The rigorous training at the Free School was such that nearly all the boys were able to write fluent Latin.

At Pentecost, at Whitsuntide, and on many feast days the Corporation subsidized plays performed by the boys at the Free School. The subsidies probably covered the cost of the costumes, and some of these plays may have been in Latin. One such play was remembered by Shakespeare when he wrote *Two Gentlemen of Verona*:

> At Pentecost,
> When all our pageants of delights were played,
> Our youth got me to play the woman's part
> And I was trimmed in Madam Julia's gown,
> Which served me as fit, by all men's judgments,
> As if the garment had been made for me:
> And at this time I made her weep agood,
> For I did play a lamentable part:
> Madam, 'twas Ariadne passioning
> For Theseus' perjury and unjust flight,
> Which I so lively acted with my tears
> That my poor mistress, moved herewithal,
> Wept bitterly.

The story of Theseus and Ariadne is told in Ovid's *Metamorphoses*, the one book of which we can be certain that Shakespeare was a careful student, for there is scarcely a page of it which is not echoed in his poems and his plays.

The young Shakespeare in women's clothes, playing the role of Ariadne bewailing Theseus after he abandoned her, would have been worth seeing, and Ariadne's long and bitter complaints, tearing the heavens to tatters, would have been a fitting introduction to Shakespeare's experience of the stage.

But there were other plays and pageants taking place in the neighborhood. In July 1575, when Shakespeare was eleven years old, Queen Elizabeth came to Kenilworth on a state visit to her favorite, the Earl of Leicester, who put on for her benefit a pageant that exceeded all other pageants in cost and magnificence. Kenilworth Castle had recently been rebuilt; it was as large as a town, and included gardens and deer parks and what Robert Laneham, the gatekeeper, who wrote a lengthy account of these festivities, called "a goodly pool," which was in fact a vast lake. The queen was on holiday. She stayed for eighteen days, and Leicester spent a fortune in entertaining her.

The Queen arrived on her palfrey toward evening on July 9, to be welcomed by giant trumpeters with silver trumpets standing above the main gate. "These trumpeters, being six in number, were every one eight feet high, in due proportion of person beside, all in long garments of silk suitable, each with his silvery trumpet of five feet long." Since the Queen detested loud trumpet blasts, these trumpeters welcomed her softly. She passed through the castle gate and rode to the lakeside to be greeted by a floating island blazing with torches. The island moved over the water toward her under the command of the Lady of the Lake, who was dressed in silk and attended by Nereids like Cleopatra on her burning barge. The Lady of the Lake sung the praises of Leicester and proclaimed that the lake had been in her possession since the time of King Arthur. The Queen commented mildly: "We had thought indeed the lake had been ours, and do you call it yours now?"

It was a warm evening, but the Queen was tireless. She inspected the bird cages full of singing birds, and the nearby heaps of fruit in silver bowls, and there were more silver bowls filled with wheat and barley, grapes, and fish, and all the bowls signifying the riches of her reign. That night she slept in a vast room overlooking the lake.

On the next day she watched part of a performance of a traditional play called *The Slaughter of the Danes at Hock Tide*, but it went on too long and she said she would see the rest of it later. So the days passed merrily with speeches, plays, banquets, and fireworks, which were usually accompanied by rumbling cannonades, and toward evening she usually took part in a deer hunt. One evening, when they were hunting by torchlight, she was accosted by a Hombre Salvagio dressed in moss and leaves, waving a small oak tree like a club, and while he congratulated the Queen's Majesty for entering his domain, he broke the oak tree in two and hurled the top of the tree at her, narrowly missing her. "No hurt, no hurt!" she exclaimed, and the courtiers thought this was one of the great moments of the day.

She hunted nearly every evening when it was cool, watched bear-baiting, admired an Italian tumbler, attended a bride-ale and a morris dance, saw another stage play, knighted five gentlemen of the court and cured nine poor people by touching them on the cheek, and one day she attended another pageant on the lake. First came Triton on a swimming mermaid, blowing his horn, announcing that the Lady of the Lake was in danger of Sir Bruce sans Pitee, her mortal enemy. Then came the Lady of the Lake on a flotilla of moving islands with her nymphs, followed by Arion wearing a horse's head and riding a dolphin's back. Arion came floating up to a bridge which spanned a corner of the lake. The Queen was riding on horseback over the bridge. Arion forgot his lines, and in his confusion he drew off the horse's head and shouted: "I'm not Arion, not he, but honest Harry Goldingham." Shakespeare remembered Arion when he made Bottom wear an ass's head in *A Midsummer Night's Dream*, and he remembered Arion again when he put into the mouth of Oberon the words:

> Thou rememb'rest
> Since once I sat upon a promontory,
> And heard a mermaid on a dolphin's back
> Uttering such dulcet and harmonious breath
> That the rude sea grew civil at her song,
> And certain stars shot madly from their spheres
> To hear the sea-maid's music.

Some thousands of Warwickshire people from near and far visited Kenilworth during the eighteen days of the Queen's sojourn. They came to cheer her, to feast at Leicester's table, and to watch the tableaux and the pageantry from a distance. As the son of a local dignitary, Shakespeare would have been a welcome guest. He saw a theatre expanded to include an enormous castle and a lake full of islands, and each island floated mysteriously across the lake to the sound of music and singing.

The Queen's visit to Kenilworth took place during the summer holidays. Shakespeare returned to school, the benches on the upper floor of the Gild of the Holy Cross, Thomas Jenkins wearing a long black gown and the pancake-shaped hat of a schoolmaster, and the endless study of Latin. He suffered himself to learn what he had to learn, but no more. He liked the world too much; the life on the farm, the flowers on the riverbanks, the faces of people, and all the pageantry of human existence were more appealing than a lifetime given to scholarship:

> Some to the wars, to try their fortunes there;
> Some to discover islands far away;
> Some to the studious universities.

It is interesting that he gave high place to the discovery of islands.

About the pleasures of schoolboys he has very little to say in his plays. John Aubrey, who thought John Shakespeare was a butcher—it may well have been one of his trades—wrote that when Shakespeare was a boy, "he exercised his father's trade, but when he killed a calf, he would do it in a *high style* and make a speech." It is not so improbable as some critics believe. The boy who could play the role of Ariadne could be expected to slaughter a calf in high style if an audience was present. We have few enough accounts of Shakespeare's boyhood to be able to dispense with any of them. Richard Davies and Nicholas Rowe, writing a hundred years after the event, reported that Shakespeare was in trouble with Sir Thomas Lucy for stealing venison and rabbits. I see no reason to disbelieve the story. The argument that Sir Thomas Lucy did not have an enclosed deer park at Charlecote and therefore Shakespeare could not have been caught stealing deer misses the point. Sir Thomas Lucy did not need to enclose his deer park. He was a staunch anti-Catholic, a harsh and bigoted man, who was continually increasing his estates in all the corrupt fashions of his time. The people of Stratford respected him but did not like him. He had warreners to guard his property, and anyone found there would receive short shrift. High-spirited boys, on a dare, could be expected to invade his property, which was only four miles from Stratford. They would hunt as they pleased, the warrener would take the law in his own hands, the boys would find themselves locked up in the gatehouse overnight and given a whipping in the morning. Nor would they hunt only deer and rabbits. They trapped foxes and moles for their skins, baked hedgehogs in hot clay, netted sparrows and wood pigeons, climbed trees for birds' eggs, and as boys do, they left a small train of death wherever they wandered. No doubt Sir Thomas Lucy was annoyed, but his annoyance and the punishments he inflicted would only spur them to invade his property still more, being more wary each time.

Richard Davies, the country clergyman who left so little impression on people's lives that it has proved impossible to trace his career, although it is known that he became Archdeacon of Lichfield, left at his death some ill-assorted memoranda which may be found in the library of Corpus Christi College, Oxford. He wrote about Shakespeare:

> Much given to all unluckiness in stealing venison and
> rabbits, particularly from Sir Lucy, who had him oft whipt
> and sometimes imprisoned and at last made him fly his
> native country to his great advancement, but his revenge is
> so great that he is Justice Clodpate and calls him a great
> man, and that in allusion to his name bore three louses
> rampant for his arms.

Scholars are inclined to rap Richard Davies over the knuckles for omitting the first name of Sir Thomas Lucy and for introducing Justice Clodpate instead of Justice Shallow. Justice Clodpate was a foolish and conceited squire in Shadwell's *Epsom-Wells*, first produced in 1672. A man writing a memorandum to himself is not under oath, and if he confused Clodpate with Shallow, and forgot a first name, we are not entitled to assume that he was ignorant. He had heard the story somewhere, wrote it down as best he could, remembering the three louses on the Lucy coat of arms, and told his story simply and convincingly. What is especially convincing is that Shakespeare went on doing what he was not supposed to do long after he had been punished for it.

Except for poaching and deer stealing, life in Stratford was uneventful. Occasionally there were tragedies. On December 17, 1579, a young woman, Katherine Hamlet, was found drowned in the Avon. She lived in the village of Tiddington near Alveston. She was buried in the churchyard at Alveston. As the days passed, people began to ask questions. Had she been murdered? Did she commit suicide? The rumors became so vehement that Henry Rogers, the "crowner" or coroner of Stratford, decided to empanel a special jury consisting of three gentlemen from Alveston and ten humble neighbors to inquire into the circumstances of her death. The body was dug up after it had been in the earth for seven weeks. The inquest was held on February 11, 1580. The jury examined the body for the tell-tale marks which might suggest that she died a violent death. None could be found. They returned a verdict, which Henry Rogers transcribed into dog-Latin. The verdict was that she had died by misadventure (*per infortunium*). She had not willfully drowned herself and had not been murdered, and she could there-fore be buried again in the consecrated ground in the knowledge that no ecclesiastical objection could be raised. Henry Rogers con-curred with the jurors who gave it as their opinion that the "de-ceased was going with a milk pail to draw water at the River Avon and was standing on the bank when she slipped and fell in, and was drowned, meeting her death in no other wise or fashion" (. . . *lapsit et cecidit in rivium, et non aliter nec alio modo ad mortem suam devenit*).

The jurors had arrived at a satisfactory conclusion; the matter was closed; it remained only to put the young woman back in her coffin. In fact, nothing had been decided and the death of Katherine Hamlet remained unexplained. The thirteen jurors had not so much reached a verdict as cleared the good name of two villages, Tidding-ton and Alveston, which were only a mile from Stratford.

Shakespeare was then fifteen, and he may have seen the body when it was dug up and displayed. Elizabethans were not squeam-ish about looking at bodies; on the contrary they enjoyed seeing them for their strangeness and also because they served as a proper reminder of their own mortality; they laughed in the presence of death because it was all around them. And there were many in Stratford who continued to believe that Katherine Hamlet had

committed suicide or met with foul play. As the priest says to
Laertes in *Hamlet* after the death of Ophelia: "Her death was
doubtful."

The drowning of Katherine Hamlet left a deep impression on
Shakespeare and on everyone else in Stratford. The "doubtfulness"
of her death raised profound moral issues. Many years later
Katherine Hamlet would become transformed into Ophelia, going
to her death in a rainbow flood of flowers, and almost effortlessly, as
though she were stepping from the riverbank into another life:

> There is a willow grows aslant a brook
> That shows his hoar leaves in the glassy stream;
> There with fantastic garlands did she come,
> Of crow-flowers, nettles, daisies and long purples
> That liberal shepherds give a grosser name,
> But our cold maids do dead men's fingers call them:
> There, on the pendent boughs her coronet weeds
> Clambering to hang, an envious sliver broke,
> When down her weedy trophies and herself
> Fell in the weeping brook. Her clothes spread,
> And, mermaid-like, awhile they bore her up:
> Which time she chanted snatches of old tunes,
> As one incapable of her own distress,
> Or like a creature native and indu'd
> Unto that element: how long it could not be
> Till that her garments, heavy with their drink,
> Pull'd the poor wretch from her melodious lay
> To muddy death.

Katherine Hamlet died in winter, when no flowers grew on
riverbanks and there could have been no coronet of flowers hanging
on a willow banch. In *Hamlet* she suffered a metamorphosis; and
from being a poor country girl she was transformed into a marvel-
ously beautiful legend who floated away singing to her death.

All through Shakespeare's plays there are echoes of his childhood
and youth in and around Stratford. He loved the countryside, knew the
names of all the flowers and trees, studied the habits of the beasts of the
field, and it was perhaps from the river Avon that he derived the rush,
the turmoil, and the melting sweetness of his verse.

He also came to know the women of the countryside. He was five months past his eighteenth birthday when he got a woman with child. She was Anne or Agnes Hathaway, the daughter of Richard Hathaway, a well-to-do farmer, who resided at Shottery, a mile or two from Stratford. We do not know how old she was. An inscription on her grave in the chancel of the Church of the Holy Trinity records that she died in 1623 at the age of sixty-seven, but such inscriptions are notoriously inaccurate. The letters and numerals could be rubbed smooth by human feet, and later they would be recarved: a 5 might become a 6, a 1 might easily become a 7. We have no record of her baptism, nor do we know the date of their wedding. By November 1582, when it was clear that she was pregnant, it became necessary to obtain a marriage license. Accordingly two friends of the bride, who had also been friends of her father, presented themselves at the consistory court of the Bishop of Worcester concerning a license for "William Shagspere" to marry "Anne Hathwey of Stratford in the Dioces of Worcester maiden." These two friends, Fulke Sandells and John Richardson, promised to pay forty pounds to the bishop's chancellor, Richard Cosin, and his registrar, Robert Warmstry, if the requirements for a lawful marriage were not satisfied. All this was the purest formality, for an Elizabethan marriage did not require a church ceremony and Shakespeare and his bride regarded themselves as already married. It was enough for the husband to say, "I do confirm that I am your husband," and for the wife to say, "I do confirm that I am your wife," for a marriage to come into existence. The words would be spoken in front of friends, or even by the couple alone. Marriage had not yet been completely institutionalized; a truly loving couple had nothing to fear from the Church. Once the words had been spoken, the dower rights and bench rights of the woman were safeguarded.

Richard Hathaway died during the summer of 1582, leaving to Anne the sum of £6.13.4, the same sum he left to his other daughters. In each case he stipulated that the money should be paid to them on their wedding day. Fulke Sandells was one of the two supervisors of the will, and if in his presence Anne Hathaway agreed to become the wife of William Shakespeare, the bequest would be paid over on the same day, for this was the day they were "wedded."

We know nothing about Anne Shakespeare, and the very fact that we know nothing is of some significance. If there had been scandal, someone would have remembered it. If she had been unusually beautiful, this too would have been remembered. If she had been a shrew or if Shakespeare had felt no love for her, there would not be lacking in the small market town someone who would be happy to reveal it. That she disappears so quietly into Shakespeare's shadow testifies to their continuing love for each other. Nor does it follow that she was a woman who retired into a dull domesticity. She was a farmer's daughter, the eldest of three sisters, therefore capable of managing affairs, milking cows, lighting fires, plucking a chicken, and preparing a meal, and at the same time clever and high-spirited, for otherwise Shakespeare would not have been attracted to her. Shakespeare rarely mentions farmers' daughters in his plays. Launce in *The Two Gentlemen of Verona*, the earliest of the romantic comedies, communes with himself on the subject of a milkmaid:

> He lives not now that knows me to be in love, yet I am
> in love, but a team of horse shall not pluck that from me;
> nor who 'tis I love; and yet 'tis a woman; but what woman
> I will not tell myself; and yet 'tis a milk-maid; yet 'tis not a
> maid, for she hath had gossips; yet 'tis a maid, for she is her
> master's maid, and serves for wages. She hath more
> qualities than a water-spaniel, which is much in a bare
> Christian. Here is the cate-log of her conditions. "Imprimis,
> she can fetch and carry": why, a horse can do no more; nay,
> a horse cannot fetch, but only carry, therefore is she better
> than a jade. "Item, she can milk": look you, a sweet virtue
> in a maid with clean hands.

Launce was a fool, and Shakespeare's most personal statements were nearly always placed in the mouths of fools. We may imagine that this is how he thought in his youth and how he continued to think of women until he left Stratford and encountered the intensely worldly women of Queen Elizabeth's court.

On May 26, 1583, his daughter Susanna was baptized in the Church of the Holy Trinity. An unusual name for a girl, it came from the apocryphal *History of Susanna*, which was then included in the Bible and regarded as holy writ. It tells the story of how Susanna was surprised in her garden by two elders who would have raped her but she resolutely rejected them. In their frustration they bore false witness against her, declaring that they had seen her lying in the garden with a man. She appealed to God to save her, whereupon Daniel appeared, and he questioned the elders, asking them under which tree they had seen her lying with a man, and each elder answered with a different tree. For bearing false witness against the chaste Susanna they were sentenced to death. In the Great Bible of 1539 Susanna is described as "a tender person and marvellously fair of face."

So we may imagine Shakespeare at nineteen, with a wife and child to support, working in his father's shop, writing poetry, and dreaming of the world outside of Stratford, and seeing every play that was performed within a day's journey of Stratford. Nicholas Rowe, who wrote the first brief life of Shakespeare in 1709, says he entered his father's employment after leaving school. In fact, Shakespeare came to possess a professional knowledge of the glover's trade, and he introduces technical terms connected with glovemaking at the most unlikely moments in his plays. Glovemaking interested him; a life devoted to glovemaking did not.

Reputable scholars have suggested that Shakespeare became a soldier, a lawyer's clerk, a traveler in Italy in the company of a distinguished personage of the time, or a country schoolmaster. The so-called lost years have been sifted in an effort to discover his whereabouts and these efforts have been unavailing. We are therefore forced to the conclusion that he did what we might expect him to do and that he ran off to London and joined a theatre. As soon as possible, under any conditions whatsoever, he was determined to become a player.

The
Young Poet

POETS HAVE A TENDENCY to keep their early works, even their very earliest works. These early poems are like love children conceived without benefit of marriage, unruly reminders of a misspent youth, all the more precious because they are weak and fragile. The poems are carefully preserved in safe places, and many years may pass before the poet dares to look at them again. And when at last he returns to them, he may have little hope of learning anything from them: he simply desires to keep faith with his beginnings. They are part of his youth and exist for their own sake. Sometimes it happens that the earliest work contains ideas, images, and rhythms which are recognizably the same ideas, images, and rhythms that appear in his mature work. The beginnings foreshadow the future.

There is something else about these early works that needs to be said. It often happens that the young poet shows an astonishing maturity. We know that William Blake wrote *Poetical Sketches* between his twelfth and twentieth years. Dylan Thomas wrote one of his most famous poems, "The Force That Through the Green Fuse Drives the Flower," when he was eighteen. There is scarcely a poet of any stature who did not write verses when he was in his teens, and we have no reason to believe that Shakespeare was an exception. We may expect him to have written verses from the age of sixteen or seventeen, and it would be surprising if he did not.

The youthful writings of poets are often violent and chaotic. The impulse to create poetry is there but sometimes the poet has no mastery over his emotions. The colors melt, the ideas are in conflict, the form is diffused, there are no clear outlines. Often the poetry betrays its sexual origins with abrupt, pounding rhythms, as the youthful poet wrestles with his demons. Frustration, anger, revulsion, visions of a blinding and unattainable beauty, are the marks of the young poet. Since he does not yet fully realize what poetry is about, he simply pours himself on the page, determined at all costs to give shape to his amorphous ideas, forcing the pace, reaching beyond his own grasp, and sometimes borrowing unashamedly from other poets. He writes out of desperation even when he is imitating other poets, and in his haste to see his ideas on paper he abuses and punishes words in order to make them serve his desperate purposes. Wrestling with demons is an occupation for grown men. The youthful poet wrestles without having taken full measure of the enemy.

If then we could imagine Shakespeare's earliest verses, we could expect them to be derivative, modeled on Spenser, using the somewhat archaic language of Spenser, yet recognizably containing in their embryonic form some of the images and many of the cadences of his maturity. The verses would be violent, chaotic, unresolved, perhaps coarse-grained, and we might expect to hear pounding rhythms. If the poem took the form of a narrative, we would expect many loose ends and abrupt changes of direction. Here and there we would find awkwardnesses and passages of great beauty. Above all, we would expect to find some intimations of Shakespeare's mature style hidden away in places where they are least expected.

Such a poem has survived in "A Lover's Complaint," which was first published by Thomas Thorpe in 1609 when it was bound up with Shakespeare's *Sonnets*. It is a long narrative of forty-seven stanzas in rhyme royal amounting to nearly 330 lines. We are introduced to a young woman who sits on the banks of a river tearing up her love letters and tossing them into the water. She has a basket full of jewels and baubles given to her in happier times and they too are thrown into the water. An old herdsman, a man who had known the excitement of the city and the court and who knew the ways of the world, approaches her and asks what she is doing. Her face lined with grief, she tells him that she has been abandoned by her lover, whom she had known from the beginning to be nothing more than a seducer who "preached pure maid and praised cold chastity" even as he took advantage of her. While the old herdsman sits at some distance from her sharing her sorrow, she laments her fate with tears coursing down her cheeks: tears, love letters, and jewels all fall into the river.

We see these two people vividly, the girl's face shaded by her straw hat, the old man gazing at her intensely while keeping a proper distance. We see the departed lover in the pride of his youthful beauty, a man loved by young and old, bewitching everyone with his charm, for she describes him at length. She remembers his impassioned speeches, his brilliant horsemanship, his grace of manner, his melting eyes, and as she describes him in her imagination she still yearns for him. The old herdsman comforts her in vain, and the poem ends with the girl caught up in a sudden visionary description of his eyes—the eyes that have betrayed her.

The poem begins awkwardly, the poet describing how he stood on a hill, heard the echo of her words from the hill's concave womb, and watched her tearing up her love letters and breaking her rings:

> From off a hill whose concave womb reworded
> A plaintful story from a sistering vale,
> My spirits to attend this double voice accorded,
> And down I laid to list the sad tuned tale,   ‎ _
> Ere long espied a fickle maid full pale,
> Tearing of papers, breaking rings a-twain,
> Storming her world with sorrows, wind and rain.*

*Reworded: repeated, reechoed. Shakespeare uses the word in *Hamlet*. In *Antony and Cleopatra*: "We cannot call her winds and waters, sighs and tears."

Nothing that comes afterward in the poem is quite so brutal with the sound of splintering wood and tearing of paper. It is harsh and gritty, perhaps deliberately so. The explosive poet is concerned to set the stage as simply as possible and to state his theme, which is a woman storming the world with her laments. In the following stanza we are warned that the woman in her grief looks old and raddled but her original beauty may still be seen "through lattice of seared age."

> Upon her head a plaited hive of straw*
> Which fortified her visage from the sun,
> Whereon the thought might think sometime it saw
> The carcass of a beauty spent and done:
> Time had not scythed all that youth begun,
> Nor youth all quit, but spite of heaven's fell rage
> Some beauty peeped through lattice of seared age.

"The carcass of a beauty spent and done" is already Shakespearean with its straining for the ultimate expression; *carcass, spent,* and *done* reinforcing one another, circling around *beauty,* which is wholly imprisoned. She is old but she is also young: Shakespeare liked these antitheses. To describe her as a carcass when she was perhaps twenty-two is to paint her in livid colors. But he is not so much painting her portrait as investigating her mind, her fears for her lost beauty. The straw bonnet which half conceals her face gives her physical dimension so that she is anchored to the landscape.

It is done well but it is done awkwardly. Shakespeare uses words that were already archaic in his day, and he uses images that seem forced to us but belonged to the poetical equipment of the time. He describes the woman lifting a patterned handkerchief to her eyes, thus: "Laundering the silken figures in the brine. That seasoned woe had pelleted in tears." We remember the "pelleted storm" in *Antony and Cleopatra*, where the pellets were evidently hailstones, and we remember the many baths of tears in Elizabethan poetry, but the image remains far-fetched and elusive. He is on safer ground when he describes the woman tossing into the river the many baubles and letters she received from her lover.

---

*Hive of straw: bonnet of straw.

A thousand favors from a maund* she drew
Of amber, crystal and of beaded jet,
Which one by one she in the river threw,
Upon whose weeping margent she was set,
Like usury applying wet to wet,
Or monarch's hands that lets not bounty fall
Where want cries some, but where excess begs all.
Of folded schedules she had many a one,
Which she perused, sighed, tore and gave the flood,
Cracked many a ring of posied gold and bone,
Bidding them find their sepulchres in mud,
Found yet more letters sadly penned in blood
With sleided silk, feat and affectedly
Enswathed and sealed in curious secrecy.

When Shakespeare speaks of "usury applying wet to wet," he is merely emphasizing that the bath of tears was overflowing, a fact that the reader already knows. He is saying very little in an unconscionable number of words. He is not to be blamed for it, for Spenser was far more prolix. Shakespeare was not being merely clever when he compared her with usury and a king's unpredictable bounty: the extended metaphor works well enough. It was a time when metaphors crowded on metaphors until they fused together to produce something more than metaphor: they produced spinning clusters of ideas and images. This fusion of metaphors was more characteristic of Shakespeare than of any other poet of his time, and it is already apparent in "A Lover's Complaint."

Nothing could be simpler than the picture of a girl in a straw hat leisurely tossing things into the river. But with Shakespeare, even the very early Shakespeare, simple things are suspect. We become aware that many things are happening simultaneously, and there is a sense in which she is pouring her whole life in the river and drowning in her own tears. The jewels which she tears apart and the letters torn into fragments are her own flesh and blood. Shakespeare speaks of "more letters sadly penned in blood," and describes

---

*Maund: basket. Schedules: letters. Posied: inscribed with a posy. Sleided: untwisted. Feat: skillfully.

how they are decorated with a red seal stamped over a silken ribbon, like legal documents: they are evidently the deeds and charters of her love, and the many promises of marriage. From the beginning he uses legal terms effortlessly and had more than a casual knowledge of legal terminology.

Here, too, in the stanza describing her frantic destruction of letters and jewelry, we encounter for the first time one of those clusters of images that return again and again in his work with the force of an obsession. Jewels-mud-sepulchre is one of those tightly knit clusters which remained with him through most of his life. The mud may become sea-ooze. The jewels may be pearl or coral, as here they are gold rings and ivory bracelets. The sepulchre may be a tomb or a coffin or simply a dead man or woman. He possessed a shuddering fear of death by drowning, a fear expressed in his plays whenever his characters are close to a river or the sea. These clusters are not so much the expressions of his unconscious mind as patterns within his imagination. He appears to be perfectly aware of their existence and is never more lyrical than when he employs them.

The rough-hewn beginning of "A Lover's Complaint" breaks down, the verse becomes more limpid, the pace quickens. For some thirty-seven stanzas the maiden continues her lamentations, describing every aspect of betrayal. She has the metaphysical temper: what has happened to her is more like war in heaven than a simple seduction. The metaphysical wit is held in check, sometimes bubbling up with extraordinary effect, as when she declares that so many maidens adored him that their eyes "stuck over all his face."

> But woe is me, too early I attended
> A youthful suit it was to gain my grace;
> Of one by nature's outwards so commended
> That maiden's eyes stuck over all his face.
> Love lack'd a dwelling and made him her place,
> And when in his fair parts she did abide
> She was new lodged and newly deified.

"A Lover's Complaint"—it is necessary to observe that the lover is a woman—is the work of a very young man, rejoicing in his control of verse and not too disturbed when he fails to control it. Restless and urgent, sometimes awkward and ugly, too often forgot-

ten in the vast volume of Shakespeare's work, it shows him wrestling with sexual demons and not always being overcome by them.
One can imagine him writing these verses in Stratford, when he was
still in his teens.

There are passages in the poem that are like the preliminary
rumblings of the great thunders he would later produce. What he
calls "The effects of terror and dear modesty" are examined by a
mind trained to understand every variation in the sexual atmosphere. He is writing on a very personal level, always examining
himself, distributing the praise and the blame evenhandedly. He
says of himself: "Maiden-tongued he was and thereof free," where
"thereof" means "therefore." "Maiden-tongued" has at least three
possible meanings, and he appears to have been aware of all of
them, delighting in their ambiguity.

There is one verse where he celebrates his power over language:

So on the tip of his subduing tongue
All kinds of arguments and question deep,
All replication prompt, and reason strong
For his advantage still did wake and sleep,
To make the weeper laugh, the laugher weep:
He had the dialect and different skill,
Catching all passions in his craft of will.

It was an astonishing boast, which he would repeat in the *Sonnets*.
Already there are signs of a fierce pride and a fierce impatience.
Already, too, he was capable of writing lines which are immediately
memorable:

Oh father, what a hell of witchcraft lies
In the small orb of one particular tear.

Few modern critics have any patience with "A Lover's Complaint." They forget it, or relegate it to a single line in a footnote, or
prefer to believe that it was not written by Shakespeare at all.
Edmund Malone, the greatest of Shakespearean scholars, delighted
in it, and showed how this youthful work contained the seeds of
many of Shakespeare's future poetic ideas. He thought he detected
the influence of Spenser:

"In this beautiful poem, in every part of which the hand of
Shakespeare is visible, he perhaps meant to break a lance
with Spenser. It appears to me to have more of the
simplicity and pathetick tenderness of the older poet, in his
smaller pieces, than any other poem of that time: and
strongly reminds me of our authour's description of an
ancient song, in *Twelfth Night*:

> It is silly sooth,
> And dallies with the innocence of youth
> Like the old age."

But "A Lover's Complaint" is not a dallying poem, and if it
seems to wander, it is because a metaphysical mind must follow all
arguments to their metaphysical conclusions. It is Shakespeare
exerting his poetic muscles and "catching all passions in his craft of
will."

The Death
of an Arden

ABOUT THE TIME WHEN SHAKESPEARE was leaving Stratford for London, there occurred an incident that threw panic into the family of Arden. Once more, as so often before, the Ardens found themselves on the losing side and paid the penalty.

What came to be known as the Somerville-Arden conspiracy began in the summer of 1583 shortly after Bishop Whitgift was raised to the see of Canterbury, becoming Archbishop and Primate of all England. He had long ago demonstrated his hatred and contempt for the old faith, and all Catholics realized that his elevation would lead to more savage punishments for Catholics and especially for their priests. Queen Elizabeth was in deadly earnest: she feared the Catholic alliance in Europe; she feared Mary, Queen of Scots, who was her prisoner; she feared and yet tolerated many of the great noble families which refused to convert to the new faith. She watched them closely, and Walsingham, the chief of her secret service, filled the country with informers who were well paid out of the public treasury.

The Ardens were a Catholic family closely linked with many leading Catholic families. When Robert Arden wrote his will in 1556, leaving Asbies to his daughter Mary, he began his bequests in the Catholic form: "First, I bequeath my soul to Almighty God and to our blessed Lady, Saint Mary, and to all the holy company of heaven." William Shakespeare's mother was brought up in a Catholic household and it is likely that she remained a Catholic to the end of her days. The Ardens of Park Hall near Birmingham were her kinsmen, and the Somerville-Arden conspiracy was hatched in the old moated house where Father Hugh Hall, a priest with a taste for violent action, encouraged the Ardens to work for the downfall of Queen Elizabeth.

Nearly everyone in the family seems to have been involved: Edward Arden of Park Hall, who was the head of the family; his wife, Mary, who was a Throckmorton; his daughter, Margaret, who was married to John Somerville, and John's sister. In 1583 John Somerville was twenty-four. He had inherited his father's estates when he was eighteen. He studied at Oxford University, and he was said to be a personable and handsome young man. Two children were born of the marriage. He could look forward to a quiet life managing his estates, raising a family, and attending to the social duties of a country gentleman. Instead he threw himself into the conspiracy and lost his life.

John Somerville and Edward Arden were intelligent people, and they knew that it would not be enough to kill Queen Elizabeth. The details of the conspiracy were never completely made clear, but it appears that an attempt was to be made to kill the Queen and simultaneously rescue Mary, Queen of Scots, and place her on the throne. On October 23, 1583, Somerville set out from Edstone for London, accompanied only by a boy. The thought that he would soon kill the Queen unhinged his mind; he talked about it; the boy became terrified and left him; and at a little inn on a lonely wayside road at Aynho on the Hill, near Oxford, he talked deliriously about his determination "to shoot the Queen with his dagg." A dagg was a heavy pistol. Someone, probably the innkeeper, informed on him, and on the following day, after reaching Banbury, he was arrested and taken to Oxford, where he was examined by a judge who issued a warrant for his arrest and sent him under guard to London. Since he was an important prisoner, he was guarded by twelve men. In London he was taken to the Gatehouse, questioned again, and a confession was extracted from him. He incriminated Edward Arden, Mary Arden, his own wife, his sister, and Father Hugh Hall. On October 31 a warrant was issued for their arrest and the arrest of any others who might be implicated. No less a person than Thomas Wilkes, clerk of the Privy Council, was sent to Warwickshire to investigate. He stayed with Sir Thomas Lucy at Charlecote, which became his headquarters. On November 3 a raiding party was sent to Park Hall, twenty miles from Charlecote, where Edward and Mary Arden were arrested. Another raiding party was sent to Idlicote, nine miles south of Stratford, where they found Father Hugh Hall living in the home of William Underhill, the owner of New Place, the second largest house in Stratford. On November 2 Wilkes wrote to Walsingham:

> Unless you can make Somerville, Arden, Hall the priest, Somerville's wife and sister to speak directly to those things you desire to have discovered, it will not be possible for us here to find out more than is found already, for that the papists in this country greatly do work upon the advantage of clearing their houses of all shows of suspicion.

John Somerville had been lodged in the Tower of London. He was now brought to Warwick, joining Father Hall and Edward and Mary Arden to face the indictment. Ordinarily the trial would have taken place in Warwick, but it was felt that the case was so important it must be moved to London. At this point Father Hall completely vanishes: it was said that he was murdered on the way to London. Somerville, Edward Arden, and his wife were found guilty and condemned to a traitor's death. On November 19 Somerville and Edward Arden were brought from the Tower to Newgate Prison in preparation for the execution on the following day. That night Somerville was found strangled in his cell: some believed he strangled himself, but it is more likely that he was murdered by his jailers. Edward Arden was hanged, boweled, and quartered at Smithfield. The heads of the two men were stuck up on Tower Bridge. Somerville's body was buried in Moorfields and Edward Arden's quarters were hung on the gates of the city. He forfeited his lands and properties to the Crown. The only happy part of the story concerns his wife Mary, who was released from prison a few months later.

In Holinshed's *Chronicles* the historian takes pains to paint a moral concerning God's vengeance on the wicked John Somerville:

> A dreadful example of God's heavy judgment upon those offenders but specially against the last, whom God delivered to a reprobate mind, insomuch as his own hands became his hangman, preventing the office of the common executioner who should have performed that last action on him: whereof the justice of God in vengeance made himself the finisher and fulfiller. This much by the ways of terror, that the remembrance hereof, by the reading and reporting of the same, may make men evil minded, amazed at the rigorous revengement which God taketh upon the wicked.

The people who were most amazed by the "rigorous revengement" were probably to be found in Warwickshire. For a few days in November the police scoured the countryside and turned the county upside down in an effort to discover the scope of the conspiracy. In fact, they discovered very little. The Catholics closed their ranks; the informers appear to have learned no more than Walsingham learned by putting Somerville on the rack. Shakespeare learned of the conspiracy, for it was the talk of the whole county. It was a family matter, touching him directly. The hanging, boweling, and quartering of the head of the Arden family was not something that could be easily forgotten. He was learning, at nineteen, the full extent of royal vengeance.

The execution of Edward Arden on December 20, 1583, came as a fitting conclusion to a year which the prognosticators regarded with foreboding. In that year occurred the conjunction of Saturn and Jupiter, "the greatest and most sovereign conjunction of the seven planets." They prophesied plagues, floods, strange alterations in the body politic, the deaths of kings, the destructions of climates, the coming of a prophet. People would have the same dread of 1588. But this time indeed there were no vast changes, very few conspiracies were discovered, England held her own abroad, and the Queen after reigning for a quarter of a century remained in good spirits and good health. The prognosticators were wrong but they succeeded in infecting the country with a sense of foreboding. In those days men read the astrological charts carefully, and even the wisest of them took precautions to avoid malign influences descending upon them from the planets. The Queen was learned in astrology; so were her ministers; so was Shakespeare. He was nineteen, a father, restless in a small provincial town, with no future except to work in his father's glove shop. In this year when Saturn and Jupiter were in conjunction, he probably left Stratford for London.

Shakespeare
of Shoreditch

The
First Theatre

W HILE STRATFORD LIVED IN THE MIDDLE AGES,
London lived in the high tide of the Renaissance. It
received merchandise from all over the world, and together with
merchandise came ideas, new interpretations of existing ideas,
books, pamphlets, architectural designs, maps of all known lands
and seas and of the constellations of the sky. Intellectually London
was most indebted to Italy, which had inherited the knowledge
accumulated in ancient Rome, and in addition she had become the
heir of the Byzantine tradition. Some of this knowledge filtered
through France; a little of it came through Spain and Portugal. It
was an age of translations, and the heritage of the ancient world
came to England through an astonishing number of translations
made very often by men who were ill equipped to translate accurately while making up for the inaccuracy of their translations by
their uncontrollable enthusiasm.

We sometimes forget how many books were published in the
sixteenth century. William Caxton printed the first book to appear
in English in 1474. He printed it in Bruges. He was both translator

and printer, for this book which was called *The Recuyell of the Historyes of Troye* was a translation made by him from the French. Two years later he set up his printing press in Westminster. Before he died in 1491, he had printed nearly a hundred books. Thereafter books came in spate. In the first quarter of the sixteenth century Richard Pynson and Wynkyn de Worde between them published more than 600 volumes. By the close of the century more than 10,000 volumes had been published in the English tongue.

It was a period when the language was fiercely alive, not forced into a matrix. It had directness and spontaneity, and showed its muscles. In the Great Bible, which was translated by William Tyndale and Myles Coverdale and published in 1539, we see the language in all its freshness, as though conscious of its youth. Here for example, are some passages from the Song of Solomon as it appeared in the Great Bible:

> I went down to the nut garden, to see what grew by the brooks, and to look if the vineyard flourished, or if the pomegranates were shot forth. I knew not if my soul had made me the chariot of the people that be under tribute. Turn again, turn again. O thou perfect one turn again, turn again, and we will look upon thee. What will ye see in the Shulamite? She is like men of war singing in a company.
>
> O how pleasant are thy treadings with the shoes, thou prince's daughter. Thy thighs are like a fair jewel, which is wrought by a cunning work master.
>
> Thy navel is like a round goblet, which is never without drink. Thy womb is like a heap of wheat that is set about with roses.

Such was the English language a quarter of a century before Shakespeare was born, in the freshness of the morning. It is the English spoken in the time of Henry VIII, before Elizabethan complexity and Italian rhythms changed it. If you compare the passage just quoted with the corresponding passage in the King James Version of the Bible which appeared seventy years later, you will see that in those seventy years the language gained in weight and sonority, but lost sinew. It lost its clear, early outlines; an immense number of new words were added; the simple song became a symphony. In 1539 no one could possibly have written "the multitudinous seas incarnadine." They would have asked what was wrong with "many red seas"? Shakespeare was one of those who extended the boundaries of the English language to hitherto unknown limits.

One of the best writers and speakers was Queen Elizabeth herself. She studied the cadences of the English sentence and read more books than most of her subjects. According to her tutor, Roger Ascham, she knew Greek, Latin, French, Spanish, and Italian exceedingly well. Her influence on the language was great, for she expected her servants—everyone in England was her servant—to speak well and vividly when they addressed her. She could not abide a clumsy phrase, as she could not abide bad manners. Vivid, redhaired, when flashing eyes and quick gestures, she ruled with gentleness and ironhandedness. She was Machiavelli's Prince, Plato's philosopher king, and the Tablets of the Law. She was also very fallible, and sometimes gave way to feminine rages. Yet for the most part she was cool-headed and very masculine.

Queen Elizabeth stood at the apex of the pyramid. Below her were the aristocracy, owners of large landed estates, many of them with titles created by King Henry VIII and possessing properties that had formerly belonged to the Church. William Cecil, Lord Burghley, the son of an obscure Lincolnshire farmer, was one of these plenipotentiary lords who acted like princes, lived in great state, possessed their own palaces, and kept retainers and liveried servants. These lords possessed naked power, and being Elizabethans they exerted it to the uttermost, pressing their advantages at court and sometimes acting as though there were no court, as though they themselves were the fountains of honor and preferment. Lord Burghley, and his son Sir Robert Cecil, who became Lord Salisbury, ruled in Queen Elizabeth's name. She provided the iron will; they provided the brains.

There were about forty landed families which between them owned most of England. Below them came the minor aristocracy and the gentry with their manor houses and their estates which they were continually attempting to enlarge by enclosing the common lands. Rising in power were the towns which received charters from the monarch, permitting them to rule themselves, thus placing them in a position where they could oppose the encroachments of the landowners. The bailiffs who ruled over the towns and the master craftsmen who ruled over the trade guilds would inevitably find themselves in opposition to the feudal lords.

The common people had no power, or so little that it was scarcely discernible. They were a robust people, intent on their creature comforts, proud of their traditions, despising all foreigners. We imagine they were not very different from us, since they spoke English and wrote the language in a way that still gives us pleasure. But we would find surprising differences if we met them in the flesh. They dressed gaily in all the colors of the rainbow, the men wore stockings which displayed the shapeliness of their legs and they wore ruffs to frame their faces, and if a man wore an enormous feather in his cap, it was simply because he believed that feathers provided a proper ornament. An Elizabethan galant posing for his portrait would need a whole morning to get dressed in, so many were the rings, jewels, garters, gilded buttons, and lace furbelows he must wear to appear at his best.

In the schools the monkish traditions continued; scholars were as sober-minded as the nobility and the gentry were exuberantly self-indulgent. Schoolboys worked inordinately hard. A boy might take his degree at fifteen, marry at seventeen, rise to a general's rank at thirty, and at thirty-five he might find himself a grandfather. They lived hard, at full tilt. They had voracious appetites—for food, for learning, for new costumes, for new experiences—and they quickly exhausted themselves and were old men at fifty.

Also, they were smaller than we are and more nimble. There was a solid, unyielding quality about them: they were not easily unnerved by disasters—plagues, floods, fires, epidemics of typhoid fever, the multitudinous deaths of babies and children. They put a bold face on things, expected the worst, and knew that even the best was impermanent. Thomas Nashe's song from *Summer's Last Will and Testament* shows how they were able to transform their deepest griefs into lyrical exaltations:

Adieu, farewell earth's bliss,
This world uncertain is,
Fond are life's lustful joys,

Queen Elizabeth by an unknown artist (National Portrait Gallery)

Robert Devereux, Second Earl of Essex, attributed to Marcus Gheeraents (National Portrait Gallery)

SERO, SED SERIO

Robert Cecil, First Earl of Salisbury, by J. de Critz the elder (National Portrait Gallery)

Henry Wriothesley, Third Earl of Southampton, at the age of 21 (National Portrait Gallery)

Henry Wriothesley in middle age, after D. Mytens (National Portrait Gallery)

Cripplegate, from Agass' map, circa 1560, showing Mountjoy's house at the corner of Silver Street and Monkswell ("Mugle") Street

The Curtain, Shoreditch, from a map called A View of the Cittie of London from the North towards the South, *1600. The Theatre had by this time been torn down and removed to Bankside.*

Death proves them all but toys,
None from his darts can fly:
I am sick, I must die:
   Lord, have mercy upon us.

Beauty is but a flower
Which wrinkles will devour.
Brightness falls from the air,
Queens have died young and fair,
Dust hath closed Helen's eye,
I am sick, I must die:
   Lord, have mercy upon us.

Again and again in Elizabethan times we come upon such calmly meditative lines on death that conceal a sense of total desperation, of total helplessness. Grief holds them by the throat, death is all around them, and for a few more minutes they attempt to conjure up the beauty of the world even when they are in agony. "Brightness falls from the air" has something of the effect of a Buddhist mantra, to be repeated softly until the words lose all meaning and there is only an afterglow.

These people who had little feeling for privacy and lived pell-mell on top of one another in crowded tenements had little feeling for splendor. They knew they were living in the best of times. Elizabethan England was England at its very height, and they were well aware of it. They built magnificently: Longleat House in Wiltshire and Wollaton Hall in Nottinghamshire testify to a superb mastery of architecture in a style that was entirely their own. More and more Elizabethan houses acquired grace and lightness: the many-windowed country houses of the aristocracy gazed down on quiet lakes and serene gardens. Splendor was equated with serenity. In fact, the lives of the Elizabethans were never serene, however much they pretended to a passion for serenity. The great lords walking in the quiet of their gardens were at the mercy of anxieties: the headman's ax hovered above their heads even when they appeared to be most carefree.

There was a Tudor ferocity that tends to be forgotten by scholars, and what Shakespeare called "the rash fierce blaze of riot" was never far from the surface. Punishment was deliberately slow, cumbersome, and terrible. The slow torture of the rack, to extract confessions, was commonplace. Serious crimes, from theft to high treason, were rewarded with the threefold punishment of hanging, boweling, and quartering. This terrible prolonged punishment seemed to answer to a need of their souls. They were a rough, turbulent, vivid, exasperated people who enjoyed life and death at their sharpest points and were headstrong for entertainment, especially for plays that permitted them to forget their own griefs. From John Stow's *Annales, or a Generall Chronicle of England* we learn that the theatre as we know it today came into existence in 1583, which happened to be about the time Shakespeare reached London:

> Comedians and stage players of former times were poor
> and ignorant in respect of those of this time, but being now
> grown very skilful and exquisite actors for all matters they
> were entertained into the service of divers great lords, out of
> which companies there were twelve of the best chosen, and
> at the request of Sir Francis Walsingham they were sworn
> the Queen's servants and were allowed wages and liveries,
> as Grooms of the Chamber; and until this year 1583 the
> Queen had no players. Among those twelve players were
> two rare men, viz. Thomas Wilson for a quick delicate
> refined temporal wit, and Richard Tarleton for a wondrous
> plentiful pleasant extemporal wit. He was the wonder of his
> time.

It was significant that the idea first came to Walsingham, the secretary of state, artificer of England's domestic and foreign policy, and head of her far-ranging secret service. The establishment of the Queen's Players was a political act. New plays would be written at Walsingham's orders and there was nothing to prevent him from using the players for his own purposes. He was a harsh man with a steely humor, devoted to the Queen and to the Protestant cause— when he was ambassador to Paris he had watched the St. Bartholomew Massacre and had nothing but loathing for the Catholics— and when at his orders the royal theatre came into existence he had several purposes in mind. The players would entertain the Queen, they would perform in plays celebrating the Tudor monarchy, and by implication Elizabeth herself, and there would be dramas derid-

ing the enemies of England, presenting them as murderous volup-
tuaries and intolerant boors. The playwrights would make propa-
ganda for England. He knew them well and sometimes employed
them in his secret service. He was the spider at the center of a great
web, and from time to time he could be seen gliding deftly along one
of its threads to catch another fly in his open mouth.

Walsingham gave the order early in March, but it was not until
November 28 that the royal players known as Queen Elizabeth's
Men were licensed by the City Corporation. All the twelve actors
were borrowed from existing companies. They were Robert Wilson,
John Dutton, Toby Miles, John Towne, John Singer, Lionel
Cooke, John Garland, John Adams, Richard Tarleton, John Laneham, John Bentley, and William Johnson. Robert Wilson was an
actor and dramatist, who wrote at least sixteen plays, all of them
lost. Tarleton, of course, was the most famous clown of his time,
dancing across the stage on tiptoe in his familiar russet suit and
buttoned cap, and wielding a tabor. He died in the year of Armada,
but he was not quickly forgotten. These twelve were the first wave
of great Elizabethan actors. When the second wave came, Shakespeare would be among them.

In a statement written many years later by Winifred and Cuthbert Burbage—Cuthbert being the brother of Richard Burbage and
Winifred being Richard's widow—we read: "The father of us was
the first builder of playhouses, and was himself in his younger years
a player." This was James Burbage, who built the Theatre in 1576
on property owned by Giles Alleyn, gentleman. The property was
in Shoreditch, about three quarters of a mile north of London Wall,
beyond Bishopsgate. It originally consisted of five tumbledown
houses, a large stable that had fallen into disrepair, and a horse-
pond. One end of the stable was used as a slaughterhouse.

On this disreputable site, between five tumbledown houses and
the stable, Burbage erected the Theatre, signing a lease with Giles
Alleyn by which he agreed to pay a rent of fourteen pounds a year,
and he also agreed to restore the five houses so that they could be
lived in. The lease was to last for twenty-one years, that is, until
1597. There was also a stipulation that Burbage could remove
during the term of the lease any building he erected on the site, and
he appears to have inserted this clause in the lease with the delib-

erate intention of removing the Theatre to another place whenever it suited him.

A few months after Burbage built the Theatre, a certain Henry Laneman built another theatre at Curtain Close a little to the south of it. Soon Laneman was quarreling with Burbage, who was also quarreling with his brother-in-law, John Brayne, a grocer who had advanced him some money. In 1585 Burbage and Laneman agreed to share the profits of the two theatres, and in the following year Brayne died. In that same year Philip Henslowe leased a property called "the Little Rose with two gardens," and he built the Rose Theatre. So there were three theatres catering to the general public. The Rose was set amid the stews of Bankside south of the river, while the Theatre and the Curtain were in the rather unsavory district of Shoreditch, which means Sewer's ditch, to the north of London, and all three theatres were outside the jurisdiction of the mayor of London. Out of these three theatres there emerged the massive splendor of the Elizabethan drama.

The profligacy of the players was well known; the theatres were the haunts of pickpockets and strumpets and worse; official London disapproved. Preachers inveighed against the theatres as though Satan had taken up his abode in them. The reverent and law-abiding wondered why London should be plagued with so much prodigality and folly. Preaching at Paul's Cross on November 3, 1577, John Stockwood thundered at the theatre owners who filled their theatres with thousands when the churches were nearly empty:

> Will not a filthy play, with the blast of a trumpet, sooner
> call thither a thousand than an hour's tolling of a bell bring
> to the sermon a hundred? Nay, even here in the City,
> without it be at this place, and some other certain ordinary
> audience, where shall you find a reasonable company?
> Whereas, if you resort to the Theatre, the Curtain and
> other places of plays in the City, you shall on the Lord's
> day have these places, with many others that I cannot
> reckon, so full as possibly they can throng.

From Stockwood's sermon we learn that the beginning of each play was announced by a trumpet blast that the players performed on Sundays. But we do not know what plays were acted in those early years. Stow tells us that they were comedies, tragedies, and histories, but it is more likely that they were mostly blood and thunder plays written by hacks in rhymed verse with a good deal of fighting and adultery. These secular dramas sometimes touched on contemporary problems and therefore the authorities kept a close watch on them. Many in the audience were young apprentices, skilled workmen, intelligent but uneducated except in their trades, capable of great havoc when it suited them. The government, afraid of riots, sent spies among them.

On Whit Monday in 1584, between the Theatre and the Curtain there was a full-scale battle. An apprentice had fallen asleep in the grassy fields near the two theatres. A young gentleman jumped on his belly, woke him up, and started a fight. Soon there were five hundred people, mostly apprentices, milling about and exchanging insults and blows with the city folk, who shouted that they were rascals and the scum of the earth, while the apprentices roared back even more devastating insults. Heads were broken, blood was spilled, some apprentices were carried off to prison. On the following day the prison was attacked by the apprentices who wanted to rescue their fellows. On Wednesday there was another small riot outside the door of the Theatre. Chief Justice Anderson, sitting in judgment over the arrested apprentices, was so disturbed by the affair that he sent two aldermen to the Privy Council to demand that the Theatre and the Curtain be torn down because they were dangerous to the Queen's peace. The Council agreed over the objections of the Lord Chamberlain. The theatres appeared to be doomed. All that was needed was for the Council to issue the order for their destruction and they would be leveled within twenty-four hours. But the Lord Chamberlain at this time was Lord Howard of Effingham, soon to become supreme commander of the English fleet against the Spanish Armada, and he refused to permit a warrant to be issued. The actors at the Theatre were the Queen's Men, the actors at the Curtain were under the protection of the Earl of Arundel, and Burbage was under the protection of Lord Hunsdon. Too many high officials possessed an interest in the actors for there to be any hope of a simple, destructive solution to the problem.

The chief magistrate of London then and now was known as the Recorder. He sent for the actors and interrogated them; he also sent

for Burbage, who refused to come, saying in a lordly manner that he
intended to write on the following day to his patron, Lord Hunsdon.
The Recorder was not impressed and sent an undersheriff to arrest
him. He was ill-tempered and threatening, when he appeared
before the recorder, but he calmed down when the recorder began to
list the punishments he might suffer for further disobedience. The
recorder complained to Lord Burghley, Queen Elizabeth's secretary
and Lord High Treasurer: "At his coming he shouted me out, very
hasty, and in the end I showed him my Lord his master's hand, and
then he was more quiet, for to die for it he would not be bound."

Burbage was "a stubborn fellow" who held out for his rights,
and he saw no reason why the theatres should be torn down just
because the apprentices and the gentlemen had bloodied a few
heads. He was to remain in litigation for the rest of his life. His son
Richard, born about 1568, was equally stubborn and if offended at
anyone would threaten him with a broom and send him packing.

About 1586—the exact year is unknown—there appeared at the
Theatre a play called *The Spanish Tragedy*, by Thomas Kyd, a
Londoner, and almost simultaneously a play called *Tamburlaine
the Great*, by Christopher Marlowe, who was about to receive an
M.A. under very peculiar circumstances, for the Privy Council
insisted that the degree be granted to him although he had done
little studying and had spent many months on secret business on
behalf of the Crown abroad. Kyd and Marlowe were friends, and
they appeared to have vied with one another to produce plays of an
extreme violence. This was blood and thunder drama elevated to the
highest art. These two plays had the effect of volcanic explosions,
and thereafter English drama would continue to exist in the ruddy
light of these volcanoes.

Kyd's play moved fast, one act of vengeance following on another. Hieronimo, marshal of Spain, sees his hapless son Horatio
hanging on a tree, blood pouring from his many stab wounds. He
becomes obsessed with the determination to find out what has
happened, uncover the conspiracy, punish the criminals. His wife,
Isabella, goes mad and stabs herself in the place where her son's
body was found. Bel-Imperia, who loved Horatio, offers to help,
and Hieronimo induces her to act in a play which will outline the
course taken by the conspirators and the real conspirators are

induced to act out their roles. This play within a play is performed with great realism, Hieronimo taking a leading role and arranging that all the conspirators shall be killed on stage, not as actors are killed, but as real people are killed. Bel-Imperia stabs herself, while the dead conspirators lie dead around her. When the play ends Hieronimo attempts to hang himself. He is prevented but succeeds in biting off his tongue. Given a pen, he says he will write out a full confession and asks for a knife to sharpen the pen. With the knife he lunges forward and stabs Lorenzo, the brother of Bel-Imperia, and then he stabs himself to death.

The single theme of the play was revenge pursued until all the evildoers to the very last one and to their most remote assistants have been as foully murdered as Horatio. It is a study of the pure pleasure of revenge, the absolute sweetness of it. From time to time the audience is reminded that revenge has its own laws, its own logic, its own magic. After trumpeting revenge throughout the play, Hieronimo, surrounded by dead bodies on the stage and soon to bite off his tongue, declares to the viceroy of Portugal:

> I tell thee, Viceroy, this day I have seen revenge,
> And in that sight have grown a prouder monarch
> Than ever sat under the crown of Spain.
> Had I as many lives as there be stars,
> As many heavens to go to as those lives
> I'd give them all, ay, and my soul to boot
> But I could see thee ride in this red pool.

Marlowe's *Doctor Faustus* was also a play about revenge—the revenge God takes on Faustus for selling his soul to the devil. Marlowe has the sharper mind, the finer ear, the subtler music. He was born at Canterbury in February 1564, and was therefore the same age as Shakespeare. Kyd was five or six years older. Unlike Kyd, who permits his plays to drift awkwardly, Marlowe wrote *Doctor Faustus* in a more or less direct line, adding comic interludes at the appropriate moments, and always remaining in complete command of the situation. Kyd's revenge-seeker has little poetry in him. In Marlowe's play Mephistopheles and Faustus have magnificent lines. Here is Faustus in his last hour, complaining bitterly about God's revenge:

Stand still, you ever-moving spheres of heaven
That time may cease and midnight never come!
Fair nature's eye, rise, rise again and make
Perpetual day, or let this day be but
A year, a month, a week, a natural day—
That Faustus may repent and save his soul!
O lente lente currite noctis equi!
The stars move still, time runs, the clock will strike:
The Devil will come, and Faustus must be damned!
O, I'll leap up to Heaven! Who pulls me down?
See, see where Christ's blood streams in the firmament!
One drop of blood will save me. O, my Christ!
—Rend not my heart for naming of my Christ,
Yet will I call on him! O spare me, Lucifer.

Faustus, contending with God and Lucifer, makes the heavens
ring with the violent arguments of his soul. Tamburlaine could do
the same with his Lucifer-like boasting, but Marlowe also possessed
a voice of melting sweetness and gentleness which charms the soul
and seems to echo heavenly voices. Here is Tamburlaine's invoca-
tion of the dying Zenocrate:

Now walk the angels on the walls of heaven
As sentinels to warn the immortal souls
To entertain divine Zenocrate.
Apollo, Cynthia, and the ceaseless lamps
That gently looked upon this loathsome earth,
Shine downwards now no more, but deck the heavens
To entertain divine Zenocrate . . .
The cherubins and holy seraphins
That sing and play before the King of Kings,
Use their voices and their instruments
To entertain divine Zenocrate.

In an extraordinarily short period of time English dramatic
poetry had found a voice, a form, and a stage. Shakespeare had
arrived at exactly the right time to take full advantage of them. He
reached London in the heroic decade which saw the destruction of a
Spanish fleet at Cádiz and the defeat of the Spanish Armada. He
could not have come at a more propitious time.

The
Apprentice

FOR FOURTEEN YEARS, half of his working life, Shakespeare was attached to two theatres, the Theatre and the Curtain, which stood close together in the parish of Shoreditch in the Liberty of Holywell. From 1584, when he probably came to London for the first time, to the winter of 1598 when the Curtain was broken up and removed piecemeal to Bankside to be reerected as the Globe Theatre, he worked in these two theatres, receiving there his apprenticeship in drama under James Burbage, the former carpenter, and there his first plays were performed. These theatres were the training ground where he first learned to walk across the stage and deliver his lines. If Stratford was the place where he was born, the small village of Shoreditch was the place where he was born into the theatre.

We are so accustomed to thinking of Shakespeare in Stratford and at the Globe Theatre that we forget the many years spent in Shoreditch. But these were the crucial years that saw the shaping of his genius. Here he wrote nearly half his plays and first saw them performed. When he spoke about "this wooden O" in *Henry V*, he was speaking about the Curtain or the Theatre, not about the Globe. Eight of his English historical dramas were first performed in Shoreditch, and here Falstaff first made his appearance.

There were advantages in having two theatres under the same management at a stone's throw from one another. Since the theatres were popular, and every afternoon the crowds streamed out of London to watch the performances, he was in a position to be saturated in drama. He might direct a play at the Curtain and act in a play at the Theatre, while composing a play of his own to be performed the following week. At one or other of these two theatres *The Comedy of Errors, Love's Labour's Lost, Titus Andronicus, The Taming of the Shrew, The Two Gentlemen of Verona, Romeo and Juliet, A Midsummer Night's Dream, The Merchant of Venice, Much Ado About Nothing*, and *Henry V* were all performed for the first time. With *Julius Caesar*, first performed at the Globe, there comes a sudden shift in emphasis, a new, deeper, and more tortured poetry. It was as though the geographical journey from Shoreditch, north of London, to Bankside, south of the river, worked a sea change in him. To the extent that it was possible the Shoreditch plays were about other people; the Bankside plays were more resolutely concerned with aspects of himself. There is an openness, an expansion in the Shoreditch plays, while in the great tragedies there comes a concentration, a continual movement toward the center, toward the glowing heart of things.

I am not suggesting here that Shakespeare spent all his time in Shoreditch. He performed for the Queen as a member of Burbage's company and later as a member of the Lord Chamberlain's Men, and there were performances in the private houses of the nobility, but the Theatre and the Curtain were his base of operations throughout his early years in London. Nor did he necessarily have any deep roots or a permanent residence in Shoreditch. James Burbage owned a tavern in the village; Shakespeare would eat and sleep there, or he would go and stay with friends like Richard Field, the young printer from Stratford, who would offer him lodging whenever he wanted to stay within the city walls. He continued to visit his family at Stratford. In London he was free of matrimonial ties and could wander wherever he pleased, staying now with one friend, now with another. He was not a scholar, owned very few books, and was therefore not burdened with a large library, which tends to keep a man fixed and immovable. Since so many historical plays were being performed, it is likely that Burbage kept a library in his theatres.

According to a tradition preserved by Dr. Samuel Johnson, handed down to him by Alexander Pope, who in turn received it from Nicholas Rowe, the first critical editor of Shakespeare, the coming of Shakespeare into the theatre was something of an accident. Johnson tells the story of the young man earning a little money by taking care of the horses of gentlemen who rode out to the theatre to see the plays. Johnson continues:

> In this office he became so conspicuous for his care and readiness, that in a short time every man as he alighted called for *Will. Shakespear*, and scarcely any other waiter was trusted with a horse while *Will. Shakespear* could be had. This was the first dawn of better fortune. *Shakespear* finding more horses put into his hand than he could hold, hired boys to wait under his inspection, who when *Will Shakespear* was summoned, were immediately to present themselves, *I am* Shakespear's *boy, Sir*. In time, *Shakespear* found higher employment, but long as the practice of riding to the play-house continued, the waiters that held the horses retained the appellation of Shakespear's *Boys*.

The story has the ring of truth. It is a simple story which would not be altered very much in the retelling. Rowe probably got the story from Thomas Betterton, the actor and dramatist, who in turn may have got it from Sir William D'Avenant, who was said to be Shakespeare's godson. But however it was got, it was all of one piece. Shakespeare's introduction to the theatre consisted in holding the horses of gentlemen attending the theatre. Many years after Johnson wrote it, it was discovered that James Burbage, owner of the Theatre and lessee of the Curtain, and owner of the Shoreditch tavern, also rented premises near Smithfield where he "usually kept horses at livery for sundry persons," the manager of the stable being "a northern man usually called by the name of Robin." Now Smithfield, which lay outside the city walls to the north of London, was the permanent horse and cattle market; every kind of horse was bought and sold, and a man riding to London from Stratford would, if he had need of ready money, sell his horse at Smithfield and walk to his lodging on foot. Shakespeare could have met Robin on his first day in London and on the second day he could have met James Burbage, that unscrupulous and rather forbidding man who stood at the beginning of the English theatre. On that same day he might be given attic space under the roof of Burbage's Red Lion Inn, which stood hard by the two theatres.

We have a good idea what the village of Shoreditch looked like in Shakespeare's time from Ralph Aggas' map made about 1560 and from an engraving made about 1595, of which a single copy survives inset in a manuscript journal kept by Abram Booth, a factor of the Dutch East India Company. The engraving, now in the library of the University of Utrecht, shows a rather drab street lying below scrub-covered foothills, with the houses standing cheek by jowl, and a little way away from them the Theatre faces the Curtain across a field which appears to be about the length of a tennis court, and the stables and the horse pond are exactly where we would expect to find them. Both theatres have their flags flying, and the Curtain appears to be much smaller than the Theatre.

From Ralph Aggas' map we see that most of the houses look over Bishopsgate Street, the main thoroughfare, but here and there we find a house set back from the road. To the west are Finsbury Fields, which was common land extending up to the very walls of London, where in summer the citizens went out to enjoy the countryside. To the north, on the edge of the village, was Holywell Priory, built around a well that gave sweet water to the villagers, dismantled in the time of Henry VIII and transformed into a private residence. Maps in Tudor times were more informative than they are today. Aggas shows people going about their daily business. We see women laying out clothes in the fields in order to bleach them, and men playing quarterstaff, which was one of the chief sports of the time, and very dangerous, for many heads were broken by those thick staffs. We see men walking across the fields toward the archery butts, where they would attach a target to a wooden post, and practice for hours. These posts were decorative, with serpents or birds or dragons carved on top of them, and there were hundreds of these posts set up on the commons around London. A man had to walk carefully not to be wounded. Shoreditch was famous for its archers ever since the day when Henry VIII, riding in the countryside, saw some people at the butts and sent one of his bodyguards, a Shoreditch man called Barlow, to see whether he could do better than everyone else. "Win them," the King shouted to Barlow, "and thou shalt be Duke over all archers." Barlow won and was dubbed Duke of Shoreditch. The title was handed down from one Barlow to another but it was not a title of nobility.

Shoreditch was famous for other things. Thomas Nashe wrote that every other house was a whorehouse. The village rivaled Westminster, Spitalfields, and Bankside as a nest of iniquity, whose prostitutes were to be avoided by those who valued their health. According to John Aubrey, who wrote an invaluable one-page life of Shakespeare, prostitution and debauchery left him totally disinterested. He was, wrote Aubrey, "the more to be admired *quia* he was not a company keeper; lived in Shoreditch; wouldn't be debauched, and if invited to, writ: he was in pain." These last words, which at first seem so mysterious, become clear when we realize that "writ" in Shakespeare's and Aubrey's time had the meaning of "specified" or "explained." Accosted by a prostitute, he would say he was sick and go on his way.

Aubrey, who acquired his information from William Beeston, the son of Christopher Beeston, who was one of the Chamberlain's men in 1598, was curious about Shakespeare's address in Shoreditch. William Beeston gave him the information: "He lives in Shoreditch at Hog Lane within 6 doors from Norton Folgate." Hog Lane was a narrow road turning off Bishopgate Street, which was also known as Norton Folgate. Today a small stretch of this street, originally a Roman military road, is still called Norton Folgate.

Most of the actors in Burbage's company had lodgings in Shoreditch. Among those who lived there was the great comedian, Richard Tarleton, the happiest of mortals, for he could undump anyone, even Queen Elizabeth, with his jests and calculated lunacy. He was a small man with a round face far too large for his body. He had a flat nose, thick lips, and a long moustache as curly as his hair. In addition he had a hump. He was the spirit of the purest comedy, always dressed like a rogue, with stockings down at heel, his hair crowned with straw and feathers. He lived in Holywell Street in the house of Em Ball, a prostitute, with his young son Philip, the godson of Sir Philip Sidney. His wife had died; he was alone with his son and with Em Ball; and he died of a broken heart at the end of the summer of 1588, the year of the Armada. He was buried in St. Leonard's church, Shoreditch, and Shakespeare remembered the death of the great comedian when he wrote *Hamlet*. For Tarleton was Yorick, "a fellow of infinite jest, of most excellent fancy."

Richard Tarleton died on September 3, 1588. A month later a huge crowd came "nigh the Theatre" to watch the execution of William Hartley, who had been sentenced to death with two others, John Weldon and Robert Sutton, for high treason. The government wanted to publicize these executions among the working-class population of London, and therefore ordered that they should take place in three separate places. Weldon was hanged at Mile End, Sutton at Clerkenwall, and Hartley at Shoreditch. Stow, who records the event briefly, notes that they were all priests who had come secretly to England from Paris and their crime was that they had disobeyed the statute by which no priests were permitted to step on the soil of England without the permission of the Council. When Stow wrote that the hanging of William Hartley took place "nigh the Theatre," no one had the least doubt what he meant, for in all of London there was only one place called the Theatre.

Nearly every afternoon people came streaming across Finsbury Fields to see the plays. Later in the afternoon they would repair to the taverns in Shoreditch, and the young men would go off to the whorehouses. A few would go sightseeing and gaze at the old, dismantled Priory of St. John the Baptist, filled with the residences and gardens of the nobility, and the more ambitious might go in search of the holy well to the west of the priory wall and find it covered with discarded stones and broken bricks. In the eyes of the Protestants, the holy well was a Catholic institution. The healing waters were no longer permitted to work miracles.

Shakespeare, living in Burbage's tavern or in his own residence on Hog Lane within a three-mile walk from the Theatre—Hog Lane formed the southern boundary of the extensive priory estates—found himself at the heart of the mysterious phenomenon which as yet had no name. Ben Jonson would give it a name and call it "the drama." It was a mystery in the same sense that the mystery plays were mysteries; the playwright was a kind of priest performing a secular rite on the open stage. He was trafficking in exaltations and revelations, in the power of spoken verse to create images of reality, and in the magical power of the actor to hold the audience in a trance. All this was new, and was only now coming into focus. It had been willed into existence by James Burbage, who believed that the people were in need of entertainment. Great plays demand great audiences, and soon the great plays would come and the audiences would rise to them.

Previously the village of Shoreditch had been dominated by its priory; now it was dominated by the Theatre and the Curtain, standing like fortresses on the edge of the rolling fields. On the days when plays were being presented, the flag would be run up on a mast and people outside the walls of London three quarters of a mile away would see it and come running. Before the end of the century the theatre would be regarded as the greatest single artistic achievement of the Elizabethan age; in the lives of Londoners it played the same role as the theatre in ancient Athens. The Armada had come and gone; *The Spanish Tragedy* had been performed and would continue to be performed for another fifty years; Shakespeare's historical plays with their fire-breathing Talbots and Percies and his tragedy of the house of Montague would continue to be played. In 1598 an unknown author of considerable talent and great charm wrote a series of satires, which he called *Scialetheia, or A Shadow of Truth*. In his snapdragon verses he described the vanity of the times. Staying late after the play at the Curtain, he had the wit to see that the dark theatre, vast and secret, represented something unfathomably precious.

> The City is the map of vanities,
> The mart of fools, the magazin of gulls,
> The painter's shop of Anticks: walk in Paul's,
> And but observe the sundry kinds of shapes
> Th' wilt swear that London is as rich in apes
> As Africa Tabraca. One wries his face.
> This fellow's wry neck is his better grace.
> He coined in newer mint of fashion,
> With the right Spanish shrug shows passion.

There comes on in a muffler of Cadiz beard,
Frowning as he would make the world afeard;
With him a troop all in gold-daubed suits,
Looking like Talbots, Percies, Montacutes,
As if their very countenances would swear
The Spaniard should conclude a peace for fear:
But bring them to a charge, then see the luck,
Though but a false fire, they their plumes will duck.
What marvel, since life's sweet? But see yonder,
One like the unfrequented Theatre
Walks in vast silence and dark solitude,
Suited to those black fancies which intrude
Upon possession of his troubled breast:
But for black's sake he would look like a jest,
For he's clean out of fashion: what he?
I think the Genius of antiquity,
Come to complain of our variety
Of fickle fashions.

Such as the unknown poet's salute to the vanities of London and the riper wisdom of the Theatre, where the genius of antiquity had at last found itself.

Not that Shakespeare, when he first came to work at the Theatre, was in the least concerned with the genius of antiquity. From being a horse-holder he progressed to being a "serviture," which means a servant or a messboy to the actors. Nicholas Rowe, writing in 1709, says he was "received into the Company then in being, at first in a very mean rank." Many actors have begun in that way. He was learning his trade by taking on all the menial tasks. Rowe continues: "His admirable wit and the natural turn of it to the stage soon distinguished him, if not as an extraordinary actor, yet as an excellent writer." Since he had wit to spare, it is likely that he wrote and acted within a year or two of reaching Shoreditch. We must think of him as stage-struck from the beginning.

Shoreditch provided him with experience and an enveloping atmosphere. Writers and actors were all around him. Christopher Marlowe lived for a while on Norton Folgate. Richard Burbage, who was about fifteen when Shakespeare came to Shoreditch, already had the makings of a great actor. They grew up together, Shakespeare and Burbage. They had much in common: an innate sense of drama, a feeling for verse, a knowledge of intellectual violence. Studying James Burbage's youngest son, Shakespeare would compose roles that exactly suited him. They were close friends and their friendship endured. By luck, from the very beginning, the dramatist had found his principal actor.

Shoreditch was close enough to London for a man to feel that he was part of the metropolis, but it was also far enough away for a man to feel that he was in the open country. Here, among rolling hills, were meadowlands, wild flowers, small streams, windmills, millponds, vegetable gardens, clumps of trees. Here John Gerard, the herbalist, found a strange form of wild crow's-foot flower which resembled the normal form but differed in some remarkable particulars:

> His leaves are fatter, thicker and greener, and his small twiggy stalks stand upright, otherwise it is like; of which kind it chanced that, walking in the field next unto the Theatre by London in company of a worshipful merchant named Master Nicholas Lete, I found one of the kind there with double flowers, which before that time I had not seen.

Shakespeare found the wild flowers he loved in Shoreditch as well as in Stratford. He was a country man, with the country man's suspicion of the city. He was both in London and out of London, and from the point of view of a young playwright about to embark on his career, he was in an enviable strategic position.

Map of Shoreditch and Finsbury Fields by Ralph Aggas, about 1560

...hortly before the Theatre and the Curtain were erected.

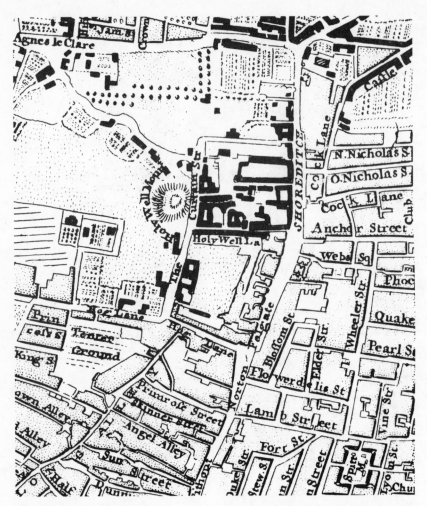

From a map of London by John Rocqueland, Surveyor, published in 1741, showing Holywell Priory, Holywell Mound, and Holywell Lane. The Curtain Theatre was opposite The on The Curtain Street and the Theatre in the field marked Tenter Ground. Hog Lane, where Shakespeare lived, is clearly visible.

War
Hath Made
All Friends

THE FIRST PLAYS WRITTEN BY SHAKESPEARE after his apprenticeship at the Theatre were almost certainly histories.
Londoners possessed a vast appetite for history, especially English
history and most especially the history of their kings and the usurpers
who proclaimed themselves kings. They were nearly always violent
men, quick to murder, quicker to form conspiracies, fathering illegitimate children as though it was demanded of them, coarse, high-
spirited, brutal in their daily affairs. They resembled hungry lions
prowling across England with their claws as sharp as swords. They
were not lovable, or likable, but in their continual rages they were
undeniably fascinating and they brought to the stage the excitement of
clashing words, much bloodletting, and stupendous speeches. They
were the Vices of the old morality plays made incarnate.

The Tudor age accepted the dissolution of the monasteries and
the collapse of the Catholic Church in England without a qualm
and without protest. As Henry VIII had foreseen, the power of the
Church could be broken by the simple process of sending emissaries
to the churches and monastic foundations with a royal warrant

proclaiming that all their lands, property, treasure, and vestments were henceforth the property of the King. The monks quietly walked away after surrendering everything they possessed to the King's commissioners. At Canterbury the jewel-studded relic-tomb of Saint Thomas à Becket was smashed at the order of the commissioners and the jewels were torn out of it and thrown into the King's jewel box. It was the same all over England, wherever there were monasteries. The people were apathetic; the commissioners enjoyed their good fortune; the monks vanished or went into hiding. The King had conquered the Church, and there would be no more Wolseys and Cranmers to share the royal power.

In Shakespeare's historical plays the Church plays a political role. The Pope, though beyond the Alps, wields power in England and in a ghostly way walks over the English fields. Yet it is notable that Shakespeare is never deeply engaged with the problems of the papacy, for the good reason that he is intimately engaged with the problems of kingship. Shakespeare has a passion, almost an obsession, for kings, and is much more at ease among them than he is with the common people. His kings are three-dimensional, larger than life, and they are seen in the lightning flash. Even when they are overwhelmed, when their downfall and servitude become inevitable, they carry with them the glow of irrefutable majesty.

Majesty in Elizabethan times was something we can scarcely hope to understand. The modern dictator armed with his secret police, insisting that his portrait should hang on every wall, that all his acts should be shrouded in silence, that he alone shall possess power although at all times he speaks of the people's power, inspires awe and terror. Elizabeth also inspired awe and terror. She, too, had her secret police, and many of her political acts were shrouded in silence. But there was a vast difference between her and the dictator. There was a love bond between herself and the people; there was the understanding that she ruled in their name, for them and with them, and that she was duty-bound to them in friendship and affection. She was Queen not by divine right—this supremely dangerous concept emerged only in the reign of her successor—but by a kind of divine rightness: not that she was infallible but that with God's help she walked surefootedly through a troubled time and that peculiar characteristic of her called "majesty" signified

God's helping hand, His superhuman aid. Since she was, like Henry VIII, "the only Head of the Church," the word "only" in those days meaning "unique" or "preeminent"—her association with God remained unquestioned except by the Catholics who associated her with the devil. Her unique relationship with the people and with God gave her the role of the mediator, the same role played by the Virgin Mary in the Catholic Church: She was King and Virgin. In the eyes of the Elizabethans she was an all-pervading presence, wise and judicious above mortal men, being herself mortal and godlike. It was this Elizabethan aspect of kingship that Shakespeare sometimes projected on the earlier kings of England.

With the coming of Henry VIII to the throne and the Act of Supremacy, kingship suffered a profound change. Since he was both head of the Church and head of the State, the King assumed the powers of an absolute monarch, and like the Byzantine emperors he must evolve elaborate rituals and formalities to reinforce his sacrosanct position. The confiscated treasures of the Church decorated his crown; church plate decorated his table; church hangings and vestments served as royal tapestries; church lands were distributed to the royal favorites. When the players mounted performances in the palace, they were helping to fill the vacuum caused by the absence of Catholic ritual. Into this vacuum marched, a little unsteadily, drunk with new wine, and waving banners, the new breed of players who were still uncertain about exactly what role they were expected to play. Were they merely entertainers? Were they the makers of dreams? Were they the King's servants with the duty of celebrating kingship? Were they the inheritors of ancient Roman dramas and of the dramas of ancient Greece? When *The Spanish Tragedy* and *Tamburlaine* were staged, it became clear that the theatre possessed a life of its own and obeyed no laws except those it invented for itself. *The Spanish Tragedy* was a story of revenge to the uttermost degree, and *Tamburlaine* was the story of a merciless and bloody-minded emperor who conquered half the earth and amused himself by building towers of skulls. Conquered kings drew his chariot; he boasted that the whole world belonged to him and all men were his slaves. At first sight these plays appear to have little to do with the preoccupations of Englishmen in the later years of Elizabeth's reign. But when we look again, we recognize that they possess in common a prodigious celebration of the powers of the human creature. Hieronymo and Tamburlaine are men of superb energy and daring. A new secular religion was coming into existence, celebrating human courage and human dignity, and the courage and dignity of kings. Just as the Elizabethan manor house was provided with vast windows to let in the sunlight, so the Englishman was beginning to learn that he, too, was the heir of the light of heaven and that all things were possible for him.

But when Shakespeare began to write plays for the Theatre in Shoreditch, he commanded neither the violence of *Tamburlaine* nor the vigorous melodrama of *The Spanish Tragedy*. The white-hot fire came later with the great tragedies. It is generally agreed that his first plays were *The Comedy of Errors, Love's Labour's Lost*, the three parts of *Henry VI, Richard III*, and *Titus Andronicus*, and that they were written between 1588 and 1594. In all of them, even in *Richard III*, we are aware of a young mind continually improvising and rejoicing in his skill but without the complete mastery of the stage we see for the first time in *Romeo and Juliet*. These are the prentice works, with *Richard III* standing high above the rest because it presents a convincing psychological portrait of the King caught in his own toils, made dizzy by his own ambiguities. The gaiety is present from the beginning, the wit is fully formed, the prose is as swift-paced as it ever will be, the drums and the violins are heard clearly, but he cannot yet play the full-throated trumpets nor can he yet dare himself to pull out the stops of the organ. Sometimes we hear the characteristic resonance of Shakespeare, the line clanging like metal, but it is always intermittent, in passing. We count *Titus Andronicus* a dramatic failure. The Elizabethans rejoiced in it, but they rejoiced more in *The Spanish Tragedy*, which was even more violent, more bloody. The four plays on English kings are full of promises which will be redeemed in later years, but none of the three plays devoted to Henry VI can be regarded as works of art. There is a strange heaviness about them, like wagons toiling uphill.

It would be foolish to contest the judgment of Heminge and Condell, who included the three parts of Henry VI in the First Folio. That they were wholly or substantially written by Shakespeare is indisputable. He knows his stage; he knows how to move his characters about; the confrontations are contrived with a proper dramatic feeling. Although the characters are often wooden, and although these plays are prentice work, they give evidence that they are by no means the first of his attempts to write historical drama. He has reached, as it were, the second stage of his apprenticeship. Does anything remain of the first stage?

There exists in the British Museum a manuscript in an excellent and well-preserved sixteenth-century hand called *War Hath Made All Friends*, dealing with the struggle for the English throne following the death of Ethelred the Unready on April 23, 1016. The struggle is between Ethelred's son Edmund Ironside and Canute, Prince of Denmark, whose forces already occupy large areas of England. The Danes crown Canute King of England in Southampton, and Edmund Ironside is crowned King of England in London. The battle lines are drawn. Canute will attempt to destroy Edmund Ironside, not only with his formidable army but also by bribery, subversion, and treachery. It was a time of great disorder and many traitors could be found.

So the play begins with Canute in his council chamber in Southampton proclaiming his intention to destroy his adversary in the presence of the Archbishop of Canterbury, his Danish courtiers, and disaffected English noblemen. One of them is Edric, Duke of Mercia, another is the Earl of Southampton, still another is Leofric, Earl of Chester. Finally there is Turchill, who has served Canute well and now ponders with Leofric the need to serve the man they regard as the real King of England—Edmund Ironside. They have both left hostages to Canute. If they go over to the other side, their children will be killed. They confront this dilemma, and calmly decide to join forces with the English King.

Leofric.   We two trusty subjects
   Are feared, suspected, and have liberty
   Only to live, yet not in liberty:
   For what is it but prisonment or worse
   Whenas our children, blood of our own blood,
   Are kept close prisoners, pledges for our faiths?
   King Edmund—who indeed is our true king
   For good regard of merit and desert,
   For honour, fame, and true nobility—

Is rightly termed mirror of majesty.
Canutus is a prudent, noble prince,
And loves to hear him called so—too, too much.
But I will tell you this: as long as we
Take part against our sovereign Ironside
We are but traitors; therefore—

Turkillus.   Stay, noble Chester, for I spy your drift.
To heap as many titles on your head
As you have poured on mine were but your due,
Yet to cut off such troyting thieves of time
I say "Amen" to your intention,
Which is to leave Canutus and his court,
And fly to Edmund, our true and lawful king,
But lest you should suspect my secrecy
By being won so soon to your device,
I here assure you that this very plot
Hath long been hammering in my troubled brain,
And had not you prevented my intent
I should ere long have moved you herein;
But what shall then become of our two boys
Which are our pledges? They shall surely die.

Leofric.   Tut, 'tis no matter; if they die, they die.
They cannot suffer in a better time,
Nor for a better cause, their country's good.
We gave them life; for us they shed their blood.

In this rollicking fashion Turkillus and Leofric go off to join
Edmund Ironside, leaving their sons to pay the penalty for their
treachery. Edric, Duke of Mercia, has observed the traitors and
seizes the opportunity to denounce them to Canute. He is himself a
traitor who gloats over his own wickedness in long soliloquies.
Dressed in black, looking like a crow or a vulture, immersed in
intrigues, supremely satisfied with himself, hoping that Canute and
Edmund will destroy each other, thus leaving him in a position to
seize the crown, he bids fair to dominate the play. And when Canute
learns of the treachery of the two nobles, Edric revels in his
newfound power, insists on the exaction of the full punishment, and

selects the executioner, a young man called Stitch, the son of a
cobbler, a coarse-grained clown who is handy with a sword. Edric is
a Machiavellian character, a man who lives only for power and
exults over every sliver of power that falls into his lap. Canute, less
worldly, yet determined to be the King of all England, seeks the
advice of his courtiers and enters into a long debate with himself on
the necessary punishment for traitors:

> *Canutus.* A traitor may be likened to a tree
> Which being shed and topped when it is green,
> Doth for one twig which from the same was cut
> Yield twenty arms—yea, twenty arms for one—
> But being hacked and mangled with an axe,
> The root straight dies and piecemeal rots away.
> Even so of traitors. Cut me off their heads,
> Still more out of the selfsame stock will sprout,
> But plague them with the loss of needful members,
> As eyes, nose, hands, ears, feet, or any such—
> O, these are cutting cards unto their souls,
> Earmark to know a traitorous villain by
> Even as a brand is to descry a thief.
> These desperate persons for example's sake,
> These ruffians, these all-daring lusty blades,
> These court appendixes, these madcap lads,
> These nothing-fearing hotspurs that attend
> Our royal court—tell them of hanging cheer,
> They'll say it is a trick or two above ground;
> Tell them of quartering or the heading axe,
> They'll swear beheading is a gallant death
> And he is dastard that doth fear to die;
> But say to them: You shall be branded,
> Or your hands cut off, or your nostrils slit—
> Then shallow fear makes their quivering tongues
> To speak abruptly: "Rather let us die
> Than we should suffer vild ignomy."
> But honorable minds are jealous
> Of honorable names, then to be marked
> Which robs them of their honors, likewise robs

Their hearts of joy, and like to irksome owls
They will be bashful to be seen abroad.

Canute's argument, impressively stated, resembles an abstract
design of justice, a balance sheet drawn up in cold blood. The scales
of justice waver. Out of his magnanimity Canute decides not to kill
the boys but to cut off their noses and their hands. Stitch regards the
boys with his head a little to one side. " 'Twere pity, in faith, to mar
two such faces. Boys, will you change beards with me?" he remarks.
The amputation scene becomes, in the Elizabethan manner, a comic
interlude. We would regard it as bad taste; the Elizabethans reveled
in such scenes. When one of the hostages offers to cut off his own
hands with an axe without explaining how after cutting off one
hand he will be able to cut off the other, Stitch, the comic bungler,
offers him the axe, saying: "You save me the labor." Canute takes
fright and abuses Stitch, saying that the boy with the axe in his hand
might attack the King. Stitch does his bloody work, Edric laughs
villainously, and the boys stumble away with sheep's blood smeared
on their noses and their hands tucked into their sleeves to show the
bloody stumps. And when this comic interlude is over, we see the
Archbishops of Canterbury and York, who have taken opposite
sides in the quarrel between the two kings, cursing each other to
high heaven. When we next see Canute he is encamped outside the
walls of London with the Danish army. A herald sent by Canute
summons the Londoners to surrender or to see London razed to the
ground. A bailiff answers defiantly:

> Go tell your master that we answer him:
> His ships that proudly ride upon the Thames
> Shall anchor on the ground where he abides,
> Borne by the bloodshed of our carcases,
> And we compelled by thirst to suck the stream
> Of this fair river dry, so that his men
> May dryshod march over the floating deeps,
> Ere we will let him enter in these gates.

The scene ends with a skirmish outside the walls, Edmund
advancing and Canute thrown back.

Thereafter come running battles, more acts of treachery, more bumbling by Stitch, Edric cheering on the combatants but taking care that he will gain the advantage. On the battlefield Edric finds the head of an Englishman, sticks it on a pike, and proclaims that it is the head of Edmund Ironside, but the English see through the stratagem. He goes in disguise to Edmund, offering to deliver secrets about Canute's army. He also offers to lead the English forces against the Danes. There are more interludes with Stitch, who speaks happily about the uses of horns, inkhorns, blackhorns, and every other kind of horn, and having exchanged clothes with Edric demands subservience from Edric's servants: "Why, ye shake-rag! Had ye never a lord under your girdle? Plain 'Sir Stitch' without welt or gard? Why, how now, you malapert knave! Have you forgot all good manners?" Edric, too, is capable of poetry and at a time of defeat flatters Canute by comparing him with the sun:

You are the sun, my lord, we marigolds:
Whenas you shine we spread ourselves abroad
And take our glory from your influence;
But when you hide your face or darken it,
With th'least encounter of a cloudy look
We close our eyes as partners of your woes,
Drooping our heads as grass down-weighed with dew.
Then clear ye up, my lord, and clear up us,
For now our valors are extinguished,
And all our force lies drowned in brinish tears
As jewels in the bottom of the sea.

As the play draws to a close the villainous Edric resolves the conflict by insisting that Canute and Edmund fight in single combat, the winner to be acknowledged the only King of England. The duel on the Elizabethan stage was the occasion for magnificent displays of swordsmanship, and since the fate of England depended on the outcome of the duel, it was necessarily prolonged to extract the utmost excitement from the audience. But Canute eventually tires and is about to have a sword driven through his heart when Edmund Ironside magnanimously announces that he wants no more bloodshed. Let Canute live, let there be friendship between the English and the Danes, and let each king take whatever part of England he chooses. Turkillus and Leofric return from the shadows to lament their sons and to vow vengeance on Canute; and Edric, maintaining to the last his inviolable malice, promises that there will be no peace in England as long as he is alive.

How much of the play is historical? In fact, a surprisingly large amount. Edmund Ironside was a doughty and chivalrous king. Edric, Duke of Mercia, was a notorious traitor who possessed a lifelong craving for power. Canute, elected king by the Witan in Southampton, did bring his army up to the walls of London, and was repulsed, and later fought a long series of battles with Edmund Ironside throughout the spring and summer of 1016. Stitch, the cobbler's son, is imaginary and so of course are many of the minor incidents in the play, but the main drive of the play follows closely on Holinshed. Here is embattled England in those last days when the English and the Danes were fighting for power, a power which would soon be taken away from both of them by the Norman, William the Conqueror.

That Shakespeare wrote the play *War Hath Made All Friends* in his prentice years seems to me indisputable. On nearly every page there are speeches that will be filled out and painted in deeper colors in later years. The peculiar Shakespearean resonance can be heard, and here and there we find him consciously or unconsciously echoing Ovid's *Metamorphoses*, the one book above all others that Shakespeare liked to keep at his side. Such a play is exactly what we might expect from the young Shakespeare with his pride of ancestry, the knowledge that he was descended from Anglo-Saxon kings. When he settled down to write his first full-length play, we would expect him to write about the period when Turchill flourished, and he would introduce Turchill into it, however briefly, and there would be all the tumult of the English wars. We would expect him to write speeches celebrating the glory of England, and this he does, and to depict a king so magnanimous that the glory is incarnate in him. His historical plays are often meditations on the theme of treachery, and here at the very beginning he puts into the mouth of Canute one of the finest of his many statements on treachery. We would expect, too, to find some of those powerful and obsessional images that remained with Shakespeare throughout his life. "You are the sun, my lord, we marigolds" has the authentic Shakespearean ring, and when Edric declares,

And all our force lies drowned in brinish tears
As jewels in the bottom of the sea,

we recognize Shakespeare's signature, for no other poet was so
obsessed with the vision of the jewels at the bottom of the sea.
Shipwreck and the treasures spilled from shipwreck are recurrent
images he will employ throughout his poetic life. Sometimes the
treasure is seen as though through a reversed telescope, very small
and distant, glittering amid the darkness of sea slime, and sometimes
he will see the treasure directly in front of him, as though he were
walking on the bottom of the sea.

Thus in *Richard III* we find George, Duke of Clarence, telling a
strange dream to the Keeper of the Tower, where he is imprisoned.
In the dream he sees himself escaping from the Tower and taking
ship with Richard, Duke of Gloucester, who was his brother:

Methought that I had broken from the Tower,
And was embark'd to cross to Burgundy,
And in my company my brother Gloucester
Who from my cabin tempted me to walk
Upon the hatches. There we look'd toward England,
And cited up a thousand heavy times
During the wars of York and Lancaster
That had befallen us. As we paced along
Upon the giddy footing of the hatches,
Methought that Gloucester stumbled, and in falling
Struck me (that thought to stay him) overboard
Into the tumbling billows of the main.
Oh Lord, methought what pain it was to drown,
What dreadful noise of water in mine ears,
What sights of ugly death within mine eyes.
Methought I saw a thousand fearful wrecks,
A thousand men that fishes gnaw'd upon,
Wedges of gold, great anchors, heaps of pearl,
Inestimable stones, unvalued jewels,
Some scattered in the bottom of the sea,
Some lay in dead men's skulls, and in the holes
Where eyes did once inhabit, there were crept
(As 'twere in scorn of eyes) reflecting gems,

That wooed the slimy bottom of the deep
And mocked the dead bones that lay scattered by.

Soon Clarence would be murdered atrociously in the Tower at the orders of the same brother he had seen drowning in his dream.

War Hath Made All Friends is a staccato play, the scenes so short that there is never any time to develop the characters. We come to know Edric well, and all the varying depths of his malicious temperament, but Edmund Ironside remains a stock character, a youthful English king armed only with his virtue, brave and resourceful to the uttermost, while the shifty-eyed Canute draws courage from his own fears like a man accustomed to lying to himself and believing his own lies. They are not complicated characters, they rarely draw long breaths, and there are so many battles and skirmishes that the characters are almost lost among the waving flags and the clash of arms. Shakespeare's battles will always be tumultuous, with much stamping of feet, dipping and raising of battle flags, sound of drums and hoofbeats of horses, soldiers shouting themselves hoarse, blood flowing richly, headless bodies on the ground and heads stuck on pikes. In Elizabethan times battle scenes were choreographed, and a play might be quite short on the written page, but if there were ten battle scenes, it would last into the late afternoon.

At the end of the play Edric hints at a sequel in which he will play a major role. According to the historian John Stow, Edric contrived the death of Edmund and was himself put to death by Canute. He was in his palace in London when the King's emissaries caught up with him. They burned him with firebrands and beat him with iron chains, and then they flung his body on the walls of London so that all men could revile the traitor who had done so much harm to the country. Edric would have been the subject of a good play.

After *War Hath Made All Friends* Shakespeare turned to another king, who was also valorous and virtuous in matters of war, though less virtuous in the bedchamber. This was *The Reign of King Edward the Third*, probably performed in 1588, when Shakespeare was twenty-four years old. Stow describes Edward as "rather like an angel, in which did shine such a marvellous grace that such as dreamed of him hoped the day following for good luck." He was a fine soldier, an excellent horseman, an expert falconer, and a consummate politician. In his reign the English won the battles of Crécy and Poitiers, suffered the Black Death, lost Aquitaine, allied themselves with the Flemings, fought the Scots to a standstill, and saw Geoffrey Chaucer coming to his maturity. It was an exciting period, and Edward took care that he should always be in the midst of the excitement. Stow finds fault with him only in his sexual behavior. "But yet he did not refrain riotous lust, carnal concupiscence, nor motions of the flesh even in his extreme age."

Edward's lust was sufficiently well known for Shakespeare to be able to devote much of the early part of the play to the King's encounter with the beautiful Countess of Salisbury. As the King describes her and as the countess reveals herself, her beauty is such that all the beauty of the world seems to be present in her face. The King threatens her, commands her, badgers and torments her, and then changing his strategy in midcareer, he begs for her favors, and though she seems sometimes to be on the point of yielding and though she genuinely admires the King and is flattered by his attentions, she refuses him. The love duel is fought with great delicacy, and for the first time we are brought into the presence of Shakespeare's lovers reveling in the ambiguities of love. The constancy of the countess trembles in the balance. She will give herself, but on conditions so terrible that the King does not dare to think of them. Meanwhile her constancy is itself a provocation, and she taunts him with it:

> The love you offer me you cannot give,
> For Caesar owes that tribute to his queen;
> That love you beg of me I cannot give,
> For Sara owes that duty to her lord.
> He that doth clip or counterfeit your stamp
> Shall die, my lord; and will your sacred self
> Commit high treason against the King of Heaven
> To stamp his image in forbidden metal,
> Forgetting your allegiance and your oath?
> In violating marriage sacred law

You break a greater honour than yourself;
To be a king is of a younger house
Than to be married; your progenitor,
Sole reigning Adam on the universe,
By God was honoured for a married man,
But not by him anointed for a King.
It is a penalty to break your statutes,
Though not enacted with your highness' hand:
How much more to infringe the holy act
Made by the mouth of God, sealed with His hand?

The privileges of the marriage state provide the countess with an excuse for introducing a new music, which is only hinted at in *War Hath Made All Friends*. The appeal to tradition and revealed morality works wonders on the poetry. The bell-like sound is heard clearly when the countess accuses him of rebellion against Heaven "to stamp his image in forbidden metal."

We hear this note of music again when the countess appeals to the Earl of Warwick for his advice and protection, and he answers:

I am not Warwick as thou thinkst I am,
But an attorney from the court of Hell.

We hear it again when the Countess learns that the King has assented to her two conditions—that the Queen and her husband shall both be killed before she will go to bed with him.

Countess.   O perjured beauty, more corrupted judge:
    When to the great Star Chamber o'er our heads,
    The universal sessions call to count
    This packing* evil, we both shall tremble for it.

Edward.   What then, my fair love? Is she resolute?

Countess.   Resolute to de dissolved, and therefore this:
    Keep but thy word, great king, and I am thine.
    Stand where thou dost, I'll part a little from thee

*Conspiring.

And see how I will yield me to thy hands.

(Draws daggers)

Here by my side doth hang my wedding knives.
Take thou the one, and with it kill thy Queen,
And learn by me to find her where she lies;
And with the other I'll dispatch my love—
Stir not, lascivious King, to hinder me;
My resolution is more nimbler far
Than the prevention can be in my rescue,
And if thou stir, I strike; therefore stand still,
And hear the choice that I will put thee to:
Either swear to leave thy most unholy suit
And never henceforth to solicit me;
Or else by heaven this sharp-pointed knife
Shall stain thy earth with that which thou would stain,
My poor chaste blood.

The countess with the two daggers in her hands was a fit subject
for Elizabethan tragedy, and Shakespeare, though still unsure of his
powers, still wavering on the edge of melodrama, is already in
command of his craft. Already he is illustrating one of the insistent
concepts of his plays: the heroines always take the initiative. They
are women of great beauty and razor-sharp will, dominating the
men and always a match for them. Since these roles were played by
fifteen-year-old-boys, he was making his task more difficult, since
the boys would need to be trained and directed more rigorously than
if they were acting simple women. He must have known many
imperious women to have rendered them so faithfully.

The best of *The Reign of King Edward the Third* is contained in
the long-drawn duel between the Countess and the King. Defeated
by the Countess, Edward goes off to France in the hope of defeating
the French. There are battle scenes written by a man who has never
seen battles, though he had read deeply in Froissart. There is a fever
in his battle scenes. Everything is a little too bright, the focus is a
little too sharp, and when people express fear, they do it in the epic
manner, as when the Black Prince in sight of the French army turns
to Lord Audeley and says:

Audeley, the arms of death embrace us round,
And comfort have we none, save that to die
We pay sour earnest for a sweeter life.

And when Audeley lies dying and is rescued from the thick of the
battle by two squires, we hear the authentic Shakespearean note
again when he says:

Good friends, convey me to the princely Edward,
That in the crimson bravery of my blood
I may become him with saluting him.

There is scarcely a moment in the play when there is not some
king upon the stage. It is a feast of kings attended by King
Edward of England, King John of France, King David of Scotland, the blind King of Bohemia, and enough attendant queens,
princes, and dukes to crowd the stage with the blinding light of
royalty. Some excellent lines are given to King David as he stands
defiantly on the walls of Roxborough Castle in the company of
the French ambassador:

Touching your embassage, return and say
That we with England will not enter parley,
Nor never make fair weather, or take truce,
But burn our neighbour towns, and so persist
With eager rods beyond their city York,
And never shall our bonny riders rest,
Nor rusting canker have the time to eat
Their light-borne snaffles nor their nimble spurs,
Nor lay aside their jacks of gymauld mail,
Nor hang their staves of grained Scottish ash
In peaceful wise upon their city walls,
Nor from their buttoned tawny leathern belts
Dismiss their biting whinyards*, till your king
Cry out: "Enough, spare England now for pity!"

King David's defiance is short-lived, for a few moments after

*Short swords.

making his speech an English army is seen advancing on Roxborough and he takes to flight.

The Reign of King Edward the Third was published in 1596. Another edition was published three years later. Nothing more was heard of it until Edward Capell, the first of the great Shakespearean scholars, rediscovered it, reprinted it, and pronounced that no one but Shakespeare could have written it. Tennyson agreed with Capell; Swinburne disagreed; C.F. Tucker Brooke thought it was written by "one of the truest poets and most ardent patriots" of the time, and concluded that it may have been written by George Peele, who in fact could scarcely have written a single line of it. A modern critic, Kenneth Muir, has written: "If Shakespeare had no hand in the play he was at least intimately acquainted with it, more intimately than with any known Elizabethan play." I believe Shakespeare was intimately acquainted with it because he wrote it, as he wrote *War Hath Made All Friends*, in the days when he was still attempting to master his sullen and majestic craft.

The Flowering
of Melancholy

ON JULY 12, 1588, the Invincible Armada sailed out of Corunna with orders to invade England, depose Queen Elizabeth, and convert the English people to the Catholic faith. England would become one more of the principalities ruled by King Philip II of Spain from his palace near Madrid.

The Armada consisted of nearly three hundred supply ships and ships of war, well armed and armored, manned by about 24,000 sailors and soldiers under the command of the Duke of Medina Sidonia. This was only one part of a huge invasion fleet. Under the command of the Duke of Parma there was another fleet of 350 flat-bottomed boats preparing to ferry 30,000 soldiers to the coasts of Essex and Kent. In due course there would be more landings in Devonshire and Yorkshire. England had never been in such danger since the time of William the Conqueror.

Sir Francis Walsingham's spies were well informed. Queen Elizabeth was aware that the fate of England might depend on a single throw of the dice. Her nerves were steady. What she feared most of all was the Duke of Parma's fleet based on Dunkirk and

Nieuport, not the Armada. Orders were given to blockade the Parma fleet at all costs; not a single boat must be allowed to leave port. The task given to the Armada was to protect the invasion fleet while the soldiers were being ferried to England. The Queen had more faith in her sailors than in her soldiers. Her sailors received few orders, for they knew what needed to be done. The Armada sailed close to Plymouth on July 20. The Duke of Medina Sidonia would have been wiser if he had commanded his ships not to come in sight of land. The English ships sailed out of Plymouth harbor in pursuit; there were battles off Portland and the Isle of Wight, the Armada was mauled, the lighter English ships darted around the heavier Spanish galleasses, and very early in the combat it seems to have occurred to the English captains that the Spanish captains had lost their nerve, did not know what to do, and were curiously incapable of carrying out a logical plan of action. It was observed, and remembered, that the Armada pursued a strange zigzag path up the English Channel, now veering close to England, now almost touching the coast of France, and then veering back toward England again. Seven days after sailing past Plymouth, while the Armada was anchored in Calais roads for a breathing spell, the English struck the first of the two powerful blows which brought about the destruction of the Armada. The fire ships were sent in. These ships did no physical damage but caused the Spaniards to weigh anchor and sail away from Calais in confusion, pursued by the English who now engaged them while keeping to windward and bombarding them. Sir Francis Drake, off Gravelines, flew at them, savagely mauled them, punched a hole through them, and sent them scattering into the North Sea. The English ships chased them as far as the Orkneys and then abandoned the hunt, while the Armada continued its melancholy progress off the shores of Ireland. Of that vast Armada only a handful of ships returned to Spain.

The triumph of England was complete; her enemies were scattered and her pride in her sailors was justified. A well-planned invasion timed to coincide with a rebellion in Ireland and the raising of armies in France and the Netherlands had failed ignominiously. Medals were struck in honor of the victory, while the Earl of Essex supervised the victory celebration that took place in the Tilting Yard in Westminster. England lost her fear of Spain and saw herself capable of wresting from the Spanish Crown all her vast possessions abroad.

So great a triumph exacted a high price; the exaltation was short-lived. Soon exhaustion set in, almost a sense of defeat. It was as though Spanish melancholy was a communicable disease that now infected the English. There arose a strange feeling of the vanity of all victories and the uselessness of all effort under the sun. After the defeat of the Spanish Armada there can be detected an abrupt change in the weather of the English soul. Melancholy became fashionable: the poets spoke about it openly; playwrights reflected it; students in the universities debated it; high officers of state complained about it; and learned books were written on the subject of the melancholy temperament. England turned inward and became more insular. The Armada had worked a curious miracle: it had made the English less sure of themselves just at the moment when they had demonstrated their utmost strength.

In 1588 Queen Elizabeth was fifty-five years old and had been on the throne for thirty years. She was at the height of her intellectual powers and her prestige had never been greater, but although she was still loved and admired and the poets continued to write voluminous odes in her honor, the love and admiration were beginning to grow stale and the odes in her honor were becoming empty and repetitious. Her power, beauty, and virginity were continually being celebrated, but the reader of these odes would not have the slightest understanding of this woman who was losing her beauty, who smiled with blackened teeth, and whose face was concealed under thick layers of paint.

What was especially disturbing about Queen Elizabeth was precisely what the poets celebrated so fervently—her virginity. She was past childbearing age; she had no heir; she had never indicated her preferences with regard to the succession. At her death the country was likely to be torn apart in civil war, as several pretenders to the throne, each with his private army, fought for the throne. There was the growing realization among Englishmen that the government of England suffered from an irremediable sickness. The Queen's very virtues had become vices.

Titus Andronicus, which we may regard as the third of Shakespeare's plays, tells the story of a Roman general who possessed all the virtues and as a result plunged Rome into fratricidal struggle and horrors which can scarcely bear thinking about.

The exact date of *Titus Andronicus* is unknown. In the induction to his play *Bartholomew Fair*, Ben Jonson mentions it in passing as contemporary with *The Spanish Tragedy*, adding disparagingly that both plays "hath stood still these five and twenty or thirty years." Since the induction was written in 1614, this places the date between 1584 and 1589, during the first years of Shakespeare's apprenticeship.

The great general Titus Andronicus does all the right things according to Roman custom. When one of his sons was killed in the Gothic wars, it became necessary that one of the captured Gothic princes should be sacrificed. Tamora, Queen of the Goths, also a prisoner, appealed for mercy on behalf of her eldest son but no mercy was given to her: her son was hacked to pieces with a sword and his remains were thrown on the sacrificial fire. Although he has been proclaimed Emperor, Titus Andronicus refused to accept the title. Saturninus, the legitimate Emperor, offered to marry Lavinia, Titus's daughter, and Titus gratefully accepts this tribute to himself, finding more satisfaction in being the father of an empress than in becoming an emperor.

Lavinia is beautiful, and the Emperor's brother Bassianus lusts after her. He makes her marry him, and not surprisingly the emperor is distressed and turns for solace to the beautiful Gothic captive, Queen Tamora, who soon becomes his wife. To revenge the death of their brother and to harm Titus, Queen Tamora's two younger sons surprise Bassianus and Lavinia. Bassianus is quickly killed. A more terrible punishment is reserved for Lavinia, who is raped and mutilated, her tongue torn out and her hands cut off. She can no longer speak nor write. Yet she succeeds in making her meaning clear. With her stumps she opens up the pages of Ovid's *Metamorphoses* and indicates the passage where Tereus tears out the tongue of Philomela and then ravishes her. In the end Queen Tamora's younger sons fall into the hands of Titus, who cuts their throats, grinds them to mincemeat, and bakes them in a pie. Dressed as a cook, with Lavinia beside him wearing a veil, the great general enters the palace of Saturninus and places the pie before the Emperor and the Empress. He waits until Tamora has eaten the pie before he announces that the mother was eating "the flesh that she herself hath bred." The play ends in a great stabbing match, for Titus stabs Tamora, Saturninus stabs Titus, and Saturninus in turn is stabbed by Lucius, who is one of Titus's surviving sons.

An important character in the play has not yet been mentioned. This is Aaron the Moor, the lover of Queen Tamora, who has a small dark-skinned baby by him. He is the instigator of her crimes and the crimes of her sons, a murderer for the sake of murder, a man with "a deadly standing eye." He is evil incarnate, enjoying his silence and his melancholy. On the stage he appears to have been portrayed not as a Moor but as a Negro, for there survives a drawing of the scene which shows Queen Tamora pleading for the lives of her sons. Aaron is black, wears a Greek fillet in his hair, a white shirt, a Roman kilt, and leather boots. He is seen defying Titus, who wears a Roman toga. The drawing was made in 1595.

Aaron is the first of Shakespeare's excursions in pure evil. He is a first sketch for Iago, a man who raises malice to the height of passion, whose desire to destroy is absolute, who refuses to accept any limitation in determination to annihilate his enemies. King Canute in *War Hath Made All Friends* and King Edward in his scenes with the Countess of Salisbury were both malicious, but their malice has a primitive quality. Aaron is a sophisticated conspirator, aware that conspiracy is an art that follows precise rules, and like all great conspirators he gets other men to do his dirty work for him. Having prepared his first murders and given orders how they should be brought about, he repairs to his mistress, Queen Tamora, who addresses him tenderly:

> My lovely Aaron, wherefore look'st thou sad
> When every thing doth make a gleeful boast?
> The birds chaunt melody on every bush,
> The snake lies rolled in the cheerful sun,
> The green leaves quiver with the cooling wind
> And make a checkered shadow on the ground:
> Under their sweet shade, Aaron, let us sit,
> And whilst the babbling echo mocks the hounds,
> Replying shrilly to the well-tuned horns

As if a double hunt were heard at once,
Let us sit down and mark their yellowing* noise:
And after conflict such as was supposed
The wandering Prince and Dido once enjoyed,
When with a happy storm they were surprised
And curtained with a counsel-keeping cave,
We may, each wreathed in the other's arms,
(Our pastimes done) possess a golden slumber,
Whiles hounds and horns and sweet melodious birds
Be unto us as is a nurse's song
Of lullaby to bring her babe asleep.

The Queen has spoken so tenderly that we scarcely realize that every word is loaded. The murders Aaron has plotted will take place in the forest during the hunt, Lavinia will be raped and mutilated, Titus's sons will be killed, and the Queen of the Goths will be on her way to becoming the Empress of the Roman Empire. All this is Aaron's work. When the worst happens to him, Titus will remain firm, though fearful:

For now I stand as one upon a rock,
Environed with a wilderness of sea,
Who marks the waxing tide grow wave by wave,
Expecting ever when some envious surge
Will in his brinish bowels swallow him.

Like Hamlet, Titus is a man of peace who genuinely detests bloodshed but is nevertheless forced to commit murder in order to punish the Goths who are creating chaos within the Roman Empire. He sees with clear eyes that chaos came out of his victory and there might have been no chaos if he had not insisted on the sacrifice of Queen Tamora's eldest son, a sacrifice demanded by Roman law. What Shakespeare called in *The Reign of King Edward the Third* "the imperial victory of murdering death" thereupon becomes the main subject of the play. When Titus's brother Marcus kills a fly by stabbing at it on a plate, Titus is in agony:

*Yelling.

Titus.   What dost thou strike at, Marcus, with thy
              knife?

Marcus.   At that that I have killed, my lord—a fly.

Titus.   Out on thee, murderer! Thou kill'st my heart;
My eyes are cloyed with view of tyranny:
A deed of death done on the innocent
Becomes not Titus' brother. Get thee gone;
I see thou art not for my company.

Marcus.   Alas, my lord, I have but killed a fly!

Titus.   "But!" How, if that fly had a father and mother?
How would he hang his slender gilded wings,
And buzz lamenting doings in the air!
Poor harmless fly,
That with his pretty buzzing melody
Came here to make us merry! And thou hast killed him.

But it is in the nature of things that Titus must eventually
become a killer and that the Roman state must sit in judgment on
Aaron, commanding that he should be buried "breast-deep in
earth" and starved to death. So the play ends like all good melodra-
mas in a heap of corpses.

Titus Andronicus was not history; there was no Roman Emperor
of that name; and there is no known source for the play unless it is
the brief prose tale called *The Tragical History of Titus Andronicus,
the Renowned Roman General*, of unknown authorship and unknown date, of which a single copy survives in the Folger Library in
Washington. But it is just as possible that the prose tale was based
on Shakespeare's play.

When Shakespeare's works are assessed, it is customary to put
Titus Andronicus at the bottom of the list. Samuel Johnson thought
it so barbarous that it was inconceivable to him that Shakespeare
could have written it. T. S. Eliot described it as "one of the stupidest
and most uninspired plays ever written, a play in which it is
incredible that Shakespeare had any hand at all, a play in which the
best passages would be too highly honored by the signature of
Peele." Hazlitt felt sick at the thought of it, and Coleridge intensely
disliked it, and all of them in their different ways showed that they

had failed to understand what Elizabethan drama was all about. Shakespeare was writing for the theatre and it was very far from his mind that literary critics would ever concern themselves with his plays. He was writing for an audience of apprentices, small shopkeepers, soldiers, sailors, young gallants, prostitutes, common laborers, the riffraff of London. He had a political point of view and *Titus Andronicus* is full of political doctrine. He had poetry in his veins, and it was continually spilling over. Above all, he possessed something that can only be called *theatricality*, and this he possessed in abundance. The play was important to him and he gave it the full measure of his young genius; and the characters of Queen Tamora, Aaron, and Titus would reappear in various disguises in many of his subsequent plays. *Titus Andronicus*, far from being stupid or uninspired, was in fact an exceedingly intelligent and poetic study of chaos and evil, of disorder in the body politic and of human courage in adversity, written in accordance with the traditions of his age. It was flamboyant, and the Elizabethans loved flamboyance. It was crude in the Elizabethan way, and it was designed to shock and to keep the audience breathlessly on the edge of their seats, and it succeeds in all these things. This play contains the seeds of his great tragedies.

Queen Tamora and Aaron had a son who would become Richard III.

When Laurence Olivier portrayed Richard III, he quite properly transformed himself into a human spider moving with a spider's quick jerking gait. He was a caricature of a man, a caricature of a king. The hump back, the hook nose, the lame leg, the hungry thinness of his body, suggested a spawn of Satan; and if his clothes were stripped from his body, you expected him to be covered with fine black fur. He was a monster of evil, predatory, obscene. And when at last he was killed in battle on an open field, he looked like a squashed insect.

One imagines that Shakespeare would have approved highly of this interpretation and he would have enjoyed the camera work which gave depth and brilliance to the spider. Olivier was evil incarnate, "hell's black intelligencer." He had no saving graces. Power had fallen into his hands: his sole use of power was to wreak vengeance on real or imagined enemies, and for him the imagined ones are the most dangerous of all. He is a spider with a serpent's head, spitting poison on everything he touches. His crimes fascinate us because they are accomplished with a clear intelligence. Like an African dictator he relishes the suffering he causes and is never happy until he has convinced himself that the utmost suffering has been exacted from his victims.

Shakespeare based his portrait of Richard III largely on Raphael Holinshed's *Chronicles of England, Ireland and Scotland*. Holinshed's summing up of Richard's appearance and character describes him pitilessly:

> As he was small and little of character, so he was of body greatly deformed; the one shoulder higher than the other; his face was small but his countenance cruel and such that at the first aspect a man would judge it to savour and smell of malice, fraud and deceit. When he was musing, he would bite and chew busily his nether lip, as who said that his fierce nature in his cruel body always chaffed, stirred, and was ever unquiet; beside that, the dagger which he wore, he would (when he studied) with his hand pluck up and down in the sheath to the midst, never drawing it fully out; he was of a ready, pregnant and quick wit, wily to feign and apt to dissemble; he had a proud mind and an arrogant stomach.

Holinshed was not in any strict sense a historian; he was an apologist for the Tudor cause, capable of bending any fact to his purpose. Richard III was a legitimate king of England, while Henry Tudor, the head of the Lancastrian party, had only a murky claim to the throne. Ultimately Henry's claim derived from his remote descent from John of Gaunt, who was himself illegitimate. In fact he claimed the throne by right of conquest, having defeated Richard at Bosworth Field. It was therefore necessary for the Tudor cause that he should be depicted in the brightest colors and that Richard should be depicted as a man of the utmost evil. Shakespeare, fascinated by evil, had no qualms in depicting an outrageously evil king. He was not writing history. He was writing drama in the light of his own persuasions and the demands of the audience, and if there was evil anywhere, then it was his task to make it blacker, and if there was good, it was always transcendently good.

Shakespeare's historical plays form long meditation on the subject of kingship, and inevitably this meditation involves further meditations on power, treason, rebellion, duty, death, patriotism, England. They are subjects worth talking about and Shakespeare enjoys talking about them at great length. *King John*, which he seems to have embarked upon without enthusiasm, provided him with an opportunity to meditate upon all these themes, and as he warmed to the play he struck off wild sparks that danced wonderfully in the air before they faded away. Darkness falls over the play; only a fitful light shines; a king mourns his approaching death in one corner, a queen sorrows over a dead child in another corner, and somewhere in the center of the stage the gravediggers are at work. Here Queen Constance mourns over the death of Arthur:

Grief fills the room up of my absent child:
Lies in his bed, walks up and down with me,
Puts on his pretty looks, repeats his words,
Remembers me of all his gracious parts,
Stuffs out his vacant garments with his form:
Then have I reason to be fond of grief!
Fare you well: had you such a loss as I,
I could give better comfort than you do.
I will not keep this form upon my head,
Where there is such disorder in my wit:
O Lord, my boy, my Arthur, my fair son,
My life, my joy, my food, my all the world:
My widow-comfort, and my sorrows' cure.

The words spoken by Queen Constance were very close to Shakespeare's heart, for he had also lost a son. Of Hamnet Shakespeare we know nothing except that he was christened at the Church of the Holy Trinity on February 2, 1585, and died probably on August 10, 1596, for he was buried on the following day. Shakespeare's grief for his dead son pours out of his works.

With grief went the horror of death, decay, the reduction of the body to a stiffened corpse. So Constance in the presence of the papal legate Pandulph, who would prefer not to take death seriously, laments the dead body of her son, which she has not seen:

Death, death; O amiable lovely death!
Thou odoriferous stench, sound rottenness,
Arise forth from the couch of lasting night,
Thou hate and terror to prosperity,
And I will kiss thy detestable bones,
And put my eyeballs in thy vaulty brows,
And stop this gap of breath with fulsome dust,
And be a carrion monster like thy self;
Come, grin on me, and I will think thou smil'st,
And buss thee as thy wife: Misery's love,
O come to me.

Death in its utmost horror: life in its utmost excellence. Sometimes in these plays of his early middle period he resembles a pendulum swinging between these two extremes.

The Elizabethan melancholy pervades all the writers and dramatists of the period. It is rich in irony, and sometimes moves lightly like a fencer across the stage, helplessly parrying the enemy but determined to keep on fighting. Out of this horror Shakespeare extracts a profound poetry:

O death, made proud with pure and princely beauty! . . .
'Tis strange that death should sing.
I am the cygnet to this pale faint swan,
Who chants a doleful hymn to his own death . . .
Gaunt am I for the grave, gaunt as a grave . . .
Even through the hollow eyes of death
I see life peering . . .

But the truth was that Shakespeare saw very little life peering through the hollow eyes of death. Death haunted him; it was as though there had been planted in him, in the deepest recesses of his body and his soul, a sense of outrage against death's dominance. In *King Lear* the sense of outrage reaches formidable proportions. And together with this extreme cry against death there would sometimes come a more sinister cry: that the whole world and the whole universe should be destroyed because both life and death are unbearable. Sometimes too there comes a quiet acceptance of death, as when the Nurse in

Romeo and Juliet recites a strange litany on her dead daughter Susan
born about the same time as Juliet; and in the recital of how Juliet falls
and hurts her forehead, there is a sense of fatality, a foretelling of
Juliet's death and a backward glance at Susan:

> Come Lammas-eve at night shall she be fourteen.
> Susan and she—God rest all Christian souls!—
> Were of an age: well, Susan is with God;
> She was too good for me: but, as I said,
> On Lammas-eve at night shall she be fourteen:
> That shall she, marry: I remember it well.
> 'Tis since the earthquake now eleven years;
> And she was wean'd,—I never shall forget it,—
> Of all the days of the year, upon that day:
> For I had then laid wormwood to my dug,
> Sitting in the sun under the dove-house wall;
> My lord and you were then in Mantua:—
> Nay, I do hear a brain:—but, as I said,
> When it did taste the wormwood on the nipple
> Of my dug and felt it bitter, pretty fool,
> To see it tetchy and fall out with the dug!
> "Shake," quoth the dove-house: 'twas no need, I trow,
> To bid me trudge:
> And since that time it is eleven years;
> For then she could stand alone; nay, by the rood,
> She could have run and waddled all about;
> For even the day before, she broke her brow:
> And then my husband—God be with his soul!
> 'A merry man—took up the child:
> "Yea," quoth he, "dost thou fall upon thy face?
> Thou wilt fall backward when thou hast more wit.
> Wilt thou not, Jule?" and, by my holidame,
> The pretty wretch left crying and said "Ay."
> To see, now, how a jest shall come about!
> I warrant, an I should live a thousand years,
> I shall never forget it: "Wilt thou not, Jule?"
>   quoth he;
> And pretty fool, it stinted and said "Ay."

In this way Susan lives on in memory, and the three-year-old Juliet comes to life, while the death of Cleopatra is foreshadowed in the bitter dug, and there is an aching sadness in the story of a child's fall. The Nurse—she is so much the Nurse that we learn with surprise that she has a first name: Angelica—is one of the supreme characters of Shakespeare. Dr. Johnson described her as "at once loquacious and secret, obsequious and insolent, trusty and dishonest." He was wide of the mark. She was one of those who bring joy to life, being affectionate, lovable, bawdy, and wonderfully at ease in the world.

Shakespeare was not at ease with melancholy, but he possessed useful weapons against it. Whenever he pleased he made a headlong plunge into fantasy. He could conjure up fantasies by the score, lace them together, and make a cage out of them. In the first act of *Romeo and Juliet* he has Mercutio describing the coming of Queen Mab:

> She is the fairies' midwife, and she comes
> In shape no bigger than an agate-stone
> On the forefinger of an alderman,
> Drawn with a team of little atomies
> Athwart men's noses as they lie asleep;
> Her waggon-spokes made of long spinners' legs,
> The cover of the wings of grasshoppers,
> The traces of the smallest spider's web,
> The collars of the moonshine's watery beams,
> Her whip of cricket's bone, the lash of film,
> Her waggoner a small grey-coated goat.
> Not half as big as a round little worm
> Prick'd from the lazy finger of a maid;
> Her chariot is an empty hazel-nut
> Made by the joiner squirrel or old grub,
> Time out o'mind the fairies coachmakers.
> And in this state she gallops night by night
> Through lovers' brains, and then they dream of love . . .

These plunges into fantasy are always reckless and dangerous, but they kept the evil spirits at bay. Out of Mercutio's speech came half of *Midsummer Night's Dream*. In fairyland melancholy vanished, for there was no death among the fairies.

Shakespeare's melancholy only increased as he grew older. His outward circumstances, so far as we know them, did not contribute to it. He became rich and famous. He was already famous in 1598 when Francis Meres published *Palladis Tamia: Wit's Treasury*, listing six comedies and six tragedies of Shakespeare, and adding that "the Muses would speak with Shakespeare's fine filed phrase, if they could speak English." Of his family life we know nothing, but we know that after Hamnet's death there were no deaths in the family until his father died in 1601. He lived very quietly, occupying himself with his plays and poems, his family and his friends, attracting no attention to himself.

So we may believe, remembering always the rage and violence underneath. In 1930 Dr. Leslie Hotson discovered two writs of attachment issued to the sheriff of Surrey in the winter of 1596. They were written in Latin, and could be translated:

1. Be it known that Francis Langley craves sureties of the peace against William Gardener and William Wayte for fear of death, and so forth.

2. Be it known that William Wayte craves sureties of the peace against William Shakspere, Francis Langley, Dorothy Soer wife of John Soer, and Anne Lee, for fear of death, and so forth.

Such writs of attachment were issued by justices of the peace to people who felt in fear of their lives or of bodily hurt. The justice had to be convinced that the danger was very real before issuing them. William Gardener was a scoundrelly Surrey justice, William Wayte was his disreputable stepson, Francis Langley was the owner of the Swan Theatre, and we know nothing at all about Dorothy Soer or Anne Lee. We know there was a violent quarrel and that William Wayte, once described as "a certain loose person of no reckoning or value," stood in deadly fear of Shakespeare. He had the luck to go down in history as one of those who quaked in their shoes when Shakespeare entered the room.

The
Armored Poet

THE ANTIQUE WORLD NEVER PERISHED. The world of goddesses, nymphs and dryads, of phoenixes and unicorns, of horned devils and shapeless *incubi*, survived the establishment of the Church of England. The medieval imagination was still thriving; so were the ancient gods of England. The rediscovery of the ancient world gave new life to mythologies. A cultivated Elizabethan gentleman lived on many levels: he believed in scientific discovery, he was entranced by the finding of a new continent beyond the Atlantic, he attended church regularly, he went about his affairs with stoic dignity, took his pleasures seriously, celebrated Dionysus when he was drunk and Apollo, the god of literature, self-knowledge, and self-control, when he was sober, and he believed that Christ died for him on the Cross in order to bring him to salvation. He found no difficulty in reconciling his many enthusiasms and beliefs. Indeed, he was not very interested in men's beliefs. What interested him most of all was man himself. "Man himself" was the discovery of the Renaissance, and men were still a little dazzled by this new discovery of their humanity.

The training in the English schools led Englishmen to a formidable knowledge of the Greek and Roman classics. Ovid among poets and Plutarch among historians impressed themselves deeply on the English imagination. Ovid was not the greatest Roman poet nor was Plutarch the greatest of Greek historians, but the Elizabethans found themselves in their works. They read Ovid and Plutarch voraciously, in the original and in translation. Ovid's *Metamorphoses* had been translated by Arthur Golding in 1567, and twelve years later Sir Thomas North published *The Lives of the Noble Grecians and Romanes* in an English translation based on Jacques Amyot's French version. North's *Plutarch* was Shakespeare's source for all his Greek and Roman tragedies. Shakespeare read Ovid's *Metamorphoses* in the original but sometimes consulted Golding's translation. One has the feeling that Ovid became a drug; he was wholly immersed in the Latin poet, adored him this side of idolatry, and never abandoned him. To the very end of his life Shakespeare would show, sometimes in very obscure ways, how deeply indebted he was to Ovid.

It was from Ovid ultimately that both Marlowe and Shakespeare derived the sweet, concise, rippling line that gives a glancing life to landscapes and describes people as though they were landscapes. In Ovid landscapes came alive, and walked, and ran, and there was always something fluid in them. People, in Ovid, are larger than life-size, and they glow with an intense light. Sometimes, too, Ovid will introduce a word of sudden power to break the mood of enchantment he has created so skillfully, thus shocking the reader into an awareness that behind these gods and goddesses, whose transformations he recounts with so much care and excitement, there lie terrible unseen forces, nightmares, chaos, the very heavens erupting like volcanoes. Ovid's world was a very particular world, but the Renaissance scholars found themselves at home in it. In Marlowe's "Hero and Leander" we see Ovid's world wearing an English dress:

At Sestos, Hero dwelt; Hero the fair,
Whom young Apollo courted for her hair,
And offered as a dower his burning throne,
Where she should sit for men to gaze upon.

The outside of her garments were of lawn,
The lining purple silk, with gilt stars drawn,
With wide sleeves green, and bordered with a grove,
Where Venus in her naked glory strove
To please the careless and disdainful eyes
Of proud Adonis that before her lies.
Her kirtle blew, whereon was many a stain
Made with the blood of wretched lovers slain . . .

Shakespeare's genius was more abstract and at the same time more physical. He was impatient with flowing descriptions; he likes to get at the heart of the matter as quickly as possible. Marlowe seduces; Shakespeare rapes. Yet both had the long breath and could spin out a tale at interminable length for the pure pleasure of it.

Shakespeare's long poem "Venus and Adonis" was published by Richard Field and sold at the Sign of the White Greyhound in Paul's Churchyard in 1593. It was "registered" on April 18, 1593, shortly before Shakespeare's twenty-ninth birthday. Richard Field was the son of Henry Field, a Stratford tanner well known to John Shakespeare, who did business with him. The book was superbly printed; it was carefully proofread; and went into seven editions during Shakespeare's lifetime. It was printed again in 1617, the year following his death.

To the modern taste it is a very strange book indeed, for though the adventures of Venus and Adonis are told as a narrative, there are very few adventures and Venus spends most of her time lamenting the chastity of Adonis, who refuses to fall into her snares. Shakespeare has not entirely rid himself of a certain charming awkwardness—the same awkwardness he showed in "A Lover's Complaint," which is also a lament—but there is an increasing command of music. Embedded in the poem are verses which appear to belong to a first juvenile rendering of the story and we can discern at least three poetic strata: Early Juvenile, Late Juvenile, Mature. The poem took many years to write, and was probably begun before he left Stratford. Unfortunately the greater part of the poem was written in the Late Juvenile style, and of the two hundred or so verses scarcely thirty are worth reading.

To the Late Juvenile style belong the superb erotic passages:

"Fondling," she saith, "since I have hemmed thee here
Within the circuit of this ivory pale,
I'll be a park, and thou shalt be my deer:
Feed where thou wilt, on mountain or in dale:
   Graze on my lips, and if those hills be dry,
   Stray lower, where the pleasant fountains lie.

"Within this limit is relief enough,
Sweet bottom-grass, and high delightful plain,
Round rising hillocks, brakes obscure and rough,
To shelter thee from tempest and from rain.
   Then be my deer, since I am such a park;
   No dog shall rouse thee though a thousand bark."

The mature style appears chiefly in passages where the poet no longer engages in metaphysical subtleties but instead rejoices in things seen in the countryside. When he writes an apostrophe to Death or to the Curse of Love or describes in almost mathematical terms the convulsions of Venus' soul, he can be as forbidding as any other metaphysical poet of his time; he is happier when he writes of snails, rabbits, wild boars, and horses. Birds delighted him, and he wrote of the elusive bird called the dive-dapper or dive-dipper, which liked to fly low over the water:

Like a dive-dapper peering through a wave,
Who, being look'd on, ducks as quickly in,

where the movement of the verse consciously imitates the quick, darting movement of the bird.

Keats, who was Shakespeare's wisest critic, almost shouted with joy when he came upon:

Or as the snail, whose tender horns being hit,
Shrinks backward in his shelly cave with pain,
And there, all smother'd up, in shade doth sit,
Long after fearing to creep forth again;
   So at the bloody view her eyes are fled
   Into the deep-dark cabins of her head.

Shakespeare obviously had very little patience with Venus, describing her perfunctorily and with a certain detachment. She is not really present in the story; she is more a symbol of eroticism than eroticism itself. And just as her failure to arouse Adonis shows that she is neither very serious nor very beautiful, so Adonis' chastity becomes at first curiously disturbing and finally ridiculous. But let Shakespeare describe a horse, and there is a real horse standing in the courtyard just below your window:

> Round-hoof'd, short-jointed, fetlocks shag and long,
> Broad breast, full eye, small head, and nostril wide,
> High crest, short ears, straight legs and passing strong,
> Thin mane, thick tail, broad buttock, tender hide;
>   Look what a horse should have he did not lack,
>   Save a proud rider on so proud a back.

He gave to his horse more life than he gave to Venus or Adonis, because it was something familiar to him. The horse is painted in broad strokes, and the love affair of the horse is considerably more energetic than the love affair of Venus and Adonis:

> He looks upon his love and neighs unto her;
> She answers him, as if she knew his mind.
> Being proud, as females are, to see him woo her,
> She puts on outward strangeness, seems unkind,
>   Spurns at his love and scorns the heat he feels,
>   Beating his kind embracements with her heels.

> Then, like a melancholy malcontent,
> He vails his tail, that, like a falling plume,
> Cool shadow to his melting buttock lent;
> He stamps, and bites the poor flies in his fume.
>   His love, perceiving how he was enraged,
>   Grew kinder, and his fury was assuaged.

Shakespeare dedicated the poem to the twenty-year-old Henry Wriothesley, Earl of Southampton and Baron of Titchfield, whose singular beauty and intelligence together with his wealth and vanity marked him as the leading member of the *jeunesse dorée*, the one young man at court who would turn all the ladies' eyes and receive the envy of every middle-aged man. He was a favorite of the Queen, a close friend of the Earl of Essex, a patron of poets, a student of

Italian literature and history—John Florio, the translator of Montaigne, was his private tutor—and a celebrator of all that was new, fresh, and distinguished. No one quite like him had yet appeared in London, for he combined to an extraordinary degree the roles of dandy, connoisseur, bon vivant, politician, arbiter of taste, soldier, and hardheaded thinker. He had a rather long, narrow face, sculptured lips, a fine nose, arrogant nostrils, large eyes, a soaring forehead, and a huge mane of thick reddish-gold hair brushed back and flowing over his left shoulder. In later years his face took on a somewhat saturnine appearance, as of a man who had seen and known too much for any comfort life could bring him.

Shakespeare's dedication of "Venus and Adonis" was couched in properly respectful terms. He had evidently met Southampton and through Florio or someone else had obtained permission to dedicate his verses to the young lord. Earls, and especially an earl so much in favor at court, were regarded wih awe, and Shakespeare was still in awe of him when he wrote:

TO THE RIGHT HONORABLE
HENRY WRIOTHESLEY, EARL OF
SOUTHAMPTON, AND BARON
OF TITCHFIELD

Right Honourable, I know not how I shall offend in dedicating my unpolished lines to your Lordship, nor how the world will censure me for choosing so strong a prop to support so weak a burthen, only if your Honour seem but pleased, I account myself highly praised, and vow to take advantage of all idle hours, till I have honoured you with some graver labour. But if the first heir of my invention prove deformed, I shall be sorry it had so noble a godfather, and never after ear so barren a land, for fear it yield me still so bad a harvest, I leave it to your Honourable survey, and your Honour to your heart's content, which I wish may always answer your own wish, and the world's hopeful expectation.

Your Honour's in all duty,
William Shakespeare

In Elizabethan times such dedications were written with great care, every word being weighed, calculated, placed in exactly the right setting. Thus, when Shakespeare wrote "if the first heir of my invention prove deformed, I shall be sorry it had so noble a godfather," he was insisting that Southampton had indeed "stood godfather" and was in some direct way responsible for the existence of the poem. By publicly humbling himself Shakespeare was in fact praising himself, for to humble oneself in the presence of the great was to pronounce favor on oneself. In this dedication Shakespeare also promised "some graver labour," which would inevitably be dedicated to Southampton.

In the following year Shakespeare published through Richard Field "to be sold at the Sign of the White Greyhound" another work called "The Rape of Lucrece," which purported to tell the story of Sextus Tarquinius' rape of the virtuous Lucrece and the revenge taken by the Roman people against the conquering Etruscans. Lucrece killed herself to expiate a crime she had not committed and the Romans rejoiced in this final proof of her virtue. Shakespeare favors virtue but at too great a length, for the poem consists of enormous soliloquies and endless declamations. Lucrece devotes eighty lines to telling Tarquinius all the reasons why he should not rape her. Her speech is convoluted, her arguments legalistic, her demeanor that of a prosecuting attorney who in order to confuse the jury deliberately speaks at great length. The argument is very tortuous:

> "Thou art," quoth she, "a sea, a sovereign king,
> And lo, there falls into thy boundless flood
> Black lust, dishonor, shame, misgoverning,
> Who seek to stain the ocean of thy blood.
> If all these petty ills shall change thy good,
>   Thy sea within a puddle's womb is hearsèd,
>   And not the puddle in thy sea dispersèd.

There is more than a suspicion that Shakespeare is playing five-finger exercises with metaphysical ideas, which become increasingly tenuous as the poem continues. There is a falling away, a retrogression. The rape itself is mismanaged, becoming an abstraction:

> But she hath lost a dearer thing than life,
> And he hath won that he would lose again.

This forcèd league doth force a further strife;
This momentary joy breeds months of pain;
This hot desire converts to cold disdain;
    Pure Chastity is rifled of her store,
    And Lust, the thief, far purer than before.

Strangely Shakespeare appears to have assured himself that he
has improved on "Venus and Adonis," and his dedication to the
Earl of Southampton is written on a note of triumph. If, as we may
expect, the words were carefully weighed, they are weighed on
metaphysical scales. The dedication reads:

> The love I dedicate to your Lordship is without end;
> whereof this pamphlet without beginning is but a
> superfluous moiety. The warrant I have of your honorable
> disposition, and the worth of my untutored lines, makes it
> assured of acceptance. What I have done is yours; what I
> have to do is yours; being part in all I have, devoted yours.
> Were my worth greater, my duty would show greater;
> meantime, as it is, it is bound to your Lordship, to whom I
> wish long life still lengthened with all happiness.
>
>   Your Lordship's in all duty,
>   William Shakespeare

It is customary to read this dedication as a declaration of love and
to suggest that Shakespeare's relations with Southampton were, if
not intimate, at least on a close and friendly basis. But it is just as
likely that the words concealed a mounting fear that their relationship was coming to an end. Shakespeare was making great claims
on Southampton's affection; he was asserting himself as one who is
"bound to your Lordship" and possessing the warrant of "your
honorable disposition," thus including himself in the circle around
Southampton. But it is curious that no document survives to show
any further contact between Shakespeare and Southampton.

In 1709 Nicholas Rowe told the story that "my Lord Southampton, at one time, gave him [Shakespeare] a thousand pounds to
enable him to go through with a purchase which he heard he had a
mind to." This story, which was handed down by Sir William
D'Avenant, who sometimes claimed to be Shakespeare's natural

child, defies belief. Southampton was wealthy; he was quite capable of giving large sums of money away; but a thousand pounds was a fantastically large sum, equivalent to $100,000 in our money. The legend that Shakespeare was on such close terms with Southampton that he could expect to receive an outright gift of a thousand pounds is one that has no basis in probability.

Shakespeare knew Southampton: this is certain. It is also certain that he was never in Southampton's intimate circle, and his further relations with Southampton are unknown.

Ever since 1817, when Nathan Drake first advanced the theory that Henry Wriothesley was the "Mr. W.H." of the *Sonnets*, commentators have continued to link Southampton with the young man addressed in the first 126 sonnets in spite of the fact that the handsome youth described by Shakespeare has very little in common with Southampton as known to history. According to these commentators there was a prolonged love affair between Shakespeare and a young nobleman, and the sonnets are the record of the varying movements of the affair, its triumphs and defeats. It would seem to be much more likely that Shakespeare was writing about an idealized youth, who may have had some of the characteristics of Southampton, may even have resembled him in some aspects, but was not in any real sense the young Earl of Southampton and Baron of Titchfield.

Curiously, no one has suggested that the idealized young man of the *Sonnets* might be modeled on Richard Burbage, with whom it is certain that Shakespeare was in daily contact in Shoreditch, for the plays were written for him to act the leading roles. His name appears immediately below Shakespeare in the "Names of the Principal Actors in all these plays," listed in the 1623 Folio, and they are coupled together by a massive initial which separates them from the other players. Burbage was three or four years younger than Shakespeare, a man of enormous charm and powerful presence. He played Hamlet, Lear, Othello, and Richard III so effectively that his performances became legendary. Shakespeare remembered him and only two other actors in his will.

The search for the identity of the young man and the dark lady of the *Sonnets* must continue to be an exercise in futility. There is no evidence to link the *Sonnets* to anyone, and this is as it should be.

They were poems written in honor of an idealized love affair and they were arranged in the form of a drama, because Shakespeare was a dramatist.

It must be admitted that the *Sonnets* are curiously uneven, and include some of the worst sonnets ever written in the English language. About fifty of them show Shakespeare at the height of his powers, and another fifty pass muster, while the rest are second- and third-rate. Published in 1609, they appear to belong to a period extending from about 1595 to 1605 with a few much earlier sonnets included for full measure. They are evidently printed from Shakespeare's manuscript, and it is possible and even probable that he read the proofs carefully, for the text is remarkably clean. The printer's errors, when they occur, are precisely the kind of calamitous errors that occur when an author corrects his own work at the last moment: *beautits treasure* (Sonnet 6), *forrwes* (Sonnet 22), and *Bare rn'wd quiers* (Sonnet 73). There are also slips like those that authors habitually make: *hundreth* (Sonnet 59) and *When in dead night their faire imperfect shade*, where he obviously meant *thy faire imperfect shade*: the sounds of *their* and *faire* helping to compound the error.

Ben Jonson wrote of Shakespeare's *Sonnets* that they were "serene, clear and elegantly plain, such gentle strains as shall recreate and not perplex your brain, no cloudy stuff to puzzle intellect." This verdict surprises modern commentators, who find puzzles everywhere and wonder why the richly orchestrated music should be described as "gentle strains." We must realize that in the perspective of their times the *Sonnets* were exactly as Ben Jonson assessed them, and it was their serenity first, and then their clarity and elegance, which attracted the readers. Where we hear organ notes, Shakespeare's contemporaries heard the music of the lute, the viol, and the virginal. Once we find ourselves removing the imaginary organ notes from the *Sonnets,* we will be in a better position to understand how they sounded to their first readers. Almost they are songs, and should be read as songs are read:

Like as the waves make towards the pibbled shore,
So do our minutes hasten to their end.
Each changing place with that which goes before,

In sequent toil all forwards do contend.
Nativity once in the main of light
Crawls to maturity, wherewith being crowned,
Crooked eclipses 'gainst his glory fight,
And time that gave doth now his gift confound.
Time doth transfix the flourish set on youth,
And delves the parallels in beauty's brow,
Feeds on the rarities of nature's truth,
And nothing stands but for his scythe to mow.
    And yet to times in hope, my verse shall stand
    Praising thy worth, despight his cruel hand.

Throughout the *Sonnets* the word "time" beats like the ticking of a clock, insistently present, hauntingly clear, terrifying in its intensity. Time, that "ceaseless lackey to eternity," is the enemy, but Shakespeare was half in love with it, as the Elizabethans were half in love with "that sweet enemy France." Time was dangerous and horrible, perversely destructive of youth and beauty; it was the creator of corpses; but it was also the creator of the seasons and the dawns. So Shakespeare, while appalled by it, makes his peace with it with an almost Oriental sense of fatality, asking no more of it than that it should sometimes give him a breathing space to study the unchanging face of perfect beauty. Sometimes, but very rarely, this serenity is exchanged for a violent rage, as in the first four lines of Sonnet 19:

Devouring time, blunt thou the lion's paws,
And make the earth devour her own sweet brood,
Pluck the keen tooth from the fierce tiger's jaws
And burn the long-lived Phoenix in her blood.

It should be remarked that these lines belong to the poetry of pure irrational rage, for no viable meaning can be extracted from them. They are overwhelmingly powerful: they speak of Doomsday, the end of the world, the earth devouring her own, the Phoenix never to rise again. But it is beyond belief that the blunting of the lion's paws and the removal of the tiger's teeth will in any way accomplish these ends. What Shakespeare has done is to evoke a series of powerful images: devouring time, blunt lion's paws, the earth devouring her own, pluck, tiger's teeth, the final burning of the Phoenix. The images are powerful enough to carry the weight of the emotion, but the emotion itself breaks under the strain.

In a surprisingly large number of sonnets Shakespeare's purest poetry comes in the first four lines. These are the "god-given" lines: the rest must be worked out with circumspection and patience, with luck and infinite labor. These "god-given" lines are among the most memorable Shakespeare ever wrote. Here are the first four lines of Sonnets 29, 30, and 33:

> When in disgrace with fortune and men's eyes,
> I all alone beweep my outcast state,
> And trouble deaf heaven with my bootless cries,
> And look upon myself and curse my fate . . .

> When to the sessions of sweet silent thought,
> I summon up remembrance of things past,
> I sigh the lack of many a thing I sought,
> And with old woes new wail my dear time's waste . . .

> Full many a glorious morning have I seen
> Flatter the mountain tops with sovereign eye,
> Kissing with golden face the meadows green,
> Gilding pale streams with heavenly alchemy . . .

What they have in common is a soaring and apparently effortless flight. Mannerisms and facile five-finger exercises have gone. The mood is remote from "Venus and Adonis" and "The Rape of Lucrece"; he is astonishingly at ease on the sunlit plains. Even when he is cursing himself or suffering in his poetic fashion the extremities of a lover's despair, he is in full control of the inner music. Only in one sonnet do we hear the hard cutting edge of sexual despair:

> The expense of spirit in a waste of shame
> Is lust in action, and till action, lust
> Is perjured, murderous, bloody, full of blame,
> Savage, extreme, rude, cruel, not to trust . . .

Hazlitt called "Venus and Adonis" and "The Rape of Lucrece" "a couple of ice-houses, as hard, as glittering, and as cold." It is a

strange verdict, since the pages blaze with sexual heat and the
poems in their own time served as aphrodisiacs. In Thomas Middleton's play *A Mad World My Masters*, Harebrain says "Venus
and Adonis" and "Hero and Leander" were "two luscious marrow-
bone pies for a young married wife; and therefore (thought Harebrain) to be conveyed away from her." The *Sonnets*, too, have been
credited with aphrodisiac powers and there is not the least doubt
that they are love poems, but they are love poems with a difference.
The troubled lover possesses an enviable serenity; he has worked
out in great detail the mythology of his love affair; he is armored
with love and knows exactly where he is going. Not the least of
Shakespeare's gifts to the world was the self-assurance he has given
to lovers everywhere.

Shake-speare's Sonnets, Never before Imprinted, consisting of a
complete sonnet sequence of 154 poems, was published by Thomas
Thorpe, together with the early work called "A Lover's Complaint." He was a reputable bookseller, who became a freeman of
the Stationer's Company in 1594. At least twenty-nine works are
known to have been published by him, nearly all of them important
works. They include three plays by George Chapman, four works
by Ben Jonson, and translations of Epictetus and Saint Augustine's
The City of God. Thorpe liked to preface his books with somewhat
sententious dedications in epigrammatic form. His dedication to
Shakespeare's *Sonnets* has perplexed many scholars and reduced
others almost to madness.

We know the quality of Thorpe's mind, which delighted in
exuberant flattery, quips, and ostentatious praise. In this he differed
scarcely at all from the other writers of his age. Thus when Ben
Jonson dedicated his play *Volpone, or the Fox* to the two universities of Oxford and Cambridge in gratitude for their applause when
the play was presented to them, he wrote:

To the
Most Noble and Most Equal Sisters
The Two Famous Universities
For Their
Love and Acceptance Shown to His Poem
In the Presentation:

Ben. Jonson
The Grateful Acknowledger,
Dedicates Both It And Himself.

By our present tastes the Grateful Acknowledger was a little too grateful, a little too self-serving. The monumental inscription is too heavy for the play he had written. *Volpone* was published by Thomas Thorpe in 1607. Jonson was well served by his publisher, who printed the book with his usual good taste.

The dedication of Shakespeare's *Sonnets* was considerably more complex although shorter by six words. It was printed in capital letters with a period after each word such as sometimes appeared in memorial inscriptions carved on stone. One can imagine Ben Jonson composing his dedication in a few moments, while Thorpe's dedication to Mr. W.H. was just as obviously conceived with great care and minute attention to detail and the proper balance of words, with Shakespeare, though unnamed, in the place of honor in the center. Like Jonson's dedication to *Volpone* it is composed in three clauses so arranged that each clause has its own impact. With Thorpe's dedication the impact is all the greater because the words have an engaging metallic ring and something of the music of verse. They could be arranged in four lines of passable verse. Instead Thorpe chose to arrange them monumentally in twelve lines, five of these lines being only one word long.

TO. THE. ONLIE. BEGETTER. OF
THESE. INSVING. SONNETS.
MR. W. H. ALL. HAPPINESSE.
AND. THAT. ETERNITIE.
PROMISED.
BY
OVR. EVER-LIVING. POET.
WISHETH.
THE. WELL-WISHING.
ADVENTURER. IN
SETTING.
FORTH.

T.T.

There still exists a surprisingly large number of people who have persuaded themselves that Mr. W.H., "the onlie begetter," must be one of Shakespeare's patrons, either William Herbert or by reversing the initials Henry Wriothesley, forgetting that Herbert was third Earl of Pembroke and Wriothesley was the third Earl of Southampton, and neither under any circumstances would be addressed as "Mr." It was left to Sir Sidney Lee, who carefully studied the dedications in hundreds of Elizabethan and Jacobean books, to solve the mystery. He discovered that a certain William Hall, a printer, worked for Thomas Thorpe as a procurer of manuscripts. Hall was "the only begetter of these insuing sonnets" in the sense that he was their procurer or the agent between Shakespeare and Thorpe, if as seems probable Shakespeare set about finding a publisher. The dedication, which appears so mysterious at first sight, becomes on examination curiously commonplace. "All happiness" was a common greeting in a dedication. Robert Greene would usually address his dedicatee in the form. "To————————Robert Greene wisheth increase of honour with the full fruition of perfect felicity." In 1606 Thorpe published a collection of poems by the Catholic poet Robert Southwell. Called *A Fourefould Meditation*, it was dedicated

TO THE RIGHT WORSHIPFULL AND
VERTUOUS GENTLEMAN, MATHEW
SAUNDERS, ESQUIRE.
W.H. wisheth, with long life, a prosperous
achievement of his good desires

The rather quirky dedication of the *Sonnets* betrays the hand and style of Thorpe and Hall working together, amusing themselves for the occasion with a more than usually exotic dedication. Hall would remain wrapped in a transparent garment of anonymity, his name nicely embedded in the third line, and Thomas Thorpe, "the well-wishing adventurer," by which he probably meant "the hopeful speculator and publisher," would remain cautiously hidden behind his initials, which also appeared on the title page. "That eternity promised by our ever-living poet" was most likely an ironic tribute to Shakespeare as he announces in about twenty sonnets that his verses are written for everlasting, will outlive all time, and threaten to outlive eternity.

The sonnets, which had circulated in manuscript long before they were published, appeared in a precise order which could only have been the order Shakespeare designed for them. It is a perfectly satisfactory arrangement and no one has been able to improve on it. In 1639 John Benson's pirated edition of the *Sonnets* was an attempt to improve on the original order but failed miserably. He omitted six sonnets for no obvious reason and sometimes bowdlerized the text, so that some of the poems addressed to a young man would appear to be addressed to a young woman. Thus in Sonnet 108 "sweet boy" became "sweet love" and in Sonnet 104 "fair friend" became "fair love." The *Sonnets*, of course, survived Benson as they survived Thomas Bowdler, who published his *Family Shakespeare* in 1818, hoping to provide a text in which all profanities and indecencies were omitted. He knew so little about the usage of words in Elizabethan and Jacobean times that some of the most hair-raising indecencies remained.

"Venus and Adonis," "The Rape of Lucrece," and the *Sonnets* are all love poems, and it would have been remarkable if they contained no indelicacies. Shakespeare presented himself as the indefatigable lover constantly examining the nature of love and celebrating its splendor.

Shakespeare of the Streets of London

The Coming
of Falstaff

OF ALL SHAKESPEARE'S EARLY INVENTIONS, Falstaff is the most formidable. He comes running onto the stage like an express train, drowning out all the voices around him, superb in his ready wit and rough-hewn arrogance. Fat and lecherous, dripping with sweat, wheezing and coughing, he takes command of the stage and demands our instant obedience. He plays his role in kingly fashion, possessing a divine impudence and a divine sweet temper. When he is on the stage, we have eyes only for him.

Where does he come from? He is, of course, part clown, part strutting soldier, but he is also something so much more that we are startled into acquiescence to all the outrages he commits on the world and on himself. He speaks some of the most glorious prose ever written. He is a coward, a liar, an imposter, a rakehell of no mean accomplishment, and at the same time he is a man without vices. He exults in his humanity, as he has a perfect right to do, being more essentially common clay than anyone in Shakespeare's plays with the sole exception of the dying Lear. There he stands, a huge jelly of a man defying the world to do its worst to him, not caring overmuch what the world thinks of him, at ease with himself, self-deceiving but deceiving no one, and his own self-deceit is scarcely sufficient to penetrate his disguise of himself as the most worldly of men and the most enchanted knight. But what is most apparent in him is precisely his ease with himself, for he is the only man in Shakespeare's plays who is entirely at home in the world. He is *filius terrae*, the laughing son of the earth, close brother to Pan, and cousin to Laurence Sterne's Uncle Toby and Dickens's Samuel Pickwick. He is *l'homme moyen sensuel* raised to the pitch of genius. Round as a wine barrel, with bulging eyes and nimble feet, he surveys the world with a kind of happy disdain and a fervent astonishment. Emerson wrote beautifully that when Shakespeare was writing comedy, he lived in a gale. Falstaff is the gale at full force.

In fact, Falstaff is well aware that he is a force of nature: he will have everyone believe he is a hurricane. He has the waywardness of a hurricane, striking where least expected, and like a hurricane he dies at last. Mortality troubles him, but only a little bit. Doll Tearsheet describes him admiringly: "Thou whoreson little tidy Bartholomew boar-pig, when wilt thou leave fighting o' days and foining o' nights, and begin to patch up thine old body for heaven?" He is not little, he is not tidy: the words are ironical and affectionate. He is a boar-pig because he eats for preference at the Boar's Head Tavern at Eastcheap, and Bartholomew is added for good measure to signify the plenty at the Bartholomew Fair. He enjoys life too much to patch up his old body for heaven, yet he pays mortality its due and sometimes talks about it. What he asks of life is what all men ask of life: laughter, good companionship, good food, women. "Peace, good Doll!" he exclaims. "Do not speak like a death's head; do not bid me remember mine end." And even when Doll Tearsheet is kissing him, he is overwhelmed by the passion of mortality. "I am old, I am old," he murmurs in a frenzy of self-disgust over his white hairs. But the self-disgust is fleeting. Women will always take him into their beds because of the joy in him.

Falstaff knows himself well and he can calculate to a hair breadth how far he can go in any of the adventures he undertakes. When he boasts—and he is continually boasting—he boasts truthfully:

Men of all sorts take pride to gird at me: the brain of this foolish-compounded clay, man, is not able to invent anything that tends to laughter more than I invent or is invented on me. I am not only witty in myself, but the cause of wit in other men.

Although the statement is true, it is also troubling. Suddenly, with the words "or is invented on me," we are made aware of ambiguities. The words invented on him were invented by Shakespeare. Falstaff is acknowledging the presence of the puppetmaster, or rather, since Falstaff is a character wholly invented by Shakespeare, we are hearing once more Shakespeare's own voice. This leads us to suspect that there may be more of Shakespeare in Falstaff than we ever guessed. It is not an unreasonable suspicion. Falstaff is so much more alive than all the other characters in the plays where he appears that we are entitled to believe that Shakespeare may be recognizing something of himself. "I am not only witty in myself, but the cause of wit in other men."

We know how Falstaff came to birth, and his many names. Originally he was Cuthbert Cutter, alias Gad's Hill, alias Sir John Oldcastle, alias Jockey. His complicated origins are to be found in a strange play called *The Famous Victories of Henry the Fifth containing the Honourable Battle of Agincourt*, first printed in 1598, though it was certainly in existence ten years earlier, for we know that the great clown Richard Tarleton acted in it at the Bull in Bishopsgate before his death in the autumn of 1588. Thomas Nashe enjoyed the play, saying in 1592: "What a glorious thing it is to have Henry V represented on the stage, leading the French King prisoner and forcing him and the Dolphin to swear fealty!" But that was perhaps as far as its glory went. The play meanders along drunkenly, spirited only in coarse-grained invective, resembling nothing so much as a midnight reveler roaring to the high firmament as he makes his way home. A poor carrier called Derick has been robbed by a thief on Gad's Hill. Not long afterward the thief blunders into the group of men around Derick, asks an innocent question, and is quickly overwhelmed. The conversation between the thief and the men surrounding him is slapstick comedy dating from the time of the morality plays:

Thief.   Here is a good fellow. I pray you which is the way
to the old tavern in Eastcheap.

Derick.   Whoop hollo, now Gadshill, knowest thou me?

Thief.   I know thee for an ass.

Derick.   And I know thee for a taking fellow.
Upon Gad's hill in Kent
A bots lights upon you.

Thief.   The whoreson villain would be knockt.

Derick.   Masters, villain, and ye be men stand to him,
And take his weapon from him, and let him not pass you.

Arrested and brought before the Court of the King's Bench, the
thief is commanded by the judge to give his name. He answers
impudently: "My name was known before I came here, and shall be
when I am gone, I warrant you." It transpires that his real name is
Cuthbert Cutter. When he hears his name in court, he flies into a
temper and shouts: "What the devil need you ask, and know it so
well?" When he is asked: "By whom wilt thou be tried?" he
answers that he wishes to be tried either by himself or by Prince
Henry, who providentially enters the court immediately after Derick has announced that the thief has also stolen the great ginger root
"that Bouncing Bess with the jolly buttocks should have had."
Prince Hal quarrels with the judge, boxes his ears, and finds
himself committed to the Fleet Prison. The thief fades away, and Sir
John Oldcastle enters the prison to commiserate with the prince. Sir
John is a sycophant who adds to the scene only the scraps that fall
from the sycophant's table but the name hovers in midair like
brightly colored balloons. Shakespeare used it until the family of Sir
John violently objected, remembering that their ancestor was a close
friend of Prince Hal in his youth but was burned as a heretic by
order of the same prince when he became King. In the first edition
of the play we see Sir John Oldcastle very briefly; by 1623, when
the First Folio appeared, Sir John Oldcastle has become Sir John
Falstaff and is larger than life.

The vicissitudes of Sir John Falstaff continued. He not only
changed his name; he changed his character. He appears in four
plays: *Henry IV Parts 1 and 2; The Merry Wives of Windsor;* and

briefly and off-stage in *Henry V*. There are traces of Cuthbert Cutter in *Henry IV Part 1* but there are no traces of him in *Henry IV Part 2*. He has grown immoderately in the interval. He grows smaller in *The Merry Wives of Windsor*. He glows brightly in the brief passage devoted to his deathbed in *Henry V*.

But whether he grows or is diminished he is always a familiar and recognizable presence. Shakespeare doted on him. If his character changes, it is no matter: the boundaries are firmly sketched and his heavy bottom rests easily in any chair. He will change his opinions on all things if it suits him, and hold defiantly to the one opinion that comes from the core of his being: that life is made for human enjoyment and the rest is folly and darkness. In spite of his joy in living, he is terrified by life's impermanence and will give himself up to an agony of nihilism at the least reminder of the poverty of the human condition. The prince complains: "I never did see such pitiful rascals," and Falstaff answers for all the oppressed people of the world:

> Tut, tut; good enough to toss; food for powder,* food for
> powder; they'll fill a pit as well as better. Tush, man,
> mortal men, mortal men.

Falstaff, of necessity, includes himself among the tortured and the damned. His verdict on suffering humanity is a profound nihilism and a raging thirst. These are echoes of Fallstaff's end in the ending of *King Lear*. Like Don Quixote he is a tragic as well as a comic character.

Shakespeare offers Falstaff the tribute of his most abundant affection, loving the man this side of idolatry and encouraging him to acts of folly that rarely go beyond speech making. Falstaff's crimes, even the crime of saying he killed Hotspur, which was to claim for himself one of those acts that change the destinies of nations, belong to the category of errors of judgment. In his own eyes he is honest and true-hearted, especially at those moments when he is blatantly dishonest and downright evil-minded. He is by nature ambiguous and has the best of both worlds. He resembles a

---

*Falstaff is not thinking about cannon-fodder. Powder = salt. He is thinking about salted meat kept in pits.

walking whale, but there is no gainsaying his joy in life. He claims
what few people have dared to claim—that his belly is preeminent
throughout the world:

> I have a whole school of tongues in this belly of mine,
> and not a tongue of them all speaks any other word than
> my name. And I had but a belly of any indifferency, I were
> simply the most active fellow in Europe: my womb, my
> womb, my womb undoes me.

So it does, but his undoing is never for long. He sails through the
plays like a full-masted galleon, the sails filled with wind, his little
pig eyes gazing out delightedly through his forest of hair, while he
proclaims himself to be the most modest of men or alternatively to
be a paragon of mankind, and we are made surprisingly aware that
he must have obtained his command of English at the school of John
Lyly, though Lyly was never so lewd nor would he take off in such
monumental flights of fancy.

"My womb, my womb, my womb undoes me." Falstaff's womb
contains millions: like Pistol it "speaks of Africa and golden joys." The
memory of these joys and the prospect of even greater joys urges him on. If
Shakespeare speaks through him, it is always because Shakespeare is
enamored of his Fools and takes them so seriously that he serves them with
his greatest art, knowing that the Fool is Everyman, that in fact the Fool is
the most serious thing in creation. When two Fools come together,
Shakespeare has a roaring time. This happens when Sir John, while
recruiting soldiers in Gloucestershire, falls into the company of Robert
Shallow, an old friend of his youth, now a doddering justice with only a
few stray wisps of his wit about him, having lost his juices and his wit
simultaneously.

Shallow.   O, Sir John, do you remember since we lay all
    night in the Windmill in St. George's Field?

Falstaff.   No more of that, Master Shallow.

Shallow.   Ha! 'Twas a merry night. And is Jane
    Nightwork alive?

Falstaff.   She lives, Master Shallow.

Shallow.   She never could away with me.

Falstaff. Never, never, she would always say she could not abide Master Shallow.

Shallow. By the mass, I could anger her to th' heart. She was then a bona-roba.* Does she hold her own well?

Falstaff. Old, old, Master Shallow.

Shallow. Nay, she must be old; she cannot chose but be old; certain she's old; and had Robin Nightwork by old Nightwork before I came to Clement's Inn.

Silence. That's fifty-five years ago.

Shallow. Ha, cousin Silence, that thou hadst seen that this knight and I have seen! Ha, Sir John, said I well?

Falstaff. We have heard the chimes at midnight, Master Shallow.

It is one of those moments in literature when the words vanish and only the sorrow remains. It would seem unlikely that we should be moved by two old men discussing the brothels they frequented in their youth, but we are. Poor Shallow comes to life, aided by the energy pouring out of Falstaff and the remembered energy of a whore. "I could anger her to th' heart," he says, meaning that he could enflame her to the quick. It is not surprising, since in Shakespeare all whores are lusty, made for the enjoyment of mankind.

Falstaff never reaches this height again except on his deathbed. Yet he comes perilously close at times, especially when he delivers his long speeches on the comforts and advantages of good sherris or the strange addiction of old men to lying about their youth. They are set pieces, delivered in front of the stage before an audience spellbound by his vast presence, and we must imagine the clowning, the sniffing, the solemn pauses and the sudden racing of words, the eyes lifted to heaven and then roving wildly over the audience, all the repertoire of buffoonery at his fingertips, while we hear the midnight chimes in the distance. Justice Robert Shallow has gone on his way and Falstaff is left alone to contemplate the vices of old men.

---

*John Florio defines bona-roba as "good stuff" or "a good wholesome plum-cheeked wench."

Falstaff.   Lord, Lord, how subject we old men are to the
vice of lying! This same starved justice hath done nothing
but prate to me of the wildness of his youth and the feats
he hath done about Turnbull Street, and every third
word a lie, duer paid to the hearer than the Turk's
tribute. I do remember him at Clement's Inn like a man
made after supper of a cheese paring. When 'a was
naked, he was, for all the world, like a forked radish,
with a head fantastically carved on it with a knife. 'A
was so forlorn that his dimensions to any thick sight were
invisible. 'A was the very genius of famine, yet lecherous
as a monkey, and the whores called him mandrake. 'A
came ever in the rearward of the fashion, and sung those
tunes to the overscutched huswives* that he heard the
car-men whistle, and sware they were his fancies or his
goodnights. And now is this Vice's dagger become a
squire, and talks as familiarly of John a Gaunt as if he
had been sworn brother to him, and I'll be sworn 'a
never saw him but once in the Tilt-yard, and then he
burst his head for crowding among the marshal's men. I
saw it, and told John a Gaunt he beat his own name, for
you might have thrust him and all his apparel into an
eel-skin—the case of a treble hautboy was a mansion for
him, a court. Well, I'll be acquainted with him, if I
return, and 't shall go hard but I'll make him a
philosopher's two stones to me. If the young dace be a
bait for the old pike, I see no reason in the law of nature
that I may snap at him. Let time shape, and there an
end.

In the end Falstaff dismisses Robert Shallow handsomely, with a
sweet temper. He is laying plans, of course. He proposes to use
Shallow as a butt to entertain Prince Hal: hence his sweet temper.
Shallow will become "a philosopher's two stones" with a vengeance,
and Falstaff will die laughing.

*Worn-out hussies.

The famous speech on the joys of drinking sherris is a more serious matter. A young rock star has recently decided to exclude the speech from his repertoire because it is a powerful incitement to alcoholism. So it is, but there are extenuating circumstances. It is Falstaff in his prime, in lustful command of the English language, ogling the audience and reducing them to helpless laughter not only because he is funny but also because he pretends to a scholastic argument: this is a fact, *ergo* it follows by the purest logic that—and thus the happy inventions follow one another. Falstaff's logic is embroidery, and we believe none of it. He is one of those who come to the right conclusions from the wrong premises. Once again he is alone on the stage, leaning forward a little, engaging the attention of the audience conspiratorially.

Falstaff.   A good sherris-sack hath a twofold operation in it. It ascends me into the brain, dries me there all the foolish and dull and crudy vapours which environ it, makes it apprehensive, quick, forgetive, full of nimble, fiery, and delectable shapes, which, delivered o'er to the voice, the tongue, which is the birth, becomes excellent wit. The second quality of your excellent sherris is the warming of the blood, which, before cold and settled, left the liver white and pale, which is the badge of pusillanimity and cowardice. But the sherris warms it and makes it course from the inwards to the parts extremes. It illumineth the face, which as a beacon gives warning to all the rest of this kingdom, man, to arm, and then the vital commoners and inland petty spirits muster me all to their captain, the heart, who, great and puffed up with this retinue, doth any deed of courage, and this valor comes of sherris. So that skill in the weapon is nothing without sack, for it sets it a-work, and learning a mere hoard of gold kept by a devil, till sack commences it and sets it in act and use. Hereof comes it that Prince Harry is valiant, for the cold blood did naturally inherit of his father, he hath, like lean, sterile, and bare land, manured, husbanded, and tilled with excellent endeavour of drinking good and

good store of fertile sherris, that he is become very hot
and valiant. If I had a thousand sons, the first humane
principle I would teach them should be to forswear thin
potations and to addict themselves to sack.

By the nature of things this speech was inflammatory, if only
because it is the most potent defense of drinking in the English
language. No doubt Englishmen drank too much: it is reliably
reported that the alehouses of London were the centers of whatever
riot and disorder there was. Defending the drunkards, however, was
one of the things Falstaff was born for, and it is not surprising that
he pointed to their valor and their courage. These were exactly the
virtues Falstaff found in himself.

We see him as a mountain of a man, nimble on his feet, quick to
dance and ogle, quick to advance on any unsuspecting women, boon
companion of the heir to the throne, and not above using his
proximity to the throne to his own advantage. All that is the familiar
Sir John. The unfamiliar Sir John appears when we remember that
he confessed to being sixty and was therefore white-haired and in
Elizabethan terms a very old man indeed. "Falstaff, the old white-
bearded Satan," Prince Hal calls him, and with bowed head
Falstaff agrees that there is a certain amount of Satan in him: Satan
being one of the Elizabethan terms for a whoremaster, although it is
not that aspect of Satan that interests him. He admits only to being
devilishly full of life. Prince Hal also accuses him of being a
"villainous abominable misleader of youth," which places him in
the same category as Socrates. Falstaff denies everything, while
admitting only his white hairs.

> *Falstaff.*   That he is old (the more the pity), his white hairs
> do witness it; but that he is (saving your reverence) a
> whoremaster, that I utterly deny. If sack and sugar be a
> fault, God help the wicked! If to be old and merry be a
> sin, then many an old host that I know is damned. If to
> be fat is to be hated, then Pharaoh's lean kine are to be
> loved. No, my good lord: banish Peto, banish Bardolph,
> banish Poins; but for sweet Jack Falstaff, kind Jack
> Falstaff, true Jack Falstaff, valiant Jack Falstaff, and
> therefore more valiant being as he is, old Jack Falstaff,

banish not him thy Harry's company. Banish plump Jack,
and banish all the world!

The cards, of course, are stacked against Falstaff; he will be
banished when his time comes. His bosom friend, Prince Hal, will
inevitably become his enemy and his King. At the end of the play
Prince Hal becomes Henry V; the time is past when he can
encourage the "tutor and feeder of my riots." Instead, the King
sends him to the Fleet Prison to cool his heels and says the most
chilling words ever addressed to Falstaff: "I know thee not, old man.
Fall to thy prayers." It is a wound from which Falstaff will never
recover: this time he will not wear his martyrdom bravely.

There is a curious phenomenon known to everyone who has been
close to men in power. There comes the need to humanize them, to
make them reveal themselves, to ask pointed questions verging on
impertinence, to search for the mysterious depths where motives and
ultimate ambitions are nourished. To enter their presence is to enter
a world where nothing is what it seems to be. Men in power, kings,
presidents, and prime ministers, are not like other men. They lie
concealed in their own secrets and subterfuges: the moment they
achieve power they are compromised. Falstaff has made it his aim to
humanize Prince Hal, to make a man of him, to guide him, if need
be, through the intolerable deceits of kingship. He succeeds insofar
as Prince Hal sometimes speaks in the authentic language of
Falstaff and promises when he is king, to command all the good lads
of Eastcheap. Falstaff even sees himself *in loco parentis* to the young
Prince of Wales and says as much in one of the livelier scenes in
Henry IV Part 1.

> *Falstaff.*   That thou art my son I have partly thy mother's
>   word, partly my own opinion, but chiefly a villainous
>   trick of thine eye and a foolish hanging of thy nether lip
>   that doth warrant me. If then thou be son to me, here lies
>   the point; why, being son to me, art thou so pointed at?
>   Shall the blessed sun of heaven prove a micher* and eat
>   blackberries? A question not to be asked. Shall the son of
>   England prove a thief and take purses? A question to be

*Truant.

asked. There is a thing, Harry, which thou hast often heard
of, and it is known to many in our land by the name of
pitch. This pitch, as ancient writers do report, doth defile;
so doth the company thou keepest. For, Harry, now I do
not speak to thee in drink, but in tears; not in pleasure, but
in passion; not in words only, but in woes also: and yet
there is a virtuous man whom I have often noted in thy
company, but I know not his name.

The spectator, of course, knows the name only too well. He
knows that Falstaff will plead his own cause; he has a great fear of
being banished from the prince's society and he will again ask not to
be banished. He will assert his living dignity against the stupidity of
servitude and death. He stands up for himself. This is his badge of
honor.

The King, the court, society, and even Prince Hal have other
views on honor. When Falstaff comes upon the dead body of a brave
soldier, Sir Walter Blunt, he shows a grave distaste for the grinning
horror that faces him. "Give me life," he says, "which if I can save,
so; if not, honor comes unlooked for, and there's an end." His
catechism of honor remains one of his bravest statements:

> *Falstaff.* Can honor set a leg? No. Or an arm? No. Or
> take away the grief of a wound? No. Honor hath no skill
> in surgery then? What is honor? A word. What is in that
> word honor? What is that honor? Air—a trim reckoning!
> Who hath it? He that died a Wednesday. Doth he feel
> it? Doth he hear it? No. 'Tis insensible then? Yea, to the
> dead. But will it not live with the living? No. Why?
> Detraction will not suffer it. Therefore I'll none of it.
> Honor is a mere scutcheon—and so ends my catechism.

The groundlings must have loved him for it, for he was saying
what men believe in their heart of hearts, and saying it brilliantly.
Hotspur will say: "Doomsday is near; die all, die merrily," when he
hears the news of his father's and Glendower's defection. But the
common people were not in love with Doomsday, they were weary
of interminable civil wars, and they may have enjoyed thinking that
Falstaff killed Hotspur.

Falstaff is one of those blessings which are visited from time to time on a world that has too few. Shakespeare created him from the whole cloth, modeling perhaps on Henry Chettle's fat body and the face of a laughing soldier the portrait of a lecherous, good-tempered drunkard, who is every man's brother.

Falstaff. Go thy ways, old Jack, die when thou wilt; if manhood, good manhood, be not forgot upon the face of the earth, then am I a shotten herring. There lives not three good men unhanged in England, and one of them is fat, and grows old. God help the while!

The
Roaring Boys

TRADITIONALLY BOY ACTORS HAVE BEEN HELL-raisers, impudent, dangerous, capable of every mischief, never more mischievous than when they are on holiday. From an impeccable source we learn that when the great French poet François Villon was living in retirement at Saint-Maixent in Poitou, he was given the duty of producing and directing the annual passion play. He went to the sacristan to borrow robes to be worn by the old peasant who would play the role of God the Father, but the sacristan refused to lend them. Villon in a furious temper let loose on the sacristan his own roaring boys, the young actors of the passion play.

Villon planned his strategy carefully. He learned that on the following Saturday the sacristan would be riding out to the nearby village of Saint-Ligaire on a young mare for the purpose of begging alms. Villon decided to ambush the sacristan in the village. He commanded his young actors to wear the costumes they would wear on the stage: wolfskins and goat skins, horns on their heads, mule bells and cowbells, and each had a sheep's head dangling from a rope around his shoulders. This formidable army of devils waited in ambush until the sacristan came into view, ambling along on his mare. Suddenly the boys were all over him. They made a horrible noise, and the mare panicked and rushed headlong down the road. The sacristan was thrown. Unfortunately he had roped himself to the mare, and he was dragged over ditches and through hedges. His skull was broken, his legs and arms crushed to pulp, his intestines were pounded to a jelly. By the time the mare reached the stables at Saint-Maixent all that was left of the sacristan was his right foot and a shoe caught in the stirrups. Villon was overjoyed: he had exacted the supreme penalty. "You played your roles very well," he told his young actors. "You acted splendidly. You outdevilled the devil. I defy the most talented actors to do as well, wherever they come from. Actors? No, you have lived your roles!"

Such at any rate is the story told by François Rabelais in the thirteenth chapter of the fourth book of *Gargantua and Pantagruel*.

High-spirited and audacious, the young actors in the Shakespearean theatre were a race apart. They were highly skilled performers, accomplished transvestites, dedicated to playing roles demanding an extreme elegance and refinement. They were trained in dancing and musicianship; an abundant vocabulary of gestures was provided for them; they were learned in deportment; and they were given impossibly difficult roles to play. A boy scarcely in his teens was asked to play Lady Macbeth or Cleopatra and to make the groundlings believe they were in the presence of long-dead queens. The Elizabethans were not of course alone in following this convention: the Chinese and Japanese were accustomed to seeing boys acting women's roles and men who were grandfathers were known to play youthful heroines.

The training was rigorous and relentless. It is often assumed that Shakespeare deliberately cut down the roles of the boy actors because they were incapable of sustaining lengthy and complicated roles, but in fact Rosalind in *As You Like It*, Imogen in *Cymbeline*, Portia in *The Merchant of Venice*, and Helena in *All's Well That Ends Well* do have lengthy roles which are central to the development of the drama; and although it is true that Cordelia speaks only 109 lines in *King Lear*, she, too, is central to the development of the play and must react by gesture and deportment to the speeches of many others. As a stage presence Cordelia is second only to King Lear, for the eyes of the audience are riveted on her.

According to the English stage tradition, the boy actors deliberately overacted; they minced and simpered, and were famous for their shrill voices. Almost they were more than women. When Cleopatra complains of the fate awaiting her in Rome, as a prisoner made to march through the streets in Caesar's triumphal procession, she speaks of their "squeaking" voices:

> And quick comedians
> Extemporally will stage us, and present
> Our Alexandrian revels; Antony
> Shall be brought drunken forth, and I shall see
> Some squeaking Cleopatra boy my greatness
> I' the posture of a whore.

It is an extraordinary speech, for she is projecting herself into the future, seeing herself in the procession and simultaneously seeing herself portrayed by the revelers who accompanied the procession and who acted out Caesar's triumph, and at the same time Cleopatra assures herself that she will never see these things. Shakespeare, enormously self-conscious about the drama, continually refers to the stage when he is dealing with historical events, seeing all life and all history as drama. Caesar and Cleopatra live in the knowledge that a playcart is following them.

We imagine Cleopatra being played in Egyptian costume with the double crown of Egypt on her head, with the instruments of kingship in her hands, sitting on an Egyptian throne. But in fact very little was known about Egyptian costumes when Shakespeare was writing, and we must imagine her dressed like Queen Elizabeth, wearing a red wig adorned with jewels and in characteristic Elizabethan costume, and there would be much hand-kissing and kneeling before her, and her throne would be the same throne on which the English kings had sat. No attempt was made to create an Egyptian atmosphere.

The boys who acted these royal roles had ample opportunity to study royalty. The meaningful gestures, the faint inclinations of the head, the way a queen would suddenly stretch out her hands after a long silence and by that sudden show of motion produce a dramatic effect, the way a queen walked as though always in procession and the way she talked as though always in command, not only in the sense of commanding others but in the sense of commanding destinies, all these things were studied closely by the boy actors who would see the real queen at the private performances offered in one of her palaces. Queen Elizabeth and Queen Anne, the wife of James I, were not likely to approve of performances lacking in royal dignity. In Elizabethan and Jacobean times royalty meant power in its utmost aspect. Royalty was like the sun radiating life and death, and even the lords of the realm trembled in its presence.

The same boy who portrayed Cleopatra one week might play Doll Tearsheet the next week. Shakespeare was prodigal with his female roles. The intellectual Portia would probably not be played by the same boy who played the passionately innocent Perdita, for they stand at the extreme limits of the spectrum of feeling. Cleopatra and Doll Tearsheet had enough in common to permit them to be acted by the same boy.

Here and there in his plays Shakespeare gives some indication of the training the boys received. Here, for example, in the Induction to *The Taming of the Shrew*, a lord sends his page to seek out old Christopher Sly, pretending to be his wife, the page's task being to seduce the drunken tinker into believing he has a beautiful young wife and together they are looking at a play about the taming of a shrew. A servant is sent to the page to explain how he should play his role:

Sirrah, go you to Bartholomew my page,
And see him dressed in all suits like a lady.
That done, conduct him to the drunkard's chamber,
And call him "madam," do him obeisance.
Tell him from me, and he will win my love,
He bear himself with honourable action,
Such as he has observed in noble ladies
Unto their lords, by them accomplished.
Such duty to the drunkard let him do
With soft low tongue and lowly courtesy,
And say "What is 't your honor will command,

Wherein your lady and your humble wife
May show her duty and make known her love?"
And then with kind embracements, tempting kisses,
And with declining head into his bosom,
Bid him shed tears, as being overjoyed
To see her noble lord restored to health,
Who for this seven years hath esteemed him
No better than a poor and loathsome beggar.
And if the boy have not a woman's gift
To rain a shower of commanded tears,
An onion will do well for such a shift,
Which in a napkin being close conveyed
Shall in despite enforce a watery eye.
See this dispatched with all the haste thou canst.
Anon, I'll give thee more instructions.
I know the boy will well usurp the grace,
Voice, gait, and action of a gentlewoman.

A few minutes later we see Christopher Sly and the page together, the old tinker radiant with the discovery that he has acquired a long forgotten bedmate only to learn that the lord has expressly instructed him not to sleep with her; and so they sit together to watch the unfolding of the play.

The lord's instructions to the page are clearly of the same kind as the instructions to the boy actors. The page is told how to behave; his deportment is indicated in some detail; we learn how tears are produced; embracements, kisses, the lowering of the head upon the bosom, and all the devices of pretended affection are shown, as the director would demonstrate to his young pupil on the stage. It is the only time in Shakespeare's works when we see the director at work with his "young eyases." When Hamlet plays the role of the director, he speaks more generally and is concerned with young actors only to complain against "the children of Paul's," where even the leading men's roles are played by boys with squeaking voices.

Ben Jonson is more prodigal with information about the training of boys. He tells a story of his play *The Devil Is an Ass* about one of his favorite young actors, Richard Robinson, who was capable of passing himself off as a woman both on the stage and in real life:

> But there be some of 'em
> Are very honest lads: there's Dickey Robinson
> A very pretty fellow, and comes often
> To a gentleman's chamber, a friend of mine. We had
> The merriest supper of it there, one night,
> The gentleman's landlady invited him
> To a gossip's feast: now he, sir, brought Dick Robinson,
> Drest like a lawyer's wife, amongst 'em all:
> I lent him clothes. But to see him behave it,
> And lay the law, and carve and drink unto them,
> And then talk bawdy, and send frolics! O
> It would have burst your buttons!

The Devil Is an Ass was presented at the Blackfriars Theatre in the autumn of 1616, not long after the death of Shakespeare. It was the most important play of that melancholy season and included one of the loveliest of Ben Jonson's songs—"Have you seen but a bright lily grow?" Robinson played the part of the greedy squire's wife, just as he had played the lawyer's wife in the gentleman's chamber. To be dressed like a lawyer's wife meant to be dressed in the height of fashion, for lawyers were rich. A few years earlier Robinson may have played Miranda in *The Tempest*, and it is almost certain that he played the Jailor's Daughter in *The Two Noble Kinsmen*. He was born about 1597. He was about ten years old when he became Richard Burbage's apprentice; he was in good hands, for Burbage was the greatest actor in England. In March 1619 Burbage suddenly became ill, drew up his will, and left everything to his wife, Winifred. Among the witnesses of his will was Richard Robinson, who later married Winifred and settled down to become one of the leading actors of the King's Men. Young Richard Robinson was mentioned in the First Folio as among the principal actors of Shakespeare's plays and must therefore have been among those who were close to Shakespeare.

From being a boy actor who played women's roles Robinson graduated into playing fatherly roles. He appears to have been one of those accomplished actors who rarely play leading roles but are content to play the second lead. He, too, had his apprentices. Among them was Charles Hart, the grandson of Shakespeare's younger sister, who became a formidable actor during the Restoration. When the Civil War broke out, Robinson and Hart both fought on the royalist side. Robinson died miserably, for he laid down his arms and surrendered but was immediately shot in the head by a fanatical Puritan soldier called Harrison, who cried out: "Cursed be he that doth the work of the Lord negligently!" There were witnesses to the cold-blooded murder, and Harrison was afterward hanged at Charing Cross. Charles Hart fared better. He became a lieutenant of horse in Prince Rupert's regiment, survived the war, and the interregnum when Cromwell ruled over the Republic of England, and joined Killigrew's Company, the leading actors' company of his time. He discovered Nell Gwyn, trained her as an actress, and became her first lover.

For the greater part of his life Richard Robinson lived quietly in Shoreditch, acting at the Globe and at Blackfriars, looking after the considerable Burbage interests inherited by his wife, and training his apprentices. He became a fully-fledged Sharer in the King's Men by 1619, for his name appears in the royal patent given to the actors in that year.

Although the Puritans thundered against the boy actors and held them up as children of the devil given to all manner of vices, the truth was that they were less dangerous than the crowds of young workingmen who attended the plays. The young actors lived with their teachers, studied hard, worked off their animal spirits in swordplay and dancing, and were kept busy. Some of the boy actors were notorious ladies' men as soon as they came of age. Nathan Field, who was also included among the principal actors of Shakespeare's plays, was famous for his seductions but eventually settled down to married life and had children. Richard Burbage painted a portrait of him which now hangs in Dulwich Gallery: he has the matinee idol look, saturnine, darkly handsome; his moustache was carefully trimmed and he wore the little tuft below the lower lip that was also affected by Shakespeare. He is seen wearing a heavily embroidered silk shirt open at the neck and his hand lies over his heart in the attitude of an actor taking his bow. His hands are almost as beautiful as his face, and it is easy to imagine him playing female roles in his youth.

Field's beginnings are curious. According to a certain Henry Clifton, Field was a schoolboy in "a grammar school in London kept by Mr. Mulcaster" when he was kidnapped, taken to the playhouse, and forced to act in plays. Field enjoyed the experience and may have been privy to his own kidnapping. Henry Clifton's son Thomas did not enjoy the experience, according to his father. The boy was walking from his house near Great Saint Bartholomews to the grammar school at Christchurch when Henry Evans and James Robinson, who were agents of the theatrical group known as the Children of the Chapel Royal, impressed him and carried him off to their playhouse in Blackfriars, where Henry Clifton at last found him and vigorously protested the abduction of his only son and heir. This happened on December 13, 1600.

Henry Evans on behalf of the Children of the Chapel Royal claimed that there existed a royal patent permitting him to "take up" children for the company. In fact, there existed a loosely worded patent permitting the choirmaster of the Chapel Royal, Nathaniel Giles, to take up children in cathedrals, churches, and chapels for the Queen's better service. The patent was not a license to kidnap schoolboys. Henry Clifton argued with Evans and Robinson. He claimed that they had acted contrary to the law and they replied that they had the right to take up even noblemen's children, and then Evans turned to the boy, gave him a play script to read, and ordered him to learn it by heart or receive a whipping. Henry Clifton vowed to rescue his son and applied to Sir John Fortescue* for a warrant, but it was a day and a half before the boy was released.

Quite properly the father, who had powerful connections, appealed to the Queen. In his curiously worded protest, full of sudden indignation and hatred of all "lewd and dissolute mercenary players," he appealed for redress and the punishment of the guilty. He wrote:

*Sir John Fortescue (1531–1607) was one of the most powerful men in England. He was related to Queen Elizabeth through his grandmother, Alice Boleyn. He was simultaneously Master of the Great Wardrobe, Chancellor of the Exchequer, Chancellor of the Duchy of Lancaster, member of the Privy Council and of the court of the Star Chamber, and an ecclesiastical commissioner.

In a place between your subject's said house and the said grammar school called Christchurch Cloister, the said Thomas Clifton with great force and violence did seize and surprize, and him with like force and violence did, to the great terror and hurt of him the said Thomas Clifton, haul, pull, drag and carry away to the said play-house in the Blackfriars aforesaid, and him the said Thomas Clifton, as a prisoner, committed to the said play-house among a company of lewd and dissolute mercenary players, purposing in that place (and for no service of your Majesty) to use and exercise him, the said Thomas Clifton, in acting of parts in base plays and interludes, to the mercenary gain and private commodity* of the said confederates.

The case of *Clifton v. Robinson and Others* was heard in the Star Chamber, which corresponded to the Supreme Court. The kidnappers were merely censured and no other punishment was handed down to them.

Henry Clifton discovered that Nathan Field had been abducted while on his way to school. He also discovered that a certain Salmon Pavy, "apprentice to one Peerce," had been abducted in a similar fashion. Ben Jonson doted on both these actors, and they played leading roles in his plays *Cynthia's Revels*, performed in 1600, and again in *the Poetas*, which appeared the following year. Salmon, or Salomon Pavy, died in 1602 at the age of thirteen.

Ben Jonson was heartbroken by the boy's death, and in his epitaph he especially remembered how well the boy played old men.

> Weep with me, all you that read
>   This little story:
> And know, for whom a tear you shed,
>   Death's self is sorry.
> 'Twas a child that so did thrive
>   In grace and feature,

*Advantage.

As Heaven and Nature seem'd to strive
  Which owned the creature.
Years he numbered scarce thirteen
  When Fates turn'd cruel,
Yet three fill'd Zodiacs had he been
  The stage's jewel;
And did act (what now we moan)
  Old men so duly,
As, sooth, the Parcae thought him one,
  He play'd so truly . . .

The three-year career of Salomon Pavy was unique in theatrical history. No other actor became so famous in so brief a life. That small boys could portray old men and mature women need not surprise us: they were trained in gestures, possessed precocious gifts of mimicry, and were natural actors. We have a glimpse of their acting ability in an account of a performance of *Othello* at Oxford in 1610, where we learn that the King's Men "moved the audience to tears, not only by their speech but by their gestures as well." One spectator was deeply moved by the performance of the boy actor playing Desdemona "especially when she lay in bed, moving the spectators to pity solely by her face."

The implication is very clear that Desdemona's long-drawn death could provide a boy actor with a wonderful opportunity to hold the audience spellbound. With writhings and jerkings and small spasmodic twitchings, he would have them looking at him, and at him alone. It would be a virtuoso performance calculated to the last tremor and the last sigh. This was stylized acting, carefully choreographed, and practiced to perfection. The morbid imagination of a boy would find itself enthralled by the spectacle of his own death. Above all, his training would be such that every ounce of his skill was employed to sustain the fiction that he was dying.

We know how well the actors were trained on the London stage. A German visitor to England, Johannes Rhenanus, commenting on the superiority of English actors to German actors, wrote:

As for the actors, they (as I have noted in England) are
instructed daily as though at school: even the most
prominent actors must permit themselves to be instructed in

their parts by the poets, and this is what endows a
well-written comedy with life and grace. Thus it is no
wonder that the English comedians (I speak of the practical
ones) are more excellent than others.

Rhenanus was writing in 1613, in the ripest period of Jacobean
comedy and tragedy, but what he said applied equally to the
Elizabethan theatre. Professional acting demanded the highest discipline; it was abundantly necessary that the boy actors playing
women's roles should be rigorously trained. The tragedy was that
they were boys for so short a time and had to be trained all over
again when their voices broke. Winifred Burbage said it most
succinctly. In an official complaint written when she was suing for
her shares in the Blackfriars Theatre, she wrote: "The boys [are]
daily wearing out."

We would like to be sure we knew the names of the boy actors in
Shakespeare's plays, but even when we know the names we cannot
attach them with any certainty to their roles. The roaring boys with
their bright faces vanish too soon into the shadows of the Elizabethan stage.

The Beast
with
Two Backs

ALTHOUGH ELIZABETH RULED OVER HER COURT with moral passion, angered by the slightest evidence of immorality among the women of the court and incensed by the extramarital affairs of her male courtiers, she was not herself a moral person. Technically she remained a virgin throughout her life, but the technicality was at odds with her nature. If Leicester and Essex were not her lovers, they were as close to it as made little difference. Alençon, too, was permitted to fondle her and slaver over her to the amusement of the Spanish ambassador, who was well aware that the Queen's principles were at war with her sexual desires. She was the Virgin Queen, chaste as the moon, vigorous as the sun of majesty. Power streamed from her five-bladed hands and was all the more menacing because the hands were so delicate and virginal. With these hands she signed death warrants without a tremor, with flourishes. This, too, was part of her moral passion.

Morality, in Elizabeth's time, was a many-sided thing. Church-men thundered on behalf of purity, thundering indeed so vehemently that one suspects they knew the battle was already lost. Strangely the homily against adultery read in every parish church of England appealed to pagan example. "Among the Arabians, they that were taken in adultery had their heads stricken from their bodies. The Athenians punished whoredom by death in like manner. So likewise did the barbarian Tartarians. Among the Turks even at this day they that be taken in adultery, both men and women, are stoned straightway to death, without mercy." Adulterers in the congregation might take comfort from the fact that these punishments were administered far away to unknown people.

When the churchmen thundered against immorality and the lusts of youth, they seemed to do so in tones of plaintive regret. They were accustomed to use the word "whoredom" rather than "adultery." "Whoredom" has the appropriate solemn sound, and they could do much with it in their incantatory prose:

> What patrimony or livelode, what substance, what goods, what riches doth whoredom shortly consume and bright to nought? What valiantness and strength is many times made weak and destroyed with whoredom? What wit is so fine that it not besotted and defaced through whoredom? Is not whoredom an enemy to the pleasant flower of youth, and bringeth it not grey hairs and old age before the time? What gift of nature (although it were never so precious) is not corrupted with whoredom? From whence come so many bastards and misbegotten children, to the high displeasure of God and dishonor of holy wedlock, but of whoredom? How many consume all their substance and goods, and at the last fall into such extreme poverty that afterward they steal, and so are hanged, through whoredom?

The long litany is not entirely convincing: the parson is too obviously enjoying the rise and fall of his own voice. We know what his congregation thought of it. They went on committing adultery as passionately as ever with little regard for the eternal damnation that awaited them. The parson dared not comment on still greater sins of the flesh and prudently avoided them, although the inquisitive Elizabethans knew all about them and would not have been surprised if the parson had inveighed against them.

For Shakespeare these homilies were as familiar as the Bible and he frequently echoes them. His own attitude toward immorality was ambiguous; like Saint Augustine in his youth he praises chastity "but not yet." No one ever wrote so sensually, yet his lovers are nearly always "stainless." Romeo proclaims his virtue to the skies but employs images that show he is well acquainted with vice. "The ice of chastity" is in the lips of Orlando. Coriolanus tells Virginia that during the entire time of his absence from her his lips "have virgin'd it." His lovers pay tribute to chastity, but it is no more than tribute. Shakespeare is the bawdiest of the Elizabethan playwrights; he is bawdy with pure enjoyment, without apology and without regret. His bawdiness flows so naturally that sometimes we are scarcely aware of it. Sometimes, too, we have forgotten the meanings of the words he uses. Eric Partridge wrote a whole book on Shakespeare's bawdy, which has long been out of date: more recent scholarship has unearthed many more examples of his command of bawdy. The sauce is added to the dish with a far more prodigal hand than modern readers had ever suspected.

In retrospect we can see that it could hardly be otherwise. The actors in the Elizabethan theatre, especially the young actors, were not renowned for their virtue. The roaring boys took their pleasure where they could find it among those who were as disenchanted as themselves. The theatres on Bankside were surrounded by stews. Vice flourished under the protection of the bishop of Winchester, whose palace overlooked the brothels and who exacted a tax on the brothel-keepers. When the theatres closed late in the afternoon, the brothel doors swung open. The brothels were bare and uncomfortable but served their purpose. "Every room with bare walls, and a half-headed bed to vault upon (as all your bawdy houses are)," wrote Thomas Dekker in *An Honest Whore*. Spider webs hung on the walls, there was dirt underfoot, the whores were thieves and thought little of emptying a man's pockets before they let him loose. London whores had a reputation for being vigorous in bed and for possesing a rough good humor.

Shakespeare was intrigued by women's plackets, for he mentioned them five times in his plays. A placket was a slit in the skirt and petticoat which permitted free access to her private parts, thus saving time and energy. It was a common device in Elizabethan times, not only among loose women. This device celebrated unencumbered sexuality.

Of lovemaking and the game of the beast with two backs Shakespeare has much to say. "The beast with two backs," mentioned in *Othello*,* was not his invention; he derived it from Rabelais, from whom he also derived Holofernes, originally the teacher of the young Gargantua. For Gargantua Shakespeare showed a proper respect, placing in the mouth of Celia in *As You Like It* the words: "You must borrow me Gargantua's mouth first: 'tis a word too great for any mouth of this age's size." Rabelais was a kindred spirit, for he exulted in the flesh and its eccentricities and was never happier than when he was describing the body's impatient ribaldry. Shakespeare and Rabelais echo one another and are happy in each other's company.

"Shakespeare may sometimes be gross, but I boldly say he was always moral and modest." So wrote Coleridge while at war with his own demons, affronted by those passages of *The Tempest* that demonstrate the contrary. He found obscenities that cut him to the quick and he shielded himself from them as best he could, for it was inconceivable to him that "noble Shakespeare" would ever depart from the moral law. In fact Shakespeare was neither moral nor modest. He was gross for the fun of it, immoral because it pleased him to rip morality to shreds, and immodest because bodily functions delighted and amused him and he saw no reason to conceal them. Shakespeare drank deep at the well of Rabelais, much deeper than we often suspect. The ribaldry of Falstaff derives as much from Rabelais as from the overhead conversations of Elizabethan soldiers and apprentices waiting impatiently outside the stews of Southwark. Shakespeare enjoyed obscenity for its own sake. In those passages of *Hamlet* and *King Lear* where he appears to reveal himself more urgently than elsewhere, where for a few moments the

---

*The phrase first appears in *Gargantua*, I, i, 3: How Gargantua was carried Eleven Months in his Mother's Belly. "In the vigour of his age Grangousier married Gargamelle, daughter of the King of the Parpaillons, a jolly pug, and well-mouthed wench. These two did oftentimes do the two-backed beast together, joyfully rubbing and fretting their bacon against one another, in so far that at last she became great with child of a fair son, and went with him unto the eleventh month."

veil is lifted from his eyes and we see them naked, at such moments obscenity takes wing and becomes the purest art.

> The codpiece that will house
>   Before the head had any,
> The head and he shall louse:
>   So beggars marry many.
> The man who makes his toe
>   What he his heart should make
> Shall of a corn cry woe,
>   And turn his sleep to wake.

The Fool comes with the storm; it is as though he had been hiding in the storm. His mission is clear; it is to turn men's sleep to wake.

Hamlet's indecencies are of another kind, abrupt and chilling, spoken in a foul, spitting humor.

Hamlet.   Lady, shall I lie in your lap?

Ophelia.   No, my Lord.

Hamlet.   I mean, my head upon your lap?

Ophelia.   Aye, my Lord.

Hamlet.   Do you think I meant country matters?

Ophelia.   I think nothing, my Lord.

Hamlet.   That's a fair thought to lie between maid's legs.

Ophelia.   What is, my Lord?

Hamlet.   Nothing.

Ophelia.   You are merry, my Lord?

Hamlet.   Who, I?

Ophelia.   Aye, my Lord.

Hamlet.   Oh God, your only jig-maker: what should a man
      do, but be merry?

What indeed? But Hamlet is not talking of merriment; he is talking about something so terrifying that it can hardly be talked about: the destruction of his enemies. And when Ophelia says, "I think nothing, my Lord," the words could have an interpretation that may never have occurred to her. "To be nothing with" or "to be naught with" meant "to copulate." Hamlet was deliberately showing the worst side of himself to Ophelia, perhaps because she was the most vulnerable of his enemies. There are only two women in the play, Queen Gertrude and Ophelia, and Hamlet claims to despise both of them for their lechery.

Lechery, indeed, was a subject that fascinated Shakespeare and he talks about it on all levels: intellectually, sensually, admiringly, and reprovingly, according to his mood or the mood of the play. In *Troilus and Cressida* he entertains himself with arguments on the mathematics of sexual love, saying in the words of Troilus: "This is the monstruosity of love, Lady, that the will is infinite and the execution confin'd; that the desire is boundless and the act a slave to limit," while Cressida comments: "They say all lovers swear more performance than they are able, and yet reserve an ability that they never perform: vowing more than the perfection of ten, and discharging less than the tenth part of one." But both Troilus and Cressida are capable of abandoning the roles of mathematicians for the direct evocation of love's progress:

> *Troilus.*   I stalk about her door
>   Like a strange soul upon the Stygian banks
>   Staying for waftage. O be thou my Charon,
>   And give me swift transportance to those fields,
>   Where I may wallow in the lily beds
>   Proposed for the deserver.

Once more, as so often in Shakespeare, death is implicated in the act of sexual love. While Pandarus in the uniform of a pander is preparing Cressida for his bed, Troilus muses on his forthcoming encounter with her.

>   I am giddy; expectation whirls me round,
>   The imaginary relish is so sweet
>   That it enchants my sense: what will it be
>   When that the watery palate tastes indeed
>   Love's thrice reputed nectar? Death, I fear me,
>   Sounding destruction, or some joy too fine,
>   Too subtle, potent, and too sharp in sweetness

For the capacity of my ruder powers.
I fear it much, and I do fear besides
That I shall lose distinction in my joys,
As doth a battle, when they charge on heaps
The enemy flying.

Pandarus is of much the same opinion, for when he leads them to their bedroom he gives them dangerous advice: "I will show you a chamber, which bed, because it shall not speak of your pretty encounters, press it to death."

Shakespeare's bawdy has two voices: the elegant voice of the middle and upper classes with its play on words and subtle suggestiveness and the course, raucous voice of the poor devils who lurk at the bottom of society. Doll Tearsheet, Mistress Quickly, Pistol, Bardolph, Falstaff, and all the rest are direct and high-spirited in their sexual affairs. They are not burdened by having a conscience, and they are lacking in any desire to indulge in word play. Nell Quickly is well named: sex is a quick and hurried thing without any need for elaborate soliloquies. The cut and thrust is hard and vulgar-playing:

Falstaff.   Welcome, Ancient Pistol. Here, Pistol, I charge you
   with a cup of sack. Do you discharge upon mine hostess.

Pistol.   I will discharge upon her, Sir John, with two
            bullets.

They will continue arguing, but the flash of the fire is over once Pistol, living up to his name, has spoken his mind in Mistress Quickly's tavern. He has taken the measure of his companions: he knows what is at stake and will proceed as carefully as a man can when confronted by men as drunken and lecherous as himself. They are all playing dangerous games in the brothel. Love has its heartaches; it also leaves sores, pustules, scabs, and fevers in its train:

Enter Falstaff

Falstaff.   "When Arthur first in court"—Empty the
   jordan!—"And was a worthy king"—How now, Mistress
   Doll!

Hostess.   Sick of a calm: yea, good sooth.

Falstaff.   So is all her sect. And they be once in a calm, they are sick.

Hostess.   A pox damn you, you muddy rascal, is that all the comfort you give me?

Falstaff.   You make fat rascals, Mistress Doll.

Doll.   I make them? Gluttony and diseases make, I make them not.

Falstaff.   If the cook help to make the gluttony, you help to make the diseases, Doll. We catch of you, Doll, we catch of you. Grant that, my poor virtue, grant that.

Doll.   Yea, joy, our chains and our jewels.

Falstaff.   "Your brooches, pearls, and ouches." For to serve bravely is to come halting off, you know. To come off the breach with his pike bravely, and to surgery bravely; to venture upon the charged chambers bravely—

Doll.   Hang yourself, you muddy conger, hang yourself.

It is all much too authentic for us to believe that Shakespeare was a rare visitor to brothels. He caught the voices and intonations of the whores to a nicety, each one different, whereas Pistol, Poins, Bardolph, and the rest resemble younger versions of Falstaff, being the products of his capacious womb. If they have their own individuality, it is only because Falstaff has enough for all.

Once he has invented Falstaff, Shakespeare's bawdy assumes another dimension. It is full-throated, heavily masculine, rich in its evocation of female flesh. We are far removed from the somewhat feminine sensuality of Mercutio who conjures up a curious picture of Romeo sighing for sexual love.

Mercutio.   Now will he sit under a medlar tree,
   And wish his mistress were that kind of fruit
   As maids call medlars when they laugh alone.
   O Romeo, that she were, O, that she were
   An open, or thou a poprin pear.

This is indelicacy of a major sort: not obscenity, which is more direct and heavier. Mercutio is playing lightly with the image of the poprin pear, said to be long and juicy, and no doubt the groundlings went off into gales of laughter.

Mercutio talks with the fever of an adolescent, still eager to discover. Falstaff has no need to discover, for he knows everything and has never been jaded. Compare Mercutio's delicate improprieties with Falstaff's full-throated roar in *The Merry Wives of Windsor*.

> *Falstaff.*   The Windsor bell hath struck twelve; the minute
> draws on. Now, the hot-bloodied gods assist me! Remember,
> Jove, thou wast a bull for thy Europe, love set on thy horns. O
> powerful love, that in some respects makes a beast a man; in
> some other, a man a beast. You were also, Jupiter, a swan for
> the love of Leda. O omnipotent love, how near the god grew to
> the complexion of a goose! A fault done first in the form of a
> beast. O Jove, a beastly fault! And then another fault in the
> semblance of a fowl; think on't, Jove; a foul fault! When gods
> have hot backs, what shall a poor man do? For me, I am here a
> Windsor stag; and the fattest, I think, i' th' forest. Send me a
> cool rut-time, Jove, or who can blame me to piss my tallow?
> Who comes here? My doe?

Falstaff's is the more honest way. It is not lust so much as lustiness, and there is joy in it. He compares himself with Jove, and why not? One can imagine him transformed into a bull but not into a swan or a goose. He wages war against all the follies of the earth, and in his eyes continence is a profound sin and a folly that sends the gods shaking from their thrones. In this he agrees with the mischievous Parolles who engages in *All's Well That Ends Well* with the equally mischievous Helena.

> *Parolles.*   Are you meditating on virginity?
> *Helena.*   Ay, you have some stain of soldier in you; let me
> ask you a question. Man is enemy to virginity, how may
> we barricado it against him?
> *Parolles.*   Keep him out.
> *Helena.*   But he assails, and our virginity, though valiant in the
> defence, yet is weak. Unfold to us some warlike resistance.

Parolles. There is none. Man, setting down before you will undermine you and blow you up.

Helena. Bless our poor virginity from underminers and blowers-up! Is there no military policy how virgins might blow up men?

Parolles. Virginity being blown down, man will quicklier be blown up. Marry in blowing him down again, with the breach yourselves made, you lose your city. It is not politic, in the commonwealth of nature, to preserve virginity. Loss of virginity is rational increase, and there was never virgin got, till virginity was first lost. That you were made of, is metal to make virgins. Virginity, by being once lost, may be ten times found. By being ever kept, it is ever lost. 'Tis too cool a companion. Away with 't!

According to Parolles, virginity "should be buried in highways, out of all sanctified limit, as a desperate offendress against nature," and goes on to explain how virginity breeds mites, like cheese, and dies feeding its own stomach. It is a proper conclusion, and Helena makes the most of it by disguising herself as Diana of Florence and slipping into the bed of Bertram, who wants nothing of her. Coleridge imagined that Helena was Shakespeare's "loveliest character," a statement so bold and improbable that one may be sure he knew very little about young women and had not sufficiently appreciated Marina, Perdita, or Miranda.

In Shakespeare's eyes the beast with two backs was a beast to be prized and nurtured. Like the unicorn and the phoenix, to which it was related, it added to the joy of creation.

The Hanging
of Dr. Lopez

AN EXECUTION IN LONDON WAS A PUBLIC AFFAIR, yet very private, almost intimate. The populace crowded round to gape at a grotesque ceremony which consisted of killing a criminal three times over, first by hanging, then by disemboweling, and then by cutting off his head and quartering the body so that the legs and arms and the adjoined flesh could be exhibited on the city gates. The head, fixed on a pike, was given the crowning privilege of being exhibited on one of the towers of London Bridge for the birds to peck at. The threefold execution appeared to answer to some strange need. It was not enough to kill the offender with a stab at the heart: instead he must be killed at the slow pace of an incompetent butcher.

The crowds who gathered at Tyburn or wherever the execution took place rarely showed any compassion for the condemned man. They laughed, jeered, cursed, and reviled him; if he tried to speak, they refused to listen and drowned his voice with catcalls, and even if he was very brave, showing by his bearing that he was quietly resigned to his fate, they despised him. It was a kind of hatred. They were absorbed in the spectacle of the execution as though they were attending a play, with the condemned man playing the role of the villain whose savage death in the last act was the consequence of his own villainies in the earlier acts. But curiously the general public had very little knowledge of the crimes committed by the men who were publicly executed. They knew that a man was being executed because he had been convicted of high treason, or had committed a murder or a theft, but the details were lacking. A man sentenced to death for high treason in Queen Elizabeth's time might be a Catholic priest whose only crime was that he was a priest. There were no newspapers to acquaint the public with the charges of the prosecution and the rebuttal of the defense. A vulgar, lusty, improvident people, voracious for spectacle, enjoyed every moment of an execution.

Usually the condemned prisoner was driven in a horse cart from his prison to Tyburn. He was bound hand and foot, and made to stand in the cart. At the Church of St. Sepulchre the cart stopped and the prisoner listened to a sermon summoning him to repentance and promising him an eternity of hellfire if he did not make his peace with God. The crowd following the tumbril was impatient; they wanted to see him hang, and they had heard the same sermon many times before. Then off to Tyburn, the crowd becoming more jubilant. The prisoner stood on the cart, a rope was tied around his neck and fastened to one of the heavy branches of a tree. The cart would move away, leaving him dangling, and sometimes the hangman would pull at his legs. While he hung there gasping and choking, his tongue protruding from his mouth and his eyes swelling out of their sockets, he was suffering his first death. It was a symbolic death, for he was still alive, though sometimes unconscious, when he was cut down.

The hangman's task was over; it was the turn of the man with the knife. The condemned man was thrown down on a hurdle, his clothes were cut away, and with a single stroke of his razor-sharp knife the executioner slit open the body from the chest to the crotch. The slitting was performed skillfully, the vital organs were avoided, the dead man was encouraged to suffer for a few moments longer the illusion that he was alive. The executioner reached down and pulled out his entrails, for it was part of the punishment that a man should see his own entrails spilling out of him. Stories were told of priests who were heard reciting prayers in a clear voice after they were disemboweled and when the executioner's bloody hands were clasped around their hearts. There were other stories of men who were hanged and thrown down on the hurdle, and suddenly they jumped up and fought ferociously with the executioner.

First the rope; then the knife; then the ax. The final death came when the head was cut off and immediately afterward the body was axed into four pieces which were tossed into a basket. What had once been a man consisted of five separate lumps of flesh and bone. The executioner bowed to the crowd. If he had performed well, he was applauded. There were many in the crowd who regarded themselves as connoisseurs of executions. "And so to Tyburn, and there hanged, cut down alive, holden down by strength of men, dismembered, boweled, headed, and quartered, their quarters set on the gates of the City."

In this way the calm and judicious John Stow describes the execution of Dr. Roderigo Lopez and two other Portuguese, which took place on June 7, 1594.

Dr. Lopez was a physician and surgeon at St. Bartholomew's hospital, where he was regarded as among the most eminent doctors in London. He was the personal physician of the Earl of Leicester. After Leicester's death he became the personal physician of Queen Elizabeth, who trusted him and was on fairly intimate terms with him. In 1590, when Don Antonio Perez, a pretender to the Portuguese throne, arrived in England and was taken up by Essex in the hope of stirring up anti-Spanish feeling, Dr. Lopez was asked to act as interpreter. Don Antonio was an ineffective conspirator but an effective troublemaker, who had once been a political secretary in the office of Philip II of Spain until he was arrested for murdering another secretary. Escaping from prison, he made his way to France, where he was well received, for he had many political secrets to sell. In London he was received with some suspicion until Essex took up his cause. Then, for a short while, Essex, Perez, and Dr. Lopez were inseparable. Soon Perez quarreled violently with Dr. Lopez, and Essex felt he was being slighted by the doctor, who had the audacity to inform the Queen about the conversations between them. Dr. Lopez could hardly do otherwise. Essex was unforgiving and set about destroying one of the most famous doctors in England.

It was not very difficult, and Don Antonio Perez proved to be exceedingly helpful with the suggestion that Dr. Lopez, as one of those who had daily access to the Queen, was in a position to poison her. "I have discovered a most dangerous and desperate treason," Essex wrote to Antony Bacon in January 1594. "The point of conspiracy was her Majesty's death. The executioner should have been Dr. Lopez, the manner poison. This I have so followed that I will make it as clear as noonday." Elizabeth soon heard the accusation; Lord Burghley, Sir Robert Cecil, and Essex examined Dr. Lopez at her command and were unable to find the least evidence of his guilt. Cecil hurried to Elizabeth to be the first to tell her the good news. It was assumed that Essex made the accusation out of pure malice and because Dr. Lopez was so close to the throne. Elizabeth summoned Essex into her presence and rounded upon him, "calling him rash and temerarious youth to enter into a matter against the poor man which he could not prove." Essex stormed out of her presence without pretending to disguise his anger, and when he came to his own chamber he slammed the door shut with extraordinary violence.

Essex remained a "rash and temerarious youth" to the end. Determined to vindicate himself, he discovered or pretended to discover new evidence confirming Dr. Lopez's guilt. He believed or pretended to believe that Spanish agents in London were offering Dr. Lopez a large bribe to murder the Queen. Don Antonio Perez was helpful. So were various justices. Dr. Lopez was arrested and arraigned at the Guildhall on the last day of February 1594 and convicted of treason for "conspiring her Majesty's destruction by poison." Essex's satisfaction was nearly complete; he felt he had been vindicated in the Queen's eyes. But the Queen was not yet convinced of the doctor's guilt. She obstinately refused to sign the death warrant, ordering that the prisoner should be committed to the Tower. She made a habit of temporizing before she signed death warrants. She wanted proof, further proof. None came. She ordered the lieutenant of the Tower to refuse to surrender Dr. Lopez for execution under any conditions. Three months passed. Essex returned to the Queen's favor. She gave him £4,000 to pay off his debts and in addition she gave him what he wanted most of all—the execution of Dr. Lopez.

A huge crowd assembled to watch the hanging, boweling, and quartering of the Portuguese Jew. The common people of London hated foreigners, and the fact that Dr. Lopez had risen high in the Queen's favor had not made them love him better. They observed that he was terrified when he saw his executioners, and screamed and pleaded for his life in a thick foreign accent. "I love the Queen as much as I love Jesus Christ," he said, and the crowd shouted in derision. They were happy with his execution and grateful to Essex for providing them with a holiday.

The Queen liked to collect relics. She began to wear at her girdle a jewel said to have been given to Dr. Lopez by Philip II through the intermediary of Spanish agents in London. The jewel had been given to her by Essex. In later years she kept in a drawer of her desk, within easy reach, another relic—the skull of Essex, who was once her lover. Six years after the execution of Dr. Lopez she signed the death warrant of Essex.

At this time there were very few Jews in England. They were disliked, as the Huguenots were disliked, because they were strangers who did not adapt themselves easily to the English scene. Like the Huguenots, the Jews possessed special skills as jewelers, doctors, and usurers. Their presence in England was tolerated, but they were not liked. Many members of the nobility were heavily in debt to Jewish moneylenders, and this too left a legacy of hatred. "Bottlenosed" Barabas, the Jew of Malta in Christopher Marlowe's play, was represented in odious caricature, a monster of cruelty and avarice, outwardly friendly to Christians while inwardly thirsting for their blood, fawning like a spaniel when it suited his purpose and smiling as he sank his teeth into the enemy's flesh. He is Machiavellian in his vast intrigues, and Marlowe emphasizes the Machiavellian aspect in his prologue, which shows Machiavelli himself coming forward to the edge of the stage and pronouncing that the Jew of Malta is his spiritual brother. *The Jew of Malta* was written about four years before the execution of Dr. Lopez. *The Merchant of Venice* was written a year or two after the execution, when the mood of the English people toward Jews had considerably changed largely as a result of second thoughts about Dr. Lopez.

Shylock, so evil, so vulnerable, so pathetic, and so magnificently installed at the center of the play, can be understood only in the context of Dr. Lopez, whose strange destiny was vividly remembered.

There appears to be no plausible explanation for the choice of the name Shylock. Shakespeare appears to have chosen the name at random or because he liked the sound of it. It was a not uncommon English name of the period.

In *The Merchant of Venice* Shakespeare asserts his right to tell the story of a tragedy to the haunting music of his romances. Echoes of *Romeo and Juliet* and *A Midsummer Night's Dream* are continually being heard. The Prince of Aragon, having opened the silver casket, speaks with the authentic voice of Puck:

> Some there be that shadows kiss;
> Some have but a shadow's bliss.
> There be fools alive iwis,
> Silvered o'er, and so was this.
> Take what wife you will to bed,
> I will ever be your head.
> So be gone; you are sped.

The enchanted gardens of Verona are transported to Belmont when Lorenzo-Romeo sings his love to Jessica-Juliet without mentioning that he is in love with her:

> *Lorenzo.*   The moon shines bright. On such a night as this,
>   When the sweet wind did gently kiss the trees
>   And they did make no noise, in such a night
>   Troilus methinks mounted the Troyan walls,
>   And sighed his soul toward the Grecian tents
>   Where Cressida lay that night.
>
> *Jessica.*   In such a night
>   Did Thisbe fearfully o'ertrip the dew,
>   And saw the lion's shadow ere himself,
>   And ran dismayed away.
>
> *Lorenzo.*   In such a night
>   Stood Dido with a willow in her hand

Upon the wild sea banks, and wait her love
To come again to Carthage.

Jessica.   In such a night
Medea gathered the enchanted herbs
That did renew old Aeson.

Lorenzo.   In such a night
Did Jessica steal from the wealthy Jew,
And with an unthrift love did run from Venice
As far as Belmont.

Jessica.   In such a night
Did young Lorenzo swear he loved her well,
Stealing her soul with many vows of faith,
And ne'er a true one.

Lorenzo.   In such a night
Did pretty Jessica, like a little shrew,
Slander her love, and he forgave it her.

The mood of *Romeo and Juliet* hovers over *The Merchant of Venice* and takes the sting away from Shylock, the gaunt philosopher who will carry logic to the final solution of a pound of flesh. The Elizabethans probably found his Machiavellian arrogance more troubling than the fact that he was a Jew. Marlowe pictures the Jew of Malta as a bestial creature who is deservedly drowned in a cauldron while the house collapses over him. Shakespeare's Jew of Venice suffers little more than hurt pride and the loss of half his fortune. Cruel and vindictive, mercilessly logical, he is yet portrayed with dignity, as a man who feels justified in his own being by "an oath in heaven." He speaks eloquently, conscious of the justice of his cause; and if he is until the very end incapable of remorse and repentance, we should not be surprised, since we know him to be the brother of Machiavelli's Prince. We do not ask the Prince to be contrite or merciful, or to surrender his gains to others. Shylock is defeated by a trick; it is a good trick, and he withdraws from the scene quietly:

I pray you give me leave to go from hence.
I am not well. Send the deed after me,
And I will sign it.

After the tumult of the trial he is chastened but still holds himself upright, conscious that he is in the right. As he declared at the trial: "What judgment shall I dread, doing no wrong?" It will occur to him that he is defeated but not that he has deserved defeat. Of mercy he has no conception at all, and Portia, it seems, has no conception of a world without mercy. So they are at loggerheads, while Portia pleads for the divine right of mercy to manifest itself and Shylock pleads for the strict letter of the law only to discover that the strict letter is subject to interpretation. Portia's speech is passionately expressed and yet so personal that it seems to be Shakespeare's own judgment on the law.

> The quality of mercy is not strained;*
> It droppeth as the gentle rain from heaven
> Upon the place beneath. It is twice blest;
> It blesseth him that gives and him that takes.
> 'Tis mightiest in the mightiest; it becomes
> The throned monarch better than his crown.
> His scepter shows the force of temporal power,
> The attribute to awe and majesty,
> Wherein doth sit the dread and fear of Kings,
> It is an attribute to God himself,
> And earthly power doth then show likest God's
> When mercy seasons justice.

Biblical scholars who study Shakespeare are sometimes of the opinion that Shakespeare spent a good part of his life studying the Bible in order to insert biblical tags in his plays, and there exist entire concordances of biblical phrases used by Shakespeare. Many of these correspondences are illusory and melt into nothingness when closely observed. But in this instance there can be no doubt that Shakespeare derived Portia's speech from the apocryphal *Book of Jesus the Son of Syrach*. In his time the apocryphal works were always included in the Bible. He read in the thirty-fifth chapter: "O how fair a thing is mercy in the time of anguish and trouble! It is like a cloud of rain that cometh in the time of a drought." This was the springboard; once he had made the leap, the rest followed.

*Constrained.

The Merchant of Venice is a play without a center. Shylock dominates, but only when he is present. The story of the caskets seems to belong to another play altogether, and the love story of Lorenzo and Jessica appears to have strayed from *Love's Labour Won*, the lost play mentioned by Francis Meres in *Palladis Tamia*. John Masefield has reminded us that Jessica, for all her poetry, was a thief and a domestic traitor, and Tudor justice would have brought her to the gallows, and Lorenzo would also have been hanged as a receiver of stolen goods "well knowing them to have been stolen." This is true but scarcely matters, for Lorenzo and Jessica have only one purpose: to speak the most melodious love poetry written in an age of accomplished love poets:

> How sweet the moonlight sleeps upon this bank!
> Here will we sit, and let the sounds of music
> Creep in our ears—soft stillness and the night
> Become the touches of sweet harmony.
> Sit, Jessica. Look how the floor of heaven
> Is thick inlaid with patens of bright gold,
> There's not the smallest orb which thou behold'st
> But in his motion like an angel sings,
> Still quiring to the young-eyed cherubins;
> Such harmony is in immortal souls!
> But whilst this muddy vesture of decay
> Doth grossly close it in, we cannot hear it.

The flowery bank with the lovers lying on it, the moonlight, and the stars—it has been done so many times before but never so poignantly or with such shining ease. Not even in *Romeo and Juliet* did love poetry reach these heights. These lines have nothing to do with Ptolemaic constructions of the universe: their purpose is to evoke the lovers in the starry night. They are love in the making, love in exaltation, and they sing like a chorus of angels.

The Merchant of Venice is a play of many moods, of many patchwork pieces sewn together. Venice, of course, is London, and Belmont no farther away than Shoreditch. We forget sometimes that Shylock, as played by Burbage in a red wig and with a long red beard, was both a tragic and a comic figure, being himself a patchwork. Shakespeare may have played the minor part of Salerio,

who takes the stage to announce one of Shakespeare's most solemn
obsessions—drowning, the tempest, the ship plunging to the bottom
of the ocean, all her rich cargoes lost, himself among them. This
time the obsession is described with a kind of amused detachment.
Salerio-Shakespeare imagines he has blown violently on a bowl of
soup, creating waves; and seeing the soup billowing in front of his
eyes, he imagines the shipwreck, the drowned silks and spices, all
his treasure lost forever beneath the seas:

> My wind cooling my broth
> Would blow me to an ague when I thought
> What harm a wind too great might do at sea.
> I should not see the sandy hourglass run
> But I should think of shallows and of flats,
> And see my wealthy *Andrew* docked in sand,
> Vailing* her high top lower than her ribs
> To kiss her burial. Should I go to church
> And see the holy edifice of stone
> And not bethink me straight of dangerous rocks,
> Which touching but my gentle vessel's side
> Would scatter all her spices on the stream,
> Enrobe the roaring waters with my silks—
> And in a word, but even now worth this,
> And now worth nothing? Shall I have the thought
> To think on this, and shall I lack the thought
> That such a thing bechanced would make me sad?

From blowing on some soup to make it cool, the poet in free
association conjures up (1) great waves, (2) time flowing in an
hourglass, (3) shallows and flats, (4) a ship beached on a shore with
her broken mast falling against the rib strakes, (5) a church, (6)
dangerous rocks smashing against the ship's side, (7) the cargo of
spices scattered into the sea, (8) a cargo of silks "enrobing" the sea,
(9) nothing. He conjures up emblems of mortality in a kind of
algebraic sequence = zero. It is all seen in silence, like a dream,
until at the very end the sound of roaring waters breaks through.
The beached ship with the broken topmast is seen vividly, for the

*Lowering.

mast forms a cross over a tomb, "to kiss her burial." Shakespeare is riding his imagination lightheartedly; he is not deeply engaged; no sparks fly; there is no sudden confrontation and fusing of images, no "I am bound upon a wheel of fire." He is contemplating death somewhat desultorily, watching the images of death pass one by one.

Not until *Timon of Athens* would there appear from Shakespeare's hand another play quite so disorganized. While there is dramatic tension in the court scene and in the casket scene, there is very little tension elsewhere. Portia is charming, but remains two-dimensional. Only Shylock is seen in the round, unloved, unredeemed, unmerciful, as evil as Richard III, as proud as Lucifer. William Camden, the antiquarian who was a friend of Ben Jonson, attended the hanging of Dr. Lopez and remembered the derisive laughter of the crowd. The sad truth is that Shakespeare had little sympathy for Shylock and made him a laughing-stock. In the eyes of Shakespeare, Shylock was a clown.

A Coat
of Arms

FALSTAFF, IN A GREAT SOLILOQUY, pronounced judgment on honor in all its forms. Shylock, too, was entangled in questions concerning honor and was at last shown to be lacking in that commodity which played such a vast role in Elizabethan thought. But while Falstaff could dismiss honor with a shrug of his shoulders, he was not averse to having honors poured on him. He was, after all, Sir John Falstaff, and it would never have occurred to him to refuse a knighthood with all its attendant privileges. Shakespeare, too, sought for honors: if not a knighthood, at least the honor of being called a gentleman with an appropriate coat of arms.

Under Elizabeth a coat of arms implied power and privilege, an accepted place in the upper reaches of society. It was carved over doorways, embroidered on linens, incised on signet rings, cut into pewter pots, and marked on tombstones. A family with a coat of arms would hang a banner in the hallway or the living room, thus reminding all visitors of its importance. This was not thought to be especially self-serving, for the whole purpose of a coat of arms was to display it. In Elizabethan times men wore their badges of honor prominently.

Because he was an actor and wrote historical plays, Shakespeare was knowledgeable in heraldry, for every king or bishop, every duke or captain-in-arms as he strode across the stage would be accompanied by standard-bearers who displayed their coats of arms in square, stiff, brightly painted banners. Even when the plays dealt with ancient kings who lived before the art of heraldry was invented, there would be standard-bearers. The Elizabethan stage was often a feast of banners.

Shakespeare, landowner and son of a landowner, descended on his mother's side from an ancient and honorable family, had as much right to a coat of arms as most of those who possessed one. John Shakespeare's claim was equally impressive, for he had been at various times principal burgess, chamberlain, alderman, and finally head alderman or bailiff of Stratford. In fact, he had made an application for a grant of arms in 1576 to Robert Cook, the Clarenceux herald, but nothing came of it. John Shakespeare continued to live in Stratford and apparently made no effort to enforce his claim by journeying to the College of Heralds in London. A note attached to his son's application made twenty years later offered a design for the coat of arms and some information on his worthiness:

> This John showeth a pattern hereof under Clarenceux Cook's handpaper, xx years past.
> A Justice of Peace, and was Bailiff, the Queen's officer and chief of the town of Stratford upon Avon xv or xvi years past.
> That he had lands and tenements of good wealth and substance £500.
> That he married a daughter and heir of Arden, a gentleman of worship.

That John Shakespeare did not pursue the matter any further may be explained by his growing distaste for public affairs and by the fact that the College of Heralds charged high fees for the comparatively little work involved. He was not a man to spend money needlessly. Soon he would find himself in financial difficulties, and the prospect of acquiring a coat of arms was indefinitely postponed.

By 1596 William Shakespeare was a famous poet and an even
more famous playwright with friends in high places with access to
men in still higher places. He had performed before Queen Elizabeth and already he had become almost a national institution.
Although the actor's trade was still frowned upon, and the Puritans
thundered against it, and the Lord Mayor of London took care that
no theatres should be built within his jurisdiction, the theatre was
becoming respectable. The request for a coat of arms could be
resumed with the certainty that it would be granted. William
Shakespeare now applied for it, and in accordance with the custom
that still prevails he made the application in his father's name. A
document was drawn up by William Dethick, the Garter principal
King of Arms—heraldic experts granted themselves resounding
titles— and an acceptable coat of arms was designed. The language
of the grant was magniloquent, as though something of enormous
importance was being discussed:

> To all and singular Noble and Gentlemen: of what
> estate, degree, bearing arms to whom these presents shall
> come. William Dethick, Garter principal King of Arms,
> sendeth greetings.
> Know ye that whereas by the authority and ancient
> privileges pertaining to my office from the Queen's most
> excellent Majesty and by her Highness' most noble and
> victorious progenitors, I am to take general notice and
> record and to make declaration and testimony for all causes
> of arms and matters of gentry through all her Majesty's
> kingdoms, dominions, principalities, isles and provinces to
> the end that as many gentlemen by their ancient names of
> families, kindreds, and descents have and enjoy certain
> ensigns and coats of arms, so it is very expedient in all ages
> that some men for their valiant feats, magnanimity, virtue,
> dignities and deserts may use and bear such tokens of
> honour and worthiness, whereby their name and good fame
> may be the better known and divulged, and their children
> and posterity in all virtue to the service of their prince and
> country encouraged.
> Wherefore being solicited and by credible report

informed that John Shakespeare of Stratford upon Avon
in the county of Warwick, whose parents and late
grandfather for his faithful and valiant service was
advanced and rewarded by the most prudent prince King
Henry the Seventh of famous memory, sithence which
time they have continued in those parts being of good
reputation and credit, and that the said John hath
married the daughter and one of the heirs of Robert
Arden of Wilmcote in the said county esquire, and for
the encouragement of his posterity to whom these
achievements by the ancient custom of the Law of Arms
may descend. I the said Garter King of Arms have
assigned, granted, and by these presents confirmed:

This shield or coat of arms, viz. Gold, on a bend sable, a
spear of the first steeled argent. And for his crest or
cognizance a falcon his wings displayed argent standing on a
wreath of his colours: supporting a spear gold steeled as
aforesaid set upon a helmet with mantles and tassels as hath
been accustomed and doth more plainly appear depicted on
this margin: Signifying thereby and by the authority of my
office aforesaid ratifying that it shall be lawful for the said
John Shakespeare, gentleman, and for his children, issue
and posterity at all times and places convenient to bear and
make demonstration of the same blazon or achievement
upon their shields, targets, escutcheons, coats of arms,
pennons, guidons, seals, rings, edifices, buildings, utensils,
liveries, tombs, or monuments or otherwise for all lawful
warlike feats or civil use or exercises, according to the Laws
of Arms, and customs that to gentlemen belongeth without
let or interruption of any other person or persons for use or
bearing the same.

In witness and perpetual remembrance hereof I have
hereunto subscribed my name and fastened the seal of my
office endorsed with the signet of my arms. At the Office of
Arms, London, the 20 day of October, the 38th year of the
reign of our Sovereign Lady Elizabeth by the grace of God
Queen of England, France and Ireland, Defender of the
Faith etc. 1596.

Such was the imposing document which charted out in proper heraldic form the whole extent and interstices of the honor granted to the former bailiff of Stratford. It has survived in a first draft on a single large sheet of paper. At the upper left hand corner there was a drawing of the shield with a spear diagonally across it while above it a rather tame-looking falcon brandishes another spear. It is an effective design, simple and cogent, without the elaboration which reduces so many heraldic devices to absurdity. The falcon was "shaking" the spear. With its outspread wings it has a proper heraldic look about it. In fact, a falcon was one of the badges of Queen Elizabeth and it appeared on the arms of Shakespeare's patron, the Earl of Southampton: *Azure, a gold cross between four silver falcons, their wing closed and their bells of gold.*

Above John Shakespeare's coat of arms the motto was written three times: *Non, sanz Droict*, and then again *Non, sanz Droict*, and then in large capital letters, NON SANZ DROICT. The motto is old French for "Not without Justice." No one has yet come up with a satisfactory explanation for a motto which seems to conceal a wound. It is just possible that *Non sanz* is intended to have an affirmative meaning, the two negative words combining to form a positive assertion of the primacy of justice, as in the catalogue of virtues in *Macbeth*:

> Justice, verity, temperance, stableness,
> Bounty, perseverance, mercy, lowliness,
> Devotion, patience, courage, fortitude.

But while the motto leaves many things unexplained, the shield and crest are brilliantly clear. A gold shield with a black bar diagonally across it, and within the bar a silver spear; on the crest above a silver falcon brandishing a gold spear. It was very simple until it occurred either to Shakespeare or the College of Heralds to impale the new coat of arms with the ancient arms of Arden. This was done three years later, for the original application appears to have been pigeonholed. In 1599, when the new application was made, there was some dispute about which of the variations of the Arden arms should be used. In that large and powerful family with many branches cousins were accustomed to making modifications of the arms as they pleased. The Ardens of Park Hall, regarded as the main descendants of Turchill, were entitled to their own coat of arms: *Ermine a fess checky gold and azure. Ermine* meant black spots on a white ground, a *fess* was a broad band across the middle, *checky* meant checkered. But there was another Arden coat of arms worn by another branch of the family which had survived since the time of the Dunstable tournament of 1308 and the siege of Calais in 1345 where it is known to have been worn by an Arden. This was *Gules, three cross-crosslets fitchy gold, and on a gold chief a martlet gules.* This is not as complicated as it sounds, *Gules* meant red, a *cross-crosslet fitchy* was a cross somewhat lengthened and pointed at the lower end, a *mantlet* was a swift. The coat of arms therefore consisted of a red shield with the gold bird on top and the three fitchy crosses below. It was believed by some that this was even more ancient than the coat of the Ardens of Park Hall.

There exists at the College of Arms in London an experimental design of the quartered arms of Shakespeare and Arden. The designer first drew the *Ermine a fess checky* coat of arms, then drew a line through, substituting the *Gules, three cross-crosslets* coat of arms as being more appropriate for the occasion. The experimental design is dated 1599. Shakespeare seems never to have used the quartered arms either out of modesty or because the quartered arms did not form as pleasing a design as the single spear surmounted by a falcon. About this time the formal offer of a coat of arms was granted to John Shakespeare and his issue forever. The design was quite simple, although the description was sufficiently complicated to please William Dethick and William Camden, who had recently been appointed Clarenceux King of Arms for the south, east, and west parts of England.

> In a field of gold upon a bend sable a spear of the first
> the point upward headed argent, and for his crest or
> cognizance a falcon with his wings displayed standing on a
> wreath of his colours, supporting a spear armed headed or
> and steeled silver upon a helmet with mantles and tassles.

In the 1599 grant the qualifications of John Shakespeare were again spelled out but in a slightly different form. Previously it was stated that his ancestors had been rewarded during the reign of Henry VII. Now we learn that they had received "lands of tenements." We learn too that John Shakespeare while bailiff of Stratford had apparently possessed a coat of arms and presumably displayed it. This former coat of arms appears to have been exactly the same as the one now granted officially by William Dethick and William Camden.

While all this may be boring in the extreme to those who do not care about coats of arms and think the world would be well served if all such honors and titles were abolished, it is beyond dispute that the Shakespeares, father and son, were determined to acquire a coat of arms and the honor of always describing themselves as gentlemen. They were proud of their rank, and they were perfectly aware that they were now in a better bargaining position when dealing with financial affairs. Contemporary records show that Shakespeare was busily investing in property in the years immediately before receiving the grant. Thus we learn from the letter of a former bailiff, Abraham Sturley, addressed on January 24, 1598, to Richard Quiney "that our countryman Mr. Shakespeare is willing to disburse some money upon some odd yardland or other at Shottery or near about us; he thinketh it a very fit pattern to move him to deal in the matter of our tithes." Shakespeare was also in the business of lending money. The same Richard Quiney wrote the only letter addressed to Shakespeare which has survived:

To my loving good friend and countryman Mr. Wm. Shakespeare deliver this.

Loving countryman, I am bold of you as of a friend, craving your help with £30 upon Mr. Bushell's and my security, or Mr. Mytton's with me. Mr. Rosswell has not come to London as yet and I have especial cause. You shall friend me much in helping me out of all the debts I owe in London, I thank God, and much quiet my mind which would not be indebted. I am now towards the court in hope of answer for the dispatch of my business.

You shall neither lose credit nor money by me, the Lord willing. And now but persuade yourself so as I hope, and you shall not need to fear; but with all hearty thankfulness I will hold my time and content your friend, and if we bargain further you shall be the paymaster yourself. My time bids me hasten to an end, and so I commit this [to] your care and hope of your help. I fear I shall not be back this night from the court. Haste. The Lord be with you and with us all, Amen.

From the Bell in Carter Lane, the 25th October 1598.

Yours in all kindness,
RYC. QUYNEY

Curiously, this letter was never delivered, for on the same day Quiney caught up with Shakespeare and obtained the promise of the required loan, and immediately wrote a letter to Abraham Sturley to announce the good news. Sturley wrote from Stratford on November 4, acknowledging receipt of the news "that our countryman Mr. Wm. Shak. would procure us money, which I will like of as I shall hear when, and where, and how." Meanwhile, on or about October 30, Adrian Quiney, soon to become bailiff of Stratford, wrote to his son Richard explaining that he hoped that some of the money borrowed from Shakespeare might be invested in knit stockings bought in Evesham:

If you bargain with Mr. Sha or receive money therefor, bring your money home if you may, I see how knit stockings be sold, there is great buying of them at Evesham.

Edward Wheat and Harry, your brother's man, were both
at Evesham this day senet, and, as I heard, bestowed £20
there in knit hosings, wherefor I think you may do good, if
you can have money.

Adrian Quiney was a dealer in silks and textiles, and a business-
man of considerable acumen, always on the lookout for bargains. It
seemed to him very natural that money borrowed from Shakespeare
should be employed to make a killing in knitted goods.

Shakespeare, gentleman and landowner, and owner of the finest
residence in Stratford, possessing extensive theatrical interests in
London, author of many poems and dramas, a moneylender who
lent his money at the usual usurious rates, was a man of many
trades, like his father. Among other things he was a maltster who
held back his supplies of malt from market in the hope that there
would be a sharp rise of price in a time of scarcity. We know he was
doing this because the civic authorities compiled on February 4,
1598, a list of thirteen hoarders in the Chapel Street ward, and
Shakespeare's name is included as one who was hoarding ten
quarters of malt. Very few were hoarding more. Thomas Dixon
was hoarding seventeen quarters for himself, sixteen for Sir Thomas Lucy, and ten for Sir Edward Greville. Shakespeare's friend July
Shaw was hoarding seven quarters. Most of them were hoarding
comparatively small amounts. Dixon was clearly the chief culprit
and chief organizer. The common people were understandably
incensed, and there is a letter from Abraham Sturley describing the
popular outrage over the high prices of corn and malt. There was
talk of drastic action, even of an uprising. Sturley quoted his friend
Thomas West as saying "he hoped within a week to lead some of
them in a halter, meaning the maltsters," and John Grannams said:
"I hope if God send my Lord of Essex down shortly, to see them
hanged on gibbets at their own doors." Although he did very little
for them, Essex had always presented himself as the head of the
popular party defending the poor and oppressed. Shakespeare himself was one of those whom John Grannams hoped to see hanging at
his own door.

Honor was always a variable commodity: it was honorable to
become rich, dishonorable to be a hoarder and to acquire riches by

manipulating prices. It was honorable to acquire a coat of arms but dishonorable to acquire it by false pretenses. In 1602 Peter Brooke, York herald, drew up a statement in which he accused William Dethick and William Camden of exceeding their authority by granting coats of arms to people who were unworthy of them. Fourth on the list was Shakespeare. Brooke was a contentious man, always at loggerheads with Dethick, who was no less contentious and much more dangerous. Dethick was capable of flying into sudden inexplicable tantrums. He once struck his own father with his fist, he stabbed his own brother with a dagger, and it was said that at the funeral of Sir Henry Sidney he was so annoyed by the behavior of the minister that he flew at him inside the church while the funeral ceremony was still going on. Dethick was just as violent inside the Heralds' office. He was totally unlike the mild and sweet-tempered William Camden, appointed Clarenceux King of Arms by the Earl of Essex, who was Earl Marshal in 1597 and therefore chief of the Heralds' College. Camden was a man with a prodigious capacity for suffering fools gladly out of Christian charity. He was therefore a match for both Dethick and Brooke. He was the friend and teacher of Ben Jonson, and it is likely that he was also a friend of Shakespeare, and he was probably the person chiefly responsible for the final official grant of a coat of arms to John Shakespeare. Nothing came of Brooke's seventeen-page statement attacking the legitimacy of twenty-three heraldic grants. It vanished among all the musty documents of the Herald's office, coming to rest at last in the Folger Library in Washington.

It was not only Peter Brooke who inveighed against the improper grants of coats of arms. Ben Jonson, too, raged against them. In *Every Man Out of His Humour*, which was performed in 1599 by the Lord Chamberlain's Players with the chief roles being played by Richard Burbage, Augustine Phillips, William Sly, John Heminge, Henry Condell, and Thomas Pope, all of them close friends of Shakespeare, Ben Jonson permitted himself a long diatribe against improper grants, putting the words in the mouths of Sogliardo, who is "so enamored of the name of a Gentleman that he will have it, though he buy it," Puntarvolo, who is described as "a vainglorious knight," and Carlo Buffone, who is described as "a public, scurrilous, and profane jester."

Sogliardo.   Nay, I will have him, I am resolute for that. By this parchment, gentlemen, I have been so toil'd among the Harrots* yonder, you will not believe, they do speak in the strangest language, and give a man the hardest terms for his money that ever you knew.

Carlo.   But ha' you arms? ha' you arms?

Sogliardo.   Y faith, I thank them, I can write myself gentleman now, here's my patent, it cost me thirty pounds by this breath.

Puntarvolo.   A very fair coat, well charg'd, and full of armory.

Sogliardo.   Nay, it has as much variety of colours in it as you have seen a coat have. How like you the crest, sir?

Puntarvolo.   I understand it not well, what is 't?

Sogliardo.   Marry, sir, it is your Bore without a head rampant. A bore without a head, that's very rare.

Carlo.   Aye, and rampant too. Troth, I commend the Herald's wit, he has deciphered him well. A swine without a head, without brain, wit, anything indeed, ramping to gentility. You can blazon the rest, signior? Can you not?

Sogliardo.   Oh, I, I have it in writing here of purpose, it cost me two shillings the tricking. . . .

Puntarvalo.   Let the word be *Not without mustard;* your crest is very rare, sir.

It is all good-humored raillery with more than a hint of venom. Ben Jonson was clearly outraged with Shakespeare's assumption of gentility: *Not without mustard* is *Non sanz Droict* with a vengeance. Carlo's words "ramping to gentility" best describe the process by which men aspire to coats of arms. And now that Sogliardo-Shakespeare had acquired his coat of arms, what then? Carlo provides the appropriate lesson in the form of a homily:

*Heralds.

Carlo. Nay, look you, sir, now you are a gentleman, you
must carry a more exalted presence, change your mood
and habit to a more austere form, be exceeding proud,
stand upon your gentility, and scorn every man. Speak
nothing humbly, never discourse under a noble man,
though you ne'er saw him but riding to the Star
Chamber, it's all one. Love no man. Trust no man.
Speak ill of no man to his face: nor well of any man
behind his back. Salute fairly on the front, and with 'hem
hang'd upon the turn. Spread yourself upon his bosom
publicly, whose heart you will eat in private. These be
principles, think on 'hem, I'll come to you again
presently.

They were angry words tricked out in enough good humor to
make them palatable. Jonson had no use for gentility; like his
mentor, William Camden, who was offered a knighthood and
refused it, he would remain plebeian to the end. "Ben Jonson,
Gentleman" is a contradiction, and "William Shakespeare, Gentleman" seems in our eyes perverse and meaningless, the word "Gentleman" being no more appropriate addition to his name than a
little rat's tail attached to a huge, lumbering elephant painted and
caparisoned for a royal progress.

Shakespeare
of Bankside

The
Great Globe
Itself

THE YEARS OF SHOREDITCH CAME TO AN END on a night of darkness and violence.

On December 28, 1598, the Theatre in Shoreditch was torn down and its timbers and ironwork were carried off triumphantly to a field in Southwark south of the Thames. According to the landowner Giles Alleyn, who had been feuding with the Burbages for twenty years, his own people had attempted to prevent the Theatre from being demolished. He was himself not in Shoreditch at the time—he was enjoying his Christmas holiday elsewhere—and he had to rely on eyewitnesses for details. His own eyes told him that where there had been the Theatre, the most famous playhouse of all and said to hold two thousand people, not a stick remained.

According to Giles Alleyn, some sixteen people were involved in pulling down the Theatre. They were Richard Burbage, his brother Cuthbert, William Smith, who was a friend of the Burbages, Peter Street, a well-known carpenter, and twelve others described as "laborers such as wrought for wages." James Burbage had died the previous year, but his widow was among those who watched the demolition. "She did see the doing thereof, and like well of it," Giles Alleyn wrote in his complaint to the Privy Council. Shakespeare and the other actors were certainly present and lent a helping hand. The sixteen men who actually tore the Theatre to pieces, with Peter Street acting as the foreman of laborers, were not the only ones involved, for in addition there were carters, carriers, and boatmen. Alleyn had friends in Shoreditch; the names of the more obvious culprits were taken down; and though he would dearly have loved to know the rest of the names he was unable to find them. His complaint was addressed to the Privy Council of Queen Elizabeth. It was drawn up by a lawyer, who made great play of the "outrageous, violent, and riotous" behavior of Richard Burbage and his demolition crew.

The lawyer who drew up the complaint was well aware that the Privy Council regarded riotous behavior with extreme suspicion and was prepared to punish severely anyone who rioted against the Queen's peace. He therefore stressed the riotous element and said very little about the work of carrying off the timbers. There must have been some violence, but he may also have exaggerated the extent of it for legal purposes and in the hope of doing the greatest damage to Richard Burbage and his brother Cuthbert. Richard was one of the most famous actors in England; he had acted before the Queen; and he was under the protection of the Court. The lawyer knew he would have to fight hard to win the case.

The most interesting part of the complaint describes the assault on the Theatre:

> The said Cuthbert Burbage, having intelligence of your subject's purpose herein, and unlawfully combining and federating himself with the said Richard Burbage and one Peter Street, William Smith, and divers other persons to the number of twelve, to your subjects unknown, did about the eight and twentieth day of December, in the one and fortieth year of your highness' reign, and sithence your highness last and general pardon, by the confederacy aforesaid, riotously assembled themselves together, and then and there armed themselves with divers and many unlawful

and offensive weapons, as namely swords, daggers, bills, axes, and such like, and so armed did then repair unto the said Theatre, and then and there armed as aforesaid, in very riotous, outrageous, and forceable manner, and contrary to the laws of your highness' realm, attempted to pull down the said Theatre. Whereupon, divers of your subjects, servants and farmers, then going about in peaceable manner to procure them to desist from that unlawful enterprise, they, the said riotous persons aforesaid, notwithstanding procured then therein with great violence, not only then and there forcibly and riotously resisting your subjects, servants, and farmers, but also then and there pulling, breaking, and throwing down the said Theatre in very outrageous, violent and riotous sort.

For the purpose of understanding what really happened, we should observe the weapons said to be employed—swords, daggers, bills, and axes. A bill was a heavy wooden staff with a blade or ax head attached to it. Quite clearly the axes and the bills were used for demolishing the building: they were not in themselves weapons used for rioting; nor at a time when most gentlemen carried swords and most workingmen carried daggers could it be said that Richard and Cuthbert Burbage were well armed. They had planned the maneuver with great care, posted some guards around the building, and hoped to tear down the building as quietly as possible. They were not accused of using the weapons people would normally use in really riotous behavior. They were not using pistols or muskets. They were tearing down a building and hoping to transport all its timbers and ironwork south of the Thames before Giles Alleyn would get wind of it.

It was not an easy task; it had to be managed very craftily, with a well-organized company of professional carpenters and ironsmiths. Horse carts had to be loaded and sent on their way; dispatchers had to be sent on ahead; bargains had to be struck with the boatmen; a large shed in Bankside must be erected to house the timbers, the ironwork, the actor's costumes, the records of the acting company, the stage properties, and a hundred other things. "The great house called the Theatre" was not a small building. It was like tearing down a mansion and carrying it, with all its bits and pieces, across the river. And the horse carts clearly did not travel across the City of London and across London Bridge; to avoid tollgates and inspectors they drove across Finsbury Fields and proceeded westward in sight of the city walls, and then when the city was safely passed, they would turn south, perhaps at the village of Charing Cross, where all the iron and timber would be transferred to boats.

Giles Alleyn's complaint listed all the damage done to him by the loss of the building which was never his own property. Had they not injured his grass to the extent of forty shillings? Had they not terrified his good neighbors? Had they not brought riot into the heart of the quiet village of Shoreditch? And was not riot very close to treason?

On the night of December 28, 1598, the Theatre died. A few months later there arose on Bankside a new theatre called the Globe, which was to become the most famous of all English theatres. The Globe flew at its masthead a flag showing Hercules carrying the weight of the whole world on his shoulders.

About this time a nursery rhyme was being recited in London. Like nearly all nursery rhymes it took the form of an invitation to pleasant nightmares:

Oranges and lemons
Say the bells of St. Clement's.

You owe me five farthings
Say the bells of St. Martins's.

When will you pay me?
Say the bells of Old Bailey.

When I grow rich,
Say the bells of Shoreditch.

When will that be?
Say the bells of Stepney.

I'm sure I don't know,
Say the great bell of Bow.

Here comes a candle to light you to bed,
Here comes a chopper to chop off your head.

Shakespeare would no longer hear the bells of St. Leonard's in Shoreditch. Instead he would hear the great bells of St. Mary Overies, the huge church, now known as Southwark Cathedral, which greeted all travelers who came over London Bridge. He had grown rich and famous, and was entitled to show his coat of arms, and from being a common player he had become a member of the gentry.

The Globe came to Southwark because this part of London was becoming increasingly the entertainment area of London. It was not a very salubrious area: swamps, marshes, open drains, a row of houses along the riverbank, and here and there were the whorehouses where a whore would sell herself for a penny. Here was the Bear Garden, built in the form of a theatre, where bears had been baited by huge mastiffs for nearly a century: it was the common English blood sport enjoyed by Queen Elizabeth and all her subjects. Ambassadors were taken to it and the finer points of bearbaiting were demonstrated to them. A poster announcing a bear baiting has survived:

> Tomorrow being Thursday shall be seen at the Bear
> Garden on the Bankside a great match played by the
> gamesters of Essex who have challenged all comers
> whatsoever to play five dogs at the single bear for five
> pounds and also to weary a bull dead at the stake and for
> your better content shall have pleasant sport with the horse
> and ape and the whipping of the blind bear.

The blind bear was known as Harry Hunks and he was whipped "till the blood ran down his old shoulders." Four or five dogs were set on the tied bull, and usually the bull succeeded in tossing them into the air with his horns. "To weary a bull dead at the stake" meant a long and exhausting performance, the bull eventually weakened through loss of blood. The Elizabethans took their blood sports seriously.

The Globe, which stood quite close to the Bear Garden, was not the only theatre on Bankside. We have records of the Swan Theatre built by Francis Langley, a rich draper and goldsmith, in 1596, and the Rose Theatre built by Philip Henslowe and John Cholmley in 1587. Henslowe was a dyer and a pawnbroker, Cholmley was a grocer, who supported the venture in order to have the right to sell refreshments. The exact site of the Globe has been disputed, but it appears to have been just south of Maid Lane and was the most easterly of the Bankside theatres. Much of the theatre was simply the Theatre reconstructed on a new site, for Peter Street is known to have been one of the most capable carpenters in London, and by numbering all the timbers, beams, joists, planks, and floorboards of the Theatre he would be able to reassemble it into the Globe. So skilled a carpenter might make changes during the reassembling; he might enlarge it or make structural alterations; and it appears that the Globe was somewhat larger and more imposing than the Theatre, although it was substantially built from the same timbers.

A visitor to the Globe from the city of London would take a wherry across the Thames or ride across London Bridge. The theatre was only a short distance from the river. If it had been raining the roads would be deep in mud, but there would be some shelter from the trees, for Bankside, like Stratford, was almost a forest. He would find the Globe looming above the treetops, a huge building daubed with white plaster, with small square windows and a small doorway, and an enormous flag fluttering from the tiring houses high above the stage. The presence of the flag signified that a play was being performed that day. The visitor would pay a penny to enter the theatre, and this would permit him to stand among the groundlings in the open space in front of the stage, and for another penny he would be permitted to climb the steps to the galleries. Cushions were lent out for a fee, the book of the play was on sale, and hawkers moved about selling bottles of ale, cakes, pies, apples, and comfits. The crowd was usually boisterous, and a good deal of shouting went on. At exactly two o'clock, after the third sounding of the trumpet, a lean figure in a cloak of black velvet advanced majestically across the stage, gazed imperiously at the audience until he had reduced them to silence, and began to speak. He was the Prologue. The performance had begun.

The modern visitor transported to Elizabethan London would have been surprised to discover how little stage equipment there was. There were no stage sets, no scenery, and very few props. There was a trapdoor, through which the Devil might appear or the damned might be seen going down to Hell, and chairs and thrones or even a table covered with food might be let down from the roof. Doors opened on the stage; an inner room, concealed by a tapestry or a curtain, stood at the back of the stage. No one came on the stage bearing a sign saying: "Agincourt," "Elsinore," or "The Senate House in Rome." "What country, friends, is this?" Viola asks, and the sea captain answers matter-of-factly: "This is Illyria, lady." No one in the audience may have known where Illyria was, but it was not a matter that deeply concerned them. They knew they were somewhere, and the place had a name attached to it, and this was enough.

Props existed, but as we know from a famous inventory found among the *Henslowe Papers* they were often little more than adjuncts to the costumes. A crown, a Pope's miter, a bull's head, a helmet with a dragon, Mercury's wings, a vizard, a lion's skin, a bearskin, a buckler, greave armor, a pair of wrought gloves, by which was meant gloves made of metal. A few were more complicated. Thus we find "a tree of golden apples" and "a chain of dragons." There was also "a moss bank" and "a great horse with four legs," both presumably made of painted wood. Finally there was "a frame for the heading," which was a device for producing the illusion of a beheading. There was a great deal of blood on the Elizabethan stage and the actors would conceal under their clothes little balloons filled with sheep's blood, and the blood would pour out of them as they lay dying. Among the first plays performed at the Globe was *Julius Caesar*, and the blood of the dying Caesar spilled all over the stage.

Stage machinery except for ropes and pulleys scarcely existed. Ben Jonson, whose play *Every Man in His Humour* was also acted at the Globe, had no great fondness for it and said so in his prologue:

He rather prays you will be pleased to see
One such today, as other plays should be;
Where neither chorus wafts you o'er the seas,
Nor creaking throne comes down the boys to please,
Nor nimble squib is seen to make afeard
The gentlewomen, nor rolled bullet heard

To say, it thunders; nor tempestuous drum
Rumbles, to tell you when the storm doth come.

Then, as now, a Shakespearean production would be accompanied by elaborate trumpet calls, the same trumpeter who announced
the beginning of the play being employed whenever a king made his
appearance or when an army was being rallied or marched into
battle. Sound effects were carefully studied. The threatening voices
of the crowd, the drum roll before an execution, the winds whistling
in the dark forests, and the sound of an army on the march were
heard by the spectators with extraordinary immediacy and clarity,
for the shape of the theatre made it a sounding box, the sounds
seeming to come from all directions. The sound of a naval battle
off-stage was not beyond the capacity of the sound engineers of the
Elizabethan theatre.

Probably the first of the Shakespearean plays to be acted at the
Globe was *Henry V*, an exultation over the life of a good king and
his ferocious sword. He is warm, human, sensual, witty—*l'homme
moyen sensuel* raised to the pitch of kingship, as far removed as
possible from King Richard III. When Fluellen, the robust and
jaunty Welshman, stubbornly proud of his gift for words, comes
upon the King during the battle of Agincourt, it occurs to him to
remind the King that they share the same blood, are companions in
arms, are almost equals on the battlefield:

> *Fluellen.* All the water in Wye cannot wash your
>   Majesty's Welsh plood out of your pody, I can tell you
>   that: God pless it, and preserve it, as long as it pleases
>   his Grace, and his Majesty too!
>
> *King.* Thanks, good my countryman.
>
> *Fluellen.* By Jeshu, I am your Majesty's countryman, I
>   care not who know it! I will confess it to all the world; I
>   need not be ashamed of your Majesty, praised be God, so
>   long as your Majesty is an honorable man.
>
> *King.* God keep me so!

"God keep me so!" in its brevity and revelation of character, is
wonderful theatre. Fluellen is a superb foil for the King, and quite

properly receives from the King's hand a favor to stick in his cap. He is a Fool, and Pistol is another Fool, and both are happy on the battlefield. In France, in the English camp, Pistol learns that his wife, Mistress Quickly, has died in hospital of the "malady of France" and makes his firm resolve to take vengeance on the world:

Pistol.   News have I that my Doll is dead i'th' spital
  Of malady of France;
  And there my rendezvous is quite cut off.
  Old I do wax, and from my weary limbs
  Honor is cudgeled. Well, bawd I'll turn,
  And sometimes lean to cutpurse of quick hand.
  To England will I steal, and there I'll steal;
  And patches will I get unto these cudgeled scars,
  And swear I got them in the Gallia wars.

One need have no pity for Pistol, bawd, thief, and braggart. He had a good time serving as Falstaff's "ancient," by which he meant "ensign." They were both close to Prince Hal in the happy days when the prince was also a thief and a braggart, and it was Pistol who heard Mistress Quickly's great description of Falstaff's death and who helped in the baiting of Falstaff in Windsor Forest. "Honor is cudgeled," he says, but honor is the least of his preoccupations. He will die at Tyburn with a rope around his neck, a braggart to the end.

With all its pageantry and heraldry, *Henry V* deals with very real issues. What is kingship? Why should a man die on a battlefield for a king? What are justice, honor, duty, love? Shakespeare's own preoccupations are heard during the night vigil when Henry V is seen wandering in disguise around the silent camp. Michael Williams, a soldier, asks the King about the prospects of the coming battle. The King replies: "Even as men wracked upon a sand, that look to be washed off the next tide." John Bates, another soldier, says: "He may show what outward courage he will: but I believe as cold a night as 'tis, he could wish himself in Thames up to the neck; and so I would he were, and I by him, at all adventures, so we were quit here." Bates may have been talking about the pirates whose bodies hung from posts until the tides had wasted them away.

There is generosity and great sweetness and much fear in *Henry V*, but it is not a play in the sense that *Othello* and *King Lear* are plays. The characters do not move toward great confrontations. It is more like Shakespeare's *Henry VIII* than any other play: all pageantry, a steady progress, a royal march through history in the company of a young king who could tell his bride Katherine, Princess of France:

A good leg will fall; a straight back will stoop; a black
beard will turn white; a curl'd pate will grow bald; a fair
face will wither; a full eye will wax hollow; but a good
heart is the sun and the moon, or rather the sun and not the
moon, for it shines bright and never changes, but keeps its
course truly.

Julius Caesar was also a pageant, but it was far more complex and tendentious than *Henry V*. Julius Caesar stands at the center of the play, but he is not the chief character; he is the somber tyrant who must be killed at all costs. All the arguments for killing tyrants are ruthlessly presented, and only Caesar himself, so proud that he cannot believe that any man's hand will be raised against him, is impervious to these arguments. While *Henry V*, in spite of the famous night scene, seems to be played in sunlight, *Julius Caesar* appears to be played at night, by the light of sheet lightning and to the sound of rolling thunder. The characters are caricatures possessed of a psychopathic intensity. They are sharp-edged, ungainly, their faces white with horror as they walk toward their predestined ends.

Shakespeare does not warm to the Romans, and it is not until *Antony and Cleopatra* that any real warmth spills over them, and then only over Antony. Even Cassius, with his lean and hungry look, flawed by envy and hatred, an anguished and human man who happens to be an arch-conspirator, is represented as a person who acts out of spite rather than out of social duty. Thus Cassius addresses the heroic Brutus in a long speech describing the character of Caesar:

Why, man, he doth bestride the narrow world
Like a Colossus, and we petty men
Walk under his huge legs and peep about

Richard Tarlton, from Harleian Ms. 3885

William Sly (*Dulwich College Picture Gallery*)

Nathaniel Field (*Dulwich College Picture Gallery*)

John Lowin (*Ashmolean Museum, Oxford*)

Richard Burbage (*Dulwich College Picture Gallery*)

Benjamin Jonson (*National Portrait Gallery*)

John Fletcher (*National Portrait Gallery*)

From J. C. Vissher's View of London, *1616, showing the Bear Garden and the Globe*

To find ourselves dishonorable graves.
Men at some times are masters of their fates:
The fault, dear Brutus, is not in our stars,
But in ourselves, that we are underlings.

There is more than a suspicion that Cassius is envious and would like to be Caesar.

John Masefield, in a brief commentary on *Julius Caesar*, insisted that Shakespeare was on the side of order and therefore of Caesar. "He saw life," wrote Masefield, "for what it was, an order of intense power, revolving with immense energy around a centre or axle, like a spinning wheel. Any upsetting of that spinning, from whatever motive is devilish and from a hellish source of broken rhythm and disharmony." But this is not quite true. Shakespeare sometimes puts his finger on the scales and presses down. He is all for Caesar; he is also all for Cassius and Brutus. He is for order, but there are times when order becomes a prison, and he turns to Cassius and Brutus. He is haunted by the fearfulness of Caesar but he is also haunted by the prospect of civil war and chaos. He wrote the play when the possibilities of civil war in England were very real, and when the old and dying Queen was surrendering her power to able and unprincipled lieutenants. *Julius Caesar* is among other things a tract for the times. It was also an extraordinarily penetrating study of Caesarism and of those who were prepared to sacrifice their lives in order to destroy it. Finally, Shakespeare entered into the minds of the conspirators, knowing them so well that it seems likely he had some inner knowledge of the workings of Essex's conspiracy, either through the Earl of Southhampton or some of the disgruntled soldiers who flocked to join Essex. The highest poetic moment of the play comes when Brutus says:

I have not slept.
Between the acting of a dreadful thing
And the first motion, all the interim is
Like a phantasma, or a hideous dream:
The Genius and the mortal instruments
Are then in council; and the state of man
Like to a little kingdom, suffers then
The nature of an insurrection.

Among those who saw the play at the Globe was a Swiss doctor, Thomas Platter, who wrote an account of a month's visit to London during the autumn of 1599:

> After dinner on the 21 September, at about 2 o'clock, I
> went over the river with my companions and in a
> straw-roofed house saw the tragedy of the first Emperor
> Julius Caesar, with at least 15 characters acted very well.
> At the end of the play 2 of the characters in men's clothes
> and 2 in women's clothes performed a dance, as is their
> custom, wonderfully well together.

The play ends with Brutus running onto the sword of a slave, dying in agony. Then Octavius and Antony enter with their train and briefly survey the dead body of the man they had defeated. Then comes the dance. Sometimes Shakespeare could make a whole play out of a simple and charming dance set to music.

Twelfth Night moves like a pavane, gaily, somberly, the most artificial of Shakespeare's entertainments and the most highly choreographed, so that we know at every moment where the dancers are going and where they are coming from. The night music is court music, and we are as much aware of the courtly audience in ruffs and pearls as we are aware of the players. It is not so much that the play is artificial as that it is deliberate artifice raised to the height of perfection, a work of art composed out of gossamer threads that will blow away if you breathe on them. It was Shakespeare's last comedy. Indeed it is his farewell to comedy, and what we call his last comedies were not comedies at all but records of wanderings in strange kingdoms lit by the light we see in dreams.

In *Twelfth Night* we are not asked to believe in the existence of the characters, for they have no existence. They will never sweat, and no blood will flow from them. They are music and gesture. The music is enervating and the gestures are rarely what they seem to be; and if they seem to be talking at cross-purposes, it is not so, for their talk is designed to decorate their nothingness, to encircle it, to give it a shape it cannot possess. They are knowledgeable about nothingness. The Clown, lording it over the Duke of Illyria, says very properly:

Now, the melancholy god protect thee, and the tailor make thy doublet of changeable taffeta, for thy mind is a very opal! I would have men of such constancy put to sea, that their business might be everything, and their intent everywhere; for that's it that always makes a good voyage of nothingness.

As the play develops we discover that there are many other things that make a good voyage of nothingness. Malvolio's preposterous pride eats upon itself until he is entirely consumed in a room which is brightly lit but which he believes to be dark: he falls into his own nothingness with no great grace. Others fall more gracefully and purposely but none with his eagerness. If Malvolio derives from the Italian *malavoglia*, meaning "ill will" or "evil will," he is misnamed; he is not one of those who commit deadly sins and his pride is quite harmless except to himself, for there is no evil in him. Like Beelzebub he plays at evil, puts on evil airs, enjoys his hypocrisy, enjoys above all his high position of steward, but he cannot convince anyone that he possesses the powers to unlock the devils in hell. When he says in a brightly lit room, "I am not mad, Sir Topas. I say to you, this house is dark," he is saying what needs to be said only by a man who is haunted by ghosts of himself. When he says in the last scene in the play, "I'll be revenged on the whole pack of you," there is no need for anyone to take cover. He asserts himself but not sufficiently for us to believe he is alive. He is a character in a play who acts out a character in a play, so remote from real life that we ask nothing of him except that he entertain us. And so with all the others. The enchanting Viola, daughter of Sebastian of Messaline, is shipwrecked on the coast of Illyria and believes that her brother has been drowned. The themes of shipwreck and drowning will become important in later plays, but Viola's shipwreck is purely imaginary. It is simply an excuse for getting her to the court of Duke Orsino, the enchanted poet who said in the very first words of the play:

If music be the food of love, play on:
Give me excess of it, that, surfeiting,
The appetite may sicken, and so die.
That dream again! it had a dying fall:

O, it came o'er my ear like the sweet south,
That breathes upon a bank of violets,
Stealing and giving odour! Enough; no more:
'Tis not so sweet now as it was before.
O spirit of love! how quick and fresh art thou,
That, notwithstanding thy capacity
Receiveth as the sea, nought enters there,
Of what validity and pitch soe'er,
But falls into abatement and low price,
Even in a minute: so full of shapes is fancy
That it alone is high fantastical.

Having completed his "high fantastical" *Twelfth Night*, written perhaps in order to rid himself of memories of Caesar and Brutus, Shakespeare returned to the world of tragic drama, where "all the interim is like a phantasma, or a hideous dream." He wrote *The Tragedy of Hamlet, Prince of Denmark.*

Hamlet
and the
Ghost

OF ALL THE MULTITUDINOUS CHARACTERS created by Shakespeare one, in our age, towers over all the rest. We know him well, but his face is unfamiliar to us even though we might recognize his sardonic smile and the huge wide-open eyes with the steady gaze, those eyes with a glint of madness in them, and we know that the madness may be simulated and the sardonic smile does not necessarily reflect his thought or his judgment on us or his judgment on himself. We might recognize him more easily if we saw him at the end of a long, tapestry-hung corridor, and we would certainly not recognize him if we saw him on the Elizabethan stage wearing a laundered white ruff, a doublet of many-colored silk, ballooning velvet breeches, and parti-colored hose. Yet assuredly when Hamlet first appeared on the stage he wore the gala costume of a contemporary prince. To the Elizabethans he was above all a prince. To us he is more the philosopher let loose in a world of intrigue, weighing life against death, innocence against guilt, providence against the accidents of fate, eternity against time. We know him better than the Elizabethans did, for we have had more time to study and contemplate his powerful presence.

While we know him better, we also know him less. We do not always know what he is saying, not because Shakespeare is unclear but because words have changed their meaning and because we are unfamiliar with Elizabethan secondary meanings. When Hamlet says, "Get thee to a nunnery!" to Ophelia, we are shocked, and we are even more shocked when we learn from a Shakespearean scholar that the word "nunnery" could also mean "a house of prostitution." What did Shakespeare mean? A nunnery could also mean a nunnery. It is possible that he meant both nunnery and house of prostitution, and was entirely indifferent which interpretation was given to it: in both cases Hamlet consigned the beautiful and high-spirited Ophelia to an earthly perdition.

The words change their meaning, and so does Hamlet. He is always fluid. We know him and we do not know him. He is all around us, and he is inside us. In our own corrupt age, when chairmen and presidents are all liars, we have no difficulty in recognizing King Claudius for what he is. We have more difficulty in recognizing Hamlet for what he is, though he lives in all of us. We share his perplexities, his doubts, his obsession with justice, his knowledge of the ways of intriguers, his disillusion and disenchantment. The luckiest among us share his grace and courage.

On the Elizabethan stage he was highly visible, highly ornamental. It has been the custom since Victorian times to represent him in a loose white shirt open at the neck, black breeches, black hose, with something in him of the student and something of the prisoner on the way to execution; a shadowy presence as he leans against a column and all the more powerful for being shadowy. He wears black like a good Puritan; we cannot imagine him wearing a plumed hat or making a significantly graceful bow in the presence of the king. We remind ourselves that in Elizabethan times there existed an entire catalogue of graceful salutations with intricate variations depending upon the exact relationship between the subject and the king. Some went down on their knees, some bent their knees, some made flourishes, some bowed their heads and lifted their clasped hands, as though in prayer. When Princess Elizabeth, the daughter of King James, greeted the young Elector Palatine, her husband to be, by falling on her knees, lifting the hem of his gown, and kissing it, she was acting in accordance with the principles of protocol as they existed at that time. These gestures were studied, choreographed, refined to the utmost degree. Court ceremonial consisted of a dance of gestures. If we suddenly found ourselves in the court of Queen Elizabeth, we would be startled beyond measure by the elaboration of ceremonial greetings which would seem to us totally meaningless.

The actors in the Elizabethan theatre knew these gestures by heart, for they were very close to the court. They had access to the courtiers and wore their cast-off clothing. The grandees who sat on three-legged stools on the stage were their acquaintances, sometimes their friends and protectors. The beautiful fourteen-year-old boy who played Ophelia was likely to have need of a protector. The actors came from all layers of society, but by the time they were performing leading roles they had the manners of the aristocracy and were more aristocratic that the aristocrats. The roaring boys could mimic the aristocracy to perfection. Since Shakespeare crowded his plays with kings and queens, earls, dukes, princes, barons, and knights, they had ample opportunity to display their aristocratic skills.

On July 26, 1602, the printer James Roberts entered in the Stationers' Register a book called *The Revenge of Hamlet, Prince of Denmark*, "as it was lately acted by the Lord Chamberlain his servants." We may suppose it was first performed in the late spring or early summer of that year and that it was written in the early months of the year. Essex lost his head a year earlier, and there is clearly something of Essex, and more of Southampton, in Hamlet, just as there is something of Queen Elizabeth in Queen Gertrude. Lord Burleigh would serve as a model for Polonius and any young foppish courtier would serve as Osric. Queen Elizabeth was dying, the succession was not yet determined, and the people were desperately afraid that civil war would break out at her death. Something was rotten both in England and in Denmark. As Queen Elizabeth's long reign came slowly to an end, there came once more, as during the period following the defeat of the Armada, a failure of nerve amid mounting uncertainties, and *Hamlet* was the fruit of those days of uncertainty.

On the evidence of the play Shakespeare was not one of those who lost their nerve. He was far from being a man of doubt and irresolution. He worked his way through a complex plot with two separate subplots with astonishing self-reliance and a formidable sense of direction. *Hamlet* is remarkable because it is at all times urgent, vital, accomplished; Prince Hamlet speaks with authority; there is never a moment when Shakespeare loses the thread of his story. In half of Shakespeare's surviving plays we come upon moments when he obviously does not know where the story is going and uses artifice or a comic scene or simply marks time until he has resolved the difficulty. In *Hamlet* the prince is steadfast and there is no faltering. If he delays an action, it is for good cause. If he feigns madness, it is to shock his enemies into revealing their plans or simply to shock them in order to put them off base. If he rejects Ophelia, it is for the very good reason that he suspects her father and her brother are plotting against him. If he seems to be cowardly, it is sometimes because only the courageous can afford to appear cowardly. At all times on the stage he carries a long sword and can defend himself against all comers. Coleridge spoke of "that aversion to action which prevails among those as have a world in themselves." The verdict is unjust. He had no aversion to action but was averse to action at the wrong time, and although he possessed worlds in himself, it was not for those interior worlds that he fought, but for a kingdom. His task therefore was to ensure that the plotters carried out their intrigues in such a way that their plots turned against them. His assumed madness, his "antic disposition," gave him an advantage they could never possess. He could stop his madness whenever he chose; the conspirators suffered their own kind of madness but did not know how to stop, how to enter the real world where all conspiracies are seen as madness. The glint of madness in Hamlet's eyes is deliberate and contrived, painted on the eyeball. He has only to weep and the paint will fall off:

> Yet I,
> A full and muddy-mettled rascal, peak,
> Like John-a-dreams, unpregnant of my cause,
> And can say nothing—no, not for a King
> Upon whose property and most dear life
> A damned defeat was made. Am I a coward?
> Who calls me villain? Breaks my pate across?

Plucks off my beard and blows it in my face?
Tweaks me by the nose? Gives me the lie i' the throat
As deep as to the lungs? Who does me this?
Ha!
'Swounds, I should take it. For it cannot be
That I am pigeon-livered and lack gall
To make oppressions bitter, or ere this
I should have fatted all the region kites
With this slave's offal. Bloody, bawdy villain!
Remorseless, treacherous, lecherous, kindless villain!

So Hamlet speaks when his antic disposition is laid aside, when he is alone with his own thoughts, his own world. If he calls himself "a dull and muddy-mettled rascal," that is his affair and we are not compelled to believe him. This young Hamlet already has gray threads in his beard. He knows he is not a coward; nor is he mad, though he has been driven to the edge of madness. He knows, above all, that he is called upon to rescue the country from a "remorseless, treacherous, lecherous, kindless villain."

It is Kafka's world: the smell of the graveyard is everywhere, and the intriguers, like ghosts, haunt the palace corridors. Like K. in Kafka's novel he is driven to seek the judge who will sit in judgment over him. Unfortunately he is himself the judge. The tension in the play derives from the judgment that implacably hovers over him by courtesy of a moral law which is never revealed to him. He must make his own law.

In this way Hamlet becomes our brother, for now more than ever we are in this predicament: the Queen is dying, there is no government, the code of laws is rotting away in a forgotten cupboard. Grace, intelligence, agility of mind, and courage remain. They are not enough. Hamlet goes to his doom with open eyes, knowing at every moment of the game where he stands. He has useful allies. Horatio, his friend, is a man who has Hamlet's virtue of clear-sightedness. He sees the world as it is, without coloring it with his own passions:

Blest are those
Whose blood and judgment are so well commingled
That they are not a pipe for fortune's finger

To sound what stop she please. Give me that man
That is not passion's slave, and I will wear him
In my heart's core, ay, in my heart of hearts,
As I do thee.

But one Horatio is never enough, even if he is always by one's side. "You will lose this wager, my lord," he says shortly before the final duel with the poisoned sword. He had known all the time that the wager would be lost.

The Fool in the miracle play achieves new status in *Hamlet*. Hamlet and Ophelia both play the Fool when it serves their purposes; they are adepts at it; they play to each other until the thread breaks. They play the Fool for different purposes but chiefly for survival; and their folly is so rich in terror that it takes the breath away. When we read the play carefully, we realize that their folly is only another way of speaking clearly and to the point. When Polonius says: "Do you know me, my lord?" and Hamlet answers: "Excellent well, you are a fishmonger," his folly has nothing to do with the fact that "fishmonger" also means "pimp." His folly accuses and has work to do besides startling the audience with a new music. Polonius is the first to realize that there is method in this madness. Hamlet offers Polonius a lesson on growing old, while reading from a book:

> The satirical rogue says here that old men have grey
> beards, that their faces are wrinkled, their eyes purging
> thick amber and plum-tree gum, and that they have a
> plentiful lack of wit, together with most weak hams. All of
> which, sir, though I most powerfully and potently believe,
> yet I hold it not honesty to have it thus set down; for
> yourself, sir, shall grow old as I am, if like a crab, you
> should go backward.

Hamlet's folly is designed to open wounds; Ophelia's folly is made of even sterner stuff. She accuses and dooms even as she scatters flowers around the court, presenting them to people she once loved—Claudius, Gertrude, and her brother Laertes:

> There's rosemary, that's for remembrance—pray you,
> love, remember—and there is pansies, that's for thoughts.

There's fennel for you, and columbines. There's rue for
you, and there's some for me; we may call it herb of grace
o' Sundays: O you must wear your rue with a difference.
There's a daisy. I would give you some violets, but they
withered all when my father died. They say a' made a good
end.

She is throwing flowers on their graves and at the same time
reminding them of their errors and their crimes: rue in flower
language being the symbol of repentance and daisies of faithless-
ness, and so with all the others. They are Persephone's flowers,
harbingers of death. Suddenly the air is cold and the flowers have
the smell of graves.

Flowers in Shakespeare are nearly always sacramental. The
long catalogues of flowers are offerings on an invisible altar; every
flower is holiness. He comes with armfuls of flowers promising a
heavenly peace beyond all understanding; the flowers wither, and
there are only the agonized dead roots and torn, crumpled petals.
One moment we are in heaven and in the next moment we are in the
world of corruption and decay. But at least we have been to heaven
in his company.

In his portrayal of Ophelia Shakespeare has depicted the first of
those divine young women whose appearance in the later plays is
sometimes perplexing because so much innocence is demanded of
them. They come to us as though they were in their bridal robes,
veiled and shimmering, offering themselves with the eagerness that
derives from innocence, with unearthly beauty. Perdita, Imogen,
Marina, Miranda, are sexless as Blakes' angels, and almost they are
children, though they have knowledge of the world. They are
among the most ambiguous of creations, being innocent and wise in
their years, human and inhuman, as though they were born from
the flowers of the woodland, having no human parentage but
somehow acquiring humanity from contact with the world.

When Jean Simmons played Ophelia to Laurence Olivier's
Hamlet, a flower sprang to life. It is inconceivable that anyone
could play the role better. She possessed the unearthly beauty that
the role demanded, and the age-old wisdom of innocence, and the
wildness of youth. She was, of all the characters, the most credible.

Felix Aylmer's Polonius was too mannered; neither King Claudius nor Queen Gertrude seemed to be in full control of their roles, and while Olivier possessed the vigor and audacity demanded of the prince, and a wonderful Elizabethan effrontery, and studied elegance, and indeed all the qualities necessary to portray the physical person of Hamlet, he could never be taken for a philosopher. It is inconceivable that he ever studied at Wittenberg or ever read a complete book. Olivier portrays Hamlet's impatience, his determination to wrest certainties out of confusion, but when Ophelia describes the ruin of his mind we wonder what she is talking about.

> O what a noble mind is here o'erthrown!
> The courtier's, soldier's, scholar's eye, tongue, sword
> The expectancy and rose of the fair state,
> The glass of fashion and the mould of form,
> The observed of all observers—quite, quite down!
> And I, of ladies most deject and wretched,
> That sucked the honey of his musick'd vows,
> Now see that noble and most sovereign reason
> Like sweet bells jangled, out of time and harsh:
> That unmatched form and feature of blown youth
> Blasted with ecstacy.

This is Ophelia's judgment on Hamlet after long and careful consideration. It is, of course, precisely the judgment that Hamlet wanted her to make. He knows her well, contrives pitfalls and traps for the sheer pleasure of watching her fall into them. Ophelia is much more penetrating, and much more herself, when she does not make set speeches on a prince whose youth is blown and blasted with madness, but instead describes him minutely with the keen eye of a girl wonderstruck by his strange presence.

Enter Ophelia

Polonius.   How now, Ophelia? What's the matter?
Ophelia.   O my lord, my lord, I have been so
                    affrighted!
Polonius.   With what, i' th' name of God?

Ophelia.   My lord, as I was sewing in my closet,
   Lord Hamlet, with his doublet all unbrac'd,
   No hat upon his head, his stockings foul'd,
   Ungarter'd and down-gyved to his ankle,
   Pale as his shirt, his knees knocking each other,
   And with a look so piteous in purport
   As if he had been loosed out of hell
   To speak of horrors—he comes before me.

Polonius.   Mad for thy love?

Ophelia   My lord, I do not know,
      But truly I do fear it.

Polonius.   What said he?

Ophelia.   He took me by the wrist and held me hard;
   Then goes he to the length of all his arm,
   And with his other hand thus o'er his brow
   He falls to such perusal of my face
   As he would draw it. Long stayed he so.
   At last, a little shaking of mine arm,
   And thrice his head thus waving up and down,
   He raised a sigh so piteous and profound
   As it did seem to shatter all his bulk
   And end his being. That done, he lets me go,
   And with his head over his shoulder turned,
   He seemed to find his way without his eyes,
   For out of doors he went without their help
   And to the last blended their light on me.

In Olivier's film, Ophelia speaks the words while simultaneously we see the scene enacted. This could not have been done on the Elizabethan stage, where the audience is summoned to see the scene unfolding in the imagination. Yet Hamlet retreating blindly and looking over his shoulder at the stunned Ophelia is something to marvel at. Here, quite early in the play, we see Hamlet, the actor, acting madness. Often it is a very solemn madness, like a slow dance of shadows, and sometimes through the voice of the madman there can be heard the authentic tones of the Fool, the idiot keeper of the world's mysteries, who is far from being a madman:

Hamlet.   Nay, then, let the Devil wear black, for I'll have
a suit of sables. Oh heavens! Die two months ago, and
not forgotten yet? Then there's hope a great man's
memory may outlive his life half a year. But, by 'r lady,
we must build churches then, or else shall he suffer not
thinking on, with the hobbyhorse, whose epitaph is "For
oh, for oh, the hobbyhorse is forgot."

Ophelia.   What means this, my lord?

Hamlet.   Marry, this is miching malleco. It means
                    mischief.

Mischief, of course, is what the play is all about, and there is
mischief, too, in the play within the play. Hamlet, as the contriver of
mischief against a greater mischief, knows exactly what he is doing,
and it would be strange if he did not. "For oh, for oh, the hobbyhorse is forgot" is one of the central themes of the play. A "hobbyhorse" was a prostitute. The Elizabethans, fascinated by prostitution, possessed nearly a hundred names for prostitutes. They were
glimmerers, bawdy baskets, morts, autem morts, walking morts,
kinching morts, doxies, dells, and kinching coes. In Hamlet's eyes
Queen Gertrude had prostituted herself, was no better than a
prostitute. Ophelia, too, was a prostitute, because she served Polonius, who served King Claudius. He had declared war against prostitution, not only in the sense that he warred against the two women
but also in the sense that he warred against a world that accepted
the prostitution of society with equanimity. *Hamlet* is many things;
it is among other things a tract against the usurpation of power by
people who had prostituted themselves.

The play scene shows Hamlet as playwright, stage manager,
metteur en scène, and principal actor, although it is often forgotten
that he is himself the leading character in the play called *The
Mousetrap* concerning a murder done in Vienna. "Gonzago is the
Duke's name; his wife, Baptista." The words of the play are a
mockery; the action is all. The target of the play is as much Ophelia
as Queen Gertrude and King Claudius. Indeed, during the course of
the play, Hamlet makes an aside to Ophelia which is more cruel
and heartless than anything said by King Claudius.

Ophelia.   You are a good chorus, my lord.

Hamlet.   I could interpret between you and your love: if I could see the puppets dallying.

Ophelia.   You are keen, my lord, you are keen.

Hamlet.   It would cost you a groaning to take off my edge.

Those last words are so harsh that they are breathtaking: he is threatening rape, or worse. It is one of those moments when one imagines he is not completely in command of himself. His actors are about to show in charade how the King his father was poisoned and he is in a state of murderous excitement. A few moments later, as the King, the Queen, Polonius, and Ophelia all rise and stalk out of the chamber, having understood the play only too well, Hamlet is himself again.

Again and again Hamlet plays with the thought of his own madness, that madness which he will not admit, which he half hopes for, although it would be intolerable to him to know he was mad; and he knows he is not mad. Yet when speaking to the Queen almost as violently as when he spoke to Ophelia, he states the case for madness with high spirits:

Let the blunt King tempt you again to bed.
Pinch wanton on your cheek, call you his mouse,
And let him for a pair of reechy kisses
Or paddling on your neck with his damned fingers
Make you to ravel all this matter out,
That I essentially am not in madness
But made in craft. 'Twere good you let him know,
For who that's but a Queen, fair, sober, wise,
Would from a paddock, from a bat, a gib*
Such deep concernings hide? Who would do so?
No, in despite of sense and secrecy,
Unpeg the basket on the house's top,
Let the birds fly, and like the famous ape
To try conclusions in the basket creep
And break your own neck down.

*Tomcat.

The ape had crept into the basket and thought it would grow wings. This was his madness. But there were other kinds of madness, and in Hamlet's view it was madness for the Queen to tell King Claudius that he was "not in madness but made in craft." The Queen knew her son well; the King did not know; and it was better that he should be left guessing.

Madness hangs over the graveyard scene like a cloud. Hamlet is too much in love with death to permit it to stray for long outside his imagination. "Bestial oblivion" he calls it, and sees no reason to temper his opinion.

> *Hamlet.*　A man may fish with a worm that hath eat of a
> king, and eat of the fish that hath fed on that worm.
>
> *Claudius.*　What dost thou mean by this?
>
> *Hamlet.*　Nothing, but to show you how a king may go to
> a progress through the guts of a beggar.

But with the graveyard scene the fencing game with death acquires another dimension which is much harder and more implacable. Berowne in *Love's Labour's Lost* says: "I move with laughter in the throat of death." This is the purest abstraction and convinces nobody. The graveyard scene convinces like no other scene in Shakespeare. Hamlet, pale with consciousness of death, stares into the eyes of a skull, at all the nothingness and emptiness of a skull, and comes to the inevitable existential conclusions:

> *Hamlet.*　Alas, poor Yorick! I knew him, Horatio: a fellow
> of infinite jest, of most excellent fancy; he hath borne me
> on his back a thousand times; and now how abhorred in
> my imagination it is—my gorge rises at it. Here hung
> those lips that I have kissed I know not how oft. Where
> be your gibes now? Your gambols, your songs, your
> flashes of merriment, that were wont to set the table on a
> roar? Not one now, to mock your own grinning? Quite
> chop-fallen? Now get you to my lady's chamber, and tell
> her, let her paint an inch thick, to this favor she must
> come. Make her laugh at that. Prithee, Horatio, tell me
> one thing.

Horatio.   What's that, my lord?

Hamlet.   Dost thou think Alexander looked o'this fashion i'
th' earth?

Horatio.   E'en so.

Hamlet.   And smelt so? Pah!

Horatio.   E'en so, my lord.

Hamlet. To what base uses we may return, Horatio! Why
may not imagination trace the noble dust of Alexander
till he find it stopping a bunghole?

One reads and hears such scenes with the smell of rotting flesh in
the nostrils. He has no illusions about the falling sparrows. He
hates death with all the withering passions of his soul, and he loves
it with the same withering passion. Hence his great soliloquy has an
astonishing power of survival, although it has been repeated so often
that the stuffing has been shaken out of each word. Every time he
speaks it, he speaks it afresh. It is significant that though Alexander
has become clotted dust in a bunghole and Yorick is nothing but a
poor mud-stained skull, Shakespeare has given them the dignity due
to them.

How much of Shakespeare is there in Hamlet? Keats, writing to
Sarah Jeffrey on June 9, 1819, thought that Hamlet and Shakespeare were twins, that Hamlet was more like Shakespeare than
any of his creations. "The middle age of Shakespeare were all
clouded over," Keats wrote. "His days were not more happy than
Hamlet's who is more like Shakespeare himself in his common
every day life than any other of his characters." Keats may have
been thinking of Hamlet when he wrote that Shakespeare was "a
miserable and mighty poet of the human heart."

Shakespeare, the actor and playwright, fits tightly in Hamlet's
skin. Hamlet, the actor and playwright, sometimes finds himself
bowing respectfully to Shakespeare. They are inseparable as they
walk along the ghostly ramparts of Elsinore, and they know each
other well. Shakespeare was never so vivid as when he wrote about
Hamlet. The intense self-consciousness, the skepticism, the quick-
ness of mind, the slipping in and out of dreams, the furious pace of
action, and the abrupt, jolting pauses, the sensuality joined to a

passionate intellectuality—all this is personal to Shakespeare. The violence of Hamlet is also Shakespeare's violence. But Shakespeare was like those Indian gods who fly across the heavens, and every dust mote falling from their garments creates a world.

Hamlet is a violent presence but he is also the ghost playing out the ghost's dreams, obedient to the ghost and to no one else. That a mind so skeptical should believe in ghosts is itself something of a mystery. There is something ghostlike in him, vaporous and unreachable; his strength comes from his habitual communion with the dead. Of all the people he loves—he loves very few—the one he loves most is his father's ghost.

Keats wrote of Shakespeare: "He could do easily Man's utmost." And Man's utmost, until he wrote *King Lear*, was *Hamlet*.

The
House on
Silver Street

AT SOME TIME IN 1602 Shakespeare left the house he had been living in on Bankside and took rooms in a house in Cripplegate belonging to Christopher Mountjoy, a refugee from France, a wigmaker and tiremaker. Mountjoy's wife, their daughter Mary, and his brother Noel were living with him and in addition there were a number of apprentices who in the fashion of the time lived on the premises. The house, which stood on the corner of Mugle Street and Silver Street, was fairly large, as we can see from Aggas' map drawn about 1560. There were two gable roofs above the two-storied building and a pentice, or penthouse, which was probably occupied by Shakespeare. Here in this somewhat secluded corner of London in the shadow of London Wall he spent the next five or six years.

It was a time when wigmaking and tiremaking could provide a good living. Fashionable women followed the Queen in wearing wigs, often dyed in bright colors and adorned with jewels cunningly arranged on "tires," which were the foundation pieces for the hair's intricate adornments. Children with beautiful hair were in constant danger of being waylaid and having their hair shaved from them to supply the ever-growing market. Poor women could sell their hair for a good price. Horsehair, too, could be manufactured into wigs. But the real wealth came from tiremaking, which involved setting jewels and whatever took women's fancy in the hair in such a way that it would enhance their appearance. Philip Stubbes, the puritanical pamphleteer, inveighed against fashionable women and especially against their hairdo. "At their hair, thus wreathed and crested," he wrote, "are hanged bugles, ouches, rings, gold, silver, glasses and such other gewgaws." "Ouches" were brooches, "bugles" were glass beads. All these had to be set on gold and silver wires which could be seen glinting in those piled-high pyramids of hair.

Shakespeare had little patience with wigs and it may be assumed that he had even less patience with tires. He wrote in *The Merchant of Venice*:

> Look on beauty,
> And you shall see 'tis purchased by the weight;
> Which therein works a miracle in nature,
> Making them lightest that wear most of it:
> So are those crisped snaky golden locks
> Which make such wanton gambols with the wind,
> Upon supposed fairness, often known
> To be the dowry of a second head,
> The skull that bred them, in the sepulchre.

What then was Shakespeare doing in the house of a wigmaker and tiremaker?

He may have met Christopher Mountjoy when buying wigs for his company, since the actors necessarily wore wigs. A boy actor playing Queen Cleopatra or Lady Macbeth would wear a sumptuous tire, a thing of dropping pearls and flickering jewels, for historical characters on the Elizabethan stage wore the finery of their own time. Mountjoy was well known. He had sold wigs to the Queen. He was something of a character, loud and volatile, a heavy drinker and a man who ran after women, possessing a pretty wife who in her turn ran after other men. Simon Forman, physician and astrologer, recorded in his daybook a number of her visits to him, the first taking place on November 22, 1597, when she asked him, as an astrologer, whether she would find two gold rings and the French coin she had lost from her purse while walking along Silver Street one day in September. This seems to have been a visit of exploration to see whether she could trust him with more grave affairs. Ten days later she visited him for advice as a physician. She explained that she was suffering from stomach pains and headaches, weakness in the legs, and dizziness. Simon Forman concluded that she was pregnant and wondered whether she could be able to keep the baby for its full term, concluding, perhaps by the astrological signs, that the decisive day would come in seven weeks when there would either be a miscarriage or she would be able to proceed to a normal birth but with some difficulty and danger. In March 1598 she came to him again with a question: she wanted to know whether her husband would fall sick. This was a little sinister, for soon her lover, Henry Wood, living in nearby Swan Alley, came to Simon Forman with a question which he stated on behalf of his mistress. Marie Mountjoy wanted to know "whether the love she bears will be altered or not." Presumably she was asking about her love for Henry Wood. Then it was the turn of Mrs. Wood, who came to Simon Forman to ask whether she should keep shop with Mrs. Mountjoy. The oracle replied: "They may join, but take heed they trust not out their wares much, for they will have loss." It appears that Mrs. Wood and Mrs. Mountjoy were both growing weary of their husbands and were thinking of setting up shop together.

Henry Wood, a mercer and dealer in cloth, a highly respected member of the community, was having an affair with the wife of another highly respected member of the community. He knew Simon Forman well and had consulted him often on business transactions. His love affair seems to have ended badly, for there is a cryptic note in the daybook reading: "Mary Mountjoy alained," meaning that she was concealed or had vanished from sight, presumably to have her baby or a miscarriage.

Christopher Mountjoy also consulted the physician-astrologer. Once when he contemplated employing two new apprentices, he asked whether they would be good workers. Their names, as Simon Forman wrote them, were Gui Asture and Ufranke de la Coles, probably Guy Astruc and François de la Chaux. Simon Forman gave his verdict based on their astrological signs.

Shakespeare was a lodger in a house where a good many things were going wrong. Christopher Mountjoy worked his apprentices hard from early morning until late in the evening, for hours in Elizabethan workshops were very long. He was miserly and paid them very little. He was unruly and boisterous, far from being the typical sober-minded Huguenot refugee in England. His wife was thirty-four when Shakespeare became a lodger, and his daughter was about fourteen.

What attracted Shakespeare to the house may have been the mischief and the violence of the place where beautiful women were continually coming to buy wigs and jeweled tires; there were lengthy sittings, assignations, mysterious comings and goings, all those artifices which we associate with a high-priced couturier of the present day. Only the very wealthy could afford tires, and tiremaking was Christopher Mountjoy's main business. Shakespeare had the actor's temperament: he enjoyed being at the center of the whirlwind. Here he could meet the women of Elizabeth's court and go to bed with them, or he could bring home one of his roaring boys without raising the slightest suspicion. The tiremaker's house was both open and secret. It was a passageway to the court and a place of refuge from the theatre. He was on intimate terms with the Mountjoys and on at least one occasion did them a delicate service. He was more than a lodger; he was a part of their household.

In this house and in Stratford he wrote his greatest tragedies.

We should not be surprised that Shakespeare would choose to live in a house like this. We sometimes imagine him to have been one of those men who live calmly above the tempest, remote from life while reflecting its infinite varieties. This is to forget the evidence of his passion, his piercing intensity, his fierce sensitivity, his almost unbearable openness to sensations. His mind worked with lightninglike speed and his senses were perpetually in motion. He would go wherever the excitement was, and when he had had enough he would shut the door and write his poetry.

In the Mountjoy house there was always as much excitement as he needed. It was a turbulent family dominated by a mischievous master and a wanton mistress. There were always half a dozen apprentices, all of them French and speaking French. There were vats filled with brilliant dyes, brocades and silks, carefully guarded stores of gold and silver wire, a treasure chest of jewels and semi-precious stones, and all the bustle of a thriving business. It was colorful, charming, noisy, and absurd.

We would know nothing at all about Shakespeare's life with Christopher Mountjoy if it had not been for the formidable researches of an American professor, Charles William Wallace, who settled down in the Public Record Office in London with the deliberate intention of discovering documents that would help to bring Shakespeare to life. In 1909, after three years of work, he found among the great parchment bundles of depositions, petitions, witness lists, decrees, and summonses of the Court of Requests in the Public Record Office twenty-six documents recording the case of *Belott* v. *Mountjoy* which came to the attention of the court in 1612, though it related to matters that had occurred many years earlier. Wallace once calculated that he pored over three million documents in his search for material throwing light on Shakespeare. He was cantankerous and quarrelsome, believed that other scholars were always ready to pounce on the fruit of his researches, and that the full weight of Shakespearean scholarship had fallen on his shoulders. In later life he abandoned scholarship altogether and became a highly successful oil engineer, making a fortune from oil wells in places where no one suspected that oil existed. Luck was with him when he drilled for oil, and it was with him when he searched among the documents in the Public Record Office.

The *Belott* v. *Mountjoy* case was never resolved and was a complete waste of time for everyone connected with it, including Shakespeare. Etienne Belott was an apprentice tiremaker who began working for Christopher Mountjoy in 1602. His mother was a French widow then married to Humphrey Flood, who described himself as "one of his majesty's trumpeters," which meant that he was one of the couriers sent by the government abroad. In France he met Etienne's mother, married her, and brought her with her infant son to England. He signed the articles of apprenticeship by which Christopher Mountjoy became virtually the boy's father. By all accounts Etienne was a good worker and Christopher Mountjoy had no complaints against him. Two years later Mary Mountjoy, the daughter, appears to have fallen in love with him, but serious difficulties arose. Etienne insisted on a dowry of about fifty pounds to be paid on the day of marriage or shortly afterward and upon a legacy of two hundred pounds on the decease of Christopher Mountjoy. That some kind of arrangement had been entered into was known by many friends of the family, including Shakespeare, but there was no written agreement. Etienne was cautious, refusing to entertain marriage until he received assurances concerning the dowry and the legacy. Shakespeare was asked to act as the go-between and he appears to have convinced Etienne that everything would be worked out. He liked Etienne, describing him as "a very good and industrious servant" who "did well and honestly behave himself." There were many conferences between Etienne and Shakespeare. The marriage took place at St. Olaph Church, Silver Street, on November 19, 1604.

The dowry, however, was never paid, and Etienne, by now a very skilled tiremaker, left the Mountjoy house six months later and started his own business. His father-in-law claimed later that they parted in a friendly manner and that he gave them parting gifts: about twenty pounds' worth of household goods and equipment for pursuing their trade. He told them he would leave them "the most part of the estate which God should have blessed him with at the time of his death," but said nothing about the dowry. In fact he appeared to be incensed by their departure because they were setting up in competition with him. Etienne claimed that the parting present from Christopher Mountjoy consisted of an old feather bed, one old feather bolster, a thin green rug, two blankets, two pairs of sheets, a bobbin box, two trunks, two pairs of little scissors, and a few other odds and ends. It was not enough and he wanted more.

Marie Mountjoy, the wife of Christopher, died in 1606, and soon the young married couple moved back to the house in Silver Street and became partners in the business. Whenever they mentioned the dowry, the old man flew into a temper. "I'll rot in prison before I give you a single groat," he said. He threatened to cut them off in his will. In his misery and loneliness he became abusive, and soon Etienne and Mary left him and started up their own business again. Christopher Mountjoy was turning more and more to debauchery. Finally in 1612, having lost all patience, Etienne began the lawsuit for the dowry and the promise of the legacy. Witnesses were summoned to give their testimony. The servant, Joan Johnson, testified in his favor. Daniel Nicholas, a neighbor, testified that he had gone to Shakespeare at Etienne's request "to understand the truth how much and what the defendant did promise to bestow on his daughter in marriage" and learned from Shakespeare that Christopher Mountjoy had promised "fifty pounds in money and certain household stuff." Although it was clear that the promise had been made, Daniel Nicholas could not remember whether Christopher Mountjoy had ever set a date for carrying it out. This, of course, was the crux of the matter. Christopher Mountjoy evidently did make the promise but carefully avoided any plain statement about the time when he would pay over the money and he put nothing in writing. Daniel Nicholas also provided the useful information that Christopher Mountjoy not only owned the house in Silver Street but also "divers leases near about where he dwelleth and at Brainford worth by report thirty pounds per annum," which meant that he was a considerable property owner and far from being a pauper.

William Eaton, a nineteen-year-old apprentice, testified that Shakespeare told him he had been asked by Christopher Mountjoy to talk to Etienne and to urge him to take Mary in marriage. Shakespeare on behalf of Mountjoy had said there would be dowry. Unfortunately William Eaton had clean forgotten how much money was involved.

George Wilkins, described as a victualler, swore that he had known Christopher Mountjoy and Etienne for about seven years. After the marriage of Etienne and Mary he had taken them into his house. He remembered that they had brought with them some household goods given to them by Mary's father, "for which this deponent would not have given above five pounds if he had been to have bought the same."

Now, we know a good deal about George Wilkins, who played many roles. He was a novelist, a playwright, a pamphleteer, an innkeeper, the keeper of a bawdy house, as well as a victualler. He collaborated with Shakespeare in the writing of *Pericles* and with Dekker in writing *Jests to Make you Merrie*. He appears as an unsavory character in many court records, nearly always being accused of aggravated assault against women. Once he kicked a pregnant woman in the belly. On another occasion, according to the records, "he hath outragiously beaten one Judith Walton and stamped upon her so that she was carried home in a chair." This happened three months before he gave his deposition on behalf of Etienne. He was a violent and melancholic man whose misery sometimes flared up into a kind of poetry. In his play *The Miseries of Inforst Marriage* one of his characters says: "What's this world like to? Faith, just like an inn-keeper's chamberpot, receive all waters, good and bad. It had need of much scouring."

Humphrey Flood, Etienne's stepfather, was another witness. Christopher Mountjoy complained that when he accepted Etienne as an apprentice, it was on condition that he would not have to pay for the boy's clothes and linen. This condition had not been obeyed and he was forced to pay for these clothes and linen out of his own pocket. Humphrey Flood testified that on the contrary Etienne had been well supplied. He had himself given the boy three suits and two cloaks while Etienne's mother had given him "good store of linen with apparel." He claimed that Christopher Mountjoy had been miserly and that Etienne's mother "was fain many times to give him money and to pay the barber for cutting the hair of his head."

Christopher Weaver, a mercer of Silver Street, had some interesting things to say about Christopher Mountjoy's finances, which were apparently in a chaotic state, for though he had a good business he had little understanding of money. He had borrowed twenty pounds "and had neither paid the principal nor interest money due for the same." He had sold his plate and some household stuff; he had borrowed more money; he was receiving rent from "a sojourner in his house with him," who was evidently Shakespeare, but did not know how much rent was being paid. Weaver also deposed that he had attempted to act as go-between between the father and the son-in-law but old Christopher Mountjoy was adamant: he would have nothing to do with him.

Shakespeare's testimony follows the form of previous testimonies. He is asked to answer five questions known as "interrogatories," his answers are taken down by a law clerk, corrections are made as they go along, and then the document is signed. Here is Shakespeare's testimony:

> William Shakespeare of Stratford upon Avon in the county of Warwick, gentleman, of the age of forty-eight years or thereabouts, sworn and examined the day and year abovesaid, deposeth and sayeth

1. To the first interrogatory this deponent sayeth he knoweth the party's plaintiff and defendant, and hath known them both as he now remembreth for the space of ten years or thereabouts:

2. To the second interrogatory the deponent sayeth that he did know the complainant when he was a servant with the defendant and during the time of his the complainant's service with the said defendant he the said complainant to this deponent's knowledge did well and honestly behave himself, but to this deponent's remembrance he hath not heard the defendant confess that he had got any great profit and comodity by the service of the said complainant, but this deponent saith he verily thinketh that the said complainant was a very good and industrious servant in the said service. And more he cannot depose to the said interrogatory:

3. To the third interrogatory this deponent sayeth that it did evidently appear that the said defendant did all the time of the said complainant's service with him bear and show good will and affection toward the said complainant, and that he hath heard the defendant and his wife divers and sundry times say and report that the said complainant was a very honest fellow: and this deponent sayeth that the said defendant did make a motion unto the complainant of marriage with the said Mary in the bill mentioned being the said defendant's sole child and daughter and willingly offered to perform the same if the said complainant should seem to be content and well like

thereof: And further this deponent sayeth that the
said defendant's wife did solicit and entreat this
deponent to move and persuade the said complainant
to effect the said marriage and accordingly the
deponent did move and persuade the complainant
thereunto: And more to this interrogatory he cannot
depose:

4. To the fourth interrogatory this deponent sayeth that
the defendant promised a portion in marriage with
Mary his daughter, but what certain portion he
remembereth not, nor when to be paid, nor knoweth
that the defendant promised the plaintiff two hundred
pounds with his daughter Mary at the time of his
decease. But sayeth that the defendant was dwelling
with the defendant in his house. And they had
amongst themselves many conferences about their
marriage which afterward was consummated and
solemnized. And more he cannot depose:

5. To the fifth interrogatory this deponent sayeth he can
say nothing touching any part or point of the same
interrogatory, for he knoweth not what implements
and necessaries of household stuff the defendant gave
the plaintiff in marriage with his daughter Mary.

Willm Shaksper

Although Shakespeare's testimony is couched in the formidable
legal language of the time, which is still our own legal language, we
can watch him attempting to clarify three things: he had taken part
in the negotiations toward the marriage of Mary and Etienne, he
did not know or had forgotten how much money was involved, and
he had a high opinion of Etienne, "a very good and industrious
servant in the said service." He wanted to be scrupulously fair. He
crossed out important words concerning financial affairs because he
felt he might have gone too far. He had no desire to hurt Christopher Mountjoy. He says clearly that it was Marie Mountjoy,
Christopher's wife, who asked him to be the intermediary and he
performed this duty and was successful.

All this effort ended in nothing. The Court of Requests finally decided it had no jurisdiction in the case and on June 30, 1612, issued an order transferring the matter to the French Church in London. The hearing, ordering, and final determination of the case would be left in the hands of "the reverend and grave overseers and elders" of the church, and whatever decision they came to would be confirmed by the Court of Requests.

Christopher Mountjoy and Etienne Belott were examined by the church elders the following month. Etienne's assertions could not be proved by any witnesses. Nevertheless, the church elders were prepared to hear arguments and to set up a body of four men who would represent the plaintiff and the defendant. Abraham Hardret and Gedeon de Lanne represented Christopher Mountjoy, while David Carperau and Pierre Bauvais represented Etienne. The church elders were less than pleased with the litigants. The brief notice in the records of the church ends with the note: "Both of them, father and son-in-law, are debauched."

In May 1613 the church elders handed down their decision. Ordered to pay twenty nobles to Etienne, Christopher refused, pleading poverty. They did not believe he was poor, nor did they believe in his good faith. They believed he had fathered two bastards on his serving girl, and not merely was he lewd and debauched but he was one of those who had rebelled against God, therefore he was excluded from the French Church. They urged the parishioners to pray for his soul that God might touch his heart and bring him back to a state of grace. Shakespeare's friend and landlord was described as a man of hardened depravity, a man whose lewdness and adulteries had caused him to be brought before the magistrates, a man of rebellious temperament, without honor and beyond the reach of the church. They called him *dérégle, débordé, endurci*, as though there were not enough words in their vocabulary to describe someone so profligate and so hateful, and they washed their hands of him.

Nothing more is heard about Christopher Mountjoy after February 1614 when the church elders decreed that in spite of all their exhortations he had shown no inclination toward repentance and therefore must be publicly expelled from the church. It is possible that he never knew he had been expelled because he never went to church. Thereafter he vanishes from history. Etienne also vanishes, to emerge again briefly in July 1646, in the reign of King Charles

II, when he wrote his will on his deathbed. There is no mention of
Mary or any of the children he had from her: presumably they had
all died. He mentions his "loving wife Thomazine," a Dutch
woman who gave him three daughters. He bequeathed twenty
shillings to the Dutch Reformed Church in Haarlem. He gave each
of his daughters twenty pounds and the rest of the estate went to his
wife, who became the executrix of the will. The industrious apprentice had outlived Shakespeare by thirty years.

Silver Street in the time of Shakespeare had some pretensions to
affluence. John Stow, the antiquary, speaks of its "divers fair
houses," and he thought the street derived its name from the
silversmiths who dwelled there. Monkswell Street, usually called
Mugle Street, was well known for the twelve almshouses built by
Sir Ambrose Nicholas, who had been a mayor of London and made
his fortune through the salt trade. The poor people in the almshouses were each given seven-pence a week and five sacks of coal
every year, the endowment having been made in perpetuity. Sir
Ambrose Nicholas was the father of Daniel Nicholas who gave his
testimony in the *Belott* v. *Mountjoy* case. When Shakespeare
stepped out into the street, he saw the old pensioners sunning
themselves. Six more almshouses had recently been built nearby
from the endowment of Robert Rogers, a leather merchant who died
in 1601, leaving his vast fortune to the poor of London. Robert
Rogers and Sir Ambrose Nicholas were merchant princes whose
munificence was long remembered.

This corner of Cripplegate was somewhat secluded, for it was
situated where London Wall makes a sharp turn in the direction of
the river, and the high walls therefore had the effect of enclosing it
like protecting arms. The main traffic of the city passed it by and it
was less noisy than other parts of London, which may be one of the
reasons Shakespeare chose to live there. Richard Field and his
French wife, Jacqueline, lived on Wood Street, which was only a
block away. John Heminge and Henry Condell lived on Aldermanbury Street, which was one street farther on. They were fellow
actors and perhaps Shakespeare's closest friends. Heminge had at
least twelve children, Condell had nine, and they were both church
wardens in St. Mary Aldermanbury Church, where there was
exhibited for no reason that anyone could remember the shankbone

of a human giant. Both men were deeply religious, kindly and unassuming. Together, with Ben Jonson's help, they published the first collected edition of Shakespeare's plays "to keep the memory of so worthy a Friend, & Fellow alive, as was our Shakespeare."

On the way to see Richard Field, Shakespeare may have dropped into the house of Launcelot Young, whose possessions included the head of King James IV of Scotland. It was a very unlikely thing for a man on Wood Street to own. Launcelot Young came by the head more or less honestly. The King fought bravely at the battle of Flodden Field in 1513, but the English troops outfought him. He was killed and his body was placed in a lead casket and removed to London and then to a monastery at Shene in Surrey. At the dissolution of the monasteries, the buildings passed into the hands of the Earl of Suffolk, who had no use for the King's corpse and tossed it into an old lumber room. Later some workmen on the earl's estate amused themselves by cutting off the head.

Then it happened that a certain Launcelot Young, a master glazier to Queen Elizabeth, living in Wood Street, acquired the head, presumably when he was working on the conversion of the old monastery into the earl's palace. Young observed that the head smelled sweet and was quite dry, as though mummified. There was a full head of red hair, there was a full red beard, the face was still recognizable. Stow says he was very pleased with his possession of the head and "he kept it for its sweetness." At some later time he gave it to the local sexton for burial in a charnel house.

Such is the account that Stow drew from Launcelot Young, the only man who could have told him the whole story. The sweet-smelling head of the bravest and most intelligent of the Scottish kings vanished from sight to reappear in Shakespeare's stage direction in *Macbeth:* "Thunder. First Apparition: an Armed Head." It is likely that Shakespeare once held the head of James IV in his hands, and from this came the inspiration for the bloody heads in *Macbeth*.

Shakespeare, deeply immersing himself in Holinshed's history of England, inevitably acquired an antiquarian's interest in London. He learned, for example, that King Edward the Confessor used to pass through the Cripple Gate, and by his saintly presence he cured the cripples and gave sight to the blind. On nearby Adle or Athel

Street there was once the palace of King Athelstan who ruled Anglo-Saxon England. Closer at hand, opposite Mountjoy's double-gabled house, was Nevil's Inn, built on the gardens once owned by the powerful Nevil family. At the top of Monkwell Street was the wonderfully ornate Barber-Surgeons Hall, the headquarters of the very honorable Company of Barber-Surgeons which supervised the work of all the doctors and barbers of London. Henry VIII gave it a charter and the event was recorded in a famous painting by Hans Holbein, showing the King standing while the barber-surgeons kneel in their livery and gaze up at him worshipfully. The painting hung in the company's great hall. When Shakespeare was writing his play *Henry VIII*, he had only to walk a little way up Monkwell Street to see the King in all his glory.

So we may imagine Shakespeare at ease in Cripplegate, lodging with the tempestuous Mountjoys, being a part of the family and at the same time a little remote from them. He was affectionate toward them and amused by them. He spent many years with them, going in and out of the house as he pleased, leaving them when his company went on tour or when he felt it necessary to return to Stratford; their scandalous love affairs were nothing to him and he delighted in their baubles and their studious devotion to the art of making wigs and jeweled headdresses, which must be among the most frivolous articles of wearing apparel ever conceived. The Mountjoys talked French, and he therefore acquired a good working knowledge of their language.

His lodgings were on the third floor under one of the two gable roofs. The shop and the workshop were on the ground floor, with dining room and bedrooms on the floor above. His own rooms, consisting of a bedroom and a study, would be well furnished, with tapestries on the walls, a carpet or two, good furniture, and gilt candlesticks. Through four mullioned windows he would look out on the traffic of Silver Street and gaze across the road at St. Olaph's church, and if he craned his neck a little he would see spires and towers of twenty other churches breaking the skyline. He was not living in luxury like Lord Southampton, but he was living as he wanted to live. In Stratford he was landowner, farmer, cultivator of flower gardens, subdeacon of Holy Trinity Church. In London he was actor, playwright, sharer in the company's fortunes, and often a stage manager and trainer of actors. That he was living in the house of a French refugee showed how little he was attached to London, how easily he was able to spread his wings and fly away.

All around him were his friends. In St. Giles, Cripplegate, beyond the wall, not more than a few minute's walk away, lived Ben Jonson, Thomas Dekker, and Anthony Munday, who would all enter into the mainstream of English literature. Nathaniel Field and William Johnson, the actors, lived in St. Giles. Ben Jonson knew Silver Street and he must have known about the Mountjoys, for in his play *The Silent Woman* he had one of his characters say: "All her teeth were made at Blackfriars; both her eyebrows in the Strand, and her hair in Silver Street."

In the Great Fire of London all of Cripplegate went up in flames. Nothing was left except the names of the streets. Today with the help of old maps and the researches of John Stow we can re-create in our imaginations a square mile of London, on both sides of London Wall, where there lived for a brief period the greatest galaxy of dramatic talent to emerge since the time of the ancient Greeks. The dramatists of Cripplegate changed the world of drama, and nearly all of them were in hailing distance of the house on Silver Street.

The
Rebellion of
Lord Essex

THERE WAS ONE SUBJECT on which the Elizabethans
spoke with bated breath—rebellion. It was familiar to them,
and very close to them. It was in the air they breathed, smelling of
gunpowder and blood and charred timbers, a fetid smell that was
nevertheless curiously exciting. In the five hundred years since
William of Normandy conquered England there had been twenty
rebellions, and few kings died in their beds. The threat of rebellion
obsessed Elizabeth and it obsessed the greatest of her subjects, who
in his historical plays wrote about it endlessly.

Rebellion came in many forms, in many disguises. First, in its
most portentous form, came rebellion against God. There were
those who despised God, and about these rebels John Calvin spoke
in *The Institution of Christian Religion*, saying that their pride in
self led to gluttony for evil, and having rejected God they permitted
themselves to commit every crime under the sun. So Calvin says:
"They were despisers of God which when they heard that sin
abounded to the end that grace might more abound, by and by
objected, We will then abide in sin that grace may abound." Calvin

examines the despisers minutely; he knows them well and his horror of them is expressed in phrases that seem to be carved in bronze. The Elizabethans were aware of these arguments, for *The Institution of Christian Religion*, in more than fifteen hundred closely printed pages, appeared in an English translation in 1574 and was widely distributed. Rebellion against God was the crime of crimes, the crime that shook the earth's foundations and the walls of heaven. And in Calvin's view, it was a crime that was being committed daily by the popes, who were all Antichrist in disguise. Although Calvin stretched his net wide, he offered no sure way to combat the rebels against God.

The English Church under Elizabeth was more pragmatical. It was not concerned so much with the rebels against God as with the rebels against the Queen's majesty. Every Sunday in every church one of the official sermons printed in a book called *Certain Sermons or Homilies appointed to be read in Churches* was read from the pulpit. Many of these sermons were written in the early years of Elizabeth's reign; three of them were written by Cranmer, who was martyred under Bloody Mary, and one each by Ridley and Latimer, who were also martyred. Among the homilies written later in Elizabeth's reign were no fewer than three deploring disobedience and willful rebellion, for the times demanded that extreme measures be taken to prevent rebellion. Shakespeare knew these sermons well, for he echoes them in his historical plays whenever the question of rebellion is raised in long speeches, and kings and bishops adjure the rebellious to put down their swords and accept the providential order. Repeatedly in these sermons two arguments are displayed. First, the prince has a divine right to rule, and therefore he must be obeyed, even if he is a bad prince. The second argument is more convincing: rebellion leads to disorder, misery, famine, the usurpation of all the ordinary rights of the people. We read in the third part of the homily against disobedience and willful rebellion:

> Rebels are the cause of infinite robberies and murders of
> great multitudes, and of those also whom they should defend
> from the spoil and violence of others; and as rebels are
> many in number, so doth their wickedness and adultery
> amongst such persons as are agreeable to such wickedness,

are (as they indeed be most damnable:) what are the forcible oppressions of matrons and men's wives, and the violating and deflowering of virgins and maids, which are most rife with rebels? How horrible and damnable think you are they? Now besides that, rebels by breach of their faith given, and the oath made to their Prince, be guilty of most damnable perjury: it is wondrous to see what false colours and feined causes, by slanderous lies made upon their Prince and the councillors, rebels will devise to cloak their rebellion withall, which is the worst and most damnable of all false witness bearing that may be possible. For what should I speak of courting and desiring of other men's wives, houses, lands, goods and servants in rebels, who by their wills would leave unto no man any thing of his own?

On Sundays, through interminable drowsy sermons, Englishmen, who went to church or else paid a fine, awoke out of their slumbers when the parson read the homily against rebellion. The homilies against adultery, gluttony, drunkenness, brawling, lewdness, and the wearing of fine clothes were abysmally boring; the homily against the fear of death scarcely mentioned death at all; the homily against whoredom merely promised God's extreme displeasure of all fornicators; but the homily against rebellion was made of sterner stuff. Here the work of "our ghostly enemy the Devil" could be observed at close quarters. If they knew anything about English history, Englishmen knew that rebellion meant civil war, the burning of towns, starvation, misery, pestilence, and plague, the whole country impoverished and beggared.

The authors of the homily against rebellion went to great pains to defend the prince who "committed small errors," pointing out that the populace had lawful means of redress, and even when these means proved ineffective, it was still the duty of the Christian citizen to obey his superiors and especially to obey the prince. It was not an entirely satisfactory argument and left too many questions unanswered. Elizabeth, who was head of the Church and head of the nation, made pronouncements but rarely answered questions. In the winter of 1600 she was physically failing, although she still danced nimbly and could still dominate any company by the force of her intellect. Her skin was ravaged, her heavy eyelids drooped, her mouth was awry. Old age was unkind to the queen with the blackened teeth and red-gold wig.

The government of England was in the hands of Sir Robert Cecil, who was nearly always able to flatter the Queen into agreement with his proposals. He was determined to rule over an England which was quiet and peaceful, united against her external enemies. Dissensions within the country were mercilessly suppressed; Catholic priests were hounded; informers were paid handsomely. As Elizabeth drew closer to death, Cecil became more and more determined to be the permanent power behind the throne, the one man who would be able to choose her successor in the best interests of England. To acquire this power, it was necesary to destroy or neutralize everyone who was closer to the throne than he was.

Robert Devereux, Earl of Essex, was one of the very few who could be said to be close to the throne. He had been the Queen's favorite, and perhaps her lover. He was the darling of the poor, for he promised them whatever they wanted, and of scholars and poets, whom he rewarded liberally. He had led a charmed life. His father, the first Earl of Essex, died when he was ten years old; his mother married the Earl of Leicester, who adopted the boy, introduced him to the court, and saw that his handsome stepson would be noticed by the Queen. The young Earl of Essex, at nineteen, accompanied Leicester on his campaign to the Netherlands and distinguished himself at the battle of Zutphen, where Sir Philip Sidney was killed. He was already a marked man, obviously destined for great positions. Leicester was the Queen's conscience, her eyes and ears, the companion of her festivities. When he died in 1588, the year of the Armada, Essex was twenty-two years old. He seized his opportunity, succeeding his stepfather in the Queen's affections.

Essex was well built, broad-shouldered, with a thick reddish-gold beard, and large blue eyes which gave him an appearance of great openness and sincerity. He was passionate and direct, almost incapable of subterfuge. In 1590 he married the widow of Sir Philip Sidney, knowing full well that the Queen would be incensed but believing that he possessed sufficient power and prestige to ride out

the storm. The Queen forgave him, and then sent him off to
command troops in France. It was an English expeditionary force
sent to aid Henri IV against Spain. He seems not to have distinguished himself and was recalled to London, spending the next
years at court in attendance on the Queen. In 1596 he was one of
three men in command of the naval expedition against Cádiz, which
proved to be wonderfully successful, for the English troops paraded
through the city and knighthoods were conferred on the bravest
inside Cádiz Cathedral: later the Queen would complain that the
booty acquired during the occupation of the city made it hardly
worth the trouble. In fact, the Cádiz expedition was brilliantly
planned and executed for the purpose of delivering a profound
psychological shock on the Spaniards and succeeded beyond expectation. In 1597 Essex was appointed Master of the Ordnance, and
went off with Sir Walter Raleigh on an ill-fated expedition to
waylay the Spanish galleons sailing from the Rio de la Plata back to
Spain, laden with treasure. Essex missed the galleons by a few
hours, quarreled with Raleigh, lost his nerve, and returned to
England with nothing accomplished and no longer enjoying the
Queen's favor. She relented in the following year and made him
Earl Marshall of England. Sir Robert Cecil observed that when
Essex lost favor from the Queen, he enjoyed greater favor from
ordinary Englishmen. It was not that they were rebellious, but they
were growing impatient. Cecil found an informer who claimed that
Essex said he was determined to become King of England—had
said this even before the Cádiz expedition—and he was also telling
the common people and the soldiers that none cared for them but
himself. The second statement was as treasonous as the first.

Then Cecil played his best hand. He tricked Essex into accepting
the Lord Deputyship of Ireland with orders to put down the bloody
rebellion of the Earl of Tyrone, and he had no difficulty in persuad-
ing the Queen to set aside money for the enterprise and to sign the
appropriate documents. Fierce, vulnerable, and still youthful at
thirty-three, Essex set out for Ireland after making a processional
tour through the center of London, riding along Cornhill and
Cheapside and all the main highways, while the people cheered and
shouted: "God save your Lordship, God preserve your honour!"
Essex, who was dressed plainly, accepted their acclamations with

good grace. It was one of those calm blue cloudless days that sometimes come at the end of March. He rode off to Islington, and suddenly the sky was black with thunderheads, the lightning flashed, the thunder roared, and the rain and hail came down. The people who had come out to cheer him scattered into their own homes, wondering whether there was some augury in the thunderstorm.

Shakespeare knew Essex through his connection with the Earl of Southampton. He rejoiced in the spectacle of the youthful viceroy setting forth to reconquer Ireland. He was writing *Henry V*, and was nearly at the end of the play, when he decided to compare Henry V's triumphal return to England after conquering France with Essex's expected return to England in a few months time. In the prologue to the last act of *Henry V* he wrote:

> But now behold,
> In the quick forge and working house of thought,
> How London doth pour out her citizens!
> The mayor and all his brethren in best sort,
> Like to the senators in th' antique Rome,
> With the plebeians swarming at their heels,
> Go forth and fetch their conqu'ring Caesar in;
> As by a lower but loving likelihood,
> Were now the general of our gracious empress,
> As in good time he may, from Ireland coming,
> Bringing rebellion broached on his sword,
> How would the peaceful city quit
> To welcome him.

The Londoners cheered, Shakespeare applauded, the Queen seemed to be relieved that Essex would be usefully employed out of her sight, and the Earl of Southampton, appointed Master of the Horse to Essex—in those days Master of the Horse was equivalent to a present-day chief of staff—amused himself with some skirmishes against the rebels and writing letters to his wife. For reasons of her own Elizabeth did not want Southampton in Essex's company and had expressly forbidden the appointment. Essex tested the Queen's resolution; her will prevailed; Southampton later returned to London. The only person at ease in all these follies was Sir

Robert Cecil, who was beginning to open the black bag into which Essex would disappear.

Essex fell into all the traps laid for him. He was like someone sleepwalking to his death: brilliant, intelligent, handsome, a Hamlet figure, at odds with himself and with the Queen, he found himself in the midst of conspiracies over which he had no control. There could have been no Prince Hamlet without the Earl of Essex. He had wealth and vast ambitions and great power, but lacked reason. The Earl of Tyrone invited him to a parlay at a ford on the river Lagan on the borders of Ulster to discuss a truce. On the English side only Essex and Southampton rode into the ford, and Southampton was given the task of ensuring that their conversations were not overheard. Someone overheard them, or perhaps Cecil's informers invented the treasonous words Essex is supposed to have uttered to Tyrone about the succession, speaking of his own correspondence with James VI of Scotland and his own claim to the throne. Cecil would say later that Essex had thought of himself as the future King of England as far back as 1594. Soon after the meeting with Tyrone, it was agreed that there should be a six-week truce renewable by letter and that the troops should remain in their present positions: an advantage to Tyrone who was waiting for reinforcements from Spain to launch an annihilating attack on the English. And then, realizing that his mission to Ireland had hopelessly failed and that his enemies were pursuing their intrigues against him in England, Essex decided on an impulse to leave Ireland and to throw himself on the Queen's mercy.

It was, of course, the worst thing he could have done; the Queen, though she had once loved him, was merciless to those who disobeyed her orders. He had been ordered to destroy the Irish rebels; instead he had formed a truce with them. He arrived at Nonsuch Palace in the morning of September 28, 1599, entered the palace, marched straight into the Queen's bedchamber, and surprised her while she was still dressing and preparing her toilet. Travel-stained, kneeling at her feet, he talked to her in private for some minutes about his tumultuous affairs and she appeared to calm him. She dismissed him, then called for Sir Robert Cecil, and together they discussed the strange and sudden arrival of Essex in England. Later that day Essex had another audience with the Queen. This time her mind had hardened, and later that night she ordered him confined in his quarters. Sir Robert Cecil had the pleasant task of drawing up a bill of particulars against the former Viceroy of Ireland.

On the following day the Privy Council met and charged Essex wth six crimes. First, he had disobeyed the Queen's instructions in returning to England. Second, he had written many presumptuous letters to her from Ireland. Third, he had acted in Ireland contrary to his instructions. Fourth, he had left Ireland in a rash manner. Fifth, he had dared to force his way into the Queen's bedchamber. Sixth, he had created far too many knights in Ireland against the Queen's express instructions. In fact, he had created more than seventy knights, more than the Queen had created in the same period. The privy councilors took only fifteen minutes to announce their verdict. The Queen sentenced him to imprisonment at York House. There he remained under guard for nearly a year, writing imploring letters to the Queen, requesting an audience or even to be permitted to stand mute in her presence as long as he could set eyes on her, but her heart had hardened against him. He formerly possessed the farm of sweet wines which enabled him to build a vast income based on a tax on all sweet wines sold in England. Elizabeth refused to renew it. He was suffering from melancholy, fevers, the stone, and even more serious ailments. He was permitted to return to Essex House, closely watched by Cecil's spies and informers. Whatever he said about the Queen was reported to Cecil the same day, and he said many things that were better left unsaid. He said, for example: "The Queen is an old woman, who is no less crooked and distorted in mind than she is in body." The Queen had been hard on him; now she was like granite. With Cecil at her side, quietly and patiently, she awaited the time when Essex would accomplish his own downfall.

She did not have long to wait. Essex was keeping open house for his supporters, disaffected soldiers, puritans, and the riffraff of London. The Earls of Southampton, Worcester, Sussex, Rutland, and Bedford called on him, offered him their assistance and loyalty, flitting in and out of the great house like messengers of doom. Essex compiled a list of 120 noblemen, knights, and gentlemen who could be counted upon to help him overthrow the government of Elizabeth. He was talking rebellion before he had any clear idea how to rebel. In debt, sick with the misery of his estrangement from the Queen, in acute agony from the stone, he held court, plotted, took more and more men into his service, listened to every whisper of gossip, and somehow convinced himself that the people of London would rise at his command.

In those dark days of winter a visitor to London might have thought nothing had changed, but in fact everything was changing. The mood of Londoners, humorous and rough-tempered, in love with brawls and in fear of riots, cold sober every morning and drunk by evening, quick to shout applause or blame, was becoming unnaturally quiet and restrained; and especially near Essex House people were behaving strangely. The blind beggar thrusting his clap box under your nose was neither blind nor a beggar; the old man browsing amid the bookstalls of St. Paul's Churchyard was not reading for his own enjoyment; instead he was searching for inflammatory pamphlets and he carried the warrant of the Archbishop of Canterbury which permitted him to arrest any bookseller selling forbidden books; and the young gallant who was escorting his lady to Goldsmith's Row in West Cheap was not looking for necklaces: he was trying to find out whether there had been any large sales of gold coins in recent days, and from Goldsmith's Row he would saunter along to the shops of the armorers and swordsmiths to find out whether they were making any unusually large sales of weapons. In a small building in Westminster lists of names, dossiers, bundles of letters, were being examined by a small, hunchbacked, spindly man whose purpose was to know every detail of the conspiracy, which was not so much being instigated by Essex as forming around him. He was the contagion which attracted all other contagions, or the vacuum which all the conspirators of England rushed to fill.

For centuries anyone who wanted to learn the news of England had only to walk at noonday along the huge nave of St. Paul's Cathedral. Here businessmen congregated, hucksters sold their wares, whores paraded, lawyers set up their offices, soothsayers and astrologers consulted the spirits and the stars, and young gallants in all their finery strode about for the pleasure of being seen. Here you would find a scribe to write a love letter or a poet to compose a poem on order. In this great open mall, which thousands entered every day, the life of London was concentrated. Foreign agents listened carefully to the rumors that sped along the nave of St. Paul's, and Sir Robert Cecil's informers were always in attendance. Now there were more of them.

Shakespeare was at this time living on Bankside close to the Globe Theatre. He could feel the waves of excitement washing across the river. He observed from his upper windows the passing of the coal scows, the barges, the wherries filled with passengers, the merchantmen gliding in their stately fashion to their berths, and he could hear the terrible loud clattering of the waterwheel recently installed under one of the nineteen arches of London Bridge. He could also see the heads of traitors stuck on poles above the great gateway of the bridge on the Southwark side. Paul Hentzner, the German traveler, wrote that there were thirty heads standing there in 1598, and there were probably more of them in the following years. From Bankside, too, Shakespeare was able to observe the strange movements of ships outside Essex House, some passing very close, others anchored in midstream, and still others arranged in a kind of holding pattern in case Essex should attempt to escape. All the traffic to the house was being observed. While the sun slanted into his study window and the grays and browns of London shone on the opposite shore, while the swans moved in procession on the river and the gulls swooped down, he would inevitably find himself gazing at Essex House with the high walls and the arched water-stairs facing him across the river.

Rebellion was in the air: it was almost tangible. It was a subject Shakespeare probably knew more about than any other person in England. He knew the motives and the causes, he knew the intricacies and the labyrinthine ways, for he had studied rebellion minutely in his historical plays. In his own handwriting, in the play *Sir Thomas More*, there survive some 150 lines composed by him. They include a speech delivered by Sir Thomas More to the rebels, warning them that they would ultimately devour one another after they had destroyed the monarchy:

> *More.* Grant them removed, and grant that this your noise
> Hath chid down all the Majesty of England,
> Imagine that you see the wretched strangers,

Their babies on their backs and their poor luggage
Plodding to the ports and coasts for transportation,
And that you sit as Kings in your desires,
Authority quite silenced by your brawl,
And you in ruff of your opinions clothed,
What had you got? I'll tell you. You had taught
How insolence and strong hand should prevail,
How orders should be quelled, and by this pattern
Not one of you should live an aged man;
For other ruffians as their fancies wrought
With selfsame hand, self reasons and self right
Would shark on you, and men like ravenous fishes
Would feed on one another.

There was no doubt where Shakespeare's sympathies lay. He detested and feared rebellion: not that kings were virtuous but that rebels were worse. Rebellion by its very nature ordained that the rebels would rebel against each other.

On the morning of Friday, February 6, 1601, a small group of Essex's men came to the Globe Theatre. They were Lord Monteagle, Sir Charles Percy, Sir Jocelyn Percy, and three others. They spent some time talking to the actors, sounding them out, and urging them to put on Shakespeare's *Richard II* on the following day. Being told that it was stale and that the actors would get little money for it because few would come to see it, and it was not in the current repertory, they were offered forty shillings "more than their ordinary." Augustine Phillips, the actor who was also manager of the playhouse, agreed to their terms, little realizing that he was putting himself in danger. He probably knew very little about his distinguished visitors and it never seems to have occurred to him that while Essex House was being transformed into an armed camp, there might be some people who would want to see *Richard II*, which describes the deposition and killing of the King. He accepted the money and on the afternoon of the following day the play was performed.

On that afternoon many of the conspirators from Essex House dined at Gunter's Tavern near Temple Bar and then made their way across the river to the Globe. Sir Gilly Merick, Sir Christopher

Blunt, Henry Cuffe, all three of them being very close to Essex, attended the play with about a dozen other members of the Essex circle. Sir Francis Bacon wrote later that Sir Gilly Merick brought "a great company" to watch the play, but since it was in his interests to exaggerate every aspect of the rebellion when it occurred, it is not necessary to believe him. If he had brought "a great company" to the play—say, fifty men—Sir Gilly Merick would be tipping his hand. It is more likely that he took a small group and they all went to the Globe not in order to advertise themselves but in order to savor in advance the downfall of the monarch.

On Saturday, February 7, 1601, the day when the play was performed, Essex made his final arrangements. There had been some talk of an escape to Wales and the capture of Welsh ports and the possibility that the army in Ireland could be ferried over the Irish Sea to take part in the uprising, and of the intervention of King James VI of Scotland on the side of the rebels, and of whether they should seize both the Tower of London and the Palace of Westminster, where the Queen was in residence, and of what they would do with the Queen once they had captured her. But all these questions were still unresolved at dawn on the following day, and the final arrangements could be stated very simply: Essex and his followers would seize power, no matter how, depending on the circumstances of the moment.

Sir Walter Raleigh, who was Captain of the Guard, sent a message to Essex House, saying he wanted to talk with Sir Ferdinando Gorges, one of Essex's most trusted lieutenants, before it was too late. More messages were exchanged, and it was decided that Raleigh and Gorges should meet on a boat moored in the river "upon equal terms." Raleigh warned Gorges that he would be ruined if he continued to remain at Essex House. Were there any armed men preparing an uprising? Gorges appears to have said that the armed men were there only for the protection of Essex and no uprising was intended.

At ten o'clock in the morning the Queen sent four of her most important dignitaries to Essex House. They were Sir Thomas Egerton, who was Lord Keeper of the Privy Seal; Sir William Knollys, Comptroller of the Queen's Household; Lord Chief Justice Popham; and the Earl of Worcester. They all knew Essex well, and

Egerton in particular had a fatherly feeling for the red-haired young nobleman who was causing so much trouble. The main gates of Essex House were closed; they were led through a wicket gate which permitted them to enter one by one, and in this way it was possible to cut off their armed escort. Inside the courtyard Egerton saw a confused rabble, all armed to the teeth, with Essex and Southampton in the midst of them. In the name of the Queen, Egerton asked Essex the cause of this extraordinary gathering. If he was expecting to ward off any hurt or injury, then surely it would be better to seek redress, the Queen would help him, he had only to submit himself to her, as he had done in the past. Essex answered with a tirade: there were people who would murder him in his bed, false documents had been written in his name, he was being condemned without fair trial. Egerton promised that he would receive a full hearing and justice, but first he must disarm his men. Voices from the crowd were saying: "They are abusing you!" "They will betray you!" "Cast the Great Seal out of the window!" The four dignitaries were in great danger, and at Southampton's suggestion they were quickly led away into Essex's study, the conversation continued for a few minutes, and suddenly Essex realized that time was running out. Meanwhile he had hostages on his hands. Egerton, Knollys, Popham, and Worcester became his prisoners, for he ordered them locked in his study, set a guard over them, and marched out into the courtyard with Southampton at his side to lead his armed followers to victory. The great gates swung open, the mob poured out into the Strand, and at this moment Essex made his greatest error. If he had turned left, he might have captured Westminster Palace and the Queen, who was defended by a royal guard consisting of two hundred men armed with halberds. Instead he turned right and marched on the city of London, hoping and believing that the Londoners would rally to his flag and acclaim him regent and then they would all march together on Westminster.

It was about ten o'clock in the morning when the desperadoes strode along the Strand and into Fleet Street, shouting: "For the Queen! For the Queen!" The Londoners cheered them, thinking there must have been a reconciliation between the Queen and Essex, and that she had appointed him to ride in this triumphant manner through the city, for there could be no other explanation for this tumultuous cry: "For the Queen!" They little realized they were witnessing a rebellion by the earls of England such as might have been seen in the Middle Ages. Essex and Southampton were both earls; they were accompanied by the Earls of Bedford and Rutland; seven or eight lords were with them. They were all sleepwalkers: neither Essex nor the other lords had worked out any concrete plans.

One of Essex's visitors the previous day had said: "All London is with you, and Sheriff Smith will have arms waiting for you." In his folly Essex believed the man, who was perhaps an agent of Sir Robert Cecil. Essex and his followers passed through Ludgate, one of the great gates leading into the city, and soon they were marching through Cheapside, which was thronged with people heading back to their homes after listening to the morning sermon at St. Paul's Cathedral. It was Sunday; the churchbells were ringing; the Londoners liked to wear their best suits and walk in the streets with their families and friends on Sundays. Essex's followers shouted: "Murder! There is a plot against the life of my Lord Essex!" No one was paying much attention. Essex pushed eastward toward Fenchurch Street, where there were many armorer's shops and where Sheriff Smith had his residence. The shops were closed, and Sheriff Smith had just been warned against Essex by Sir William Rider, the Lord Mayor of London. Instead of giving arms to Essex, he was ordered to send them at once to Whitehall; and when Essex arrived at his house, Sheriff Smith set about entertaining him, sitting him down to table and offering him good ale, for he was sweating hard and appeared to be exhausted. Sir Charles Blount and a small group of desperadoes broke into an armorer's shop nearby, but all he could find were half a dozen old halberds. Essex left the house on Fenchurch Street and rode back to Ludgate; a chain had been thrown across the street, and soldiers were on guard. As he tried to make his way through the gate, there was a skirmish; Sir Charles Blount was wounded and captured; one of the soldiers was killed, and Essex's page, known as "young Mr. Tracy," was also killed. Two bullets went through Essex's hat. His task now was to reach Essex House as soon as possible, and at Queenhithe he took a boat that brought him to the waterstairs of his own house. There he discovered that in his absence his four captives—Egerton, Knollys, Popham, and the Earl of Worcester—had all been freed. Only about forty of the two hundred followers who set out with him in the morning were still with him.

Essex had often thought of dying in glory on the battlefield; he was more likely to die ingloriously in his own house, for guns were being wheeled into position, companies of loyal soldiers were stationed on the landward side of his house, and there were ships on the river waiting to fly in pursuit if he attempted to escape by river to the continent. The brief siege was begun at about four o'clock, when it was growing dark. The Queen and Sir Robert Cecil had given orders that at all costs Essex and Southampton must be captured alive and put on trial. The conspirators debated among themselves whether to die fighting or to surrender. The main gates were broken down, loyal troops poured into the courtyard, there was fighting inside the vast house, the women who included Essex's wife panicked and "filled the place with their shrieks and cries," and Essex and Southampton, separately and together, appeared on the roof to parley and seek terms with their enemies. Finally, at six o'clock in the evening, when it was quite dark, they surrendered. It was decided not to take them to the Tower through the streets of London; there might be demonstrations in their favor. Because a storm was coming up, it would be dangerous to "shoot" the archways under London Bridge. It was decided to keep them overnight in the palace of the Archbishop of Canterbury at Lambeth. Essex, Southampton, and the rest of the conspirators were put on trial. Essex was beheaded on February 25, and for a while the life of Southampton hung in the balance. He remained a prisoner in the Tower through the remaining days of Elizabeth's reign. Sir Gilly Merick, who had attended the performance of *Richard II* at the Globe, was beheaded; Lord Monteagle was made to pay a fine of £8,000, and Sir Jocelyn Percy and Sir Charles Percy paid fines of £500. On the night before the execution of Essex, Shakespeare and his players performed before the Queen at Whitehall.

Four months later the antiquary William Lambarde, who had been appointed Keeper of the Records at the Tower of London, had a strange conversation with Queen Elizabeth. He was showing her the long strips of parchment recording events during the reign of

Richard II. The Queen said: "I am Richard II, know ye not that?"

Lambarde knew she was thinking about the Essex conspiracy and thought it prudent to tell her what he thought of Essex.

"Such a wicked imagination," he said, "was determined and attempted by a most unkind gentleman, the most adorned creature that ever your Majesty made."

The Queen replied: "He that will forget God will also forget his benefactors. This tragedy was played forty times in streets and houses."

She showed no animus against the author of the play or the actors, but she was clearly annoyed and disturbed by the popularity of the play.

In the year of Essex's execution there appeared a strange volume called *Loves Martyr: Or, Rosalins Complaint*, by Robert Chester, a minor poet, who celebrated in his poem the singular beauty and constancy of his patron's marriage. His patron was Sir John Salisbury, whose wife, Ursula, had given him a daughter, Jane. The turgid poem described the metaphysical adventures of the Turtledove (Constancy) and the Phoenix (Love). Robert Chester solicited other poems on the same subject from his friends, and Shakespeare gave him an extraordinary work of eighteen verses which have always delighted and puzzled commentators:

Beauty, truth and rarity,
Grace in all simplicity
Here enclosed in cinders lie.

Death is now the Phoenix's nest,
And the Turtle's loyal breast,
To eternity doth rest.

Leaving no posterity,
'Twas not their infirmity,
It was married chastity.

Truth may seem, but cannot be,
Beauty brag, but 'tis not she,
Truth and beauty buried be.

To this urn let those repair,

That are either true or fair,
For these dead birds sigh a prayer.

No one now knows what the poem is all about, and these last five verses are like magical incantations, beyond all meaning. The accepted legend describes how the Phoenix always rises from her own ashes. Shakespeare has changed the legend: the Phoenix has come to her ultimate death and will never rise again. The poem is the flowering of Elizabethan melancholy in its most precise and most mysterious form.

Some have seen in the poem a reference to Elizabeth and Essex, and nearly everyone is agreed that it cannot have been composed in honor of John and Ursula Salisbury. One has the feeling that for a brief moment Shakespeare unlocked his heart and then closed it again; and if the marvelous poem has any meaning at all, it seems to announce the coming end of an age.

Shakespeare
of the
High Mountains

The Coming
of James

ON MARCH 24, 1603, the old Queen who had ruled over England and Ireland for nearly forty-five years died quietly in her palace at Richmond. For many days she had been sitting on her cushions on the floor, with her eyes glazed and a finger in her mouth, not knowing or caring what was happening around her, caught up in a stupor. She refused food with the result that she was emaciated, skull-like, with sunken eyes and trembling chin, and the courtiers around her were terrified by the changes time had wrought on her. Sometimes, very briefly, the old fire returned. After she had spent ten days on the cushions, Sir Robert Cecil told her she must go to bed to reassure her people that everything was being done to maintain her strength. "Little man, little man, the word 'must' is not to be used to princes!" she replied. "If your father had lived, you durst not have said so; but ye know I must die and that makes thee so presumptuous." And to Lord Nottingham, she said: "My Lord, I am tied with a chain of iron around my neck. I am tied, I am tied, and the case is altered with me."

Sir Robert Cecil was presumptuous as long as she lived; he was the government of England, and all decisions were being made by him. He had decided long ago that James VI of Scotland should be her successor, and in the last hours of Queen Elizabeth he arranged a little charade, himself and the Lord Keeper and the Lord Admiral gathering around her bed and delicately questioning her about the succession. According to the official version she said: "I tell you my seat hath been the seat of Kings. I will have no rascal to succeed me; and who should succeed me but a King?" Sir Robert Cecil asked her to be more precise. "Who, but our cousin of Scotland?" she said, and a little later: "I pray you, trouble me no more."

The official account of her naming of her successor is not entirely credible. Sir Robert Cecil was quite cabable of lying in his own interest. He was in communication with James, and had horses ready to rush the news of her death to James the moment it occurred. "Who, but our cousin of Scotland?" she is supposed to have said, but it is more likely that she remained silent, with her finger in her mouth, to the very end. When she died, the people were stunned: they had no way of knowing what was happening behind the scenes; Cecil acted so deftly and quickly that James was safely on the throne before the people fully realized what had happened. Elizabeth was embalmed and buried in Westminster Abbey. James VI of Scotland, whose mother had been executed by order of Elizabeth, became James I of England and Ireland and the royal possessions beyond the seas.

He was a strange man, awkward and ugly, with a huge tongue which made speaking difficult and a shambling walk which suggested that he was drunk when he was dead sober. He wore a shaggy doublet heavily quilted to protect him from an assassin's dagger. He was a coward to excess, and a voluptuary who fiddled with his codpiece with one hand while caressing the face of one of his handsome young favorites with the other. His bulbous eyes, his slavering mouth, his bandy legs, and his unwashed appearance gave him something of the look of a village idiot, but he had a Scot's canniness. Elizabeth had the splendor of a king, but there was nothing kingly in James except his title. The English found him nearly incomprehensible and were horrified when he filled the court with his Scotch catamites. Sir Robert Cecil made him king, and sometimes regretted the words he had spoken beside the Cross at

Cheapside a few hours after Elizabeth's death when he described James as a man "adorned with all the rarest gifts of mind and body to the infinite comfort of all his people and subjects." A Scotch divine once took the King by the sleeve and called him "God's silly vassal." A French statesman made a large claim for him, calling him "the wisest fool in Christendom."

James rejoiced in his new kingdom and prepared to enjoy his kingship. His leisurely progress to London took over a month. He was entertained magnificently at all the great houses on the road. At Newark he demonstrated his kingly power by ordering that a pickpocket caught in the crowd should be hanged on the spot, without trial. Later it was explained to him that English law proclaimed that a man was innocent until proven guilty and must be tried in a court of law before he may be sentenced to be hanged. James was intelligent enough not to repeat the performance. During the triumphal journey to London he conferred 230 knighthoods, and in the following months he dubbed 600 more; and he created more peerages than Elizabeth had created throughout her long reign. He reached the outskirts of London on May 7, 1603, but the plague had broken out in its most virulent form and he cautiously avoided the city until July 25, which happened to be St. James's Day. Then he was crowned and became, according to the rubric, King of England, Scotland, Ireland, and France, God's Anointed, and Defender of the Faith.

Shakespeare appears not to have grieved greatly over the death of Elizabeth. So much we learn from a collection of pious tributes and memorials in verse collected under the title *England's Mourning Garment*, where we find Henry Chettle pointing an accusing finger at Shakespeare:

> Nor doth the silver-tongued Melicert
> Drop from his honeyed Muse one sable tear
> To mourn her loss who graced his desert.

Melicert means "honeycomb": an apt name for Shakespeare, whose honey was always spilling from the comb.

At irregular intervals during the winter season Queen Elizabeth would demand to be entertained with dramas. James and his Queen, Anne of Denmark, had a voracious appetite for entertainment, encouraged actors, and rewarded them handsomely from the privy purse. James's coming was no benefit to the people but no other king has provided so many benefits to English drama. Sir Robert Cecil, now Keeper of the Privy Seal and given the title of Lord Cecil of Esingdon, taking careful note of James's passionate addiction to the drama, made haste to provide the King with a troupe of players. The patent was executed at the royal palace at Greenwich on May 17, 1603, nearly ten weeks before James was crowned at Westminster. The patent read as follows:

James, by the grace of God King of England, Scotland, France and Ireland, Defender of the Faith, &c, to all justices, mayors, sheriffs, constables, headboroughs, and other our officers and loving subjects greeting.

Know ye that we, of our special grace, certain knowledge and mere motion, have licenced and authorize, and by these presents do license and authorize these our servants, Lawrence Fletcher, William Shakespeare, Richard Burbage, Augustine Philips, John Heminge, Henry Condell, William Sly, Robert Armin, Richard Cowly and the rest of their associates, freely to use and exercise the art and faculty of playing comedies, tragedies, histories, interludes, moralities, pastorals, stage plays and such other, like as they have already studied or hereafter shall use or study, as well for the recreation of our loving subjects as for our solace and pleasure when we shall think good to see them, during our pleasure. And the said comedies, tragedies, histories, interludes, moralities, pastorals, stage plays and suchlike, to show and exercise publicly to their best commodity*, when the infection of the plague shall decrease, as well within their now usual house called the Globe within our county of Surrey, as also within any town halls or moot halls, or other convenient places within the liberties and freedom of any other city, university, town or borough whatsoever within our said realms and dominions, willing and commanding you and every one of you, as you tender our pleasure, not

*Advantage.

only to permit and suffer them herein without any your lets, hindrances or molestations during our said pleasure, but also to be aiding and assisting of them, if any wrong be to them offered, and to allow them such former courtesies as hath been given to men of their place. And also, what further favour you shall show to these our servants for our sake we shall take kindly at your hands.

In witness whereof &c. And these our letters shall be your sufficient warrant and discharge in this behalf.

Given under our Signet at our Manor of Greenwich the seventeenth day of May in the first year of our reign of England, France, and Ireland, and of Scotland the six and thirtieth.

To our right trusty and well beloved Councellor, the Lord Cecil of Esingdon, Keeper of our Privy Seal for the time being.

Such was the long, complex, and far-ranging privilege granted to the actors who would come to be known as the King's Men. It represented a formidable breakthrough, a sudden alteration in their estate. Never before had a company of actors received such an accolade from the reigning monarch. Henceforward they were the King's servants directly responsible to the King.

Exactly how this came about is still unknown. The Earl of Southampton, released from the Tower on April 10 at the King's orders, with all his privileges and possessions restored to him and soon to become a favorite of the court, may have had much to do with it. Cecil's intervention had saved Southampton from the block, and Cecil was responsible for the warrant releasing him from the Tower. But there is no evidence that Cecil showed anything more than a passing interest in drama, and there are only two recorded instances when he attended a performance of Shakespeare's plays. When he realized that James was determined to be entertained, he would have consulted Southampton and asked his advice. In this way, astonishingly quickly, the King's Men came into existence.

Lawrence Fletcher, who heads the list of the players, appears to have been a member of the King's Men *ex officio*. He was "comedian to His Majesty" when James was King of Scotland only. He

was in the King's trust, knew what the King liked, and was likely to
have been an adviser to the players rather than a leading actor. He
appears in no actor lists, and his name does not appear in the list of
principal actors in Shakespeare's plays which appears at the beginning of the First Folio. Yet he was evidently well liked by the
players, and Augustine Philips left "my Fellow Lawrence Fletcher"
a legacy of twenty shillings at his death in 1605.

The King's Men came into existence on May 17, but we hear of
no performances by them during the summer. 1603 was a plague
year, and there were no performances at all in London. The actors
went on tour in the Midlands, and we hear of performances of
Hamlet in Oxford and Cambridge. At some time in 1603, perhaps
in the last days of the year when the plague had abated, Ben
Jonson's play *Sejanus* was performed by "the King's Majesty's
Servants with the allowance of the Master of Revels." One of the
principal actors was Shakespeare, as Jonson stated publicly and
proudly when he printed the play. The actors were listed as
follows:

Ric. Burbage	Will. Shake-Speare
Aug. Philips	Joh. Hemings
Wil. Sly	Hen. Condel
Joh. Lowin	Alex. Cooke

The ordering of the names seemed to be designed to give
Shakespeare prominence. Jonson's earlier play *Every Man in His
Humour*, first acted in 1598, presented a slightly longer list of
principal actors:

Will. Shakespeare	Ric. Burbage
Aug. Philips	Joh. Hemings
Hen. Condell	Tho. Pope
Will. Sly	Chr. Beeston
Will. Kempe	Joh. Duke

In *Every Man in His Humour* Shakespeare has been given pride
of place. He evidently played the lengthy role of old Edward
Knowell, the hoary-headed London gentleman who is driven almost
to madness by the wayward behavior of his son. It was the most
popular of Jonson's plays, and there is a tradition that Shakespeare

was responsible for getting it performed at a time when Jonson was still unknown.

Too much has been made of Shakespeare's intellectual quarrel with Jonson. Their disagreements were on the surface; they had more in common than we sometimes think. They both had lyric genius and vast resources of dramatic power; they were both good actors, though not of the first class; they were both determined to write plays and poems that would endure. Jonson described his own appearance on the stage: "a raw-boned anatomy who walked up and down the stage like a charged musket." According to tradition Shakespeare played an entirely different kind of role: the Ghost in *Hamlet*, Adam the old family retainer in *As You Like It*, perhaps Prospero in *The Tempest*, roles in which he would be permitted to walk gracefully on the stage, announcing with great clarity the wisdom of the ages. He probably played old men's parts even when he was young, and it would never occur to him to march up and down the stage like a charged musket.

Jonson was a heavy-set burly man with red hair and a hot temper; one eye a little lower than the other, a thick nose, sensual lips, features of rugged granite. He had been at various times a scholar at Westminster School, a bricklayer, a soldier, a murderer, a condemned prisoner, an actor, a librarian, and a professor. Imprisoned for his part in writing the play *Eastward Hoe*, he held court in jail and was proud of the fact that his mother came to visit him, bringing with her poison to mix in his drink in case he was condemned, and he told his friend Drummond of Hawthornden that she would herself have drunk the poison if things had gone badly with him. In 1598, the year of *Every Man in His Humour*, Jonson killed the actor Gabriel Spencer in a duel, was arrested, pleaded guilty of manslaughter, was released by benefit of clergy, forfeited all his goods, and was converted to Roman Catholicism, all this in a few weeks.

Shakespeare could read a page of Plutarch and immediately the whole Roman scene would come to life in his imagination. Jonson would set himself to read a library of Latin histories, take careful notes, form a scene out of innumerable minute particulars, and produce a work that smelled of the lamp. Scholarship was his drug, his escape from present pain. It is strange that a man so adventurous should be so addicted to scholarship. He knew intimately vast areas of human experience which Shakespeare knew only in his imagination.

Originally Jonson appears to have collaborated with Shakespeare on *Sejanus*. He wrote in his introduction to the play:

> I would inform you that this book, in all numbers, is not the same with that which was acted on the public stage, wherein a second pen had good share: in place of which I have rather chosen to put weaker (and no doubt less pleasing) of mine own, than to defraud so happy a genius of his right by my loathed usurpation.

This would seem to mean that he had entirely rewritten the passages written by another dramatist, that he was determined not to share the honors with anyone, and that he was perfectly content to write the play in his own words wihout assistance, even if his own lines were weaker. The "so happy a genius" can hardly be anyone but Shakespeare, who was one of the principal actors in the play.

Inevitably Shakespeare and Jonson sometimes quarreled. Drummond of Hawthornden was told by Jonson "that Shakespeare wanted art." Jonson wrote in his *Discoveries:*

> I remember the players have often mentioned it as an honor to Shakespeare that in his writing (whatsoever he penned) he never blotted out line. My answer hath been, would he had blotted a thousand. Which they thought a malevolent speech. I had not told posterity this, but for their ignorance, who choose that circumstance to commend their friend by, wherein he most faulted. And to justify mine own candor (for I loved the man, and do honor his memory (on this side idolatry) as much as any.) He was indeed honest, and of an open and free nature: had an excellent fancy; brave notions and gentle expressions: wherein he flowed with that facility that sometimes it was necessary he should be stopped.

Jonson was writing in 1630, long after Shakespeare's death, and these words suggest a large affection and a long impatience.

Unfortunately Jonson was impatient with nearly everyone. He

was likely to quarrel with his closest friends as vehemently as he quarreled with his bitterest enemies. He quarreled with Inigo Jones, who designed the masques for King James while Jonson wrote the verses, and Inigo Jones, who had the ear of the King, saw to it that Jonson was suitably punished.

This strange King opened his money chests, scattered largess to his actors, and sometimes arranged that they should be in attendance on ceremonial occasions. Thus when Don Juan de Velasco, Constable of Castile, came to England in August 1604 as an ambassador to sign a treaty of peace, Shakespeare and eleven of his fellows, wearing gorgeous red liveries, served as grooms to the constable and his suite. It was a weighty occasion; everything possible was being done to please and impress the visitors. Don Juan was Constable of Castile and Legion, Lord Chamberlain of His Serene Majesty Philip, Duke of Frias, Earl of Haro, Lord of the House of Velasco and of the Seven Infantes de Lara, Chancellor of State and War, Presidente of Italy, and much more. The twelve players received £21.12.0 for their services over a period of eighteen days.

A few weeks after the departure of the Spanish ambassador, *Othello* was performed at court. On December 26, 1604, *Measure for Measure* was performed. King James's appetite for Shakespeare's plays increased during the winter months, for in January and February he saw *The Merry Wives of Windsor, The Comedy of Errors, Henry V, Love's Labour's Lost,* and *The Merchant of Venice,* and he liked the last so much that he saw it twice.

Under King James, Shakespeare's company went from strength to strength. It has been calculated that during the last years of Queen Elizabeth's reign, between 1594 and 1603, the company gave 32 court performances. From 1603 to 1616 they gave 177 performances. It is not to be supposed that the performances were uniformly decorous. The King was noisy and sometimes interrupted the play, or he slept through it, or he applauded too vigorously for comfort. His Scotch courtiers were rude and liable to be drunk. Queen Anne insisted on decorum, which was not always granted to her.

No account of a court performance in King James's time has survived, but we have accounts of the masques in which the King, the Queen, and the courtiers sometimes participated, acting out the roles assigned to them. An anonymous chronicler here describes the last moments of a masque designed by the young Prince Charles in 1610:

> ... There entered dancing two ballets intermingled with varied figures and many leaps, extremely well done by most of them. The Prince then took the Queen to dance, the Earl of Southampton the Princess, and each of the rest his lady. They danced an English dance resembling a pavane. When the Queen returned to her place, the Prince took her for a coranta which was continued by others, and then the gallarda began, which was something to see and admire. The Prince took the Queen for a third time for *les branles de Poitou*, followed by eleven others of the masque.
>
> As it was about midnight and the King somewhat tired, he sent word that they should make an end. So the masqueraders danced the ballet of the sortie, in which the satyrs and the fauns joined. With vocal and instrumental music the masqueraders approached the throne to make their reverence to their Majesties. The masques being laid aside, the King and Queen with the ladies and gentlemen of the masque proceeded to the banquetting hall, going out after they had looked about and taken a turn round the table, and in a moment everything was thrown down with furious haste, according to the strange custom of the country. After this their Majesties withdrew and the ambassadors took leave.

We may imagine that a Shakespearean play presented in the Great Hall at Windsor or in the palaces of Richmond or Hampton Court may have ended equally abruptly with King James halfway during the fourth act announcing that he was tired and wanted to go to bed, and immediately "everything was thrown down with furious haste." He was an exacting monarch with a ferocious temper.

Under King James, Shakespeare prospered exceedingly. He was wealthy and famous; bought land; engaged in the customary law-suits; wrote one or two plays a year; spent his winters in London and his summers in Stratford, where he watched his daughters growing up. In the summer of 1605 he bought from Ralph Huband, a wealthy landowner, his interest in a lease of tithes in Stratford,

Old Stratford, Welcombe, and Bishopton, and paid £440, which was a huge sum in those days. It was a year of great happiness, great financial success, and also of great fear.

A small band of fanatical Catholics, nearly all of them being Warwickshire gentry, was determined to destroy the King and government of England by blowing up the House of Lords on the opening day of Parliament, November 5, 1605. The plot was worked out with great skill and audacity by Robert Catesby, a distant relative of Shakespeare. More than a ton of gunpowder had been stored by the conspirators under heaps of faggots in the cellars of the House of Lords, and it needed only a match to blow the building sky-high. On November 4 the plot was uncovered, and the conspirators who were not immediately arrested ran for their lives. They met in Warwickshire; commissioners followed them into their hiding places; in a running battle Catesby was killed. Eight prisoners including Guy Fawkes, a Yorkshireman, were tortured into making confessions and executed. To this day the Gunpowder Plot is remembered in England every November 5 with the burning of the guy.

Ben Jonson was one of those examined in the course of the inquiry. He testified that he knew some of the conspirators but knew nothing of the conspiracy. Shakespeare was not examined. If he had been, he would have had to testify that he also knew some of the conspirators, and like Ben Jonson he would have been in danger of being placed on the rack until he remembered every last detail of his acquaintance with them. The Arden-Somerville conspiracy brushed very close to Shakespeare; the Gunpowder Plot also brushed very close to him. He was not a Catholic like Ben Jonson; he had powerful protectors at court and was in no real danger. Yet he was close enough to the event to smell the powder and to feel on his nerves the shuddering horror of the attempt to destroy the King and Parliament.

He was leading a charmed life, trusted by the King and secure in the King's affections, protected both as an actor and as a playwright. He had everything to gain by writing plays which would favor the King's cause. Instead, he wrote *Macbeth*, which is a study of regicide, and *King Lear*, which is about a King dethroned. He was writing what he wanted to write, reaching for the highest mountains.

The Moor
of Venice

O N AUGUST 8, 1600, there arrived at Dover an embassy from
Muley Hamet Sharif, King of Barbary, who ruled over large
areas of what is now known as Morocco, Algeria, and Tunisia. The
ambassador was Abdulla Ouahed Anoon, and he was accompanied by
two Barbary merchants. The purpose of Muley Hamet Sharif was to
bring about a treaty of friendship with England and an exchange of
ambassadors preparatory to a full-scale military alliance against
Spain. England was to provide the ships, the King of Barbary would
provide the soldiers, Spain would be invaded, the East and West Indies
would be wrested from her, England and Barbary would divide the
spoils. It was a tempting proposition: in a single stroke the power of
Spain would be destroyed and the Spanish empire wiped from the face
of the earth.

Unfortunately—or perhaps fortunately—nothing came of the
embassy. Elizabeth took pains to see that the ambassador was well
housed and entertained; she sent hangings and furniture from
Hampton Court Palace to decorate the house set aside for him, and
arranged that he should be given special facilities to view the

triumphal procession that took place on the anniversary of her coronation. She received the ambassador twice, both times with great panoply. A painting was made of him during his stay in London. He was well built and handsome in a Levantine way, with a huge coiling turban, deep-set eyes, a powerful aquiline nose, and a long, square-cut black beard. He had very long thin fingers and gestured with them eloquently. He looked impressively Mephistophelian, arrogant and intelligent. Londoners watched him closely and they found him too strange for their comfort. The Queen was surprised because he brought no presents for her, unlike the ambassador from the Ottoman Empire, who brought her "four lions royal, twelve Turkish swords, four cases of knives, four unicorns' horns, twenty hangings of cloth, a bed for a galley all of crystal and gold and two horses." The ambassador came empty-handed, for apparently no one had warned him that great princes demand to be flattered with gifts.

According to John Stow, the Londoners took a violent dislike to the ambassador. They disapproved of his manner of living, the way he said his prayers, his habit of keeping sheep in his house, his lack of common charity, his supposed Machiavellian intelligence, and there was one other reason for disapproving of him: he stayed in London for six months at the country's expense, and six months was too long. Stow draws up a catalogue of the ambassador's errors, concluding with a real or imagined error so heinous that it darkened all the rest:

> Notwithstanding all that kindness showed them together with their diet, and all other provision for six months' space, wholly at the Queen's charges, yet such was their inveterate hate unto our Christian religion and estate, as they could not endure to give any manner of alms, charity, or relief, either in money or broken meat unto any English poor, but reserved their fragments, and sold the same unto such poor as would give most for them. They killed their own meat within their house, as sheep, lambs, poultry, and such like, and they turn their faces eastward when they kill any thing; they use beads and pray to saints; and whereas the chief pretence of their embassy was to require

continuance of her Majesty's special favor towards their
King, with like entreaty of her naval aid for sundry special
uses chiefly to secure his treasure from the parts of Guinea
etc., yet the English Merchants held it otherwise, by reason
that during their half years' abode in London, they used all
subtlety and diligence to know the prices, weights, measures,
and samples of commodities, as either their Country sent
hither, or England transported thither: they carried with
them all sorts of English weights, measures and samples of
commodities. And being returned, it was supposed they
poisoned their interpreter, being born in Granada, because
he commended the estate and bounty of England . . .

We may imagine that Abdulla Ouahed Anoon was a perfectly
innocent visitor to England who offended Londoners simply because
he was a stranger in their midst and they had no way of comparing
him with anyone they had ever seen. The case against him is loaded:
he asks for samples, weights, and measures, and seems to be spying
on English merchants. He is niggardly; he turns to the East for the
same reason that Englishmen in church turn to the East, to salute
the founder of their religion. All his daily acts, including the killing
of sheep and poultry in his house, are given a sinister interpretation,
perhaps for no better reason than that they have grown weary of
him, but it is more likely that the government and Elizabeth herself
did not like him, distrusted his motives, and encouraged the people
to watch him closely and especially to observe whether he gave
money to the Christian poor.

Poor Abdulla Ouahed Anoon! And also poor Queen Elizabeth,
who was too busy entertaining the ambassador from Russia who
offered her sumptuous gifts from the Tsar Boris Godunov, to pay
much attention to the lonely ambassador from Barbary, who was
busy collecting samples to bring back to his King. The great design
of destroying Spain and her vast empire was conveniently forgotten.
The embassy accomplished nothing except to expedite the exchange
of prisoners between England and Barbary. The ambassador vanished from history, while the Londoners cursed him and spread the
rumor that his interpreter was poisoned for having said good things
about the English.

When a Londoner in the year 1600 thought of a Moor, he thought of Abdulla Ouahed Anoon, dark-skinned, black-bearded, abrupt, wearing a white turban and a white gown according to Moorish fashion, a reputed murderer, a man who had no Christian charity in him. If a Moor appeared on the stage, we would expect him to have some of these qualities, above all the quality of strangeness, as of someone who did not belong to the familiar world, someone who was irritating, confusing, and totally deplorable.

It has become the custom to play Othello as an open-hearted warrior of heroic simplicity, vehement in defense of his honor. It is possible, however, to read another character in him: sly, boastful, vengeful. When he declares, "I fetch my life and being through men of royal siege," are we to believe him? When he has murdered Desdemona and is under arrest, he shouts just as he prepares to stab himself:

> Set you down this
> And say, besides, that in Aleppo once,
> Where a malignant and a turbanned Turk
> Beat a Venetian, and traduced the State,
> I took by the throat the circumcised dog,
> And smote him thus!

Addressing Desdemona when she is dead, he says: "I kissed thee ere I killed thee," as though a kiss redeemed him from a crime. We believe neither that the kiss redeems the crime nor that the killing of "a malignant and turbanned Turk" is necessarily a matter of great service to the Venetian state. Again, when Othello explains to the Duke of Venice how he came to thrive in Desdemona's affections by telling her stories of his wars and travels, are we bound to believe that he told her the truth, the whole truth?

Many men have told many women astonishing histories of their adventures, and some have got away with it. Othello's adventures were unusually colorful:

> I spoke of most disastrous chances:
> Of moving accidents by flood and field,
> Of hair-breadth scapes i' the imminent deadly breach,

Of being taken by the insolent foe,
And sold to slavery. Of my redemption thence,
And portance of my traveler's history.
Wherein of antres vast, and desarts idle,
Rough quarries, rocks, hills, whose head touch heaven,
It was my hint to speak. Such was my process.
And of the cannibals that each other eat,
The Antropophague, and men whose heads
Grew beneath their shoulders. These things to hear
Would Desdemona seriously incline:
But still the house affairs would draw her hence:
Whichever as she could with haste dispatch,
She'd come again, and with a greedie ear
Devour up my discourse. Which I observing,
Took once a pliant hour, and found good means
To draw from her a prayer of earnest heart
That I would all my pilgrimage dilate,
Whereof by parcels she had something heard,
But not instinctively: I did consent,
And often did beguile her of her tears,
When I did speak of some distressful stroke
That my youth suffered: my story being done,
She gave me for my pains a world of kisses.

The old warrior has done his work well. He presents himself as an open-hearted man, without a trace of malice or malignancy. In Shakespeare's time it was very different, for Othello strode on the stage with an air of menace and terror. They saw the turbanned Moor in the light of the King of Barbary's embassy. They distrusted him, were quick to see evil in him, and were not misled by his gruff good humor. They saw him for what he was: desperate and cunning, but slow-witted, especially when pitted against the diabolically quick-witted Iago, who was even more desperate and even more cunning than himself. It was evident from the beginning that they would destroy each other.

So they felt apprehensive from the moment he appeared on the stage, since he was as much a stranger in their midst as Shylock, and like Shylock he would convey his foreignness with ample gestures and an Oriental disdain for those who were not as he was. Even his love for Desdemona was ambiguous: he had captivated her with his stories and placed her under his spell. The audience sympathized with Roderigo, who deserved better than to be outwitted by a foreigner. As for Iago, the Machiavellian with the sharp teeth and the ratlike smile, the man of silent action and interminable speech, "honest" Iago, who dissembles because dissembling has become a habit, and who is so adept in conspiracy that he cannot conceive of a world where he is not at the center of at least three running conspiracies all working toward the same end, this Iago is almost but not quite a Machiavellian figure raised to the level of a clown. His name is Spanish and sufficient warning that he is up to murderous mischief.

In many of Shakespeare's plays the clown plays the role of the chorus. In *Othello* there is no clown, or rather there is the very brief appearance of a clown who engages Desdemona in conversation and is then mercifully forgotten. For Shakespeare's purpose there is enough clowning going on in Iago's head to make another clown unwarrantable.

In Giraldi Cinthio's *Hecatommithi,* from which Shakespeare borrowed the main outlines of the story of the ill-fated Moor of Venice, the Ensign and the Moor together plan the murder of Desdemona. There is no grandeur in it. They propose to beat her to death with sandbags and then pull down part of the ceiling so that it will seem that she died because the ceiling caved in on top of her. This was not the kind of murder which would appeal to Shakespeare, nor could it be staged satisfactorily. In Cinthio's story the Moor and the Ensign fall out after the murder of Desdemona, and each attempts to bring about the downfall of the other. At the orders of the Signoria of Venice the Moor is arrested, brought to Venice in chains, tortured, condemned to perpetual banishment, and slain by a kinsman of Desdemona. The Ensign escapes punishment until, engaging in another conspiracy, he is accused of attempted murder and is put to the rack for a crime which has nothing to do with the murder of Desdemona. He survives the rack but dies shortly afterwards of a "ruptured body." The Moor dies by the hands of an assassin, and the Ensign dies as a result of the exertions of the official torturer.

Except for the ending, Shakespeare has followed Cinthio's text remarkably closely. The characters of Othello, Iago, and Cassio are sketched out by Cinthio with care. To Cinthio, too, we owe the handkerchief "finely embroidered in the Moorish fashion." In the story the Ensign takes his three-year-old daughter to see Desdemona, and when she lifts up the child, it is an easy matter for him to pocket the handkerchief from her sash. Shakespeare has taken the bare bones of a rather lifeless story of jealousy and intrigue and filled it with blood and sinew, with a roaring life of its own. For once there is no subplot. The play moves decisively to its inevitable conclusion. Although it is among the longest of Shakespeare's plays, it seems to be among the shortest.

Othello moves with prodigious speed, and so it must, for it is full of improbable and implausible events, each one following hard on the heels of another. Thomas Rymer's celebrated criticism of the play in his *A Short View of Tragedy,* published in 1693, is not to be dismissed lightly as a neoclassicist rebuke. Often described as a well-structured play, *Othello* is in fact structured only in the sense that a wild stallion plunging headlong across a desert in search of pasture may be said to be structured. The characters are structured; the play is not. Thomas Rymer legitimately points to the play's faults:

> Othello, the night of his arrival at Cyprus, is to consummate with Desdemona; they go to bed. Both are raised and run into the town amidst the soldiers that were afighting; then go to bed again; that morning he sees Cassio with her; she importunes him to restore Cassio. Othello shows nothing of the soldier's mettle: but like a tedious, drawling, tame goose is gaping after any paltry insinuation, laboring to be jealous; and catching at every blown surmise.

There is some truth in these rebukes, and Thomas Rymer finds many others to buttress his argument that the play is "none other than a bloody farce, without salt or savor." In this he is demonstrably wrong, for it is the salt and the savor that we remember. Othello was too wild and too preposterous a creature for the neoclassicists at the end of the seventeenth century. He lacks logic, for only an illogical man would feed on his own jealousies. He is not a tame goose but a wounded lion raging in his misery. Rymer thinks of the play as a farce, of the order of Harlequin and Scaramuccio. We, knowing what ravages jealousy can commit on the soul, are more likely to see it as great tragedy and to sit on the edge of our seats in a state of terrible excitement, wondering how it will all end, even though we know the play by heart.

The pace of *Othello* is dizzying. There is nothing else like it in Shakespeare except the last act of *Hamlet*. It is therefore not a play which permits scene changes: the scenes must follow one another without pause, as they did on the Jacobean stage. I have seen it performed by the Roundabout Theatre in New York on a vast black stage, with black curtains, the only decor being a meaningless abstraction set far in the rear. It could not be said that the actors were especially talented, though they uttered their lines with passion and conviction: Othello had an appropriate dignity, Iago was properly nervous and cunning, Desdemona was adorably beautiful, innocent, and perplexed. I do not remember Cassio, for he left no more impression on me than a face painted on wood. But the director had seen to it that there were no pauses, everything moved at vertiginous speed, the actors simply emerged from the darkness into the spotlights where they were seen clear-cut against the dark hangings, gleaming like jewels, and they communicated across the vastness of the stage, which was about forty feet deep, as though space had no meaning, as though nothing else mattered but the impact of one personality upon another. In this darkness they moved, or seemed to move, with the extraordinary vitality of angel fish in a dark aquarium.

There were advantages in this dark but brilliantly spotlit stage. The place was immaterial; the faces, the costumes, the confrontations, and the poetry were everything. The director at the Roundabout Theatre had one advantage over the director at the Globe: he had enormous depth of field, so that when Othello emerged from the rear of the stage he looked very small, almost a miniature of himself, and when he advanced toward the footlights, he gave almost the impression of a man seen in close-up. The staging of the play was an object lesson in Shakespearean direction, for not only did it have the speed of the original production at the Globe and the actors were set free from the limitations of place, but every movement was so carefully choreographed that the actors seemed to be taking part in a complex and sinister dance.

Many who saw the first production of *Othello* would remember the embassy from the King of Barbary. A few would remember that Queen Elizabeth liked to call Sir Francis Walsingham, who was her principal secretary for two decades, "the Moor." He was small and slight, dark-featured, with a heavy black bristling beard, and he was the head of her secret service and therefore more feared than any other man in England. Walsingham did not enjoy being called "the Moor," for it was a term of opprobrium directed as much to his dark ways as to his dark face. She also called him "the Spy," as though there was no other spy in the kingdom. He served her faithfully and was responsible for breaking up the adder's nest of conspiracies that threatened to destroy her.

We should be on our guard with Othello: there was something of the conspirator in him, something of the rakehell, something of madness. He can play Hamlet's game, though he lacks Hamlet's fine-drawn intelligence. The Jacobean audience would have wondered whether Othello's epileptic fit was feigned and whether all the passionate abuse directed at Desdemona was meant to be taken at face value. A man may roar abuse at his wife and still love her. He can suggest that she has committed the most abominable crimes only to taunt her. How much is irony? How much is bluster? And when Othello is being seduced by Iago into the belief that his wife is a whore and all the demonstrable proofs are presented to him, we should not expect him to be entirely credulous, to fall into every trap opened for him. What appears to be rage in Othello is often irony, though it becomes rage later. He is more clear-headed than we think: he gulls Iago when we think he is being gulled, and after the shock of murder he knows exactly what is demanded of him, for murder has brought him to his senses.

But it is Othello in his madness who creates the greatest poetry. Shakespeare follows the Senecan tradition, for madness allows the poetry to break free of logical flesh and logical intelligence. The soaring speeches of Shakespeare's madmen take off like curlews that even in their rising change direction suddenly. Othello, appealing to the cause of justice, is in fact appealing to everything except justice: terror, revenge, ferocious indignation, remorse before the act is accomplished. The pounding rhythms are sexual: his desire for her is as great as the desire to see her dead.

It is the cause, it is the cause, my soul.
Let me not name it to you, you chaste stars.
It is the cause. Yet I'll not shed her blood,
Nor scar that whiter skin of hers than snow,
And smooth as monumental alabaster.
Yet she must die, else she'll betray more men.
Put out the light, and then put out the light.
If I quench thee, thou flaming minister,
I can again thy former light restore,
Should I repent me; but once put out thy light,
Thou cunning'st pattern of excelling nature,
I know not where is that Promethean heat
That can thy light relume. When I have plucked the rose
I cannot give it vital growth again;
It needs must wither. I'll smell thee on the tree.
O balmy breath, that dost almost persuade
Justice to break her sword. One more, one more!
Be thus when thou art dead, and I will kill thee,
And love thee after. One more, and that's the last!
So sweet was ne'er so fatal. I must weep.
But they are cruel tears. This sorrow's heavenly;
It strikes where it doth love.

The ideas pursuing each other pell-mell through his brain seek for an anchorage in her body. The flaming sun becomes a rose, becomes her lips, becomes her breath, becomes her death. His reasons for killing her have nothing to do with what has happened. It is preposterous to kill her "else she'll betray more men." He is not in the least interested in what happens to other men. "I will kill thee and love thee after" is equally preposterous on the level of fact while comprehensible to the imagination. "She should have died hereafter." Her death, like the death of Lady Macbeth, is not explained, even though we see it happening before our eyes. She dies "for other reasons." Among those reasons is her innocence.

Othello, gazing at Desdemona asleep, caught up in the magic of her presence, celebrates her even when he is about to kill her. She is his whole world, and about to become nothing. In his regret and fear of loss there lies a wild hope that desire will be rekindled. He does not explain why or how this may be brought about except by declaring that he may restore the light of the sun by repentance. But repentance is still far away; nor does any image occur to him to suggest that life, Desdemona's life and his own, can conceivably continue. The argument he presents is all abstractions: justice, repentance, betrayal, nature, cause. In *Cymbeline* Iachimo peers down at the sleeping Imogen with a different purpose in mind:

> Cytherea,
> How bravely thou becom'st thy bed; fresh lily,
> And whiter than the sheets: that I might touch,
> But kiss, one kiss. Rubies unparagon'd,
> How dearly they do't! 'Tis her breathing that
> Perfumes the chamber thus. The flame o' th' taper
> Bows toward her, and would under-peep her lids
> To see the' enclosed lights, now canopied
> Under these windows white and azure, lac'd
> With blue of heaven's own tinct.

Iachimo, of course, has not entered Imogen's bedroom to kill her. Instead he has come to discover false evidence of her unchastity, which will benefit him only to the extent that he may win a wager. His motives are as far as possible remote from Othello's. The passage shows how Shakespeare could use in the grand baroque manner the image of a candle flame underpeeping her lids to see her naked eyes; and that surrealistic flame, leaping to her face and prizing open her lids, somehow conveys the sense of her abundant life.

In the list of actors that comes at the end of the play in the First Folio, Iago is described as "a villain." It is a suitable description of a man who might have been fathered by Richard III on Lady Macbeth. What Coleridge called "motiveless malignity" is precisely what the play is about. Iago rejoices in a conspiracy which has one aim: to destroy Othello. To that extent his malignity is not motiveless. But beyond the destruction of Othello there lie, like the rings formed when a stone is thrown into a pool, more hoped-for destructions and betrayals. His malice is assured, his motives are unmeasured, to be invented on the spur of a moment. "He is a being next to devil, only *not* quite devil—and this Shakespeare has attempted— executed—without disgust, without scandal." In this way Coleridge assures us that Iago is not Mephistopheles and affirms that Shakespeare wrote the part in cold blood, "without disgust, without scandal," as an entomologist might describe the more disagreeable habits of a beetle. In fact, Shakespeare has loaded the play with the passionate nihilism of Iago, who becomes the chief character, the hub on which the wheel revolves.

If Iago derives ultimately from the Vices of the morality plays, he reaches forward to Dostoyevsky's nihilists and to Sergey Nechayev who wrote that the task of the revolutionary was terrible, total, universal, and merciless destruction. Iago has allegiance to no one, not even to himself. He does not care, and he embraces his conspiracy only because it faintly amuses him. He enjoys destruction for its own sake; it pleases him a little that people can be so easily pushed into the abyss. When he tells a tall story about Cassio and Desdemona, he seems to be almost surprised that Othello believes it:

> I lay with Cassio lately,
> And being troubled with a raging tooth,
> I could not sleep.
> There are a kind of men so loose of soul
> That in their sleeps will mutter their affairs.
> One of this kind is Cassio.
> In sleep I heard him say, "Sweet Desdemona,
> Let us be wary, let us hide our loves!"
> And then, sir, would he gripe and wring my hand,
> Cry "O sweet creature!" and then kiss me hard,
> As if he plucked up my kisses by the roots
> They grew upon my lips, then laid his leg
> Over my thigh, and sighed, and kissed, and then
> Cried "Cursed fate that gave thee to the Moor!"

Iago is brilliant in his improvisations; he knows how to calculate the exact measure of Othello's credulity, and he knows what phrases compel belief. "Then laid his leg over my thigh" is more than improvisation; it is the most damaging blow of all, finely executed, and we see him smiling inwardly at this discovery. He is more evil than Richard III and Lady Macbeth because he is disinterested.

Othello, Iago, and Desdemona required so much of Shakespeare's genius that there was little left over for Cassio. While the three principals have a life of their own, Cassio gives the impression of being manipulated. He has "very poor and unhappy brains for drinking," but he also has very poor and unhappy brains for everything else. He is "unfortunate in his infirmity" and wishes "courtesy would invent some other custom of entertainment." "O God that men should put an enemy in their mouths." In this way he defends his own existence as a man of principle. It scarcely matters, for he is soon washed away in tides of poetry. Cassio, the soldier, proves to be no swordsman. He plays no intelligent part in the brawl that suddenly flares up at Iago's command. Shakespeare has watched many brawls, and he knows what people say when they are drawing daggers out of their sleeves. But what he knows best of all is what a heroic figure may say in the height of passion:

> O ill-starred wench!
> Pale as thy smock! When we shall meet at compt,
> This look of thine will hurl my soul from heaven,
> And fiends will snatch at it. Cold, cold, my girl?
> Even like thy chastity.
> O cursed, cursed slave! Whip me, ye devils,
> From the possession of this heavenly sight!
> Blow me about in winds! roast me in sulphur!
> Wash me in steep-down gulfs of liquid fire!
> O Desdemona, Desdemona! dead!
> O!   O!   O!

Desdemona dies on the stage, but it is a very special kind of death. "Cold, cold, my girl?" Othello says to her when she is still warm. We will not be surprised when at the end of the play she dances a jig and throws a kiss to the audience. She belongs among those innocent women who haunted Shakespeare's imagination, being half sister to Imogen, Perdita, Marina, Miranda, Cordelia, for whom innocence was a way of life. And just as she possesses a very special kind of innocence, so Shakespeare will endow her with a kind of majesty, so that she becomes the generative force that produces the innocent women of his last plays, who are more than innocent, for they are also heavenly.

But before reaching out to that perfect innocence, he felt the need to describe perfect evil. In Macbeth and Lady Macbeth he entered the heart of darkness.

The Blood
of the Poet

Othello, Hamlet, AND Macbeth are all rooms of the same
house. They lead into one another, they explain one another, and they are built of the same bricks and clamped together with
the same mortar. They are inhabited, like the old morality plays,
with virtues and vices. Time and Death stalk through them like
visible presences, and there is still another emblematic figure who
has never been properly named, because there is really no name for
him in the English language: the proud man who walks with an
intense self-awareness through the vast chambers of his own mind,
and whose awareness permits him to see the shape of unfolding
tragedies. In all three plays we are aware of the preliminary tremors
that come before the earthquake because a man has sensed them.
We are also aware that Othello, Hamlet, and Macbeth are brothers
under the skin.

They are all men of rank, flawed, resolute, irresolute, possessing
a profound instinctive feeling for the motives of others while
curiously lacking in an understanding of their own motives. They
are larger than lifesize, and Shakespeare has sculptured them in

high relief. We learn very early that all three of them are capable of
murder and they are not terrified by it: they will do what they have
to do because their own logic demands it. Each of them possesses to
an extraordinary degree the quality that was known to the Italian
Renaissance by the word *terribilità*. Each is a flare of consciousness,
a flame that bends with the wind, shoots up to incredible heights,
dies down, flickers, becomes no more than a small ember flame, and
always we are aware of the flame, even when we can scarcely see it,
even when the stage is dark. These men carry their terror with
them, as though terror was the most natural thing in the world; and
somewhere deep down in their consciousness is the knowledge that
they will inevitably be betrayed by their own weapons, their own
terror. But what is most remarkable about them is their towering
pride and self-awareness. It can be seen in their eyes, their fingertips, and above all in the words that escape from their lips. And it is
this towering self-awareness that makes them so real to us, so that
we seem to know them better than we know our friends.

Of course they are creatures of Shakespeare's imagination,
although he found them in old books. Cinthio's *Hecatommithi*,
Belleforest's *Histoires Tragiques*, and Holinshed's *Chronicles* provide merely the skeletons. Shakespeare reshaped the skeletons, gave
them muscles and nerves, clothed them with flesh, and made them
so living that they walk among us today. They share Shakespeare's
preoccupations with time and sex, his nihilism, his racing prose and
high-textured verse, which in these three plays are often interchangeable. Shakespeare evidently kept a notebook in which he
entered verses and lines of prose as they occurred to him, and at
intervals he would plunder his notebook and take what he wanted
from it. There are passages in *Othello* which look as though they
have strayed from the *Hamlet* notebook. Is it Ophelia or Desdemona who says:

My mother had a maid called Barbary.
She was in love; and he she loved proved mad
And did forsake her. She had a song of "Willow";
An old thing 'twas, but it expressed her fortune,
And she died singing it. That song tonight
Will not go from my mind; I have much to do

But to go hang my head all at one side
And sing it like poor Barbary.

Here is a passage from *Othello* which could be at ease in *Hamlet*:

Roderigo.   It is silliness to live when to live is torment; and
then have we a prescription to die when death is our
physician.

Iago.   O villainous! I have looked upon the world for four
times seven years, and since I could distinguish betwixt a
benefit and injury, I never found man that knew how to
love himself. Ere I would say I would drown myself for
the love of a guinea hen, I would change my humanity
with a baboon.

Roderigo.   What should I do? I confess it is my shame to
be so fond, but it is not my virtue to amend it.

Iago.   Virtue? A fig! 'Tis in ourselves that we are thus. Our
bodies are our gardens, to the which our wills are gardeners,
so that if we will plant nettles or sow lettuce, set hyssop and
weed up thyme, supply it with one gender of herbs or distract
it with many—either to have it sterile with idleness or
manured with industry—why, the power and corrigible
authority of this lies in our wills. If the balance of our lives
had not one scale of reason to poise another of sensuality, the
blood and baseness of our natures would conduct us to most
preposterous conclusions.

The signposts in this passage are clearly written. When the
twenty-eight-year-old Iago says "Virtue? A fig!" we know what he
is about: Hamlet also despaired over virtue. Among the preposterous conclusions reached by Iago are those which make a mock of
virtue. The great "Put money in thy purse" speech presents the
same argument that Dostoyevsky presented in *The Possessed.* If
there is no God, then everything is permissible, even suicide, and
Iago pays particular attention to suicide. "Come, be a man! Drown
thyself? Drown cats and blind puppies? . . . Seek thou rather to be
hanged in compassing thy joy than to be drowned and go without
her!" He will not commit suicide; he will certainly be hanged.

Bloodstained Macbeth, thane of Cawdor and later King of Scotland, descends from Iago. He is larger and heavier, his beard more bristling, his eyes more bloodshot; he stamps and roars, like the Vices of the morality plays; he is not so agile as Iago; he has the tyrannical and kingly manner long before he became a tyrant and a king. He is obsessed with murder as a means to power, while Iago is merely obsessed with his own murderous cleverness.

Simon Forman saw *Macbeth* at the Globe and put down his recollections of the play in his playbook. He was not a particularly attentive observer and he appears to have slept through half the performance. Nevertheless he was able to convey something of the mood of the performance. He wrote:

In Macbeth at the Globe, 1610, the 20 of April, Saturday, there was to be observed first how Macbeth and Banquo, 2 noblemen of Scotland, riding through a wood, there stood before them 3 women fairies or nymphs. And saluted Macbeth, saying 3 times unto him, "Hail, Macbeth, king of Cawdor, for thou shalt be a king but shalt beget no kings etc." Then said Banquo, "What, all to Macbeth and nothing to me." "Yes," said the nymphs. "Hail to thee, Banquo, thou shalt beget kings but be no king." So they departed and came to the court of Scotland to Duncan, king of Scots, and it was in the days of Edward the Confessor.

And Duncan bade them both kindly welcome, and made Macbeth forth with Prince of Northumberland and sent him home to his own castle and appointed Macbeth to provide for him, for he would sup with him the next day at night, and did so. And Macbeth contrived to kill Duncan, and through the persuasion of his wife did that night murder the king in his own castle, being his guest. And there were many prodigies seen that night and the day before. And when Macbeth had murdered the king, the blood on his hands could not be washed off by any means, nor from his wife's hands, which handled the bloody dagger in hiding them. By which means they became both much amazed and affronted. The murder being known, Duncan's 2 sons fled, the one to England, the [other to] Wales, to save themselves. They being fled, they were supposed guilty of the murder of their father, which was nothing so.

Then was Macbeth crowned king, and then he for fear of Banquo, his old companion, that he should beget kings but the king himself, he contrived the death of Banquo and caused him to be murdered on the way as he rode.

The next night being at supper with his noblemen whom he had bid to a feast, to the which also Banquo should have come, he began to speak of noble Banquo and to wish that he were there. And as he thus did, standing up to drink a carouse to him, the ghost of Banquo came and sat down on his chair behind him. As he turning about to sit down again saw the ghost of Banquo which fronted* him so that he fell into a great passion of fear and fury, uttering many words about his murder; by which when they heard that Banquo was murdered, they suspected Macbeth.

Then Macduff fled to England to the king's son. And so they raised an army and came into Scotland and at Dunsinane overthrew Macbeth. In the meantime, while Macduff was in England, Macbeth slew Macduff's wife and children, and after in the battle Macduff slew Macbeth.

Observe also how Macbeth's queen did rise in the night in her sleep, and walked and talked and confessed all, and the doctor noted her words.

One might have hoped that Forman would have spent more time writing up his notes. He makes some elementary mistakes: Macbeth was the thane of Cawdor, not the king; Macbeth did not himself slay Macduff's wife and children; Lady Macbeth did not hide the dagger. But these are not really mistakes; they are the errors a man makes when he is writing hastily late at night after seeing a play in the afternoon. The play as we have it is the shortest of Shakespeare's tragedies and it is certain that it was once longer. In the original version shown at the Globe Theatre there may well have been a scene in which Lady Macbeth makes the gesture of hiding the dagger.

*Affronted

Simon Forman's notes throw some light on the staging of the play. We can see now, with Forman's aid, how Banquo's ghost appeared to an Elizabethan audience. If we imagine a raised throne in the background and a table set in front of it in the middle area of the stage, with Macbeth at the head of the table on the right and all the others facing the audience, then Macbeth alone would see the ghost who suddenly appears sitting on the throne, wearing a ghostly veil over his armor, and because he is on the throne the ghost dominates the stage. He has risen silently through the trapdoor, and just as silently he would vanish while Macbeth was reciting those verses in which he screams in abject terror of the ghost. In his own time, and very briefly, the ghost would appear again and vanish again. The clue to this stagecraft is provided by the words: "the ghost of Banquo came and sat down on his chair behind him," where "his chair" can only mean "the throne," which is behind Macbeth as he sits at table.

So, too, with the witches, whom we are accustomed to regard as dark, venomous, and hag-toothed, in ragged clothes and perhaps wearing the pointed black witches' hats, evil pouring out of them like smoke. Forman saw them as three women fairies or nymphs. Must we revise our concept of the witches? I think we must, and not only because Forman described them as fairies or nymphs. In Raphael Holinshed's *Chronicles of England, Scotland, and Ireland*, first published in two magnificent illustrated volumes in 1578, there is an engraving showing Macbeth and Banquo on horseback as they encounter the Weird Sisters who have the appearance of perfectly normal matrons in richly embroidered robes, and one of them raises a warning hand to prevent the horsemen from passing them. Holinshed describes them as "three women in strange and wild apparel resembling creatures of elder world." In the illustration there is strangeness only in the flamboyance of the costumes, and although they might come from an older world, they are appropriately dressed for the world of England. Shakespeare had this volume of Holinshed in front of him while he was writing the play, for it was his chief source. He not only used the story of Macbeth but also included incidents borrowed from the lives of King Duff and King Kenneth. Without Holinshed there would have been no play, and in the illustration we are close to seeing Macbeth, Banquo, and the witches as Shakespeare saw them.

Macbeth is represented as a bearded gentleman of middle age, wearing a tall beaver hat surrounded by the spiked coronet to denote his princely rank and what appears to be a leather jerkin. He sits stiffly upright on his horse. Banquo wears a helmet and a short Elizabethan cape and the ballooning breeches and long hose of a well-dressed Elizabethan, and seems to be more at ease on his horse. Neither of them looks particularly surprised by the appearance of the Weird Sisters.

This is more or less how Macbeth and Banquo would have appeared on the stage. We should remember that the Elizabethan stage managers showed not the slightest interest in authentic costumes; there was little decor; the props were cardboard or papier-mâché; the actors sat on orange crates. There was a deliberate avoidance of naturalism. The eyes of the audience were riveted on the performers, not on the stage scenery: a tree or some bushes might be carried onto the stage to represent the forest of Birnham Wood, a tent might be folded round one of the supporting pillars, or a table and chairs would be displayed during a royal conference.

The imagery was in the poetry and in the person of the actor; and the intention of the dramatist was to create on the stage images which the audience would perceive in their imaginations, seeing crowds, towns, palaces, rivers, mountains, seas, shapes of cloud, where in fact there was nothing at all. Hence the barrenness and emptiness of the Elizabethan stage. The actor enjoyed primacy; he commanded the audience, as a conductor commands an orchestra, and played on them until he had wrung out of them the last ounce of emotion. But this could only happen through the convention that the actor assumed a reality superior to the everyday reality of the spectators, who smoked their pipes, drank bottled ale, and chewed apples throughout the play.

Macbeth takes hold of the play as only Hamlet and Lear take hold of their plays. That tremendous figure, who emerges so abruptly from Scotland's turbulent and chaotic past, acquired, as Shakespeare's thoughts played on him, a curiously modern appearance: the murderer caught in his own coils, one murder leading to another, each betrayal an invitation to an even greater betrayal. All the time the rational Macbeth looks down at himself like the thane Donwald, who also murdered his King, "though he abhorred the act greatly in heart." What he sees when he looks down at himself disgusts him, and disgust leads him to further murders. The violence of the poetry mirrors his tortured mind: and somewhere amid the cries of a murderer exulting in his crimes, there can be heard the plaintive cries of a man begging for pity.

Exultation, horror, and disgust sometimes work on Macbeth simultaneously. We have the impression that in his eagerness to understand himself he attempts to distinguish them, to isolate them, to look them in the face. He has a conscience. He at least knows he has committed crimes and must answer for them, though he feels safeguarded by the words of one of the Weird Sisters: "Fear not, Macbeth; no man that's born of woman shall e'er have power upon thee." The prophecy gives him strength but not enough to exorcise his deepest fears. Lady Macbeth has no conscience to disturb her. Even when she is attempting to rub away the imagined bloodstains on her hands, she can say: "A soldier, and afeard? What need we fear who knows it, when none can call our power to account?" Macbeth, despite prophecies, knows that his power must be accounted for.

So with the speed of darkness Macbeth goes about his bloody work with distaste and urgency. Blood, fresh-flowing around a knife, puts him in wild good humor, and with Shakespeare he stretches the language to the uttermost. Here Macbeth describes his discovery of the murdered Duncan:

> Here lay Duncan,
> His silver skin lac'd with his golden blood;
> And his gash'd stabs look'd like a breach in nature
> For ruin's wasteful entrance: there, the murderers,
> Steep'd in the colours of their trade, their daggers
> Unmannerly breech'd with gore.

Samuel Johnson could make nothing of these lines. He objected vigorously to "Here lay Duncan, his silver skin lac'd with his golden blood." It was a time when reputable scholars were busily amending Shakespeare's words in order to bring them more into tune with Augustan feeling. Alexander Pope, on an off day, suggested that the "golden blood" was an error. What Shakespeare had really meant to say was "gory blood." Johnson disapproved. The lines had no merit and therefore need not be amended. "No amendment can be made to this line," he observed, "of which every word is equally faulty, but by a general blot." He meant that these words should be stricken out.

"Breech'd with gore" was another conondrum. What Shakespeare meant was very clear: the daggers were covered with blood as with breeches. Malone thought "sheaf'd" would be an improvement. Johnson thought the word should be "drench'd." Someone else suggested "hatch'd." "Reech'd" was also proposed. At all costs "breech'd" must be avoided. The modern taste is less inclined for amendments, especially when there is nothing to be amended.

In writing *Macbeth* Shakespeare was in a mood for heaping images upon one another until they almost crushed each other, running them together so that the confrontation provides a strange and disturbing third image, which is sometimes followed by a fourth. Partly it comes from his habit of setting two nouns together to reinforce each other, as when he writes "the bank and shoal of time." He is accustomed to hurling words together, and sometimes it has the effect of torn and ripped metal and there is a clanging metallic sound. Sometimes, too, the images move with a fierce, relentless speed, as though the poet had almost lost control of his images and was hurrying after them:

And pity, like a naked newborn babe,
Striding the blast, or heaven's cherubin horsed
Upon the sightless couriers of the air,
Shall blow the horrid deed in every eye,
That tears shall drown the wind.

We can guess the origins of these compacted images with a fair certainty. The babe striding the blast comes evidently from the naked babes blowing winds from the four quarters of the earth, which appeared on ancient maps. From these babes floating in heaven he moves impatiently to the angels, the cherubin, from whom pity may be expected. "The sightless couriers of the air" cannot be winds, as Samuel Johnson supposed, but are likely to be the energy that transports the cherubin on their journeys, and it is the cherubin who convey the dreadful news across the world, bringing tears to men's eyes. But the imagery is so compacted that it becomes all one movement, one image, and the word "horsed" is here so explosive that its thrust drives "the sightless couriers of the air" at a speed which is dizzying. "Horsed" is abrupt; "Upon the sightless couriers of the air" flows like a single word. The effect is to bring us by the sheer music of the words into the presence of these angelic beings in whose existence we may believe, though they defy our comprehension.

On these verses William Blake produced one of his most miraculous color prints. With inspired literalism Blake depicted the ghostly horses streaming across the sky, bearing on their backs two angels: on one of the horses is the angel of death, supine, with outflung arms, her face turned away; on the other horse is the angel of life leaning down from the horses, gathering into her arms a naked babe, who is the soul of the dead woman we see lying on the seashore. The horses racing across the sky, the naked babe, the angels or cherubin, the sense of pity infusing the entire design, and the dark depths of unfathomable space produce the effect of an epiphany. We are seeing the birth of pity. A difficult and complex

Shakespearean text is transformed into a rich and wonderfully strange visionary painting.

Blake read *Macbeth* attentively and like many others he was fascinated by the three Weird Sisters, identifying them with Hecate, ruler of the underworld and sister of the moon. He has shown them as three beautiful women huddled together, kneeling or sitting on the earth, two of them naked, the other wearing a skirt, attended by an owl, a serpent, a donkey, and what looks like a winged cat of horrible aspect. Only the winged cat is evil. They might be three beautiful women huddled together against the cold.

In *Macbeth* Shakespeare portrays evil in its most naked form. If Macbeth himself suffers from doubts and hesitations, they are only doubts and hesitations such as a man might feel in deciding between alternative plans of murder. It is unfair to put the blame on Lady Macbeth, although she is given the best lines. Shakespeare gives an undeserved nobility to Macbeth. I remember a performance by Eric Porter and Janet Suzman where the nobility of their appearance was at odds with their infamous and venemous characters. There should, I think, be something coarse and vulgar in both of them. An Elizabethan audience would have expected Lady Macbeth to lurch drunkenly in the sleepwalking scene, while the doctor watching and taking notes would wear the appearance of Puritan sobriety.

> *Lady Macbeth.*   Out, damned spot! Out, I say! One: two: why, then 'tis time to do 't. Hell is murky. Fie, my lord, fie! A soldier, and afeard? What need we fear who knows it, when none can call our power to accompt? Yet who would have thought the old man to have had so much blood in him?
>
> *Doctor.*   Do you mark that?
>
> *Lady Macbeth.*   The Thane of Fife had a wife. Where is she now? What, will these hands ne'er be clean? No more o' that! You mar all with this starting.
>
> *Doctor.*   Go to, go to! You have known what you should not.
>
> *Gentlewoman.*   She has spoke what she should not, I am sure of that. Heaven knows what she has known.

At this moment we realize that Lady Macbeth, who plays many roles, is also the Fool, the one who has secret communication with the heavens. She is far more formidable than the witches, who have secret communication with the netherworld. The doctor says: "This disease is beyond my practice," but it is not beyond the practice of Shakespeare. Lady Macbeth knows she is doomed; it is her only satisfaction once the crime has been committed.

Shakespeare had a bloodlust while writing *Macbeth*. Hamlet, dedicated to killing his enemies, never exults in bloodshed. Othello takes care not to shed a drop of Desdemona's blood. But in *Macbeth*, as though in close-up, we see the hand gripping and squeezing the handle of the dagger, and the blood spurting. The stage seems awash with blood. Macbeth's hands are red, while Pity like a newborn babe soars into the stormstrewn heavens. If we accept Thomas Hardy's definition that tragedy describes a worthy creature encompassed by the inevitable, then it would be impossible to accept Macbeth as a tragic character, for he is neither worthy nor encompassed by the inevitable. *Macbeth* is philosophical *grand guignol*, and no worse for being less than a tragedy. One's sympathy goes out to Othello, Hamlet, Lear, Cleopatra, but to have sympathy for Macbeth is to stretch sympathy to the uttermost. What is most wonderful about him is his poetry of fear and pity and blood:

> Come, seeling night,
> Scarf up the tender eye of pitiful day,
> And with thy bloody and invisible hand
> Cancel and tear to pieces that great bond
> Which keeps me pale! Light thickens, and the crow
> Makes wing to th' rocky wood.
> Good things of day begin to droop and drowse,
> While night's black agents to their preys do rouse.

With such poetry it scarcely matters what his actions are. Like Faustus and like Tamburlaine, he becomes the vehicle for great poetry, being charged with diabolic energy. He is Lucifer rejoicing in his murderous adventures, being capable of laying half of Scotland waste, and killing everyone who gets in his way, killing mechanically in the modern fashion, slavishly obedient to his wife, yet perfectly capable of committing the murders she encourages without her assistance. He can say such things as "She should have died hereafter" or "Tomorrow, and tomorrow, and tomorrow," and reduce us to shivering tears until we realize that these heavily weighted words have a hollow sound. They are magnificent verse but they include within themselves the parody of verse.

> Tomorrow, and tomorrow, and tomorrow
> Creeps in this petty pace from day to day,
> To the last syllable of recorded time;
> And all our yesterdays have lighted fools
> The way to dusty death. Out, out, brief candle!
> Life's but a walking shadow, a poor player
> That struts and frets his hour upon the stage
> And then is heard no more. It is a tale
> Told by an idiot, full of sound and fury,
> Signifying nothing.

If this were true, tragedy—all tragedy—would be meaningless. Sometimes it is precisely because the poor player struts and frets upon the stage that life acquires meaning. No one ever wrote more nihilistically than Shakespeare, who denied his nihilism with the energy of his telling of it.

Leafing through the pages of Holinshed, Shakespeare came upon a description of King Lear. Once more he drained the dregs of his nihilism, and this time he presented a portrait of a man who is wholly convincing, wholly improbable, and witheringly alive.

King Lear
and the
Second Death

ZERO MOSTEL USED TO SAY that the most powerful dramatic scene he ever witnessed took place when the great Jewish tragic actor Solomon Mikhoels played the dying Lear. Mikhoels advanced across the stage in rags, one wavering arm stretched forward as though he was blindly attempting to clear a way for the burden he was carrying, while the other arm was uplifted high above his head, holding as though in triumph and misery the dead body of his daughter. Mostel could never explain to himself exactly why the scene was so moving, almost unbearable in its intensity. There was artifice in it: only a very strong man could support Cordelia on his upraised hand and only a genius would have thought of performing the scene in this way. The stage direction reads: *Enter Lear with Cordelia in his arms.* This is terrible enough; Mikhoels had added another dimension of terror to the scene.

Yet the more one thinks of Mikhoels' staging of the scene, the more appropriate it becomes. Suddenly Lear and Cordelia become sculptural: we see Cordelia's falling hair, her bare legs, her white face etched against the darkness of a stormy night, while below her stands Lear with his vast and ragged beard, his bulging eyes, his huge shapeless body in a rat's nest of clothes. Lear staggers across the stage, kneels under the intolerable weight of his daughter's body, and gradually brings it to earth; and in those gestures, while he howls in mingled hope and grief, knowing she is dead while not permitting himself to believe it, we see him at the very height of himself, all the more himself because he is doomed and his daughter is doomed and in his eyes the world is doomed.

> *Lear.*   Howl, howl, howl! O you are men of stones!
> Had I your tongues and eyes, I'd use them so
> That Heaven's vault should crack: she's gone for ever.
> I know when one is dead, and when one lives.
> She's dead as earth. Lend me a looking-glass,
> If that her breath will mist or stain the stone,
> Why then she lives.
>
> *Kent.*   Is this the promis'd end?
>
> *Edgar.*   Or image of that horror.
>
> *Albany.*   Fall and cease.
>
> *Lear.*   The feather stirs, she lives. If it be so,
> It is a chance that does redeem all sorrows
> That ever I have felt.
>
> *Kent.*   O my good Master.
>
> *Lear.*   Prithee away.
>
> *Kent.*   'Tis noble Kent, your friend.
>
> *Lear.*   A plague upon you murderers, traitors all.
> I might have saved her, now she's gone for ever.
> Cordelia, Cordelia, stay a little. Ha:
> What is it thou sayest? Her voice was ever soft,
> Gentle, and low, an excellent thing in woman.
> I killed the slave that was ahanging thee
>
> *Gentleman.*   'Tis true, my lords, he did.
>
> *Lear.*   Did I not, fellow?
> I have seen the day, with my good biting falchion
> I would have made them skip: I am old now,

And these same crosses spoil me. Who are you?
Mine eyes are not o' th' best: I'll tell you straight.

*   *   *   *   *   *   *   *

Kent.   That from your first of difference and decay
    Have followed your sad steps.

Lear.   You are welcome hither.

Kent.   Nor no man else: all's cheerless, dark, and deadly.
    Your eldest daughters have fordone themselves,
    And desperately are dead.

As King Lear staggers across the stage, the thunderbolts follow one after another, the stage is blinding with forked lightning, and the King whirls about to confront each new horror as it comes. He speaks of his strength, and has none. He speaks of the life stirring in Cordelia, and knows she has gone forever. He thinks the feather stirs when he places it on her lips, and pretends to hear her voice, but the feather stirs only because his hands are trembling and her voice is only the echo of his own voice. He is man reduced to his utmost misery: his family gone, his mind unbalanced, all hope destroyed, his body reduced to a rag made up of ancient skin and bone, and yet, in his wild presence, we are aware of a titanic power, of a man who is close to death but retains to the very end of his life a ferocious authority. We recognize in his words a strange nobility and grandeur even when he is most helpless, even when it is certain that the concepts of nobility and grandeur could have no meaning for him. He is in his death throes, yet he continues to struggle against all hope, against all logic, and against all the terrors the universe can hurl at him. There is nothing gentle about his death. He dies roaring. And when we see him in his helpless predicament, we are not cast down. We realize that this stupid, obstinate, foul-mouthed old man, who has brought all his troubles down upon himself, is in a curious way a triumphant figure, all the more triumphant because he is so human, because he is every man.

Nothing in all of English literature is so heavy with mortality as Shakespeare's portrait of the dying King Lear. There are many deaths in Shakespeare's plays, but this is the one that hurts most. To write this death the dramatist had almost to experience death. The

King dies like a drunken beggar who crawls into a hole and bellows abuse at the world or like a whipped dog which continues to snap and bark while it is being kicked to death. A fierce vitality, a deep consciousness of his own dignity, inform the King. There are a few moments when the energy of the King in his death throes seems to balance the energy of the universe .

There are many strange and perhaps inexplicable things in these passages. Kent, Edgar, and Albany offer in thirteen words a kind of litany:

> *Kent.*   Is this the promis'd end?
>
> *Edgar.*   Or image of that horror.
>
> *Albany.*   Fall and cease.

The words come like staccato drumbeats interrupting the flow of Lear's thoughts. One may think that Kent is talking about the death of Cordelia, but he is himself dying of a fatal wound suffered in battle. He is therefore speaking about his own death or all the deaths that follow in the train of King Lear. Beyond this there is another death, the death of the universe, the dissolution of worlds, the ultimate Doomsday, the final death that absorbs all other deaths. The brave Kent, the noble Edgar, and Albany, who has married Goneril and last realized her wickedness, come together in this brief passage to perform in poetry a kind of dance honor of the second death. We have heard this music before. When Young Clifford finds his dead father on the battlefield, he exclaims:

> O let this vile world end
> And the premised flames of the last day
> Knit earth and heaven together!
> Now let the general trumpet blow his blast,
> Particularities, and petty sounds
> To cease.

The "image of that horror" is therefore the image of the flames of the Last Day: "the great doom's image" of *Macbeth,* the Day of Judgment, which is not a day but the ending of days. This is the theme of Michelangelo's great painting of the Last Judgment on the wall of the Sistine Chapel and countless other renderings in churches throughout Christendom: God in glory, Christ, the Virgin, the Apostles, and the Saints, the blessed rising toward the heavenly throne and the damned descending into the bottomless pits of Hell. This is "the promis'd end." It is also the "image of the horror," and the "fall and cease." Implied in the words of Kent, Edgar, and Albany is the concept of damnation .

Shakespeare is using language so compacted that it is almost incomprehensible. If we did not have Young Clifford's exclamation on the battlefield, we would scarcely know what Kent and the others were talking about. We realize that "fall" and "cease" are nouns, and that "Particularities, and petty sounds" are the ultimate short-hand for creation, the history of the world, everything that men have sung or spoken, all of them coming to their "promis'd end." Kent and the others are asking whether Lear is damned, whether they are all damned, and perhaps whether the universe itself is damned. "It is a fearful thing to fall into the hands of the living God," wrote St. Paul in the Epistle to the Hebrews. Those terrible words, which are central to the Protestant ethic, are also central to the last arguments of *King Lear*.

For more than a century commentators have exerted themselves to show that *King Lear* ends on a note of redemption. The King, having passed through all his trials, achieves, so we are told, the promise of grace and redemption. He is one of those who are "saved," though he dies under abominable conditions. We are told that the terror of his death is itself a sign of redemption. He is the heroic figure who wrestles with God and Nature to be raised to a new majesty, as a saint is raised to majesty by his martyrdom.

But there is nothing in the text or in Lear's mind to suggest that a Christian interpretation is viable. It is a play about a pagan king living in an ancient, prehistoric age. When he curses, he says "By Jupiter" or "By Appolo"; priests are mentioned by the Fool, but they are pagan priests; there is no thought of Christ. In the last pages, when King Lear dies before our eyes, some elements of Christianity seem to break through like volcanic lava too long buried within the heart of the volcano, and these last pages glow in their fiery light. For the most part the play is about "unaccommo-dated man," "a poor, bare, forked animal," who has no real gods to worship nor any hope of divinity. It is a sordid pragmatical world.

"What is your study?" Lear asks Edgar, who replies pragmatically: "How to prevent the fiend, and to kill vermin." This was a study which could occupy a man for a lifetime.

It was a world much like our own of treachery and bigotry, of unbelievably cruel punishments, quick betrayals, man's life as cheap as beasts. It is not a world worth living in, but King Lear elects to live and to take vengeance on his enemies even at the price of madness:

> I will have such revenges on you both
> That all the world shall—I will do such things,
> What they are yet, I know not, but they shall be
> The terrors of the earth! You think I'll weep.
> No, I'll not weep. I have full cause of weeping.
> But this heart shall break into a hundred thousand flaws
> Or e'er I'll weep. O Fool, I shall go mad!

So he does, but like Hamlet his madness is the purest sanity. Two of his daughters seek his death; he must be more wily than they are. He chooses his companions well, even though outwardly they appear to be the least competent he could find. Gloucester, Edgar, and the Fool are men of spirit, each of them equipped with an excessive and terrible vitality. When Gloucester is betrayed by Edmund and falls into the hands of Cornwall, who gouges out his eyes, he swears he has nothing to live for and attempts to commit suicide by falling over the cliff at Dover. Edgar cures him of his despair by leading him in sound of the sea and then telling him to jump over the cliff.

> *Edgar.*   Come on, Sir,
>   Here's the place: stand still: how fearful
>   And dizzy 'tis to cast one's eyes so low.
>   The crows and choughs that wing the midway air
>   Show scarce so gross as beetles. Half way down
>   Hangs one that gathers sampire: dreadful trade:
>   Methinks he seems no bigger than his head.
>   The fishermen that walked upon the beach
>   Appear like mice: and yond tall anchoring bark,
>   Diminished to her cock; her cock, a buoy

Almost too small for sight. The murmuring surge
That on th' unnumbered idle pebble chafes
Cannot be heard so high. I'll look no more,
Lest my brain turn, and the deficient sight
Topple down headlong.

Gloucester.   Set me where you stand.

Edgar.   Give me your hand:
You are now within a foot of th' extreme verge:
For all beneath the moon would I not leap upright.

Gloucester.   Let go my hand.
Here, friend, 's another purse: in it, a jewel
Well worth a poor man's taking. Fairies and gods
Prosper it with thee. Go thou further off,
Bid me farewell, and let me hear thee going.

Edgar.   Now fare ye well, good sir.

Gloucester.   With all my heart.

It is one of the most tremendous of all Shakespeare's scenes, accomplished quietly, without any calling to high heaven. Edgar is, of course, playing a trick; Gloucester will jump, fall on his head, awaken after a moment's stupor, and Edgar will tell him that he fell the height of ten masts and was saved by a miracle. "Have I fallen, or no?" Gloucester will ask, and Edgar will answer that he fell from the dread summit of the chalk cliff. "Do but look up," Edgar says, and Gloucester replies: "Alack, I have no eyes."

There is more of Christianity, of tenderness and brotherhood, in this scene than in any of the others. If, as Albany says, "Humanity must perforce prey on itself like monsters of the deep" and the world is inexpungibly evil, there still remains the hope of brotherhood and the promise of love. Edgar is demonstrating his love for Gloucester to the highest degree by helping him simultaneously to commit suicide and to draw him back to life. In despair, for love's sake, men must play tricks on one another.

The tenderness returns in the other great scene where Cordelia finds her father, ill and exhausted by his experiences on the barren heath, lying in bed. King Lear looks up and sees her standing before him.

Cordelia.   How does my royal lord? How fares your
majesty?

Lear.   You do me wrong to take me out o'th' grave;
Thou are a soul in bliss; but I am bound
Upon a wheel of fire that mine own tears
Do scald like molten lead.

Cordelia.   Sir, do you know me?

Lear.   You are a spirit, I know; when did you die?

Cordelia.   Still, still, far wide!

Doctor.   He's scarce awake; let him alone awhile.

Lear.   Where have I been? Where am I? Fair daylight?
I am mightily abused. I should e'en die with pity,
To see another thus. I know not what to say.
I will not swear these are my hands. Let's see;
I feel this pin prick. Would I were assured
Of my condition!

Cordelia.   Oh, look upon me, sir,
And hold your hands in benediction o'er me.
No, sir, you must not kneel.

Lear.   Pray, do not mock me;
I am a very foolish, fond, old man,
Fourscore and upward, not an hour more nor less;
And to deal plainly,
I fear I am not in my perfect mind.
Methinks I should know you and know this man;
Yet I am doubtful; for I am mainly ignorant
What place this is, and all the skill I have
Remembers not these garments, nor I know not
Where I did lodge last night. Do not laugh at me;
For, as I am a man, I think this lady
To be my child Cordelia.

Cordelia.   And so I am: I am.

It is Shakespeare at his very best, using the language sparely,
matter-of-factly, to the utmost of his emotional power. There is no need
for stage directions. When King Lear attempts to struggle out of bed to

kneel to his daughter, we are not told: *The King rises and kneels;* nor are we told at the very end of the passage that Cordelia is kneeling. The stage sets itself. At such moments the actors need no instructions .

The most memorable passage in this memorable scene comes when Lear says:

> I am bound
> Upon a wheel of fire that mine own tears
> Do scald like molten lead.

The words are excessive, the concept is illogical, the ideas run one after another pell-mell, and the effect is to produce such a torn and twisted fusion of images that the mind at first rebels and then accepts them for their sheer power. A man bound on a wheel of fire, tears spurting into the fire, the sound of scalding as when a pig is scalded in boiling hot water, molten lead. We sometimes speak of the fusion of Shakespeare's images, but often there is no complete fusion: each image clangs against the next, like bells. We see them separately and together. Bound, wheel, fire, tears, scald, molten lead. Nouns and short, stripped-down words do the work, while the grammatical links are scarcely heard, vanishing in the excitement or serving as distant background music. And when Cordelia says at last: "And so I am: I am," we hear the clanging of bells again. Dante has Beatrice saying: "*Ben sem, ben sem, Beatrice,*" "It is I, it is I, Beatrice," in circumstances which are not wholly dissimilar, for Beatrice in Heaven and Cordelia on earth are both divinities for the purposes of poetry.

King Lear is of the earth, earthy: an old man stumbling toward his death. He is dragged from place to place; refused admittance at Albany's place, thrust out in the storm from Gloucester's palace, then blundering across the heath during the height of the storm; then carried away on a pallet from a farmhouse only to find himself wandering again in the fields near Dover; then we see him asleep in a tent in the French camp, and he awakes, and the soldiers lead him away in the company of Cordelia to a place of safety, which is no safety; and then King Lear and Cordelia are prisoners under guard; and when we see King Lear again, he is carrying the dead body of Cordelia in his arms and claiming that he has killed the hangman who had killed her.

Concerning this last event we have only Lear's word: it may or may not have happened as he claims. We know nothing about this event, and it is right that we should know nothing. We see him in the utmost extremity of his passion and of his misery: the tragic hero *in extremis*. He is not humbled but remains proud to the end, protesting against fate with vigor and tenderness. He addresses the dead Cordelia as "my poor fool":

> *Lear.*   And my poor fool is hanged: no, no, no, life?
>   Why should a dog, a horse, a rat have life,
>   And thou no breath at all? Thou'lt come no more,
>   Never, never, never, never, never.
>   Pray you, undo this button. Thank you, sir.
>   Do you see this? Look on her. Look, her lips,
>   Look there, look there.
>
>   *He dies.*
>
> *Edgar.*   He faints. My lord, my lord!
>
> *Kent.*   Break, heart; I prithee, break.
>
> *Edgar.*   Look up, my lord.
>
> *Kent.*   Vex not his ghost. O, let him pass! He hates him
>   That would upon the rack of this tough world
>   Stretch him out longer.

The mood of these last moments of the play is deeply religious, but it is not religious as we know religion. There is no apostheosis, no descent from the Cross followed by the ascent into eternal life. King Lear dies; and this is all; and it is enough. We can no more think of a resurrected King Lear than we can think of a resurrected King Macbeth. The gods have forsaken them both, but while one King dies gloriously in the full command of his human qualities, the other dies ignobly, like a bludgeoned rat. King Lear had sinned greatly: pride and anger he possessed, and human folly, and human weakness, but weighed against them was his generosity of spirit, his essential goodness. He was man robed in majestic humanity, and he suffered the fate that comes to most men: to die miserably. But out of that misery he extracts the utmost poetry.

There is no moral to be discovered in *King Lear,* just as there

was no moral to be discovered in Seneca's *Medea,* which ends with
the heroic Jason gazing up at Medea riding on her dragon chariot
into the heavens, throwing down on him the dead bodies of his sons.
"Ride through the lofty spaces of high heavens," says Jason, "and
wherever you go bear witness that there are no gods."

King Lear is the heart aching aloud, the tears flowing down an
old man's cheeks, an innocent girl hanged, a King gone mad. It is a
blind man attempting to jump off a cliff and falling a little way in a
field to find he is still alive. It is wandering over a blasted heath with
the happiest and wisest of fools in attendance. It is a tale set in
prehistoric England but it is also a tale of our own times with people
being murdered for no cause and against all reason, and it is two
people under sentence of death comforting one another in prison, as
King Lear comforts Cordelia:

We two alone will sing like birds i' th' cage:
When thou doest ask me blessing, I'll kneel down
And ask of thee forgiveness: so we'll live,
And pray, and sing, and tell old tales, and laugh
At gilded butterflies, and hear poor rogues
Talk of court news; and we'll talk with them too,
Who loses and who wins, who's in, who's out;
And take upon's the mystery of things
As if we were God's spies: and we'll wear out,
In a walled prison, packs and sects of great ones
That ebb and flow by th' moon.

We see them in prison briefly. When we see them again, Cordelia lies dead in the King's arms, Lear has escaped from prison, he
has reached his friends too late and has nothing left to live for. He
dies his ordinary death, while the invisible flames of Doomsday
stretch across the whole sky and the world ends.

The
Crack-up

QUITE SUDDENLY, IN MIDCAREER, with some of his greatest works yet to be written, Shakespeare suffered a crack-up, a mental depression so great and pervasive that it left him on the verge of madness. The evidence lies in the plays, in the sudden change of direction and abrupt alteration of feelings reflected in his images, in the staccato rhythms and the violence of his obsessions. "Gentle Shakespeare," "the mellifluous and honey-tongued Shakespeare" of contemporary allusions vanishes. Instead there is a gaunt face chalk-white in horror and a hand stretching out through the bars, not for help or for understanding or forgiveness, but making an obscene gesture.

What has happened to him has happened to many other men: a disintegration, a folding up and collapse at his very core. We hear the sound of splitting wood, a scream followed by the falling of an avalanche. There is a hard-edged horror of himself and all his works, and a horror of the world around him: the royal court, the stews, the taverns, the ordinary lives of ordinary people. In con-tempt of life and in terror of death he curses the world in which he sees himself as a stranger. He makes short stabbing statements which have the suddenness and the force of a sexual ejaculation. Everything he loved before is now held in derision. Since the world is nothing but sickness and corruption, not worth living in, and not worth a man's thought, he will give himself up to pure hatred of it when he is not surrendering to a violent, disgusted apathy.

It is not surprising that Shakespeare should have suffered in an extreme degree from a disease that was not uncommon in his time. A man can be destroyed by melancholy, as Robert Burton, who wrote a thousand-page study which he called *The Anatomy of Melancholy*, knew only to well. But no one seemed to know how the disease came about: Burton sought an answer by reading all the books he could lay his hands on, including Shakespeare's *Venus and Adonis*. Burton himself suffered from the disease, and he said that he found relief not in books but by listening to bargemen, notorious for their filthy language. But Burton's sufferings were not to be compared with Shakespeare's. With Shakespeare there is the sense of a titanic upheaval, a rending of the mental bones from the mental flesh. He has entered a hell from which there is usually no return.

We do not know the dates when Shakespeare completed his plays, and none of his letters have survived. We know very little about his private life, and even if we knew, it might not help us very much. But we can date the crack-up fairly accurately to 1607, the year when his younger brother, Edmund, who had followed him to London to become an actor, fathered an illegitimate child and died a few months later. The death of a younger brother can be a shattering experience even more terrible than the death of a wife or a child. I am not suggesting that grief for Edmund's death was responsible for the crack-up, but it was at least one of perhaps many contributory causes.

Edmund, as a living being, exists only in the wide margins of his older brother's life. He was christened in Holy Trinity Church on May 3, 1580. An entry in the burial register of St. Giles Church without Cripplegate for August 12, 1607, reads: "Edward, son of Edward Shackspeere, player, base-born." The names Edward and Edmund were interchangeable; "base-born" meant "illegitimate" and referred to the son, not to the father. On the last day of the same

year two entries in two registers at St. Saviour's Church, Southwark, announce the interment of the twenty-seven-year-old actor.
The first entry is found in the burial register and reads simply:
"Edmund Shakespeare a player in the Church." The second entry
is found in the fee book of the church:

Edmond Shakspeare A player Buried in the Church
with a forenoon knell of the great bell.   xx

The fee for burial in the church was two shillings, and the fee for
ringing the lesser bell was one shilling. If Shakespeare paid twenty
shillings, it meant that the burial was conducted with considerable
panoply, with many ministrants, many candles, and many choir-
boys. "Edmund Shakespeare, player," dying too young to achieve
any fame on the stage, was given a burial suitable for a rich
merchant.

Of Edmund Shakespeare's life in London we know nothing at
all, but the fact that we know nothing is itself a clue to his way of
living. It signifies that he lived wholly in his brother's shadow and
suggests that he was perfectly content to live in this way. That he
was called a "player" means that he was enrolled among the players
of the Globe Theatre, played minor roles, and occupied himself with
the business of the theatre. He had not yet reached a position where
he would be featured among the "principal players" and he evidently possessed no gifts as a dramatist. We may imagine that he
possessed some resemblance to Shakespeare, with red hair, a high
forehead, long nose, and sensual mouth. He was the youngest child
in the family, and as often happens in families he was perhaps the
most loved.

Shakespeare took death hard. "The imperial victory of murdering death" offered him no solace; he wrote about it with loathing
and horror, in fear and trembling. Death enters his histories and
tragedies with withering gestures and all-seeing gaze. Throughout
his life he was on intimate terms with it, wrestling with it until the
sweat poured out of his poetry.

"One can fall into the heights as well as into the depths," wrote
the poet Friedrich Hölderlin. In *Hamlet, Othello, Macbeth*, and
King Lear Shakespeare fell into the heights. In *Timon of Athens* he
fell into the depths.

The story begins in the outer room of a great lord who resembles the Earl of Southampton. His name is Lord Timon, an "honorable, complete, free-hearted gentleman of Athens," who would be wealthy if he had not out of generosity of spirit given most of his wealth away. In the outer room a poet, a painter, a merchant, and a jeweler are waiting upon the lord to receive his favors. The poet might be Shakespeare fresh from dedicating his Sonnets to Southampton. The painter turns to him and addresses him:

Painter. You are rapt, sir, in some work, some dedication
　To the great lord.
Poet. A thing slipped idly from me.
　Our poesy is as a gum, which oozes
　From whence 'tis nourished. The fire i' th' flint
　Shows not till it be struck, our gentle flame
　Provokes itself, and like the current flies
　Each bound it chases.

This is as close as Shakespeare ever got to describing the creative process: the oozing of gum, the striking of flint, spontaneous flame, and the sea racing to shore and bounding back again. But these conversations in the waiting room only prepare us for the coming of Lord Timon in all his magnificence to listen to their requests, their desires, their "sacrificial whisperings," himself being the sacrifice. Timon enters to the sound of trumpets, mild-mannered, the soul of delicacy and aristocratic feeling. He learns that a friend has been imprisoned and will be released only against a ransom of five talents, an enormous sum. Timon, saddened by the thought of his friend's imprisonment, gives the money willingly. An old Athenian enters and begs three talents for this daughter's dowry. The jeweler, the painter, and the merchant make their requests: all are granted. Significantly the poet makes no request. Shakespeare is brooding in a dark corner of the waiting room, watching the comedy unfold. He will vanish, and in his place there will be the crabbed philosopher Apemantus, who comments rudely during a feast:

　I scorn thy meat; 'twould choke me, for I should ne'er
　flatter thee. O you gods! What a number of men eats
　Timon, and he sees 'em not! It grieves me to see so many

dip their meat in one man's blood, and all the madness is,
he cheers them up too.

The feast is given to celebrate the arrival of Alcibiades, the general,
and Ventidius, who has been freed from prison, and certain lords of
Athens. As usual, Timon is the soul of generosity, and Apemantus, full
of foreboding, continues to warn him against flattery:

> What a coil's here,
> Serving of becks and jutting out of bums!

Supremely self-confident, Timon continues to pour out his
largess.

Suddenly Timon's debts are called in. A senator of Athens sends
messengers to Timon to demand immediate payment. One moment
Timon is saying: "I am wealthy in my friends." The next moment
he realizes that they all suffer from hereditary ingratitude, that their
blood is caked and cold, that all affection is gone, and they want
their money back. He rages, summons his former friends to one last
banquet, and when they come, he ceremonially offers them the
covered dishes while they lick ther lips. He orders his servants to
remove the covers. There is only hot water in the dishes. He rails at
them and hurls the hot water in their faces.

Timon abandoned Athens in disgust and made his way to an
abandoned place on the seashore. There, beside the vast sea, he
raged not so much against man's ingratitude as against the entire
human condition. Mortality is implicated, and so are the gods.
Chaos is come again but there is not enough chaos: he will stir the
pot. He declaims the litany of chaos:

> Maid, to thy master's bed,
> Thy mistress is o' th' brothel. Son of sixteen,
> Pluck the lined crutch from thy old limping sire,
> With it beat out his brains. Piety and fear,
> Religion to the gods, peace, justice, truth,
> Domestic awe, night rest, and neighbourhood,
> Instruction, manners, mysteries, and trades,
> Degrees, observances, customs, and laws,
> Decline to your confounding contraries,
> And let confusion live. Plagues incident to men,

Your potent and infectious fevers heap
On Athens ripe for stroke. Thou cold sciatica,
Cripple our senators, that their limbs may halt
As lamely as their manners. Lust and liberty
Creep in the minds and marrows of youth,
That 'gainst the stream of virtue they may strive,
And drown themselves in riot. . . .

There is a good deal more of it, for Timon delights in his witches' brew of curses. "Destruction fang mankind!" is one of his lesser curses. He is even more thunderous than the Sunday preachers reading from the official book of homilies. Suddenly, while grubbing among roots, he discovers gold treasure and at once realizes that the treasure can be used to destroy the human race:

This yellow slave
Will knit and break religions, bless th' accursed,
Make the hoar leprosy adored, place thieves,
And give them title, knee and approbation
With senators on the bench. This is it
That makes the wappened* widow wed again;
She, whom the spital-house and ulcerous sores
Would cast the gorge at, this embalms and spices
To the April day again. Come, damned earth,
Thou common whore of mankind, that puts odds
Among the rout of nations, I will make thee
Do thy right nature.

By the "right nature," of course, Timon means total and merciless destruction. He will not rest until the world is drowned in blood. Providentially at this moment Alcibiades, who has been banished from Athens and now thirsts for revenge, arrives outside Timon's cave accompanied by two trollops. Timon is overjoyed; Alcibiades will destroy humankind with the sword and the trollops with their diseases. He gives them gold and speeds them on their way, sure that all men will be plagued with them and that their activity "may defeat and quell the source of all erection."

*Worn-out.

Timon's rage is something to wonder at. He is coarse-humored, grimly determined, and close to madness, if he is not already mad. His feast of hate is full of rich fare. He can be as vicious as Hamlet when talking to Ophelia; there is something of Iago's craft in him. He can be the philosopher of nihilism, demanding that nature's womb shall dry up and all life come to an end. After the departure of Alcibiades, he digs for more gold and addresses the earth which is providing him with the means for earth's destruction:

> Common mother, thou,
> Whose womb immeasurable and infinite breast
> Teems and feeds all; whose selfsame mettle,
> Whereof thy proud child, arrogant man, if puffed,
> Engenders the black toad and adder blue,
> The gilded newt and eyeless venomed worm,
> With all the abhorred births below crisp heaven
> Whereon Hyperion's quick'ning fire doth shine;
> Yield him, who all the human sons do hate,
> From forth thy plenteous bosom, one poor root,
> Ensear* thy fertile and conceptious womb;
> Let it no more bring out ingrateful man,
> Go great with tigers, dragons, wolves, and bears,
> Teem with new monsters. . . .

Timon is in favor of selective destruction: man must be destroyed, but tigers and dragons may be allowed to roam the earth. Apemantus is inclined to agree with Timon's verdict, but receives no mercy when he appears at the cave. They engage in a slanging match, hating each other violently because they are in common agreement that man is hateful. But when some bandits come on the scene in search of hidden gold, Timon receives them well, for thievery is universal and to be applauded:

> The sun's a thief, and with his great attraction
> Robs the vast sea. The moon's an arrant thief,
> And her pale fire she snatches from the sun.
> The sea's a thief, whose liquid surge resolves

*Dry up.

The moon into salt tears. The earth's a thief
That feeds and breeds by a composture stolen
From general excrement.

So the thieves, like Alcibiades, are blessed and sent on their way. Other worthies come to visit Timon, including the poet and the painter, and the Athenian senators who beg Timon to take command of the city, which is in danger of being destroyed by Alcibiades. Timon refuses; he has better things to do, and the most urgent is dying. He tells the senators:

> Say to Athens
> Timon hath made his everlasting mansion
> Upon the beached verge of the salt flood,
> Who once a day with his embossed froth
> The turbulent surge shall cover. Thither come,
> And let my gravestone be your oracle.

In this way, by dissolving into sea and sand, Timon shows that he acquiesces to his own verdict on humanity. But curiously it is precisely at the moment when he prepares for death that he utters his best poetry and we remember him more for those five and a half lines than for all the rest. His curses on humankind are always ambiguous; he is never quite convincing. The hate, the hurt, the venom, and the misery are depicted in abstract speech. He broods too much, and there is little action. We see him tossing the dishes and the hot water at his guests, and later we see him grubbing for roots, but these are the limits of his action. He is so sternly stating the case for the prosecution of humanity that he scarcely leaves the center of the stage, so wrapped up is he in his own arguments. The play becomes a soliloquy, which takes many forms but always reverts to a central core: man is unworthy, man deserves to die. Shakespeare wrote the play in a state of acute depression. His energy rose when he cursed humanity and failed when it came to ordering a credible structure for the play.

Coriolanus suffers many of the same faults and crudities as *Timon of Athens*. Timon's fault was anger, one of the seven deadly sins; Coriolanus' fault is pride, the deadliest of the deadly sins. From being a man he has become "a lonely dragon"; his loneliness is something he feels on his nerves and senses. From pride comes his contempt for people and most especially his contempt for the common people of Rome, the mischievous and noisy mob. His opinion of the *plebs* is very clearly stated:

> They are dissolved: hang 'em!
> They said they are an-hungry, sighed forth proverbs,
> That hunger broke stone walls, that dogs must eat,
> That meat was made for mouths, that the gods sent not
> Corn for the rich men only—with these shreds
> They vented their complainings, which being answered
> And a petition granted them, a strange one—
> To break the heart of generosity,
> And make bold powers look pale—they threw their caps
> As they would hang them on the horns o' the moon,
> Shouting their emulation.

Like Timon, Coriolanus suffers from such an overwhelming disgust for humanity that one suspects a streak of madness in him. In his eyes nature comes to a peak of excellence in himself, in his self-portrait of a generous, bold-hearted man. How is it possible that the mob do not understand his natural excellence? Why do they not take their loving dictator into their arms? A similar question was much debated in England when the Earl of Essex was thinking of installing his own dictatorship. The question was left unanswered. In *Coriolanus* there are no answers, only arguments. As Coriolanus, in his pride and glory, surveys himself, finding no one superior to himself, withdrawn into himself to a degree that leaves him lacking in humanity, seeing the state as an abstraction and himself becoming daily more and more an abstraction of pride, we find ourselves wondering what all the fuss is about and whether there are any advantages at all in dictatorship, since inevitably the dictator must go m d. Coriolanus does go mad; he becomes a traitor by joining the Vols ians, hereditary enemies of Rome, for no better reason than that the Roman people are weary of his arrogance and contempt, and have banished him. From being the most popular and beloved man in Rome he becomes the most hated, the most despised. His own contempt for the people meets their contempt for him head on. One of the citizens sizes him up well:

Citizen. You have deserved nobly of your country,
and you have not deserved nobly.

Coriolanus. Your enigma?

Citizen. You have been a scourge to her enemies, you have
been a rod to her friends; you have not, indeed, loved the
common people.

Coriolanus defends himself as best he can, but not convincingly. He is a proud man proudly denying he is proud. He cannot conceal his withering contempt for the common people, "the beast with many heads." He possesses the least of the virtues, which is constancy.

A play written about a proud man can succeed only if the hero is abased. Coriolanus does, indeed, pretend to abase himself before the people, but they quickly detect that it is a pretense. They know him too well, and get rid of him. The Volscians also know him well, and in the end they too will get rid of him by killing him. Hidden in the last scene of the play is a defense of tyrannicide at least as cunning as John Milton's *Tenure of Kings and Magistrates*. Coriolanus was struck down because he was proud beyond human measure: he deserved to die.

Coriolanus is heavy in the way that Ben Jonson's Roman plays are heavy, which is to say that it is very nearly unreadable and unactable. The abstract arguments of Roman senators on the nature of power do not service to drama; the common people's argument against their rulers is never expressed adequately. The play is dry, leathery, full of a kind of running sore of self-disgust, self-horror, self-misery. There are memorable images in *Timon of Athens*, but there are very few in *Coriolanus*. Exhausted, saddened, and offended by the human condition, Shakespeare appears to have sunk into a stupor. He fell into the depths and then mounted into the heights.

The Crowning
of Cleopatra

B Y THE TIME SHAKESPEARE WROTE *Antony and Cleo-patra* he had recovered his spiritual health and broken away from the last vestiges of the mood of self-hatred and self-disgust that afflicted him at the time of *Timon of Athens*. He was like a patient who has come through a long illness into a calm convalescence; and as often happens during convalescence there is a strange heightening of the senses. Colors are brighter, touch is keener, taste and smell are more delicate, sounds are more piercing, and the sexual impulses are stronger. The convalescent, lying quietly in his bed, imagines himself in full vigor until he attempts to stand and put on his clothes; then he discovers that he is still weak with the after-effects of his illness.

Although the body remains weak, the imagination of a convalescent is often powerful and alert, stretching out into a newfound world of experiences. He has cut away many of the roots that attached him to the past, and some of these roots have been burned out by illness. He has the sensation of freedom; he tells himself he can accomplish anything he desires. His unbounded imagination

pours fuel on his sexual desires and these desires in turn provoke the
imagination. Sometimes the calm of convalescence is broken by
unpredictable sexual storms.

Of all Shakespeare's plays *Antony and Cleopatra* is the most
overtly sexual, not in the sense that *Romeo and Juliet, Hamlet*, and
Troilus and Cressida are filled with sexual images, but in a much
wider context. *Antony and Cleopatra* glows in the light of the sexual
imagination, and is colored by it. It is steeped in sexuality like the
sticky buds of a tree before it flowers. The sexual drive is slow and
sure and very open, like lovemaking on the banks of a river on a
summer afternoon.

It is a summery play and one may imagine it was written in
summer. There are only two characters, Antony and Cleopatra, for
the rest are spear carriers. Among them are some brilliant spear
carriers who step briefly to the front of the stage and comment at
shorter or greater length on what they see and know. We are back in
the world of "Venus and Adonis": the lovers at their play.

These lovers speak as the gods might speak if they were human.
They have no reserve; their freedom is absolute. Like the gods, they
are in a state of enchantment, so wrapped up in themselves that the
world scarcely exists for them even though the course of their love
affair involved the destiny of the world. They know from the
beginning that their love is doomed, but this is the least of their
preoccupations; it is there to be enjoyed, and the doom is also to be
enjoyed. There is very little violence. *Macbeth* and *Hamlet* crackle
with the sound of swordplay, screams in the night, alarms, sudden
forays. In *Antony and Cleopatra*, in spite of the apparent movement
of the actors across the stage—there are forty-two scenes and some
of them must be played at great speed—we are aware of a deep and
pervading silence, as the lover's talk transforms itself into the
gestures of love.

What creatures they are! Antony is strong and robust, handsome
beyond belief, youthful and majestic. Cleopatra is a whore raised to
the height of genius, splendid in her wantonness, possessing brilliant mental as well as physical powers, as majestic as Antony.
Shakespeare gives her a tawny skin, like Othello, but historically
she was of Greek descent. Plutarch, who thought Antony handsome,
though the surviving portraits show a rough and rather brutal face

without too much distinction, believed that Cleopatra was a woman of no particular beauty. Her portrait on coins shows a heavy nose and a jutting chin, but hints at an abundance of charm. Shakespeare was not writing only about the historical Antony and Cleopatra. He was imagining another Adonis and another Venus incandescent with love. A fire is burning in the center of the stage and we are the fascinated spectators of the flames.

With *Antony and Cleopatra* a new music entered English poetry. The music derives ultimately from passages in the translation of the Bible made by William Tyndale and Miles Coverdale first published in the Great Bible of 1539, especially the translation of *The Song of Solomon* and from Sir Thomas North's richly orchestrated translation of Plutarch's *Lives* first published in 1579. North, who had never read the Greek original, translated from the brilliant French version by Jacques Amyot. The result was a book of quite extraordinary coloring, with French rhythms racing alongside North's muscular but overdecorative English, somehow achieving a new balance, almost a new language. Shakespeare found himself at home in this language, which preserved echoes of ancient Greek. Indeed, he was so much at home in it that sometimes he scarcely changed a word of North's translation and set it down boldly in his play. Sometimes, too, he changed it only a little, but this little was enough to change the mood and the meaning.

It is worthwhile to watch Shakespeare closely as he turns the pages of North's Plutarch. Here, for example, is the most famous of all his borrowings:

> *Enobarbus.*   The barge she sat in like a burnisht throne
>   Burnt on the water: the poop was beaten gold,
>   Purple the sails: and so perfumed that
>   The winds were lovesick.
>   With them the oars were silver,
>   Which to the tune of flutes kept stroke, and made
>   The water which they beat to follow faster;
>   As amorous as their strokes. For her own person,
>   It beggared all description, she did lie
>   In her pavilion, cloth of gold, of tissue,
>   O'er-picturing that Venus where we see

The fancy outwork nature. On each side her
Stood pretty dimpled boys, like smiling Cupids,
With divers coloured fans whose wind did seem
To glove the delicate cheeks which they did cool,
And what they undid did.

Agrippa. Oh rare for Antony.

Enobarbus. Her gentlewomen, like the Nereides,
So many mermaids tended her i' the eyes,
And made their bands adornings. At the helm
A seeming mermaid steers: the silken tackle
Swell with the touches of those flower-soft hands
That yarely frame the office. From the barge
A strange invisible perfume hits the sense
Of the adjacent wharfes. The city cast
Her people out upon her: and Antony,
Enthroned in the market-place, did sit alone,
Whistling to the air: which but for vacancy
Had gone to gaze on Cleopatra too
And made a gap in nature.

Here is Plutarch in Sir Thomas North's version:

> . . . to take her barge in the river of Cydnus, the poop
> whereof was of gold, the sails of purple, and the oars of
> silver, which kept stroke in rowing after the sound of the
> music of flutes, hautboys, citherns, viols, and with other
> instruments as they played upon in the barge. And now for
> the person of her self: she was laid under a pavilion of cloth
> of gold of tissue, apparelled and attired like the goddess
> Venus, commonly drawn in picture: and hard by her, on
> either hand of her, pretty fair boys apparelled as painters do
> set forth god Cupid, with little fans in their hands, with the
> which they fanned wind upon her. Her ladies and
> gentlewomen also, the fairest of them were apparelled like
> the nymphs Nereides (which are the mermaids of the
> waters) and like the Graces, some steering the helm, others
> tending the tackle and ropes of the barge, out of which there
> came a wonderful passing sweet savour of perfumes, that

perfumed the wharf's side, pestered with innumerable
multitudes of people.

At first glance it would seem that Shakespeare has simply transcribed Plutarch and changed it only to suit the rhythm of his verse.
In fact he has done a good deal more: he has transformed Plutarch,
poured new paint on the canvas, invented new scenes, gestures, and
ideas, and so altered it that it has become something else entirely.
Plutarch provides the still photograph, which Shakespeare transforms into a movie.

Above all, Shakespeare has introduced the element of sexuality
and is not in the least reticent about it. The amorous strokes are not
the strokes of oars or hands. The barge which carries Cleopatra
becomes Cleopatra, swelling and glowing, pulsating with sexual
energy. "The silken tackle swell with the touches of those flower-
soft hands That yarely frame the office." A rope does not swell
when touched by flower-soft hands. "Yarely" means "nimbly, delicately"; "frame" means "perform." The Nereides, the mermaids,
are performing acts of love and bending their bodies invitingly. The
sexual imagination has taken command and thrust back the intellectual imagination. As often happens, the workings of the sexual
imagination lead to a certain confusion; we are never quite sure
what is taking place. The scene is bathed in sexual fire and we must
look between the flames to see what the lovers are up to. And
curiously, very little is happening to Cleopatra: all the lovemaking
is being done by the mermaids. As for Antony, he is sitting in
throned splendor in the marketplace, marking time. For a little
while longer he will be excluded from the sexual feast.

In this evocation of Cleopatra's barge Shakespeare's imagination
is displayed in its splendor. He does not describe Cleopatra any
more than Homer describes Helen of Troy; her beauty is charged
with the energy of everything around her. "The barge she sat in like
a burnisht throne Burnt on the water." Nothing of this was
supplied by Plutarch except the word "barge." Shakespeare's barge
becomes a burning ship, and at the same time it is a ship in full
flower, like the famous Attic vase painting which shows Dionysus
on a ship with a flowering vine for a mast. It is not in the least that
the ship has become a sexual symbol. Instead, as it moves along the

river, it becomes a sexual act performed poetically before our astonished eyes.

Such evocations are rare, and there are only three or four other places where Shakespeare performs this magic spell. It is not easy to conjure up a ship, or a house, or a landscape, and to endow them with sexual feeling. The classic example in modern literature is provided by D. H. Lawrence when he describes Lady Constance Chatterley running away from Mellors' hut: "As she ran home in the twilight the world seemed a dream; the trees in the park seemed bulging and surging at anchor on a tide, and the heave of the slope to the house was alive." Here the language of sexual love is defined. Lady Chatterley has left Mellors; their sexual encounter is over; she is living in the afterglow, while the heavens and the earth and all nature seem to be throbbing with sexual energy.

We must imagine that Shakespeare was nearly always aware of his resources and knew exactly what he was doing. His primal sexual images are deliberate, but what emerges from them is a certain confusion which is necessary for the progress of his verse and for the depiction of a mood. He was the first to use sexual images boldly. In *Macbeth* sexuality flows in the darkness; in *Othello* it seems to be exulting in the brilliant, watery light of Venice; in *Hamlet* it is always felt like the crackling in the air before the coming of the storm; in *Lear* it comes with the thunder and the lightning as the old King falls helplessly in love with his long-lost daughter; in *Antony and Cleopatra* it flows through a long summer afternoon.

Antony and Cleopatra see each other swimming in a sea of pleasure, possessing that awareness of each other that comes from loving. The sea becomes a bed, and the bed vanishes in the contemplation of the naked limbs of the beloved:

Cleopatra.　His face was as the heavens, and therein stuck
　　A sun and moon, which kept their course, and lighted
　　The little O, the earth.

Dolabella.　Most sovereign creature!

Cleopatra.　His legs bestrid the ocean, his rear'd arm
　　Crested the world: his voice was propertied
　　As all the tuned spheres, and that to friends.

> But when he meant to quail, and shake the orb,
> He was as rattling thunder. For his bounty,
> There was no winter in 't: an autumn 'twas
> That grew the more by reaping; his delights
> Were dolphin-like, they show'd his back above
> The element they lived in: in his livery
> Walk'd crowns and crownets: realms and islands were
> As plates dropp'd from his pocket.

Here, too, the sexual imagination is at work, the woman passionately observing her lover at his lovemaking. In the two great death scenes we are made aware that even death is seen in terms of the sexual climax, the man silent, the woman saying the same word again and again.

> *Cleopatra.* How heavy weighs my lord!
> Our strength is all gone into heaviness,
> That makes the weight. Had I great Juno's power,
> The strong-winged Mercury should fetch thee up
> And set thee by Jove's side. Yet come a little,
> Wishers were ever fools, O, come, come, come.

Here Cleopatra is addressing the dying Antony as he is pulled up in a bed sheet to her upper room, blood flowing from the wound he has inflicted upon himself. White-faced, with sunken eyes, he gazes fixedly at the audience as he is slowly lifted up; and in that scene, one of the most dramatic that Shakespeare ever conceived, the upward movement of the bloodstained sheet resembles a deposition in reverse. The dying hero is being lifted into the arms of his beloved, who is also dying. The theme of the *Liebestod* is continued until the very end of the play. In the most glorious passage where Cleopatra prepares herself for death and orders Charmian and Iras to place a crown on her head and to decorate her with jewels and her royal robe, we realize that she is adorning herself for her husband's sake, though he is dead. "Husband, I come," she says, and those three words, so simple and so effective, echo the previous thrice-repeated conjuration.

> *Cleopatra.* Give me my robe, put on my crown, I have
> Immortal longings in me. Now no more

The juice of Egypt's grape shall moist this lip.
Yare, yare, good Iras; quick; methinks I hear
Antony call. I see him rouse himself
To praise my noble act. I hear him mock
The luck of Caesar, which the gods give men
To excuse their after wrath. Husband, I come:
Now to that matter my courage prove my title!
I am fire and air; my other elements
I give to baser life. So, have you done?
Come then, and take the last warmth of my lips.
Farewell, kind Charmian. Iras, long farewell.
Have I the aspic in my lips? Dost fall?
If thou and Nature can so gently part,
The stroke of death is as a lover's pinch
Which hurts and is desir'd. Dost thou lie still?
If thus thou vanishest, thou tell'st the world
It is not worth leavetaking.

Charmian. Dissolve, thick cloud, and rain, that I may say
The gods themselves do weep.

Cleopatra. This proves me base:
If she first meet the curled Antony,
He'll make demand of her and spend that kiss
Which is my heaven to have. Come thou mortal wretch,
With thy sharp teeth this knot intrinsicate
Of life at once untie: Poor venomous fool,
Be angry, and dispatch. Oh, couldst thou speak,
That I might hear thee call great Caesar ass
Unpolicied.

Charmian. Oh, eastern star.

Cleopatra. Peace, peace:
Doest thou not see my baby at my breast,
That rocks the Nurse asleep?

Charmian. O break! O break!

Cleopatra. As sweet as balm, as soft as air, as gentle.
O Antony! Nay, I will take thee too.
What should I stay—   *Dies.*

Charmian.   In this wild world? So fare thee well:
Now boast thee, death, in thy possession lies
A lass unparallel'd. Downy windows, close,
And golden Phoebus, never be beheld
Of eyes again so royal: your crown's awry,
I'll mend it, and then play—

In this way with the utmost splendor Shakespeare brings Cleopatra's life to its inevitable close. It is as though he had invented it all, as though Cleopatra had no life outside his imagination. From North's *Plutarch* he found very little, only the words: "When they opened the doors, they found Cleopatra stark dead, layed upon a bed of gold, attired and arrayed in her royal robes, and one of her two women, which was called Iras, dead at her feet; and her other woman called Charmion half-dead, and trembling, trimming the diadem which Cleopatra ware upon her head." "Trimming" here means "straightening," and it was from this passage that Shakespeare derived the strange remark: "Your crown's awry, I'll mend it, and then play—" She will play the game of dying.

Prospero spoke of his own "rough magic." Shakespeare in these last scenes of *Antony and Cleopatra* plays the most delicate magic of all: he brings the divine lovers to life by putting them to death. They die, but their deaths are an apotheosis. Cleopatra knows she will die by her own hand, and all her offspring will die, and her royal line will die out, and she takes courage from mortality. Indeed, she revels in it, and all her greatest poetry is concerned with her coming death. A magical rite is being performed that will lead to the melting of her world. She is exalted by her forebodings. Her body, which Caesar and Antony had loved, which had given birth to Caesarion, and which had given her the most exquisite enjoyment, will perish utterly and become the food of insects:

. . . as it determines, so
Dissolve my life! The next Caesarion smite!
Till by degrees the memory of my womb,
Together with my brave Egyptians all,
By the discandying of this pelleted storm
Lie graveless, till the flies and gnats of Nile
Have buried them for prey.

"Discandying" means "melting," as sweets melt in the mouth, leaving nothing but their taste behind. Cleopatra sees herself melting into death, as earlier she had melted into love; and she is no more terrified by the prospect of death than a lover is terrified by a lover's pinch. It is not only that she welcomes death avidly with the sheer abandonment of a lover but she has not the least doubt that there are huge advantages to be gained by embracing death and entering immortality. Even though she is doomed to die graveless, eaten by flies and gnats like all the other Egyptians doomed by the Romans, she is superbly aware that Providence has reserved for her a special place in the visionary kingdom beyond the grave. Her death is therefore theatrical to the highest degree, as she sits on her high throne and commands her servants to perform the ultimate ministrations reserved for a great queen's death. She will die unhurt, unchanged. The asp in the basket of figs is scarcely more than a figment of her imagination. Shakespeare's last plays take place in the landscape of vision and enchantment. Real violence is laid aside. There will be no deaths, only resurrections. No blood will flow, the cutting edges of all knives will be dulled, there will be no paroxysms, no anguish, no contortions. She vanished in an explosion of pure colors, having become pure form.

In this way she enters the visionary kingdom which Shakespeare will explore in greater detail in his last plays, but never again will he explore the spiritual landscape with such calm assurance and in such a blazing light.

Shakespeare of the Enchanted Islands

The Death
of the
Prince

HENRY, PRINCE OF WALES, Knight and Baron of Renfrew, Lord of the Isles, Earl of Carick, Duke of Rothesay, Prince and great steward of Scotland, bore his resounding titles lightly. As the elder son of King James I, and heir to the throne, he showed himself in his appearance and in his actions to possess all those qualities lacking in his father. He was handsome, held himself well, made friends easily, was direct and simple in his personal affairs. James teetered when he walked; Henry strode. James was totally incapable of performing any task that required mechanical skill; Henry liked to work with shipwrights building ships and he especially enjoyed taking command of a ship. He danced well, swam well, played tennis whenever he had the opportunity, sometimes for four hours at a stretch, and it was remembered that when he lost a game he smiled as happily as when he won. The high and mighty prince sometimes showed his mettle: he had "a piercing grave eye" and "a terrible frown" when he felt that he was not receiving the respect due to him, but such moments were rare. He was tall and auburn-haired, broad-shouldered, narrow-waisted, lithe on his feet,

moved gracefully. He was so unlike his father that people sometimes wondered how such an ugly, shambling King could have
produced such a son. He had inherited only one of the King's
defects: his tongue was a little too big for his mouth, and he spoke
slowly and haltingly, and he would say he had "the most unservice-
able tongue of any man living." But when he asked questions, it was
remembered that he shaped them well and waited patiently for the
answer.

Prince Henry was very close to Sir Walter Raleigh, who wrote
his great *History of the World* to teach him history, and a book
called *Excellent Observations Concerning the Royal Navy and
Sea-Service* to teach him about warships, and a slender book called
The Prince, or Maxims of State to teach him about government and
diplomacy. George Chapman dedicated *The Tears of Peace* to
Prince Henry and earned a living as a servant in the prince's
household. Musicians, poets, and theologians dedicated their works
to the young prince. The most beautiful women of England were
available to him but he showed little interest in them, greeting them
all kindly when he attended the great balls designed to serve as
forcing grounds for his young manhood, and he favored none of
them. He was friendly with Ben Jonson, and he sometimes played
leading roles in the masques performed for the entertainment of the
King and Queen. One of his courtiers complained that he had only
two vices—an inordinate love for playing tennis and an inordinate
love for fruit.

In the summer of 1612, during the preparations for the marriage
of his sister Elizabeth to Frederick, the Elector Palatine, the
sixteen-year-old prince was seen to be pale and listless. He was well
enough for a few days to supervise the building of a huge tent of
green branches for a feast he offered for the King at Woodstock; he
went riding with the royal retinue, and seemed to be recovering.
Then he rode to London for the festivities attending the coming of
his sister's bridegroom, who landed at Gravesend on October 16 to
great acclamation. The Elector Palatine was small and dark—
Elizabeth called him "my Nigger Duckling"—but he possessed
sweetness and dignity, and he was loved because he was the grandson of the great William the Silent of the House of Orange. Prince
Henry took a great liking to Frederick. The festivities began the day

Frederick landed. During a banquet Prince Henry fainted; he was discovered to have a high fever and was put to bed in St. James's Palace. Soon it became clear that the prince was dying. His lips turned black, the fever made his skin paper-thin, and his face resembled a skull. The doctors bled him, which further weakened him. They shaved off his long hair, sliced a chicken in two, and clapped it to his head. Queen Anne, in her despair, begged Sir Walter Raleigh, who was in the Tower, to allow her son to drink some of the precious cordial called the Elixir of Life which was in his possession. Raleigh, who received daily bulletins about the prince's health, prepared the cordial, which arrived too late to do any good. James, in deadly fear of contracting his son's illness, fled from London. Princess Elizabeth, who was under orders not to go near her brother, disobeyed but was able to see him only briefly. He died on November 6, 1612, and was buried in Westminster Abbey.

With Prince Henry died the hope of England. It was as though something very precious had vanished from the scene. His promise, gaiety, youthful strength, openness of heart and mind augured well for England. James with his swollen tongue and coarse humors, eternally fiddling with his codpiece, surrounded by catamites, incompetent to deal with any matters of state in a sensible fashion, loving arguments but only on condition that he had the best of them, was generally despised. Since regicide was not yet fashionable, he had to be endured. Henry was loved extravagantly, and perhaps the hopes men had in him were also extravagant; they had less hope for his sharp-featured brother Charles. When he heard of the prince's death, Sir Walter Raleigh reached for the manuscript of his history of the world, wrote that the book had been written in "the service of that inestimable Prince," and wrote no more.

James decreed that the marriage festivities for Princess Elizabeth and the Elector Palatine should continue in spite of the death of the heir to the throne. At Christmas the court came out of mourning. At the New Year the courtiers followed the usual custom of presenting gifts to the King, and then they chose wedding gifts for Princess Elizabeth: it was an expensive winter. It was the time, too, for the Master of the Revels and his staff to prepare a long list of plays to be shown at court. That winter the King's Men performed before the King six times, and fourteen times before Princess Elizabeth, the Elector Palatine, and Prince Charles. Before the King they performed *Hotspur* and *Benedick and Beatrice,* which we know as *I Henry IV* and *Much Ado About Nothing. The Tempest, The Winter's Tale, The Moor of Venice, Caesar's Tragedy,* and *Sir John Falstaff,* which was probably *The Merry Wives of Windsor,* were performed before the young people together with the popular *Benedick and Beatrice.* For the King's Men and for Shakespeare it was a highly profitable season.

In spite of all the glittering festivities, it was a strange, feverish, and unhappy time. Plays, masques, feasts, and entertainments followed one another at a hectic pace. At the gambling tables fortunes were lost and won overnight, and sometimes James appeared at the tables not to play but to watch one of his courtiers gambling with money lent to him from the King's pocket. The young princess's marriage took place in the Chapel Royal in Whitehall on February 14, 1613. The bride and bridegroom wore robes of silver cloth, and the princess's long hair was dressed with ropes of pearls. James came in his full regalia, wearing jewels estimated to be worth £600,000, and Queen Anne wore a white satin gown weighed down with jewelry worth only a little less. On the wedding night and for two successive nights there were masques at court honoring the newly married couple.

The gaiety was a little too wild, there was too much drinking, too much laughter. The mood of excitement continued long after the wedding celebrations. Raleigh wrote in the *History of the World:* "The World's bright glory hath put out the eyes of the mind." Now very little of the glory remained; the people knew that James would continue to waste the nation's treasure; already there could be heard the first rumblings of civil war; already the Cavaliers and the Roundheads were taking up positions. Within a generation they would be at each other's throats.

For a dozen more years James would continue to reign as an absolute monarch—Parliament had been dismissed in 1611 and the King ruled through the Privy Council, which was composed of the King's favorites. The younger and more handsome of them soon succeeded in adorning themselves with titles and in fleecing the treasury. Robert Carr, Earl of Somerset, the penniless fifth son of an obscure Scottish knight, emerged as the favorite of favorites, having nothing to recommend him except his good looks. Carr ruled while James reigned, and shared the King's bed, and knew nothing about the arts of government.

In this decaying court Shakespeare thrived. He wrote, directed, and acted in plays as a member of the King's Men under the King's protection. He was present in London throughout the winter festivities, conducted negotiations with the Master of the Revels, and was inevitably summoned into the royal presence to discuss which plays should be put on. The King's Men received £153 6s 8d for the fourteen plays they presented during the festivities. Shakespeare now was rich enough to look around London for a town house.

He bought the Blackfriars Gatehouse. It was an admirable choice, close to the Blackfriars Theatre and close to Puddle Wharf, where the wherries would take him across the river to Southwark and the Globe Theatre. He bought the house from a certain Henry Walker, described as a "citizen and minstrel of London." In 1604 Walker had bought the house for £100. Thirteen years later he asked for £140. Shakespeare agreed to pay this sum, and a deed of conveyance was drawn up, dated March 10, 1613, full of the usual finely wrought legalistic language identifying the exact site of the house and the garden and introducing "all and singular cellars, sollers, rooms, lights, easiments, profits, commodities and hereditaments." The property abutted "upon a street leading down to Puddle Wharf on the east part, right against the King's Majesty's Wardrobe." The conveyance was signed by Shakespeare and by his close friends William Johnson, the vintner who kept the Mermaid Tavern, and John Jackson, merchant and landowner, who possessed a talent for light verse. The conveyance has the interesting detail that the house together with the other property of the Dominican priory had fallen at the time of the dissolution of the monasteries to the Earl of Northumberland but at some period the gatehouse was detached and came into the possession of a certain Mathias Bacon, who sold it to Henry Walker.

It is generally assumed that Shakespeare bought the house as an investment, did not live in it, and had no intention of living in it. This may be true but is highly unlikely. He needed a London residence of his own, and for his purposes the Blackfriars Gatehouse could not have been more desirable. The gatehouse of a Dominican priory would be very large and commodious, the many-windowed principal room running above the gateway, and there were kitchens, a well house, a storehouse, a buttery, lofts and sleeping quarters for the servants, stables, and shops. At this moment there was a haberdasher's shop on the ground floor. A young aristocrat would have enjoyed having such an address together with the advantages of a small income from the ground floor.

On the following day Shakespeare turned about and executed another deed which stipulated that £60 of the purchase money was to remain in mortgage until the following Michaelmas. This was simply an expedient to delay paying the full purchase price. Henry Walker insisted that there should be three, not two, witnesses to the agreement, and kindly John Hemminge obliged Shakespeare by adding his signature, thus establishing himself as a guarantor. Instead of taking full possession of the house, Shakespeare leased it to John Robinson. Three years later Shakespeare willed the Blackfriars Gatehouse to his daughter Susanna, carefully identifying the place: "All that messuage or tenement with the apurtenances wherein one John Robinson dwelleth, situate, lying and being in the Blackfriars in London near the Wardrobe."

Who was John Robinson? Then as now the name was so common that it becomes difficult to distinguish any particular person with that name. There were four John Robinsons in Stratford at the time, and at least one in Blackfriars. Most of them appear to have been common laborers and it is entirely unlikely that Shakespeare would lease the gatehouse to a laborer. It is more likely that the mysterious John Robinson was a young actor or a body servant or both, for he was clearly very close to Shakespeare. He was in Stratford when Shakespeare was dying and was one of the five witnesses to Shakespeare's will, writing his name in a firm educated hand with a large and satisfying *f* for *s* and a neat flourish to the final *n*.

One would like to know more about John Robinson, who vanishes among his namesakes, but he remains a mystery.

A few days after Shakespeare signed the conveyance for the Blackfriars Gatehouse, Thomas Screvin, one of the stewards of Francis Manners, the sixth earl of Rutland, recorded in his account book:

> Item, March 31, to Mr. Shakespeare in gold about my
> Lords impreso, 44s; to Richard Burbage for painting and
> making it, in gold 44s.

This means that both Shakespeare and Burbage were paid for making a design on an *impresa,* one of those highly decorative shields worn by knights at tourneys. They were made of paper or pasteboard, were usually carried by the knight's squire, and resembled imaginary coats of arms with real mottoes. Evidently Lord Rutland hoped to acquire an *impresa* of great charm and was prepared to pay handsomely for it. Burbage was a painter as well as an actor, and Shakespeare apparently enjoyed writing mottoes for his friends and acquaintances. No trace of the Shakespeare-Burbage design has been found among the Rutland papers. In *Pericles* Shakespeare describes six *imprese*, beginning with a black Ethiopian reaching out for the sun with the motto *Lux tua vita mihi* (Your light is life to me), and ending with a withered branch and the motto *In hac spe vivo* (In this hope I live). More complicated *imprese* are known to have been designed, but in general they aimed at poetic simplicity.

The occasion for the tourney was the tenth anniversary of King James's accession to the throne. This took place on March 24, 1613, a week before the payments were made to Shakespeare and Burbage. Sir Henry Wotton, who attended the tourney as a spectator, was not impressed by the tourney and still less by the *imprese*, for he wrote a full account of them to his friend Sir Edmund Bacon, who was living in the country and eagerly awaiting news from London. Wotton thought he had seen many of the *imprese* before and wondered why the contestants were so frugal as to show their outworn shields. There were some, he commented, "so dark that their meaning is not yet understood." This, of course, is to miss the point. Darkness, mystery, was the mark of a good *impresa*. He was, however, impressed by two *imprese* which belonged to two friends of Shakespeare, William and Philip Herbert, Earls of Pembroke and Montgomery. Sir Henry Wotton wrote: "The two best, to my fancy, were those of the two Earls brothers: the first a small, exceeding white pearl, and the words *Solo candore valeo;* the other a sun casting a glance on the side of a pillar and the beams reflecting, with this motto, *Splendente refulget;* in which there seemed an agreement, the elder brother to allude to his own nature, and the other to his fortune."

Wotton, an excellent letter writer with a proper appreciation of the dignity and splendor of the Earls of Pembroke and Montgomery, was a man with fatal defect of character. He adored everything that was fashionable; he loved baubles, delighted in mischievous gossip, and was adept at intrigues. His sins, which were many, were forgiven many years after his death when a single poem was found among his papers. The poem was entitled: "To His Mistress, the Queen of Bohemia," who was James's daughter, Princess Elizabeth, who briefly became the Queen of Bohemia:

You meaner beauties of the night,
  That poorly satisfy our eyes
More by your number than your light,
  You common people of the skies;
  What are you when the moon shall rise?

You curious chanters of the wood,
  That warble forth Dame Nature's lays,
Thinking your passions understood
  By your weak accents; what's your praise
  When Philomel her voice shall raise?

You violets that first appear
  By your pure purple mantles known
Like the proud virgins of the year,
  As if the spring were all your own;
  What are you when the rose is blown?

So, when my mistress shall be seen
  In form and beauty of her mind,
By virtue first, then choice, a Queen
  Tell me, if she were not designed
  The eclipse and glory of her kind.

To Sir Henry Wotton it was given to compose the only perfect poem in the English language addressed to a queen.

Shakespeare composed no poem for his Queen, perhaps because he knew the life of the court too well to be enchanted by her. He recorded the triumphs of the Tudor dynasty but with a sense of reluctance which can be heard throughout *Henry VIII*. The only King he seems to have unreservedly admired is Henry V. He possessed the reverence and awe before kingship that was common in his age, but he had no undue fondness for the physical persons who inhabited the royal robes.

Thomas Screvin's brief entry in his account book concerning Lord Rutland's *impresa* is the last surviving reference to Shakespeare as a Londoner. We hear of a few financial transactions in Stratford; there is his will; there is the entry in the church register at his death. We know that he wrote more plays, but the exact circumstances of his writing them are unknown.

In March 1613 Shakespeare was forty-nine years old, at the height of his powers. He had not written himself out. The sentimental view that in *The Tempest* he made his farewell to the stage, preferring to live the rest of his life as a country gentleman, can be disproved, for he went on to write with or without the assistance of John Fletcher three more plays: *Henry VIII,* the lost *Cardenio,* and *The Two Noble Kinsmen.* The first of these has an honored place in the First Folio, *Cardenio* is something of a mystery, and there is now a general acceptance among scholars that *The Two Noble Kinsmen* is very largely the work of Shakespeare.

Cardenio has an interesting history. It was performed during the festivities for the marriage of Princess Elizabeth and the Elector without attribution. In 1563 the publisher and collector of manuscripts Humphrey Moseley announced the forthcoming publication of *The History of Cardenio* by John Fletcher and William Shakespeare. It was never published, and we next hear of it in 1727 when Lewis Theobald, the Shakespearean scholar, announced that he had acquired no fewer than three manuscript copies of *Cardenio* and proceeded to stage the play at the Drury Lane Theatre, changing the names of the characters, and revising it to suit the taste of his time very much as Dryden revised *Antony and Cleopatra,* calling it *Double Falsehood or the Distrest Lovers.* Theobald published the play during the following year, describing it as "written originally by W. Shakespeare, and now revised and adapted for the stage by Mr. Theobald."

How much of truth or falsehood there is in *Double Falsehood* is a matter of dispute. Theobald was a brilliant scholar and a nearly incompetent playwright. The play reads lamely but has magnificent lines which almost certainly derive from Shakespeare:

Strike up, my Masters;
But touch the strings with a religious softness.
Teach sound to languish through the night's dull ear,
Till melancholy start from her lazy couch
And carelessness grow convert to attention.

Such miraculous things were beyond the compass of anyone except Shakespeare. Oddly enough Theobald claimed that this was one of his own additions to the play. Nothing more was heard of the three manuscripts, and it is just possible that they vanished in the famous holocaust which took place about 1730 when John Warburton, a collector of manuscripts, discovered to his horror that his collection was "unluckily burned or put under pie bottoms by his cook."

The History of Cardenio exists today in an agreeable limbo of the imagination as a collaboration between Fletcher, Cervantes, and Shakespeare. Thomas Shelton had produced a translation of *Don Quixote* in 1612. Cardenio, a fool of love, with long black matted beard and deep-sunk staring eyes, was running wild in the Sierra Morena when Don Quixote and Sancho Panza found him. Don Quixote invited him to tell his story but Cardenio was as prickly as the Knight of the Woeful Countenance. Cardenio hurled a stone at Don Quixote, threw him to the ground, and did the same to Sancho Panza before running back to his hiding place in the mountains. When they met again, Cardenio related the story of his unrequited love affair with the beautiful Luscinda, who fell prey to Don Ferdinand, the second son of a duke. A wedding was arranged, and Cardenio watched it from behind the tapestries; Luscinda swooned before the marriage ceremony was completed; her mother opened her bodice to permit her to breathe and found a letter in which she declared she loved only Cardenio and would kill herself if she was forced to marry another. Don Ferdinand swore vengeance, and Cardenio fled to the mountains and took to living in a hollow cork tree when he was not dancing from crag to crag. So the ludicrous adventures continue, and the mad Cardenio is an admirable foil for the mad Don Quixote, who refuses to believe that the age of chivalry has departed.

One would like to read the words Shakespeare put into the mouths of Don Quixote and Cardenio. Cervantes and Shakespeare were contemporaries, and they died within a few hours of one another. They would have looked well together: the neat, fastidious, high-domed Shakespeare, elegant and well groomed, rich with lands and houses, and the poor Cervantes, who struggled to make a living writing plays and failed in all of them, stoop-shouldered, heavily built, his face deeply lined, his silver beard jutting out, his left hand destroyed by an arquebus at the battle of Lepanto, his eyes glittering with a savage light in them. They were brothers in arms and gave glory to their age, so that we speak of "the Age of Shakespeare" and "the Age of Cervantes," forgetting the kings and dignitaries who thought themselves in charge of the world's destinies. Cervantes was unluckier than Shakespeare, for he never received the patronage of high personages, lived out his life in misery and loneliness, and confronted adversity with the only weapons he possessed: his doggedness and his genius. Except for a very brief period at the beginning of his career, Shakespeare lived in affluence. Cervantes, hounded by poverty, lived like a beggar. Both of them explored the undiscovered territories of the human spirit with a passionate eagerness to discover the utmost truths; they were both violent men who wrestled with angels and were merciless to themselves.

In an age of great explorations they were the greatest adventurers of all.

The Discovery
of the
Islands

IN SHAKESPEARE'S LAST PLAYS we hear a strange and unfamiliar music. This music seems to have little enough to do with drama, for it is haunting and peaceful like the sound of running streams or the wind wandering in caverns or a shepherd's piping. The music is immediately recognizable, yet nothing quite like it was ever heard before. The organ notes are rarely sounded; the clang of metal is no longer heard; the voice is whispered, very intimate. We are far from the resounding utterances of the English kings at court or on the battlefield. We have entered a new landscape, where the air is lighter and softer, and the skies more spacious. We are in the islands set in the open seas.

Shakespeare set out to explore the islands and in his own way provided a geography: the shapes of cliffs, field paths, scattered farms, and sandy beaches. It is true that the islands look remarkably like the British Isles, but they have become smaller, brighter, more accessible. We could travel over them in half a day. There are no towns, and London is nowhere to be seen. When ships come to these islands, they are always shipwrecked.

These last plays—*Pericles, Cymbeline, The Winter's Tale, The Tempest*, and *The Two Noble Kinsmen*—bear a family resemblance. They come from the same lode, the same characters appear in them, though the names change; the dead come back to life, or rather it is shown that they never died; and scenes of madness and terror are followed by pastoral interludes. The gods are present, even though we never see them, and through their oracles they announce their high and solemn purposes. In these plays there are no titanic battles of will, no ferocious denunciations of the heavens. Evil men are punished, not by being thrown into jail or sentenced to death, but by an alteration of events that prevents them from continuing along their evil paths. We are kept at a little distance from all these characters. Never for a moment do we enter into their burning hearts, as we do in *Othello, King Lear*, and *Antony and Cleopatra*. There is a fence around them. They belong to another world.

All this, of course, is a simplification, for while the plays are very similar in their music and their feeling, in their intense preoccupation with innocence and the restoration of the kingdom to the rightful king, they are remarkably different in the characterization of the minor figures. It is fashionable to say that the plays are concerned with reconciliation and moral rebirth and the artist's pilgrimage toward true happiness. A specifically Christian interpretation has often been given to them by critics who fail to observe the presence of the pagan gods. While there is no reason to believe that he is writing parables, it is certain that he is writing out of deep religious feeling. They are fables and deal with fabulous events; there is a glory in them, and they speak of heavenly things. There is no heavenly Jerusalem but there is a new heavenly world, a world of freshness and delight. Through this world, which seems to be entirely of the imagination, Shakespeare walks surefooted.

> O wonder!
> How many goodly creatures are there here!
> How beauteous mankind is! O brave new world
> That has such creatures in it!

In this world fear has vanished and the heart knows its own reasons. All those anxieties which normally beset the human creature are muted and made endurable, as though exorcised by magic spells. Off these magical islands there may be a storm at sea but over the seacoast there are summer skies.

Quite evidently Shakespeare has conjured up these landscapes for a purpose. He has decided to create dramas which are far removed from the revenge tragedies he created in his younger years. Instead of the human appetite for revenge there is the divine longing for mercy. He studies the workings of divinity to bring about the new world in which revenge and hatred will have no place, where men and women will be at peace with each other, where love will be stripped of its pretensions and all men will be ruled by their affections, without pride, without ambitions, caring for one another.

Although the new landscape is clearly defined and the new characters move about in it with ease, Shakespeare never explains why he felt so great a need for them. There are few clues, not all of them satisfactory. He was obsessed with the deaths of children, for his own son Hamnet had died when he was only eleven years old. Ophelia, Desdemona, and Cordelia were only a little older when they died. Almost they were children. They were innocent: why should death strike them? They were jewels lost in the shipwreck at the bottom of the sea: how could they be brought into the sunlight? So he imagined them as babes or children abandoned at sea or on the seacoast, miraculously found, and permitted to live in full enjoyment of their inheritance.

Grief for a dead child can shake a man for the rest of his life. Twenty or thirty years may pass, but the grief remains, growing with every passing year. Grief is a passion which can destroy a man and drive him to madness. For Shakespeare the death of Hamnet was probably the most shattering experience of his life, causing him the most suffering. Hamnet died in the summer of 1596, and the shock of the boy's death would still be vivid to Shakespeare many years later.

There appears in the burial-register of St. Clement Danes in London the entry: "Jane Shackspeer daughter of Willm. 8 Aug. 1609." We do not know how old she was, and we know nothing about her mother. This was a plague year, when the doors of the playhouses were locked, and the actors went on tour. A few weeks earlier Shakespeare's *Sonnets* were published by Thomas Thorpe, and it was possible that Shakespeare was in London during the summer.

"Jane Shackspeer daughter of Willm," carried off by the plague, is a haunting and appealing figure. Nicholas Rowe hinted at an illegitimate daughter, saying that Shakespeare had three daughters, of whom two, Susanna and Judith, lived to be married, and he said nothing at all about the third daughter. Shakespeare's brother Edmund had fathered an illegitimate son, Edward, two years earlier. There were not many William Shakespeares in London, and it is possible and likely that Jane was his daughter.

Jane Shakespeare, whose name is preserved in a single entry in a burial register, throws a long shadow over Shakespeare's last plays. Somewhere about this time there was a death of a young woman so painful to him that he had to bring her to life in his plays. He had to see her, he had to imagine her living out her life to its fulfillment, he had to hear her voice and invent her music, and he had to do this even to madness. In all these plays there is the compulsion "to bring to life." The sadness is beyond tears. Thaisa's words to Pericles:

> Did you not name a tempest,
> A birth, and death?

speak of a vast hope and a return from the grave.

Pericles, Prince of Tyre is a deeply puzzling play. Many things have gone wrong. It was not included in the First Folio for reasons that are obscure. The text is notoriously corrupt, and the organization of the play is notoriously incompetent. The first two acts could not have been written by Shakespeare, for there is not a redeeming line in either of them, and then quite suddenly with the third act Shakespeare's voice is heard distinctly like a roll of thunder and once more he is talking about a tempest:

> The God of this great Vast, rebuke these surges,
> Which wash both heaven and hell, and thou that hast
> Upon the winds command, bind them in brass;
> Having call'd them from the deep, o still
> Thy deaf'ning dreadful thunders, gently quench
> Thy nimble sulphurous flashes: o how Lichorida!

How does my Queen? Then storm venomously,
Wilt thou spit all thyself? The seaman's whistle
Is as a whisper in the ears of death.
Unheard, Lichorida? Lucina, oh!
Divinest patroness, and midwife gentle
To those that cry by night, convey thy deity
Aboard our dancing boat, make swift the pangs
Of my Queen's travels.

Pericles, after many adventures, is returning to his own city of
Tyre with his Queen, Thaisa, who dies in childbirth in the midst of
the storm to the horror of the sailors who believe that a dead body on
shipboard will bring disaster to the ship. She must be thrown
overboard, otherwise they will all drown. Pericles does not argue
with the sailors. He gazes down at Thaisa, bidding her farewell:

A terrible child-bed hast thou had, my dear,
No light, no fire, th' unfriendly elements,
Forget thee utterly, nor have I time
To give thee hallow'd to thy grave, but straight
Must cast thee scarcely coffin'd in the ooze,
Where for a monument upon thy bones,
The aye-remaining lamps, the belching Whale,
And humming water must o'erwhelm thy corpse,
Lying with simple shells: o Lichorida,
Bid Nestor bring me spices, ink, and paper,
My casket, and my jewels; and bid Nicander
Bring me the satin coffin: lay the Babe
Upon the pillow; hie thee whiles I say
A priestly farewell to her: suddenly, woman.

So Pericles places the Queen in a coffin together with a letter
giving her name and title, and calling upon those who find her to
give her proper burial, adding that the gods will reward them.
When the storm dies down, we are in the house of Cerimon, a
doctor, a man who has studied physic and learned the secret properties of metals, stones, and herbs, believing that knowledge and
virtue have the power of "making a man a god." We hear of his
charity and of how he has healed hundreds of his fellow creatures

without thought of gain. To this good doctor some servants bring the coffin that has been cast ashore by the storm. Cerimon orders them to open the coffin, revealing Thaisa, who appears to be a lifeless corpse. The doctor knows better. He orders fires to be lighted, prepares medicaments for her, commands the musicians to play for her, and soon the dead Queen begins to move and "to blow into life's flower again." And since for Shakespeare the light of life is in the eyes, we watch how her eyelids "begin to part their fringes of bright gold" to show her eyes gleaming like diamonds.

Thaisa comes to life, but her daughter Marina, "born of the sea," is condemned to a living death. For unexplained reasons she has been entrusted by Pericles to Cleon, the governor of Tarsus. As the child grows older, Cleon's wife grows jealous of her beauty and decides to kill her, and at the moment when we first hear of her decision, Marina, now about fourteen, enters with a basket of flowers, singing even more richly than Ophelia:

> I will rob Tellus of her weed
> To strew thy green with flowers, the yellows, blues,
> The purple violets, and marigolds,
> Shall as a carpet hang upon thy grave,
> While summer days doth last: Aye me, poor maid,
> Born in a tempest, when my mother died,
> The world to me is as a lasting storm,
> Whirring me from my friends.

She is singing a lament over her own murder, for she has the gift of prophecy. She sees herself buried and her grave strewn with summer flowers. But before Cleon and his wife can murder her, she is captured by pirates, taken to Mytilene, sold into a brothel, and ordered to perform the duties of a prostitute. Her innocence defends her; she does not know what prostitution is, and parries her accusers. "Whither would you have me?" she asks, and Boult, the pandar's servant, replies in his matter-of-fact way: "I must have your maidenhead taken off, or the common hangman shall execute it." Lysimachus, governor of Mytilene, comes to the brothel as a client, falls in love with her, gives her money so that she can buy her freedom, and then for some reason leaves her in the tender hands of Boult, who is all for putting her to profitable use in the shortest possible time. What he does not know, and what the reader and the spectator know very well, is that she is a divine child divinely protected and that her gift of prophecy is not always infallible. Pericles will come and take her in his arms, and the lost mother will return to do the same service. Thaisa indeed has become a priestess of Diana and is only waiting for the day when Pericles and Marina will be restored to her.

Shakespeare depicted the brothel scene with calculated cruelty and violence. This was necessary in order to establish belief in the subsequent scenes, where accidental encounters and the workings of manifest destiny play havoc with credulity. Pericles arrives by ship in Mytilene. He is a man still crazed by grief over the loss of his wife and daughter, silent as though his tongue had been torn out by the roots. Lysimachus welcomes him on shipboard. It occurs to him that there is one person on the island who might have the power to arouse him from his stupor. Providentially Marina arrives at this moment and sings a song. Pericles shows no emotion. He has heard songs before and has not yet recognized his daughter. Marina is determined to awake him, to make him look up at her, and speaks:

> I am a maid, my Lord, that ne'er before invited eyes,
> But have been gazed on like a Comet:
> She speaks my Lord, that maybe hath endured
> A grief right equal yours, if both were justly weigh'd.
> Though wayward fortune did malign my state,
> My derivation was from ancestors
> Who stood equivalent with mighty kings,
> But time hath rooted out my parentage,
> And to the world and awkward casualties
> Bound me in servitude.

The words are printed as prose, but we can detect some traces of the original verse in the corrupt text. Pericles stirs into life. It seems to him that she possesses the modesty of justice and resembles "a palace for the crowned truth to dwell in." He will believe her whatever she says. She speaks about her strange birth and her mother's death, and Pericles rouses himself, seeing at last that his daughter has come back to him. He addresses Hellicanus, one of the lords of Tyre:

Pericles. I embrace you. Give me my robes.
I am wild in my beholding. O heavens, bless
                    my girl,
But hark what music tell, Hellicanus! my Marina!
Tell him o'er point by point, for yet he seems
                    to dote:
How sure you are my daughter; but what music?
Hellicanus. My Lord, I hear none.
Pericles. None? The music of the spheres, list, my
    Marina!
Lysimachus. It is not good to cross him, give
                    him way.
Pericles. Rarest sounds, do ye not hear?
Lysimachus. Music, my Lord? I hear.
Pericles. Most heavenly music.
It nips me into listening, and thick slumber
Hangs upon mine eyes. Let me rest.

So he rests until the time comes when he, Marina, Cerimon, Lysimachus, Hellicanus, and their attendants enter the temple of Diana to find Thaisa serving as a priestess. Pericles fails to recognize her but Thaisa recognizes his voice. And thereupon Pericles utters a cry from the heart:

You gods . . . you shall do well
That on the touching of her lips I may
melt and no more be seen. O, come, be buried
A second time in my arms.

In this way the play with its melting tenderness comes to an end, yet never seems to end. It has the quality of vision, of an illumination. A double grief, for a lost mother and a lost daughter, is transformed into a double triumph; and Pericles stands transfixed with joy, his heart mended and his life restored. Never again will Shakespeare utter so piercing a cry of joy.

Pericles, Prince of Tyre has a strangeness about it, but there is as much, and more, strangeness in *Cymbeline*. Once more there is an innocent daughter who is lost and found, babes abandoned, a woman restored to life, the knowledge that the innocent daughter is under divine protection. Pericles is a strong-willed or at least determined king, who loves his daughter. In *Cymbeline* the King is lukewarm toward Imogen, who falls from favor by marrying Posthumus, "a poor but worthy gentleman," who is banished to Italy. There he meets Iachimo, who resembles Iago to the extent that he suffers from the disease of malignity. Iachimo steals into Imogen's bedroom at night, purloins her bracelet, observes a mole on her breast, and proves to Posthumus' satisfaction that she has been unfaithful to him. Posthumus sends Pisanio, his servant, to murder her.

All this is a proper subject for romance, even for tragedy. Yet Shakespeare writes in the mood of *Venus and Adonis*, without wholly believing what he is writing, conjuring up the shape of the story as he goes along, the spider spinning the web, the writer at odds with the story yet making the best of it, even when the characters are nearly unmanageable. When Pisanio tells Imogen that he will take her to Milford Haven to meet Posthumus, she accompanies him willingly and all the more so because she is being pursued by Cloten, the son of Cymbeline's present wife. When he announces that he must murder her because she has been false to Posthumus, she answers unbelievingly:

> False to his bed? What is it to be false?
> To lie in watch there, and to think on him?
> To weep 'twixt clock and clock? If sleep charge Nature,
> To break it with a fearful dream of him,
> And cry myself awake? That's false to bed, is it?

Pisanio has no appetite for murder, offers Imogen his sword, and hopes to die at her hands in expiation of a crime he was nearly forced to commit. Imogen, more concerned with her husband's madness and its causes, intrigued by his arguments and in no mood to kill the man who is her protector, decides upon flight. She will vanish so completely that no one will ever find her. She will change her sex and her name: she becomes the page boy Fidele. And since this is a romance, she will find her hiding place in a cave in the Welsh mountains with Belarius, the war chieftan, an old and kindly man, who has been banished by King Cymbeline. In addition to Belarius in the cave there are two boys, Arviragus and Guiderius, sons of Cymbeline who were long ago captured by Belarius. The boys do not know they are the sons of a king. They know Belarius by the name he has chosen for himself—Morgan. Arviragus has been given the name of Cadwal. Guiderius has been given the name of Polydore. Imogen, of course, presents herself as the boy Fidele. Thus all the people in the cave are known by names which are not their true names.

Life in the Welsh mountains has severe disadvantages, only too well known to Arviragus, who complains to the wise Belarius:

> What should we speak of
> When we are as old as you? when we shall hear
> The rain and wind beat dark December, how,
> In this our pinching cave, shall we discourse
> The freezing hours away? We have seen nothing;
> We are beastly, subtle as the fox for prey,
> Like warlike as the wolf for what we eat;
> Our valour is to chase what flies; our cage
> We make a quire, as doth the prison'd bird,
> And sing our bondage freely.

When Imogen comes to the cave, their spirits soar a little. Belarius, too, exults in this newfound companion of their miseries. "By Jupiter, an angel!" he cries. "Behold divineness no elder than a boy." But their happiness in Fidele's coming is short-lived. Soon, against all probability, Cloten, searching for Imogen, arrives near the cave, quarrels violently with Guiderius, and has his head cut off, and about the same time Imogen falls ill and takes a drug which gives her the appearance of a corpse. The boys are ecstatic at the thought of having killed Cloten and utterly downcast by Fidele's death. To Arviragus there is given the great speech comparing Fidele with the flowers he will place on her grave:

> With fairest flowers
> While summer lasts, and I live here, Fidele,
> I'll sweeten thy sad grave: thou shalt not lack
> The flower that's like thy face, pale primrose, nor
> The azur'd harebell, like thy veins: no, nor
> The leaf of eglantine, whom not to slander,

Out-sweetened not thy breath: the ruddock* would
With charitable bill (O bill, more shaming
Those rich-left heirs, that let their fathers lie
Without a monument!) bring thee all this;
Yea, and furred moss besides.

But it is given to his brother Guiderius to sing her requiem in verses that announce the heart and core of the play in a way that is not mournful. "Fear not!" he proclaims, as he gazes down at the body of the page boy he has scarcely known, not knowing that it is the body of his sister, Imogen:

Fear no more the heat o' th' sun,
   Nor the furious winter's rages,
Thou thy worldly task hast done,
   Home art gone and ta'en thy wages.
Golden lads and girls all must
Like chimney-sweepers, come to dust

Fear no more the frown o' th' great,
   Thou art past the tyrant's stroke,
Care no more to clothe and eat,
   To thee the reed is as the oak:
The sceptre, learning, physic must
All follow this and come to dust.

Fear no more the lightning-flash,
   Nor th' all-dreaded thunder-stone.
Fear not slander, censure rash.
   Thou hast finish'd joy and moan.
All lovers young, all lovers must
Consign to thee and come to dust.

It is one of Shakespeare's most magical poems, being a magic spell to cast out all fear. And indeed in these last plays Shakespeare is much concerned with fear, or rather with the spells that conquer fear. "Be not afraid: the isle is full of noises." Fear is a kind of ravishment that Shakespeare takes pains to exorcise.

*Robin.

But fear remains with Imogen. When she wakes up from the effects of the drug, she finds herself alone with the headless body of Cloten. The boys and Belarius have brought the two bodies together to bury them and have gone on their way, presumably to make coffins. Imogen thinks she sees the body of her husband, Posthumus, and cries out in an agony that begins with flowers:

> These flowers are like the pleasures of the world;
> This bloody man, the care on't. I hope I dream:
> For so I thought I was a cave-keeper
> And cook to honest creatures. But 'tis not so:
> 'Twas but a bolt of nothing, shot at nothing,
> Which the brain makes of fumes. Our very eyes
> Are sometimes like our judgements, blind. Good faith,
> I tremble still with fear: but if there be
> Yet left in heaven as small a drop of pity
> As a wren's eye, fear'd gods, a part of it!
> The dream's here still: even when I wake it is
> Without me, as within me: not imagin'd, felt.
> A headless man? The garments of Posthumus?
> I know the shape of 's leg: this is his hand:
> His foot mercurial: his martial thigh:
> The brawns of Hercules: but his Jovial face—
> Murder in heaven! How? 'Tis gone.

To the modern reader unaccustomed to stage monologues concerned with headless corpses there is a sense of anticlimax, but the Jacobean taste would see nothing anticlimactic at all. A generation brought up on *Titus Andronicus* and *The Spanish Tragedy* would revel in the invention of the new sensation of watching a boy who is a girl waking up on the stage to see the headless body of the man she believes to be her husband when in fact he is her most determined enemy, the man she has repulsed. It was *grand guignol* played within Chinese boxes, for Fidele confesses that she does not know what is real and what is unreal, and they appear to melt into one another, as they do when you are awaking from a drugged sleep. And as she contemplates the headless corpse still further, she concludes that the murderer of her husband was either Pisanio or Cloten. She could scarcely be more wrong.

Lucius, the general of the Roman forces in Britain, now enters the scene. He, too, is puzzled by the headless corpse, and inquires from Fidele what is known about it. Since Fidele does not know, she makes a wild guess, telling Lucius that it is the body of Richard du Champ. This can be translated into Richard Field, Shakespeare's friend, the printer of *Venus and Adonis* and *The Rape of Lucrece*, and it would appear that Shakespeare was doing what authors commonly do: he was enjoying a private joke about a friend. Fidele goes off to join the Roman army under Lucius.

Lucius is defeated in battle and Posthumus returns to England, where he is promptly arrested and thrown into jail. His jailers have a coarse sense of humor and busily remind him that he is surely about to be hanged. They rejoice in the advantages of hanging over all other medicines:

> *First Gaoler.* A heavy reckoning for you, sir: but the
> comfort is you may be called to no more payments,
> fear no more tavern-bills, which are often the
> sadness of parting, as the procuring of mirth: you
> come in faint for want of meat, depart reeling with
> too much drink: sorry that you have paid too much,
> and sorry that you are paid too much: purse and brain,
> both empty: the brain the heavier for being too light: the
> purse too light, being drawn of heaviness. O, of this
> contradiction you shall now be quit. O, the charity
> of a penny cord!

This was small comfort for Posthumus, who has even sadder things to worry about than his own hanging. King Cymbeline orders him to attend the court, where all the characters of the play except Cloten are assembled. There a repentant Posthumus encounters a glowing Imogen, Iachimo confesses his crimes, Belarius and his two foster sons are returned to Cymbeline's good graces, and even the Roman Empire is now on terms of harmony with Cymbeline. All are vindicated, and all are forgiven.

Nevertheless the play is incredibly disjointed: musclebound, attempting to move in contrary directions, never really moving except over a fixed spot, which is the innocence of Imogen, who alone keeps the play alive. When she is finally permitted to embrace Posthumus, he exclaims:

> Hang there like fruit, my soul
> Till the tree die,

and the passion of those words absolves him from his murderous crimes.

To the Jacobean audience the play must have been nearly as perplexing as it is to us. Simon Forman, who saw one of the early performances of the play, found it hard going. He wrote:

> Remember also the story of Cymbeline, King of England, in Lucius' time. How Lucius came from Octavius Caesar for tribute, and being denied, after sent Lucius with a great army of soldiers who landed at Milford Haven, and after were vanquished by Cymbeline, and Lucius taken prisoner, and all by means of three outlaws, of the which two of them were the sons of Cymbeline, stolen from him when they were but two years old by an old man whom Cymbeline banished, and he kept them as his own sons twenty years with him in a cave.
>
> And how [one] of them slew Cloten, that was the Queen's son, going to Milford Haven to seek the love of Imogen, the King's daughter, whom he had banished also for loving his daughter, and how the Italian that came from her love conveyed himself into a chest, and said it was a chest of plate sent from her love and others, to be presented to the King. And in the deepest of the night, she being asleep, he opened the chest, and came forth of it, and viewing her in her bed, and the marks of her body, and took away her bracelet, and after accused her of adultery to her love, &c.
>
> And in the end how he came with the Romans into England and was taken prisoner, and after revealed to Imogen, who had turned herself into man's apparel and fled to meet her love at Milford Haven, and chanced to fall on the cave in the woods where her two brothers were, and how by eating a sleeping dram they thought she had been

dead, and laid her in the woods, and the body of Cloten by her, in her love's apparel that he left behind him, and how she was found by Lucius, &c.

The best interpretation of all this is that Simon Forman was confused by the play and wrote down pell-mell what he thought he remembered, confusing Octavius Caesar with Augustus Caesar, making the boys twins, which they were not, and giving the credit for a British victory to "three outlaws," as though they were enough to destroy a Roman invasion force. But the modern reader also deserves to be pardoned for making similar errors. *Cymbeline* intrigues but does not hold the imagination; the mind wanders, and then awakes, startled by moments of great purity, those diamonds embedded in the rock face.

The discovery of the islands has ended in failure. He has mapped the enchantment but only in part, a very small part. The story proved too weak to carry the weight of his knowledge, and he must hurry over it quickly like a man hurrying over ice floes about to melt. He is writing about people seen in a visionary landscape. Sometimes he sees the vision steadily. This happens when Imogen is in absolute despair, knowing that she is completely forsaken, with no one to turn to, her husband murderous, an evil-minded half brother pursuing her. Pisanio suggests she had better leave Britain forever, and she answers:

> Where then?
> Hath Britain all the sun that shines? Day? Night?
> Are they not but in Britain? I' th' world's volume
> Our Britain seems as of it, but not in 't:
> In a great pool, a swan's nest.

The Shores
of the
Islands

WHEN SHAKESPEARE AT LAST CAME to the enchanted
islands, half suspecting they were mirages and uncertain
whether a man could return from them in this life, he was armed
with only those weapons he had forged during thirty years of
writing dramatic poetry. He had a powerful intelligence and fierce
imagination; he was astute in the practical affairs of living; he was
well known as the leading dramatist of his time. He was thus
exploring unknown territory with all the advantages that come with
earlier explorations among the mountains of passion and the forests
of suffering. Previously he seemed always to know where he was
going, even in *King Lear*, where he changed the generally accepted
legend and ended the play with such trumpet blasts of unrelieved
tragedy that even today we are terrified. But when he wrote *Pericles*
and *Cymbeline*, we are aware that he sometimes falters. There is no
certainty in these sea roads. The ship shudders; the sails fall slack;
he is at the mercy of the weather and the tides; and there is no
landfall.

Yet as the journey to the enchanted islands continues, we become aware that in a way that has little to do with human knowledge he is more surefooted, more certain of his powers, than he seems to be. Almost he falters deliberately, like a man on a tightrope a hundred feet above the earth who pretends to be about to fall and throws the audience into a paroxysm of excitement and fear. He kneels on the wire, waves his arms vigorously, slowly straightens himself, blows a kiss to the audience, and proceeds calmly on his way. So it is with Shakespeare: he is learned enough in the ways of the theatre to know that faltering also has its triumphs.

As he approaches the enchanted islands, the light changes, the structure of the verse changes, words acquire new meanings. There is the sense of trembling excitement before the appearance of a vision: the storm will end, there will be no more savage lightning strokes, the world will be glittering after rain and made more beautiful by rainbows, and there will appear "in a great pool, a swan's nest." All this will happen according to the divine will. There is a theophany but no God appears: only the certain knowledge that God is there. And this certainty, so gently expressed, has the effect of banishing all fear.

In *The Winter's Tale* Shakespeare reaches the shores of the enchanted islands. He does not yet penetrate very far into the interior. Most of his new knowledge is put into the mouth of Perdita, the daughter of King Leontes and Queen Hermione of Sicilia, and we should not be surprised to find that this knowledge is related to those images of mortality he had known in the past and now saw in another light—the drowned sailor and the grassy riverbank covered with flowers. These images, which had obsessed him in the beginning, still obsessed him. Now, the flowers on the riverbank may be used to decorate graves, but they exist supremely for their own sake and for the sake of lovers. Perdita, like Shakespeare, has acquired her new knowledge by gardening and spins out her catalogue of flowers with a kind of impatience to allow none to be forgotten, remembering how each of them bears its freight of doom but all of them form "a bank for love to lie and play on."

> *Perdita.* Here's flowers for you;
>   Hot lavender, mints, savory, marjoram;
>   The marigold, that goes to bed wi' the sun

And with him rises weeping: these are flowers
Of middle summer, and I think they are given
To men of middle age. You're very welcome.

Camillo.   I should leave grazing, were I of your flock,
And only live by gazing.

Perdita.   Out, alas!
You'ld be so lean, that blasts of January
Would blow you through and through. Now, my fair'st
friend,
I would I had some flowers o' the spring that might
Become your time of day; and yours, and yours,
That wear upon your virgin branches yet
Your maidenheads growing: O Proserpina,
For the flowers now, that frighted thou let'st fall
From Dis's wagon! daffodils,
That come before the swallow dares, and take
The winds of March with beauty; violets dim,
But sweeter than the lids of Juno's eyes
Or Cytherea's breath; pale primroses
That die unmarried, ere they can behold
Bright Phoebus in his strength—a malady
Most incident to maids; bold oxlips and
The crown imperial; lilies of all kinds,
The flower-de-luce being one! O, these I lack,
To make you garlands of, and my sweet friend,
To strew him o'er and o'er.

Florizel.   What, like a corse?

Perdita.   No, like a bank for love to lie and play on;
Not like a corse; or if, not to be buried,
But quick and in mine arms.

The magic of the poetry sustains the argument, which is concerned among other things with the nature of mortality. The gods
and goddesses of ancient Greece, who seem to be always waiting in
the wings in the last plays, are summoned to evoke the flowers.
Phoebus Apollo, Cytherea, Juno, and the tragic Proserpina keep
watch. Their task is to allow the poetry to come to its leisurely

fruition, like the argument, and the conclusion is the purest sensuality. Polixenes, the father of Florizel, is a little puzzled. He thinks of Perdita as "the prettiest low-born lass that ever ran on the greensward" and wonders whether she might not have been descended from noble parents. Florizel, who loves her, remains unconcerned with her ancestry. He sees her with his lover's eye as one who possesses a divine perfection: she moves and is motionless, like a wave of the sea:

> When you do dance, I wish you
> A wave o' th' sea, that you might ever do
> Nothing but that, move still, still so,
> And own no other function. Each your doing,
> So singular in each particular,
> Crowns what you are doing, in the present deeds,
> That all your acres are Queens.

What Shakespeare and Florizel are describing is the perfection of the human creature. He is not speaking of the ideal Perdita, an abstraction in a world of abstractions, but of a living, breathing, entirely charming, and entirely credible Perdita transformed by the power of vision. She is beautiful and moves with grace and is not entirely of this world. She is a princess in exile from her kingdom, but this may be the least important fact about her. She is a creature of the earth and of the islands. She walks in a royal way, firm in body, clear-eyed, wonderfully appealing and entertaining. She has been abandoned on the coast of Bohemia and is thought to be dead; instead, she is more alive than the living.

In *The Winter's Tale* Shakespeare has exerted himself to portray a young woman so wonderful that we shall remember her always, even though he pays little attention to her, for after her appearance with Florizel she is scarcely mentioned during the rest of the play. Yet she dominates it. She is the pole star and the universe revolves around her.

In this play the passions are subdued: there is almost no anger, no lust, no hatred, no violent indignation. Life has become ceremonial even for those who are in exile: the slow gestures have the effect of weaving magic spells. The people walk in the presence of the gods and are exceedingly aware of divine presences. But what is especially remarkable about them is that they are living in territory they know well, but it remains foreign and unfamiliar to them in spite of their knowledge of it. Cleomenes and Dion are discussing their discovery of the enchanted island:

> *Cleomenes.* The climate's delicate, the air most sweet,
>   Fertile the isle, the temple much surpassing
>   The common praise it bears.
>
> *Dion.* I shall report,
>   For most it caught me, the celestial habits,
>   Methinks I so should term them, and the reverence
>   Of the grave wearers. O, the sacrifice!
>   How ceremonious, solemn, and unearthly
>   It was i' the offering.

This "ceremonious, solemn, and unearthly" note is heard at intervals throughout the play, never more clearly than when King Leontes looks upon the statue of Queen Hermione and watches it coming to life. Sometimes the melody becomes simple and childlike. It is very like the music of Beethoven's posthumous quartets where the most solemn statements are made on the edge of vast discoveries and suddenly there is heard a simple childish melody such as might be sung by children playing hopscotch, and then the vast singing waves of time are heard again.

We hear this music in the speech of Antigonus, the Sicilian lord married to the splendidly outspoken Paulina, as he describes how he is being forced to abandon Perdita on the seacoast. He addresses Perdita in a calm sorrow, like a man speaking to himself:

>   Come, poor babe,
>   I have heard, but not believed, the spirits o' th' dead
>   May walk again. If such thing be, thy mother
>   Appeared to me last night, for ne'er was dream
>   So like a waking. To me comes a creature,
>   Sometimes her head on one side, some another.
>   I never saw a vessel of like sorrow,
>   So filled and so becoming. In pure white robes,
>   Like very sanctity, she did approach
>   My cabin where I lay; thrice bowed before me,

And, gasping to begin some speech, her eyes
Become two spouts. The fury spent, anon
Did this break from her: 'Good Antigonus,
Since fate, against thy better disposition,
Hath made thy person for the thrower-out
Of my poor babe, according to thine oath,
Places remote enough are in Bohemia;
There weep and leave it crying. And, for the babe
Is counted lost for ever, Perdita,
I prithee, call 't. For this ungentle business,
Put on thee by my lord, thou ne'er shalt see
Thy wife Paulina more.' And so, with shrieks,
She melted into air. Affrighted much,
I did in time collect myself, and thought
This was so and no slumber. Dreams are toys;
Yet for this once, yea, superstitiously,
I will be squared by this. I do believe
Hermione has suffered death, and that
Apollo would, this being indeed the issue
Of King Polixenes, it should here be laid,
Either for life or death, upon the earth
Of its right father. Blossom, speed thee well.
There lie, and there thy character; there these,
Which may, if fortune please, both breed thee, pretty,
And still rest thine. The storm begins. Poor wretch,
That for thy mother's fault art thus exposed
To loss and what may follow. Weep I cannot,
But my heart bleeds; and most accursed am I
To be by oath enjoined to this. Farewell!
The day frowns more and more. Thou'rt like to have
A lullaby too rough. I never saw
The heavens so dim by day. A savage clamor!
Well may I get aboard! This is the chase.
I am gone for ever.

Exit pursued by a bear.

This passage creates more wonder and bewilderment in the
reader than it does on stage. The scene flows on stage with the

naturalness that derives from a centuries-old convention, going back
at least to the time of Romulus and Remus, by which the casting
away of royal children is accompanied by strange portents and the
rolling of thunder. Antigonus speaks with the complete self-assurance of a true visionary. He has seen Hermione in a dream or
vision, majestic in her grief, her head leaning to one side, and he has
heard her pronounce that he will never again see his wife. The
vision has shaken him, and the casting away of the child shakes him,
and the bear will shake him to death. Antigonus is destined to an
end far more terrible than the end promised for Perdita, cast away
on a lonely shore. "There these," he says, as he sprinkles gold and
jewels on the baby in order to identify her if anyone should be so
lucky as to pass by this way. And then, as he runs offstage, an actor
wearing a bear's skin and a bear's mask jumps on him and carries
him away. The appearance of the bear breaks the spell: from
visionary tragedy we are brought into the real world where there
are no visions and everything is matter-of-fact, so matter-of-fact
indeed that immediately afterward a shepherd strolls on stage and
announces his views on lust, a subject that has fascinated him for
some time. He says: "I would there were no age between ten and
three-and-twenty, or that youth would sleep out the rest; for there is
nothing in the between but getting wenches with child, wronging
the ancientry, stealing, fighting." And as he ruminates he comes
upon the lost Perdita.

Shakespeare has been severely taken to task for introducing the
bear as a farcical *deus ex machina*. It is possible that he had no
alternative: that the bear in this context was absolutely right. Under
no imaginable conditions could a real bear be let loose on the stage:
the bears in the nearby Bear Garden could not be depended upon,
for they were trained to fight huge mastiffs to the death. A Londoner of the time, seeing the bear on the stage even if only for a moment,
would regard it as perfectly appropriate. You would expect to find
bears prowling along the seacoast of Bohemia; if not bears, there
would be lions. The effect, which is comical to us, would be just as
comical to the Elizabethans. The boy in the bearskin was a clown;
so was the ruminating shepherd; so, of course, was the clown who
comes ambling onto the stage to discuss, as clowns so often do,
questions of mortality. He is the best of clowns, for he provides

information on the fate of Antigonus, who, before being mauled to death, had time to cry out his name and proclaim that he was a nobleman. Also the ship that brought him to the coast of Bohemia had capsized in a storm, "flap-dragoned," everyone lost. The clown observed the shipwreck which the shepherd was too busy to observe, being immersed in his thoughts as he contemplates the foundling.

> *Shepherd.* Here's a sight for thee. Look thee, a
> bearing-cloth for a squire's child. Look thee here.
> Take up, take up, boy; open 't. So let's see. It was
> told me I should be rich by the fairies. This is some
> changeling. Open 't. What's within, boy?
>
> *Clown.* You're a made old man. If the sins of your
> youth are forgiven you, you're well to live.
> Gold! all gold!
>
> *Shepherd.* This is fairy gold, boy, and 'twill prove so.
> Up with 't, keep it close. Home, home, the next day.
> We are lucky, boy, and to be so still requires
> nothing by secrecy. Let my sheep go.

Except for the clown in *Othello*, all Shakespeare's clowns are welcome. They talk well about mortality; they know that gold is gold, not fairy gold; they have the advantage of knowing what is really happening as distinguished from the heroes of the play who labor under the disadvantages of guesswork. But when the scene ends, Shakespeare finds himself in a quandary. Perdita has been discovered, but she is still a baby. He wants to see her in love and therefore must jump some sixteen years. But how? He introduces Time, the Chorus. Time discusses the passing of time at some length. He is the fourth clown. Never had Shakespeare been so prodigal with his clowns. When we see Perdita again, she is sheep-shearing, and a certain Doricles, who is really Florizel, Prince of Bohemia, in disguise, has by the purest chance discovered her.

Shakespeare tells the story like a fairy tale, and yet, like children sitting by a fire on a winter evening and listening to an old man's tales, we are aware that the story has many meanings and that they touch our lives at their sharpest points. Perdita, Leontes, and Hermione are the purest fictions behaving in total disagreement with probability. They are all visionary creatures on an enchanted island, and yet they have much to tell us about the world we live in. Reading the play, we have the curious feeling that our own world is unreal and only Perdita's world is credible.

In *The Winter's Tale* Shakespeare set foot on the enchanted islands. In *The Tempest* he took full possession of them.

The
Tempest

W HEN HEMINGE AND CONDELL, together with Ben
Jonson, set about editing Shakespeare's works, they
placed *The Tempest* first, though it was neither the first nor the last
of his plays. They knew what they were about. This was the one
perfect play, the crown of all his works, being both comedy and
tragedy, and being also the most autobiographical. Here there is no
faltering, the imagination never flags, nothing is contrived, and
comedy and tragedy are held in perfect balance. Here everything
seems to flow effortlessly from the depths of his inspiration. Some
may argue that Perdita is more charming than Miranda and that
Prospero conceals his vengefulness with too much solemnity. It does
not matter. The play has so vast and wonderful a scope that it
reduces all judgment to tatters. Only the very bravest may argue
against perfection.

  The Tempest is a very literary work; the reading of many books
went into it. Shakespeare collected words, images, and ideas from a
dozen books while writing the play, but what he found he made his
own, so that it always seems strange to learn the sources. He found

Frontispiece of Sir Walter Raleigh's The History of the World, *1614*

King James I, by D. Maytens (National Portrait Gallery)

King James and Queen Anne, engraved by Ronald Elstrack, about 1608

Prince Henry, from an engraving in Michael Drayton's Poly-Olbion, *1612*

PHILIPPVS HERIBERTVS COMES DE PENBROKE ET MONGOMERY. BARO
DE CARDIFFE ET SHIRLAND. D^{ns} DE PARRE ET ROOS IN KENDALL
MARCHIO S^{ti} QVINTI. REGIS ANGLIÆ. A CVBICVLIS. EQVES PERISCELIDIS.

Ant van Dyck pinxt   Robertus van Voerst sculpsit.
                                      I. W. London f.

*Philip Herbert, First Earl of Montgomery, from an etching after Van
Dyck. Heminge and Condell dedicated the First Folio to him and to his
brother William Herbert, Third Earl of Pembroke.*

Martin Droeshout's portrait of Shakespeare in the First Folio, 1623

The same plate was used in 1685 for the Fourth Folio. An unknown engraver pointed up the eyes and firmed the lips, producing a more vivid portrait.

Shakespeare's monument above his tomb in Holy Trinity Church in Stratford. The profile shows an alertness not present when the statue is seen full face. (The Folger Shakespeare Library, Washington, D.C.)

the names Prospero and Stefano in Ben Jonson's *Every Man in His Humour,* in which Shakespeare was one of the principal actors. For other names he searched his library. Setebos came from Richard Eden's posthumously published *The History of Travayle in the East and West Indies*: it is the name given to a Patagonian devil by one of the companions of Ferdinand Magellan. Gonzalo and Ferdinand sprang to Shakespeare's attention when he was reading William Strachey's *A True Reportory of the Wreck and Redemption of Sir Thomas Gates, Knight* and found the name Gonzalus Ferdinandus Oviedus, who is mentioned as an authority on Bermuda and the island devils. The names Prospero, Ferdinando, Alonzo, and Antonio all occur in Thomas's *Historie of Italie,* published in 1561. Caliban apparently comes from the Italian Calibana, meaning the Caribbean. Ariel is a more mysterious name. Shakespeare found it in the margin of Ezekiel 29 in the Geneva Bible: "The Hebrew word Ariel signifieth the Lion of God, and signifieth the altar, because the altar seemed to devour the sacrifice that was offered to God." Ariel in the play is far from being the Lion of God or a devourer of sacrifices.* Instead, he is an enchanting sprite, all fire and wisps of smoke, who is given three of Shakespeare's most enchanting songs to sing.

Quite clearly Shakespeare liked the name and was not in the least impressed by its exalted status. There is a sense in which the whole play is written around Prospero and Ariel. They are the nucleus, and from them the play unfolds.

The sprite, still nameless, was first seen on the night of Thursday, July 27, 1609, by Admiral Sir George Somers when his ship *The Sea Venture,* caught in a storm off the coast of Bermuda, was in desperate straits. The ship was being broken apart by the storm; the heavens were black; there were no stars at night and no sun by day. He had no idea that he was close to land, and only knew that the ship had sprung many leaks and would surely founder unless his crew of 140 men continued to pump out the water in the holds. Suddenly, while he was on the watch, he saw

---

*Thomas Heywood, in *The Hierarchie of the Blessed Angells*, 1635, thought that Ariel, in the eyes of the Hebrews, was the supreme angelic master of the earth: "The earth's great lord, Ariel, the Hebrew's Rabbins thus accord."

. . . a little round light, like a faint star, trembling and streaming
along with a sparkling blaze, half the height upon the mainmast
and shooting sometimes from shroud to shroud, 'tempting to
settle, as it were, upon any one of the four shrouds. And for three
or four hours together, or rather more, half the night, it kept
with us, running sometimes along the main yard to the very end
and then returning; at which Sir George Somers called divers
among him and showed them the same, who observed it with
much wonder and carefulness. But of a sudden, toward the
morning watch, they lost the sight of it and knew not what way it
made.

So wrote the admirable William Strachey in his *True Reportory,*
being himself on *The Sea Venture* and a witness of the faint star
with a sparkling blaze. He was a minor poet, about twenty-one
years old, and he would soon become recorder of the colony of
Virginia. His short book on Bermuda took the form of a letter
addressed to an unnamed Excellent Lady, who was probably Lady
Elizabeth de Walden. It was dated July 15, 1610, and reached
England in the following September. It was not a public document
but belonged among the confidential papers of the Virginia Company. The Earl of Southampton was among the leading members of
the company and it is likely that Shakespeare found it in the earl's
library.

But it was not only the exceedingly well written account of the
storm and the faint star that seized upon Shakespeare's imagination.
Strachey goes on to tell how they waited out the storm and when the
sky cleared they saw land on the horizon, and soon Somers was
steering the waterlogged ship toward the land, looking for a safe
anchorage. By mischance the ship was caught between two ledges of
a reef some four or five hundred yards off shore. No one was hurt;
the ship remained intact; it was a simple matter to get into the boats
and land on the island at a place now known as St. Catherine's Bay.
The island appeared on Somers' maps as Bermuda, the place of
storms, and had another name, the Island of Devils. Mariners
dreaded it and avoided it. Strachey says it was "avoided by all sea
travelers above any place in the world." But when they landed, they
discovered it was a small paradise.

There were palms and cedars, and berries of all kinds, and a kind of pea as big as a Catherine pear. There were thousands of wild hogs and tortoises, fat sparrows, green and yellow robins, and a bird like an English plover that could almost be plucked out of the air. All the birdcatchers had to do was to stand on the seashore and holler at the top of their voices, and the birds would come flocking to them. The sea was brimming with fish, pilchard, bream, mullet, rockfish, swordfish, and many others, and there were oysters aplenty, and crayfish under the rocks. The reddish earth was fertile, and the new colonists planted the seeds they had brought with them: musk mellon, peas, onions, radish, lettuce, and herbs. In ten days they all came up, but worms or birds got at them. Somers planted sugarcane saved from the wreck; it was beginning to grow when the hogs rooted it up.

For most of them it was a magical island where with almost no effort at all they could live pleasantly. They built huts, hunted wild pig, which became their principal diet, and went fishing and bird catching. Bermuda is not one island but a multitude of islands, and they went exploring. The islands had only one defect: there was no fresh water, no rivers, no springs.

The Sea Venture was the flagship of a small fleet comprising seven ships and two pinnaces, that set out from Plymouth, England, on June 2, 1609, with six hundred colonists bound for Jamestown, Virginia. Six of the ships reached Jamestown. As for the flagship wedged on the reef, it was quickly dismembered by the colonists on Bermuda, who used its gear and timbers to make another ship called *Deliverance,* Which some months later sailed for Virginia, leaving some settlers behind.

Somers was not alone in charge of the expedition. In theory he commanded only the ships. The chief authority in Bermuda was Sir Thomas Gates, a somewhat irascible man who was the designated governor of Virginia. So there was some rivalry between Somers and Gates, and this was dangerous, because the settlers were typical Englishmen of the period, high-spirited, quarrelsome, quick with their weapons, and always rebellious of authority. There were small mutinies five weeks after they landed. A sailor killed another man with a shovel and was at once sentenced to be hanged at dawn. During the night he was roped to a tree, some sailors stood guard over him, and were so sorry for him that they let him loose and hid him in the woods until Somers was able to convince Gates to grant him a reprieve. There were religious quarrels and conspiracies to overthrow the governor. Henry Paine, more rebellious than the rest, and possessing a good supply of stolen swords, hatchets, and clubs which he was not quick enough to use, defied the governor in a heated speech which led to his arrest. The governor sentenced him to death, and toward evening he was shot, "the sun and his life setting together."

For Shakespears's purposes Strachey's account of the shipwreck and the faint star and the landing and the mutinies were all important, but even more important was the young writer's description of the island. Strachey had the power to evoke its strangeness and loneliness in the midst of the ocean. Others wrote about the shipwreck: late in 1610 Silvester Jourdain, who had sailed with *The Sea Venture* and returned to England, published *A Discovery of the Bermudas, otherwise called the Ile of Divels,* but it is a very brief and perfunctory work, no more than a dozen pages, and cannot compare with Strachey's book as a work of art. Jourdain emphasizes the absolute peacefulness of the island where there were no venomous creatures at all, no rats, no mice, no snakes. It was a place, he said, where "God, in the supplying of all our wants beyond all measure, showed Himself still merciful unto us." One sentence in particular may have impressed itself on Shakespeare's imagination. It occurs when Jourdain describes the discovery of pearls: "There is great store of pearl, and some of them very fair, round and oriental, and you shall find at least one hundred seed of pearl in one oyster." Such Oriental luxury was too excessive to be forgotten; out of these words there may have come the single most magical line in Shakespeare's works: "Those are pearls that were his eyes."

There are other sources for *The Tempest,* and some of them are to be found in Shakespeare's own works. Ariel is half brother to Puck:

Over hill, over dale,
    Thorough bush, thorough briar
Over park, over pale,

> Thorough flood, thorough fire,
> I do wander everywhere,
> Swifter than the moon's sphere,
> And I serve the Faery Queen,
>   To dew her orbs upon the green.
> The cowslips tall her pensioners be:
> In their gold coats spots you see;
> Those be rubies, fairy favors,
> In those freckles live their savors,
> I must go seek some dewdrops here,
> And hang a pearl in every cowslip's ear.

Ariel shows little interest in dewdrops and cowslips's ears but he will go through bush, briar, park, pale, flood, and fire in the twinkling of an eye. Puck served the Fairy Queen; Ariel's master is Prospero, who has long ago lost his throne and is almost content never to return to Milan. When Oberon in *A Midsummer Night's Dream* summons Puck into his presence, we hear words that could just as well be placed on the lips of Prospero:

> *Oberon.*   My gentle Puck, come hither. Thou rememb'rest
>   Since once I sat upon a promontory,
>   And heard a mermaid, on a dolphin's back,
>   Uttering such dulcet and harmonious breath,
>   That the rude sea grew civil at her song,
>   And certain stars shot madly from their spheres,
>   To hear the sea maid's music.

Just as Ariel is half brother to Puck, so Oberon is half brother to Prospero, who has many ancestors. He is Plato's philosopher king and the Renaissance man as described in the biographies of Leon Battista Alberti and Leonardo da Vinci. He is all that is wise and well ordered, and in addition he is a man seeking for his lost kingdom and patiently searching for revenge. Prospero, indeed, dominates *The Tempest:* he is the kingpin around which the play revolves.

Prospero has magic powers: can raise the dead, raises storms at sea, tames savage beasts, lulls people to sleep simply by gazing at them, and he possesses a powerful persuader in Ariel, his private ministering angel. We find him a little strange, but the Jacobeans would have found him less strange, while the Elizabethans would have thought him not strange at all. A modest belief in magic was a commonplace of Elizabethan life. Queen Elizabeth was devoted to Dr. John Dee, who raised spirits and helped Edward Kelly to discover the philosopher's stone. Dr. Dee was thrown into prison on the charge of uttering enchantments against Elizabeth's half sister Queen Mary, and was lucky to escape with his life. When Queen Elizabeth came to the throne, she rewarded him for his mystical devotion to her, appointed him her physician and astrologer, and seems to have been a little in awe of him. Dr. Dee died at the age of eighty-one in great poverty. It was 1608, and magic was dying out.

While Dr. Dee was the most famous of Elizabethan magicians, there were others nearly as famous. There was Abraham Savory, the son of a poor hatmaker in London. He became an actor, a dramatist, a teacher of fencing, owner of bawdy houses in Clerkenwell and Westminster, an astrologer, a practical creator of conjurations. He possessed a familiar spirit who appeared to him each night in the shape of a naked arm.

Dr Dee, teacher of Philip Sidney and deeply in the confidence of Queen Elizabeth, lived for a good part of his life in court circles. Thomas Digges, astronomer, mathematician, student of military strategy, the first in England to study the works of Copernicus and the first to use the words "the infinite universe," also moved in court circles. He was not credited with magic powers but was regarded with awe and veneration, as one who had accomplished intellectual miracles. He lived in a spacious house on Philip Lane, Cripplegate. He died in 1595, and his sons Dudley and Leonard continued to live in the house. Dudley became a member of the Virginia Company and had much to do with the sending of the *Sea Venture* to Virginia, while Leonard became Shakespeare's friend. When Shakespeare came to live in Silver Street Cripplegate, he was only a four-minute walk from the house on Philip Lane.

Thomas Digges might serve for a model of Prospero as a man of wisdom and intellectual power, while Dr. John Dee might serve as the model for Prospero as a magician. There was still another model: Shakespeare himself, the creator, who has the power to write incantations and enchantments and can raise the dead by putting them on the stage, so that they live out their lives again. He can write the word "storm," and at his bidding a storm appears. If he writes the word "green," everything is colored green. He becomes a mage and a magician through the evocative power of words. In *The Candle Bearer,* the play which Giordano Bruno wrote in 1582 during his stay in England, Bonifacio speaks of magic so powerful that "it can turn back rivers in their courses, halt the tides, make the mountains bellow, the abyss cry out, can blot out the sun, veil the moon, pluck out the stars, turn day into night." But there was another magic to which Bruno was devoted—the exploration of the heavens in search of new worlds, new creatures living in the stars, and it was his belief in the existence of these intelligent creatures which contributed to the decision of the Church to burn him at the stake in Rome in February 1600. Bruno's works were well known to the Essex Circle and there was no doubt that Shakespeare was aware of them.

Many strands went into the making of Prospero: the wise magician possessing a celestial calm was also a man of great violence and inner turmoil. Nor was the island quite as idyllic as we are accustomed to think of it. As Gonzalo said near the very end of the play:

All torment, trouble, wonder, and amazement
Inhabits here. Some heavenly power guide us
Out of this fearful country.

It is in fact a wonderfully cruel island made all the crueler by Prospero, the worker of shipwrecks, with a heavenly sprite and a demonic monster at his service. He has all the advantages of power: a kingly presence, the capacity to order everything as he pleases. When Adrian arrives on the island after the shipwreck, he observes that it seems to be desert, uninhabitable and almost inaccessible; yet the air seems sweet to him.

Adrian. The air breathes on us here most sweetly.

Sebastian. As if it had lungs, and rotten ones.

Antonio. Or 'twere perfumed by a fen.

Gonzalo. Here is everything advantageous to life.

Antonio.   True; save means to live.

Sebastian.   Of that there's none, or little.

Gonzalo.   How lush and lusty the grass looks!
         how green!

Antonio.   The ground, indeed, is tawny.

The tawny ground consisted of the bare boards of the stage: it was an actor's joke: having made their joke, they pass on to consider the fact that although they have been in a shipwreck, their clothes retain "their freshness and gloss, being rather new-dyed than stained with salt water." Obviously they are in a state of enchantment. Something strange and inexplicable is happening to them, and the owner of the island is equally strange and inexplicable. The sailors are not clowns, but intelligent creatures concerned with the mysteries around them. Sebastian and Antonio come to an exact conclusion:

Sebastian.   I think he will carry this island home in his
   pocket and give it to his son for an apple.

Antonio.   And, sowing the kernels of it in the sea, bring
   forth more islands.

Which is, of course, what Prospero will do in good time, giving his empire of islands to Miranda. The sailors are not yet aware of her presence and may be excused for not knowing of her existence.

The calm that descended on Shakespeare when he was writing the last act of *Antony and Cleopatra* returns in *The Tempest*. Antony, too, has islands dropping from his pocket: Prospero has inherited something of Antony's royal power without his fatality. Prospero has the advantage over Antony that he has no lust; his single desire is to recover his kingdom. Since he possesses such formidable power, it is somewhat surprising that he did not accomplish his aim more simply. Could not Ariel have been ordered to bring the usurper in chains into his presence? Could he not have sent a magic sword to cut off the usurper's head? All possibilities are in his keeping, and he deliberately limits himself to those possibilities that arise from his possession of the island.

In geographical terms the island must be somewhere in the Mediterranean, for Alonso, King of Naples, is shipwrecked when returning from Tunis to Naples, and the witch Sycorax came to the island from Algiers. It appears that the island must be somewhere off the boot of Italy; it might be Malta or Pantellaria if we did not know that Shakespeare showed not even the remotest interest in geography. The island of *The Tempest* is the visionary England, which appears in all his last plays.

Who really owns the island? Caliban claims it by right of inheritance; he could not be more clear or forceful in his claim:

The island's mine by Sycorax my mother,
Which thou tak'st from me. When thou cam'st first,
Thou strok'st me and made much of me; wouldst give me
Water with berries in 't; and teach me how
To name the bigger light, and how the less,
That burn by day and night; and then I loved thee
And showed thee all the qualities o' th' isle,
The fresh springs, brine-pits, barren place and fertile.
Cursed be I that did so! All the charms
Of Sycorax—toads, beetles, bats, light on you!
For I am the subjects that you have,
Which first was mine own king; and here you sty me
In this hard rock, whiles you do keep from me
The rest o' th' island.

Caliban is a magnificent conception, who almost runs away with the play. Prospero calls him "hag seed," "earth," "freckled whelp," "tortoise"; Miranda calls him "abhorred slave," "a thing most brutish," and claims she taught him how to speak. Since he speaks magnificently, she should feel rewarded for her pains. Instead, father and daughter feel only revulsion in his presence, perhaps because they are oppressed by his ugliness and by their knowledge that they are usurpers on his territory.

It would be pleasant if we had a stage designer's drawing of Caliban in his original stage costume. We may imagine him covered with scales, for he was "a strange fish," "a fishlike monster," with arms like flapping fins and a fish's head, all eyes and wide, wandering mouth, and in his movements there would be all the generous excess which the audience demanded in the clown. Although the stage Caliban was probably a fishlike monster, the original impetus was probably the manitee seen by Job Hortop and described in his account of his voyage with Diego Flores de Valdez in 1570, published by Richard Hakluyt in his monumental work *The Principal Navigations, Voyages, Traffiques and Discoveries of the English Nation:*

> When we came to the height of Bermuda we discovered
> a monster in the sea, which showed himself three times unto
> us from the middle upwards, in which parts he was
> proportioned like a man of the complexion of a mulatto or
> tawny Indian.

Job Hortop's brief glimpse of a monster "like a man" has a hallucinatory quality. We believe him totally, for he has seen the most credible monster of all.

There is much in *The Tempest* which is not credible and not intended to be credible in any realistic terms. Shakespeare's imagination glows with scenes which fade into one another and possess an imaginative logic of their own. We do not ask questions, for we are "spell-stopped" like the characters in the play. And while in *Cymbeline* we pause and ask questions and put down the book from time to time, asking ourselves why Shakespeare introduced this or that character and what on earth was his intention in writing this or that speech, in *The Tempest* he speaks with so much authority and is so much in command of the play that we have no time for questions. Sometimes the play breaks down in trivialities as when the sailors make silly jokes about the Widow Dido; and then we tell ourselves that Shakespeare like everyone else has a right to make silly jokes. We may have the feeling that Prospero is not telling the whole truth when he describes how he lost his throne, that some very important detail has been omitted or deliberately obscured. In the last act there are some curious passages suggesting that some characters have died and been brought back to life. Alonso, King of Naples, asks Prospero: "When did you lose your daughter?" and Prospero answers against all the evidence: "In this last tempest." The theme of the lost daughter remains as one of the haunting themes of the play, but Prospero loses her only to Ferdinand.

There is so much talk of Milan and Naples that we are led inevitably to the time when Lodovico Sforza usurped the throne of Giangalleazo Sforza, the rightful Duke of Milan. This act of usurpation in the last years of the fifteenth century was well known in England. Lodovico Sforza, superb, arrogant, and ignorant, dominated Milan, while Giangalleazo Sforza was permitted to live out his life in idleness in the company of the enchanting Isabella of Aragon, Princess of Naples. Giangalleazo died mysteriously. Lodovico was captured by the French King and thrown into a cavelike dungeon. Isabella of Aragon fled to the duchy of Bari, never again returning to Milan. The violence of those times is dimly reflected in the strange calm of *The Tempest*.

Almost at the very beginning of the play Shakespeare entertains us with two of his most magical songs. They seem effortless and spontaneous, as though he had lifted his eyes from the page and suddenly the songs had come into his head. Ariel sings to Ferdinand, the son of the King of Naples, as the young man wanders along the island shore, lamenting his shipwrecked father.

> *Ariel's Song*
> Come unto these yellow sands,
>   And then take hands.
> Curtsied when you have and kissed,
>   The wild waves whist,
> Foot it featly here and there,
> And, sweet sprites, the burden bear.
>   Hark, hark!
> *Burden dispersedly.*   Bowgh, wawgh!
>   The watchdogs bark.
> *Burden dispersedly.*   Bowgh, wawgh!
>   Hark, hark! I hear
> The strain of strutting chanticleer
>   Cry cock-a-diddle-do.

There are perhaps five other songs written by Shakespeare which have this perfection and this simplicity. One can know the song all one's life without knowing or caring what the word "whist" means. It means "silent" or "hushed," and the card game whist owes its name to the fact that it had to be played in silence. The song, however, does not depend upon the meaning of the words; we do not know why the dogs are barking or why they should be followed by Chanticleer. It is early morning by the seashore, the cocks are crowing, the dogs are barking; and having said this, we realize we have said nothing, for the song says everything.

"Come unto these yellow sands" seems to be song in a pure state, in the purest possible state. It can derive from nothing except itself, or so we believe until we turn to Christopher Marlowe's long poem "Hero and Leander," first published in 1598. Toward the end of the first sestiad we come upon the lines:

> Upon a rock, and underneath a hill,
> Far from the town where all is *whist* and still,
> Save that the sea playing on *yellow sand*
> Sends forth a rattling murmur to the land,
> Whose sound allures the golden Morpheus
> In silence of the night to visit us,
> My turrent stands, and there God knows I play
> With Venus' swans and sparrows all the day.
> A dwarfish beldame bears me company
> That hops about the chamber where I lie,
> And spends the night that might be better spent
> In vain discourse and apish merriment.
> *Come thither . . .*

Shakespeare has been rereading "Hero and Leander," and letting his eye wander loosely across the page he had seen the italicized words, regrouped them, allowed his mind to dwell on the shores of the mysterious island of *The Tempest,* and so there had come to him the opening words of Ariel's song. He was a man who often wrote with a book open before him. The rock, the hill, Morpheus, the turret, and the dwarfish beldame were all abandoned; in their place he put the pack of dogs whose barking, as they pursued the thieves, kept the day awake. Even the swans and the sparrows were abandoned in order to write a song which is the purest lyric.

A few moments later, turning the pages of "Hero and Leander," Shakespeare found some other verses which may have affected him even more deeply, for they describe how Leander fell to the bottom

of the sea where the shipwrecked treasure lay and entered the blue
palace of King Neptune:

> Leander striv'd, the waves about him wound
> And pull'd him to the bottom, where the ground
> Was strewed with *pearl,* and in low *coral* groves
> Sweet singing mermaids sported with their loves
> On heaps of heavy gold, and took great pleasure
> To spurn in careless sort the shipwrack treasure,
> For here the stately azure palace stood,
> Where kingly Neptune and his train abode.

Out of those two italicized words, and out of the image of sunken
treasure and Neptune's palace, Shakespeare wrote the most haunting of all his songs, placing it in the mouth of the invisible Ariel as a
warning to Ferdinand that his father lay at the bottom of the sea.

> *Ariel's Song*
> Full fathom five thy father lies;
>   Of his bones are coral made:
> Those are pearls that were his eyes.
>   Nothing of him that doth fade
> But doth suffer a sea-change
>   Into something rich and strange.
> Sea nymphs hourly ring his knell.
> *Burden.*   Ding-dong.
> Hark! now I hear them—Ding-dong bell.

Here at last, after many years, a theme that had obsessed him
found its perfect expression. Almost it is pure music. It carries its
weight of mortality lightly: the mortal image of man is wholly
transformed. The words become music; the music becomes enchantment; the enchantment remains.

Shakespeare had not stolen his ideas from Marlowe: he had
simply made them his own by a process akin to crystallization. We
can watch the formation of the crystal within the chemical solution.
In fact, the process happens all the time, and many of Shakespeare's
best speeches are crystals from other poems by other dramatists.
Thus Prospero's speech beginning "Ye elves of hills, brooks standing lakes and groves" derives from Golding's translation of Ovid's

Metamorphoses, and Prospero's farewell to the magical art, which takes place long before the ending of the play and may therefore be regarded as somewhat premature, derives from *The Tragedy of Darius,* by William Alexander:

> Let greatness of her glassy scepters vaunt;
> Not scepters, no, but reeds, some bruis'd, some broken:
> And let this worldly pomp our wits enchant,
> All fades, and scarcely leaves behind a token.
> Those golden palaces, those gorgeous halls,
> With furniture superfluously fair,
> Those stately courts, those sky-encountering walls
> Evanish all like vapours in the air.

When Shakespeare plucks the crystal from this muddy solution, we are almost blinded by the brightness of its light. He says little more than Alexander said in the two words "All fades," but that little more is a celebration of life, a hymn of praise and a solemn threnody:

> Our revels now are ended. These our actors,
> As I foretold you, were all spirits and
> Are melted into air, into thin air;
> And like the baseless fabric of this vision,
> The cloud-capped towers, the gorgeous palaces,
> The solemn temples, the great globe itself,
> Yea, all which it inherit, shall dissolve,
> And like this insubstantial pageant faded,
> Leave not a rack behind. We are such stuff
> As dreams are made on, and our little life
> Is rounded with a sleep.

Shakespeare wrote: "The scene: an uninhabited island." This was a way of saying that he inhabited it together with all the living creatures of his imagination. He had found the island at last. It was one where people sleep and wake quite suddenly and unexpectedly, but sometimes they awake into another dream, and sometimes when they seem to be sleeping they are wide awake.

Shakespeare
of the
Last Days

The Burning
of the
Globe

O N THE AFTERNOON OF TUESDAY, JUNE 29, 1613, Shakespeare's last historical play which he called *Henry VIII or All is True* was presented before a distinguished audience which included Ben Jonson, John Taylor the water poet, and Sir Henry Wotton whose permanent claim to fame rests on his statement, uttered in the presence of King James, that "ambassadors were good men sent to lie abroad for their country." The theatre was crowded; there was a feeling of expectancy in the air, for the audience had been promised a spectacular production. It was high summer in London—the loveliest time of the year—and the banner showing Hercules carrying the globe of the world waved briskly from the mast-head high above the stage.

Henry VIII was more pageantry than drama, a thing of brilliant colors, masques, dances, interludes, trials, long-drawn lamentations. Catherine of Aragon, the Duke of Buckingham, Cardinal Wolsey, all fall, but not as old apples fall. Instead they fall like meteors which blaze for a while and then vanish into nothingness. Henry VIII appears rarely but his presence can be felt throughout the play like a hungry tiger waiting for his prey. There could be no play about this king without the brisk business of the executioner's ax. Hurried scene follows hurried scene, and we rarely stay long enough with any character to know the depths of his being. There is one exception: Catherine of Aragon. The play, among other things, is Shakespeare's salute to the Queen whose sorrows wrung the hearts of her subjects who nevertheless permitted the King to commit crimes against her because he was the fountain of all power and she was powerless. Catherine addresses her serving women:

> I am the most unhappy woman living.
> Alas, poor wenches, where are now your fortunes?
> Shipwrecked upon a kingdom, where no pity,
> No friends, no hope, no kindred weep for me?
> Almost no grave allowed me? Like the lily
> That once was mistress of the field, and flourished.
> I'll hang my head, and perish.

Henry had called her "the Queen of earthly Queens," he had loved her to distraction, and now he was resolved to break all the ties that attached him to her, using Cardinal Wolsey as the instrument of his will. Very quickly we come to learn that Wolsey is as cunning as a wolf and too cunning for his own good. He will destroy her, and he will destroy himself. Catherine of Aragon laments nobly; Wolsey rages.

> O Cromwell, Cromwell,
> Had I but served my God with half the zeal
> I served my King: he would not in mine age
> Have left me naked to mine enemies.

While Catherine of Aragon and Wolsey come to life, and there is a brief moment when Anne Boleyn appears vividly on the stage, there is less drama in the play than in any of his other plays. Nor was it necessary: he was experimenting with a new kind of play, a royal masque dressed up with every known device of pageantry. We are aware of the smell of midnight oil. He opens the huge in-folio of Foxe's *Book of Martyrs* with its more than two thousand double-columned pages, and takes a phrase here and another there. He opens George Clarendon's *The Life and Death of Cardinal Wolsey* and takes a whole speech. He opens Ralph Holinshed's *The Chronicles of England, Scotland and Ireland* with its more than fifteen hundred double-columned pages and found another speech, another turn of phrase, another incident. Foxe and Clarendon wrote brilliantly; Holinshed was unforgivably dull. Shakespeare himself, the heart of him, was not deeply engaged with the words. What interested him was the panoply, the splendor, the costumes, the solemn dances, the fierce light of kingship, the flash of the headman's sword. The stage directions were long and he reveled in them. He was writing a royal pageant which by its very nature did not demand the utmost of his poetry.

The crowds who came to see *Henry VIII* on that summer afternoon saw the first of three scenes in comfort, and little more. In the fourth scene the King enters with a group of masquers, all of them disguised as shepherds, and to salute his presence guns with blank shot were fired. A spark from one of the guns set fire to the thatched roof. At first no one thought anything about the coils of smoke rising from the roof, but soon the flames began to engulf the upper stories of the theatre, sparks were flying everywhere, and the audience stampeded through the two narrow doors which led into the surrounding marshland. In about an hour the Globe Theatre was a burned-out shell.

Three days after this extraordinary event Sir Henry Wotton wrote an account of it to his friend Sir Edmund Bacon:

> Now, to let matter of state sleep, I will entertain you at the present with what hath happened this week at the Bank's Side. The King's Players had a new play called *All is True* representing some principal pieces of the reign of Henry VIII, which was set forth with many extraordinary circumstances of pomp and majesty, even to the matting of the stage, the Knights of the Order, with their Georges and Garter, the Guards with their embroidered coats, and the like sufficient in truth within a while to make greatness very familiar, if not ridiculous. Now, King Henry making a masque at the Cardinal Wolsey's house, and certain cannons being shot off at his entry, some of the paper or other stuff wherewith one of them was stopped, did light on

the thatch, where being thought at first but an idle smoke
and their eyes more attentive to the show, it kindled
inwardly and ran around like a train, consuming within less
than an hour the whole house to the very ground.

This was the fatal period of that virtuous fabric; wherein
yet nothing did perish but wood and straw, and a few
forsaken cloaks; only one man had his breeches set on fire,
that would perhaps have broiled him if he had not by the
benefit of a provident wit put it out with bottle-ale.

Sir Henry Wotton, delighting in his own wit, saw it as a merry
game. John Chamberlain, writing to Sir Ralph Winwood a week
after the fire, was more respectful. He thought the fire was caused
by the "tampling or stopple" of a cannon alighting on the thatched
roof. "It was," he says, "a great marvel and fair grace of God that
the people had so little harm, having but two narrow doors to get
out at." But the finest memorial to the burning Globe was provided
by an anonymous balladeer who wrote a ribald account of the fire as
seen by the common people of London.

A Sonnet upon the Pitiful Burning of the
Globe Playhouse in London

Now sit thee down, Melpomene,
Wrapped in a sea-coal robe,
And tell the doleful tragedy
That late was played at Globe;
For no man that can sing and say
Was scared on St. Peter's day.
  Oh sorrow, pitiful sorrow, and yet all this is true.

All you that please to understand,
Come listen to my story;
To see Death with his raking brand
Mongst such an auditory;
Regarding neither Cardinal's might
Nor yet the rugged face of Henry the eight.
  Oh sorrow, pitiful sorrow, and yet all this is true.

The fearful fire began above,
A wonder strange and true,

And to the stage-house did remove,
As round as tailor's clew,
And burned down both beam and snagg,
And did not spare the silken flag.
    Oh sorrow, pitiful sorrow, and yet all this is true.

Out ran the knights, out ran the lords,
And there was great ado;
Some lost their hats and some their swords;
Then out ran Burbage, too.
The reprobates, though drunk on Monday,
Pray'd for the fool and Henry Condy.
    Oh sorrow, pitiful sorrow, and yet all this is true.

The periwigs and drum-heads fry'd
Like to a butter firkin:
A woeful burning did betide
To many a good buff jerkin;
Then with swollen eyes, like drunken Flemminges
Distressed stood old stuttering Hemminges.
    Oh sorrow, pitiful sorrow, and yet all this is true.

No shower his rain did there down force
In all that sunshine weather,
To save that great renowned house;
Nor thou, O ale-house, neither.
Had it begun below, sans doubt
Their wives for fear had pissed it out.
    Oh sorrow, pitiful sorrow, and yet all this is true.

Be warned, you stage-strutters all,
Lest you again be catched,
And such a burning do befall
As to them whose house was thatched;
Forbear your whoring, breeding biles,*
And lay up that expense for tiles.
    Oh sorrow, pitiful sorrow, and yet all this is true.

*Boils.

Go draw you a petition,
And do you not abhor it,
And get with low submission
A license to beg for it
In churches, sans churchwardens' checks,
In Surrey and in Middlesex.
  Oh sorrow, pitiful sorrow, and yet all this is true.

This ballad wonderfully conveys the excitement of that summer day when audience and actors ran for their lives with the flames at their heels and showers of sparks falling on their heads. No wonder that "old stuttering Hemminges" stood distressed, though he cannot have been distressed for very long. A few years later he is described as a man of "great living wealth and power." Since he often played leading roles, he was probably playing Cardinal Wolsey in *Henry VIII* and had just got into his stride when in the fourth scene of the first act the theatre began to burn. John Lowin probably played the King: he had the proper majestical appearance, as we know from a portrait of him still preserved in the Ashmolean Museum in Oxford, and there is a tradition dating from 1708 that Shakespeare himself instructed Lowin in the part. Richard Burbage may have played Thomas Cromwell, and Henry Condell would be an excellent Archbishop Cranmer, while Shakespeare, who appears to have enjoyed minor roles portraying old men of great dignity and force, would have played Cardinal Capuchius, the ambassador from the Emperor Charles V.

The chorus of the ballad preserves the joke contained in Shakespeare's original title: *Henry VIII or All is True*. Shakespeare had read deeply in George Cavendish's book on Cardinal Wolsey and was evidently struck by the fact that Cavendish in his introduction asserts and reasserts with tiresome ingenuity—for the words "truth" or "untruth" appear ten times in two pages—that he alone has presented the truth, the whole truth, and nothing but the truth.* Shakespeare, for his own pleasure, is

---

*Cavendish's understanding of truth is accompanied by some remarkable circumlocutions. Here is a passage from the Prologue: "Since his death I have heard divers and sundry surmises and imagined tales, made of his proceedings and doings, which I myself have perfectly known to be most untrue; unto which I could have sufficiently answered

ironically mimicking the claims of Cavendish, knowing that in a pageant play historical truth must necessarily be abandoned for the truth of the imagination.

Cavendish's book is still the most important source for the study of Cardinal Wolsey. Secure in the knowledge of the cardinal's affection, living with him day by day during the last four years of his life and being present at the deathbed, Cavendish studied the great man minutely, weighing the good and the bad, finding more bad than good. His final conclusions were stated bluntly:

> Here is the end and fall of pride and arrogancy of such men, exalted by fortune to honours and high dignities; for I assure you, in his time of authority and glory, he was the haughtiest man in all his proceedings that then lived, having more respect to the worldly honour of his person than he had to his spiritual profession; wherein should be all meekness, humility, and charity; the process whereof I leave to them that be learned and seen in the divine laws.

Out of these lines Shakespeare drew the great speech in which Wolsey describes his own withering away, his journey from the heights to the lowest depths: his remorse, his horror of himself. He is neither more nor less pitying than Cavendish. The speech seems to come soaring out of Wolsey's heart so that we find ourselves believing that he uttered them and could have uttered nothing else.

> Farewell? A long farewell to all my greatness.
> This is the state of man; today he puts forth
> The tender leaves of hopes, tomorrow blossoms,
> And bears his blushing honours thick upon him:
> The third day comes a frost, a killing frost,
> And when he thinks, good easy man, full surely
> His greatness is aripening, nips his root,
> And then he falls as I do. I have ventured

---

according to the truth, but, as me seemeth, it was much better for me to suffer and dissimule the matter, and the same to remain still as lies, than to reply against their untruth, of whom I might, for my boldness, sooner have kindled a great flame of displeasing, than to quench one spark of their malicious untruth. Therefore I commit the truth to Him who knoweth all truth."

Like little wanton boys that swim on bladders
This many summers in a sea of glory,
But far beyond my depth: my high-blown pride
At length broke under me, and now has left me
Weary, and old with service, to the mercy
Of a rude stream, that must for ever hide me.
Vain pomp and glory of this world, I hate ye.
I feel my heart now opened. Oh how wretched
Is that poor man that hangs on Princes' favours?
There is betwixt that smile we would aspire to
That sweet aspect of Princes, and their ruin,
More pangs and fears than wars, or women have;
And when he falls, he falls like Lucifer,
Never to hope again.

It is, of course, the one great speech in *Henry VIII*, the speech in which Shakespeare has most fully engaged his imagination, and for good reason, since he may have believed that this was the last play he would ever write. Although Wolsey was not himself, and between himself and Wolsey there were only a few frail silvery threads of agreement, he appears to have seen himself or a shadowy image of himself in Wolsey. When he writes:

I have ventured
Like little wanton boys that swim on bladders
This many summers in a sea of glory,
And far beyond my depth,

the words in their rawness and nakedness appear to spring from the heart. Images of wanton boys follow one another. When King Henry learns that Archbishop Cranmer has been kept waiting in an anteroom with lackeys and footman, he compares him with "a lousy foot-boy at chamber door." A drunken porter's man tells a long story about a quarrel with the haberdasher's wife, and complains that her screaming brought on a squadron of boys against him together with two score trunchioners:

Porter's Man.   I missed the meteor once and hit that
woman, and cried out "Clubs!", when I might see from
far some forty trunchioneers draw to her succor, which
were the hope of the Strand where she was quartered;

they fell on, I made good my place, at length they came
to the broom staff with me, I defied 'em still, when
suddenly a file of boys behind 'em, loose shot, delivered
such a shower of pibbles that I was fain to draw mine
honor in, and let 'em win the work. The divel was
amongst them I think surely.

Porter.   These are the youths that thunder at a playhouse
and fight for bitten apples.

At the end of the play it remains only for Archbishop Cranmer to
praise the newly born Princess Elizabeth, daughter of Queen Anne
Boleyn, promising that the royal infant would bring upon the land
"a thousand thousand blessings, which Time shall bring to ripe-
ness." At the time of Elizabeth's death Henry Chettle and others
had remarked that Shakespeare had written nothing to celebrate her
death. Now at last Shakespeare made amends for his past forgetful-
ness, and having praised Elizabeth as though she was the goddess of
all love, truth, beauty, and wisdom, went on to praise James in a
similar fashion, granting to Cranmer the powers of a prophet. But it
is not the praise of Elizabeth and James one remembers so much as
the sudden eruption of the boys throwing stones, as related by the
drunken porter's man. Quite suddenly, in the last dying moments of
a long and ornamental pageant, we see the real faces of the boys of
summer at their deadly game, the "loose shot," throwing stones for
the fun of it, not caring whether they maim or kill; and there is more
than irony in the remark of Shakespeare wearing the mask of the
old porter: "These are the youths that thunder at a playhouse and
fight for bitten apples."

Henry VIII was the last play written wholly by Shakespeare.
This pageant-play, not *The Tempest*, was his farewell to the stage
and to the world. It is sometimes slow and sometimes creaks
awkwardly on its hinges, and like all pageant-plays suffers from the
fact that the pageantry tends to obscure the unfolding of the drama.
Groups of people form, melt into other groups, vanish as in a
dream. They are nearly always great officers of state in magnificent
costumes, gold-braided and wearing their jeweled orders, marching
a little stiffly to their doom. Shakespeare wrote it in a mood of high
seriousness. "I come no more to make you laugh," he announced in

the prologue, which concludes with words which amount to an ironic rebuke to the patient audience:

For Goodness sake, and as you are known
The first and happiest hearers of the town,
Be sad, or we would make ye. Think ye see
The very persons of our noble story,
As they were living. Think you see them great,
And followed with the general throng, and sweat
Of thousand friends. Then in a moment see
How soon this mightiness meets misery:
And if you can be merry then, I'll say
A man may weep upon his wedding day.

Once more Shakespeare was reminding them, as he had done throughout his historical plays, that "mightiness" contains the seeds of its own downfall, its own corruption. The meeting of misery and mightiness was an encounter endlessly repeated, and not a laughing matter. The solemn prologue was an invitation to watch one disaster following another, like ninepins going down. *Oh sorrow, pitiful sorrow, and yet all this is true!*

The Globe Theatre, which burned in little more than an hour, was rebuilt in less than a year. The new theatre was said to be "the fairest that ever was in London." Between the two gable roofs there was a curiously shaped admiral's walk, which perhaps also served as a skylight and a support for the flagpole. Wenceslaus Hollar, who ascended to the top of the tower of St. Mary Overies to make his wonderfully detailed etching known as *The Long View of London*, drew an admirable picture of the outside of the new theatre. Unhappily we know very little about the interior, though we can guess that the style was wholly Jacobean, heavy and ornate, every column intricately carved and gilded, and with every new device of stage machinery. The Jacobean masques had changed the essential nature of the theatre, and Jacobean taste demanded the filling up of empty spaces. The second Globe theatre, which survived for thirty years until the Puritans destroyed it, lacked Elizabethan simplicity.

Yet it was a thing to marvel at, and John Taylor the water poet regarded it as a great improvement on the old:

As gold is better that's in fire tried,
So is the Bankside Globe that late was burned,
For where before it had a thatched hide,
Now to a stately Theatre is turned:
Which is an emblem that great things are won
By those who are through greatest dangers run.

We see the "stately Theatre" again in the panoramic view of London engraved by Claesz Jans Vissher in 1616: the building looking like a fortress, a small park and trees all round it. Some men have gathered close-by and they appear to be waiting for the play to begin, and in a moment they will rush in to take their seats. Vissher's panorama shows the serried row of houses on the river-bank. These houses are small and sturdy, scarcely different from workmen's dwellings built in the Victorian era. The thatch has gone from the theatre roof; there are smooth tiles, a suggestion of opulence; and the theatre looks as though at most it could hold two hundred people, though we know that it held two thousand.

In Vissher's map we see all London laid before us on a summer afternoon, while the smoke pours lazily from the chimneys and the trees are full of leaves. The river is like a sea of glass, the ships floating on it as delicately as swans. If the panorama were colored, we would see the gray stones of Old St. Paul's, the huge Gothic cathedral which dominated London like a stern mother hen among her chicks. The river would be silvery blue, sweet and unpolluted, and the houses would be the warm red brick favored in Elizabethan times. As we see it in Visscher's engraving, it does not seem to be a city of deafening noise and incessant bustle. All that we see here within the ancient walls of London would go up in flames during the Great Fire of 1666.

About the time that the new Globe Theatre was being opened for its first performance, in the summer of 1614, there occurred a great fire in Stratford. It was the third great fire in twenty years. Sir Fulke Greville, William Combe, and other commissioners drew up a report. This "sudden and terrible fire" burned fifty-four houses, with barns, stables, rain, hay, and timber, worth eight thousand pounds, in less than two hours. It was Saturday, July 9, 1614, a market day. Once again the cause was found to be burning thatch, which flew up in a strong wind and settled on the neighboring houses. So many houses were burning at once and there was so little equipment for putting out fires that the people of Stratford could only watch helplessly as a quarter of the town vanished in the flames. The commissioners observed: "The force of the fire was so great (the wind sitting full upon the town) that it dispersed into so many places thereof whereby the whole town was in very grave danger of having been utterly consumed."

Shakespeare's house, New Place, escaped, and he was lucky, for houses very close to his were destroyed. The commissioners were concerned to prevent a recurrence of the disaster. They ordered more fire equipment: buckets, ladders, fire hooks. A royal patent granted on December 5, 1614, authorized Richard Tyler and four other Stratford worthies to seek contributions for the people who suffered in the fire. When the books of these worthies were examined, the commissioners concluded that much of the money had been wrongfully distributed: everyone was "preferring his own private benefits before the general good." Richard Tyler was one of those men who worked for their own advantage and always put a good face on things, for we find him described in a petition to the Lord Chancellor drawn up by his friends as "a man of honest conversation and quiet and peaceable carriage amongst his neighbors and towards all people." This was certainly untrue, for many people had reason to hate him. Shakespeare apparently liked him enough to mention him in his will and then abruptly crossed out the name as though he suddenly remembered that their long friendship had recently ended, presumably because Taylor had misappropriated funds.

In these last years we may imagine Shakespeare spending more and more time in Stratford, going about the affairs of a country gentleman, reading in his library, visiting friends, talking with his farm laborers, spending part of every day poring over his account books. He had not given up writing plays. In London Queen Anne, the wife of King James, busied herself with masques and plays as though her life depended on them; the theatre had never been more popular; new dramatists were coming along, and soon John Fletcher would become the leading playwright in the company of the King's Men. The death of Prince Henry and the marriage of Princess Elizabeth had sharpened sensibilities and created a strangely heightened mood among poets and playwrights in London, but these waves of grief and joy scarcely touched Stratford, which was like an island remote from the world's tempests.

Here at last Shakespeare was his own master, spending each day as leisurely as he pleased. His granddaughter Elizabeth Hall was six years old, and Shakespeare would have been an unusual grandfather if he had not doted on his only grandchild, all the more so because her birth may have had something to do with the invention of the divine children of his last plays. We may imagine him taking the short walk along the riverbank to Hall's Croft to meet her, listening to the noise of building and hammering that resounded through Stratford as the new houses were being built to replace those that had burned to the ground. He would accompany the child along the field paths, telling her the names of flowers and explaining the world's mysteries.

In that year he was confronted with the difficult and troublesome problem of the Welcombe enclosure. Old John Combe, the money-lender, died in July 1614, leaving some of his wealth to his nephew William Combe, who promptly set about infuriating his neighbors. He inherited the property in Welcombe, a hamlet about a mile from the center of the town, and now decided to enclose the common land. Nearby were open fields of two more hamlets, Old Stratford and Bishopton. In 1602 Shakespeare bought 127 acres of land in Old Stratford, and three years later he bought part of the hay and corn tithes of Stratford, Bishopton, and Welcombe. He therefore had an interest in these hamlets and would be affected by the enclosure. As a tithe-holder he would probably gain if the enclosure led to a proper cultivation of crops and he would lose if the arable land was converted to pasture. It appeared that the enclosure was illegal, and Shakespeare's kinsman, Thomas Greene, who was town clerk of Stratford and also a tithe-holder, bitterly opposed it. Shakespeare appears not to have cared very much whether the enclosure took place as long as his own interests were safeguarded, and there exists a long document drawn up by William Replingham, the agent of William Combe, guaranteeing him against any losses if the enclosure took place. This was drawn up on October 28, 1614, but Greene, who was in London on private business, did not hear about it until some time later. On November 16 Shakespeare reached

London, and Greene went to see him to discuss the enclosure on the
same day. He wrote to Stratford the next morning:

My cousin Shakespeare coming yesterday to town, I
went to see him how he did. He told me that they assured
him they meant to enclose no further than to Gospel Bush,
and so up straight, leaving out part of the Dingles to the
Field, to the gate in Clopton Hedge and take in Salisbury's
piece; and that they mean in April to survey the land, and
then to give satisfaction and not before. And he and Master
Hall say they think there will be nothing done at all.
Master Wyatt after noon told me that Master Combe
had told Master Wright that the enclosure would not be,
and that it was at an end. I said I was the more suspicious,
for those might be words used to make us careless. I willed
him to learn what he could, and I told him so would I.

Greene later learned from Master Wright that there were others
besides himself who vigorously opposed the enclosure, and they
included Lord Carew, another prominent landowner. Greene returned to Stratford on December 3 to find that William Combe was
as adamant as ever. A few days later together with the bailiff and
other prominent citizens Greene called on Combe to express "their
hearty desires that he would be pleased to forebear further proceedings touching the enclosure, and to desire his love towards the Town
as they shall study to deserve it." Combe, who was twenty-eight
years old and therefore by many years junior to the worthies who
had called on him, flew into a temper, saying they had better pray
for the continuance of the frost, for as soon as the frost was over he
would begin "to hedge in the enclosure," and those who opposed his
plans had made "almost the greatest men of England" their enemies. What he meant by "almost the greatest men of England" was
not clear, but apparently it included Shakespeare, who was still in
London, attending to his theatrical affairs and presumably working
with John Fletcher on various projects. He was obviously in continual touch with Stratford, but his letters and documents have not
survived. Greene kept him informed about what was going on.

On December 19 the frost broke and Willam Combe immediately
carried out his threat to enclose the common land. He sent laborers to

dig a ditch and raise an earthen bank around the disputed lands. Greene summoned a meeting of the aldermen and burgesses to decide on the proper course to be followed. It was decided to appeal to the important local landowners, urging them to "Christian meditation" on the subject of "the great disabling" that would occur if the common lands were enclosed, and among those disablings was the fact that there were seven hundred poor men receiving alms in the borough of Stratford and they would inevitably be affected. Greene kept a voluminous diary. He wrote on December 23, 1614, an entry to remind himself that almost all the members of the Stratford Corporation had signed an urgent message addressed to Shakespeare, adding: "I also writ of myself to my Cousin Shakespeare the copies of all our oaths made then, also a note of the inconveniences would grow by the enclosure." Early in January, while the work of hedging in the enclosure continued in defiance of the Corporation, Greene decided that the earthen walls had to be broken down and sent some of his friends to the common land with instructions to proceed cautiously. At all costs he wanted to avoid a confrontation. He failed. William Combe was there, on horseback, when the attempt was made to throw down the earthen walls. There was the inevitable riot, Combe's men fighting off the invaders and doing so well that they succeeded in knocking their adversaries to the ground. Both sides had committed a breach of the peace, and there would inevitably be a full-scale inquiry. Combe was seen laughing hugely while on horseback, but he laughed a little less when he learned that women and children from Stratford and Bishopton came *en masse* later in the day to complete the work of throwing down the earthen walls and filling up the trenches. Combe was unrelenting. He took down the names of as many "women-diggers" as he could find and saw to it that they were bound over to keep the peace.

All this was so unsatisfactory that Greene decided to appeal to Edward Coke, the Lord Chief Justice. At the assize held at War-wick on March 28, 1615, the Chief Justice handed down his verdict: no enclosure could be made by William Combe or by anyone else until he showed cause at open assizes, for such enclosures were against the law of the realm. Combe was rich, arrogant, possessed powerful friends, and determined to achieve his aim, whatever the Chief Justice said. He was elected that year to the extremely powerful position of high sheriff of Warwick and continued to make life miserable for all those who had fought against the enclosures. By September Shakespeare had been won over to the view that the enclosures were unhealthy, for there is a note in Greene's diary in September: "Master Shakespeare telling J. Greene that he was not able to bear the enclosing of Welcombe." J. Greene was John Greene, the town clerk's brother.

William Combe continued to be a nuisance in Stratford. He made life miserable for his tenants, beating them and imprisoning them. His servants acted as his bullies and he paid a small army of them to safeguard his interests. At the Lent Assizes in 1616 he confronted the Lord Chief Justice who "bade him set him heart at rest he should never enclose nor lay down his common arable land so long as he [Coke] served the King." Combe continued to do as he pleased, and it was not until 1619 that he was forced to desist by an order from the Privy Council.

Shakespeare remained on good terms with the Combe family. Thomas Combe, a year younger than William, was his special favorite. Thomas, too, had an unsavory reputation as a bully who took to his fists on the slightest provocation. In his will Shakespeare bequeathed to him the sword he wore as one of the King's Men. A few months after Shakespeare's death Thomas had a fight with a certain Valentine Taunt, or Tant, wounding him so severely that he died a few weeks later. Previously Thomas had kicked and beaten a shepherd who had the temerity to demand his proper wages. At the time of the Welcombe enclosure he called the Stratford councilors "dogs and curs." That Shakespeare liked him is certain, but it is difficult to find anything likable in him.

Life in Stratford was not uneventful. People died violently and wild passions sometimes shook the calm of the sleepy market town. Adultery, drunkenness, and contentiousness were the common-places of daily life. Evil-minded gossip, which spread through the town like wildfire, was rife at all times. Even Shakespeare's daughter Susanna was not immune from it. In June 1613 a certain John Lane asserted that she "had the running of the reins and had been naught with Rafe Smith at John Palmer." Rafe Smith was a prosperous middle-aged haberdasher, John Palmer was a well-respected country gentleman, and John Lane was twenty-three years old and a drunkard, the son of a landed proprietor. "Running of the reins" meant that she was lecherous, and "had been naught with Rafe Smith" meant that she had bedded with him. Susanna, to save her name, had recourse to the consistory court at Worcester Cathedral, which had power to investigate crimes of morality. She was represented by Robert Whatcott, who was a close friend of Shakespeare and appears as a signatory in the will. Lane refused to appear at the court. He was judged at fault and sentenced to be excommunicated. The punishment may not seem severe in our eyes, but in Jacobean times it involved some hardship, for an excommunicated man could not obtain any public office, was not permitted to take part in the communion service, and in theory he could not be married and if he had children they were all illegitimate. Lane's sister married John Greene, the town clerk's brother, and a cousin, Richard Lane, appointed Dr. Hall to be the trustee of his estate. The Halls, the Lanes, the Greenes, and the Shakespeares were very close to one another and very tolerant of one another's failings.

Shakespeare continued to live in a fair degree of state at New Place. He was a private man, and never aspired to public office, unlike his father, who climbed all the rungs of civic office. A curious entry in the Stratford archives shows that Shakespeare could sometimes be induced to play a quasi-public role. We see him offering his house as a place of entertainment for a visiting preacher, the cost of the wines being borne by the Corporation. The entry reads: "Christmas, 1614. One quart of sack and one quart of claret wine given to a preacher at the New Place. xx*d*." It was a very high price to pay for two quarts of wine, and one may imagine that the very best wines were served at New Place.

Nicholas Rowe, Shakespeare's first biographer, wrote about these last years: "The latter part of his life was spent, as all men of good sense will wish theirs to be, in ease, retirement and the conversation of friends." It was not quite true. There were theatrical affairs to be tended to, violence and riots in Stratford, visits to London, the constant care of his estates. Retirement meant hard work; nor was it likely that the creator of *King Lear* would ever be completely at ease in the world of pain and misery and death. There was no idyllic retirement, no rest. He was fifty years old and had only a few more months to live.

The Two Noble Kinsmen

JOHN FLETCHER, THE PLAYWRIGHT, was a man of considerable personal distinction. He had a long, rather narrow face, melting eyes, a carefully trimmed beard, a prominent and well-shaped nose, a fine brow, and hair which was swept back carelessly from his forehead. He possessed a studied elegance, and of all the poets of the time he was the one who most resembled Shakespeare.

He came from a distinguished family, for he was one of the eight children of Dr. Richard Fletcher, who was successively chaplain to Queen Elizabeth, Dean of Peterborough, Bishop of Bristol, of Worcester, and of London. He was the chaplain appointed to be in attendance at the execution of Mary, Queen of Scots, and her last words were spoken to him after he urged her in this last moment of her life to convert to Protestantism. The Queen of Scots dismissed him curtly, saying that she was born a Catholic and would die a Catholic, and a moment later she flung off her black robe to reveal herself in a scarlet underrobe: the color of martyrdom. Dr. Fletcher was not usually dismissed so curtly. He had the ear of Queen

Elizabeth and spent a good deal of his time furthering intrigues at court.

Almost from the time of his birth John Fletcher knew the way of the court. When he wrote plays with or without the help of his friend Francis Beaumont, he knew the precise weight of each gesture and the timbre of the royal voice. He also knew exactly what happened when a courtier fell into disgrace, for his father fell into disfavor with Queen Elizabeth when he married for a second time without asking the Queen's permission. He was about twenty-eight when he wrote his first play, *The Faithful Shepherdess*, which was an instant success. A year earlier Francis Beaumont had written his equally successful *The Knight of the Burning Pestle*. Thereafter they collaborated, and it was said that Beaumont wrote the plots and Fletcher decked them out with poetry. In fact they were true collaborators, but Fletcher was by far the greater poet.

John Aubrey told a scandalous story about their living arrangements. "They lived together on the Bankside, not far from the playhouse," he wrote. "Both bachelors; lay together; had one wench in the house between them, which they so admire; the same clothes and cloak etc. between them." In 1613 Beaumont, five years younger than Fletcher, married an heiress, Ursula Isley, and moved to the country. In the same year he wrote *The Masque of the Inner Temple and Gray's Inn*, which was produced at court during the celebrations of the nuptials of Frederick, Elector Palatine, and Princess Elizabeth. He died three years later, a month before Shakespeare, and was buried in Westminster Abbey.

John Fletcher's particular tone of voice can often be recognized. It is a voice of great clarity and sweetness, calm and assured. Here in *The Maid's Tragedy* Aspatia, who spends her time among her serving women embroidering stories of women who have been cast off by their lovers, complains that Antiphila has portrayed her in the wrong colors:

You are much mistaken, wench:
These colours are not dull or pale enough
To show a soul so full of misery
As this sad lady's was. Do it by me.
Do it again, by me the lost Aspatia;

And you shall find all true but the wild Island,
And think I stand upon the sea breach now,
Mine arms thus, and mine hair blown with the wind,
Wild as that desert, and let all about me
Tell that I am forsaken, do my face
(If thou hadst ever feeling of a sorrow)
Thus, thus, Antiphila arrive to make me look
Like sorrow's monument, and the trees about me
Let them be dry and leaveless, let the rocks
Groan with continual surges, and behind me
Make all a desolation, look, look, wenches,
A miserable life of this poor picture.

    This is Jacobean poetry in its perfection. One can get drunk with the line: "And you shall find all true but the wild Island." John Fletcher can speak as memorably as Shakespeare; his gifts would be more widely known if he was not, like all the other dramatists of his time, drowned in Shakespeare's shadow. Or take the few words of Amintor, who was once the betrothed of Aspatia, as he sums up all the categories of pride and honor in three perfect lines:

What a wild beast is uncollected man!
The thing that we call honour bears us all
Headlong into sin, and yet itself is nothing.

Or again, listen to the murderous conversation between Philaster and Bellario in the play *Philaster*, first acted at the Globe Theatre in 1608:

Philaster. Oh, but thou dost not know
  What 'tis to die.
Bellario. Yes, I do know, my lord:
  'Tis less than to be born; a lasting sleep;
  A quiet resting from all jealousy,
  A thing we all pursue; I know, besides,
  It is but giving over of a game
  That must be lost.

Here there is the illusion of effortlessness; the words fall inevitably on the page, and when they are spoken they have the effect of whispers uttered in long corridors endlessly reverberating. The charm of *Philaster* and *The Maid's Tragedy* lies in a kind of tragic gaiety very close in feeling to the last plays of Shakespeare.

Fletcher enjoyed collaboration—at various times he appears to have collaborated with Ben Jonson, Cyril Tourneur, John Ford, and Philip Massinger—and about the time that Francis Beaumont went off to live with his heiress he began to collaborate with Shakespeare. Together they wrote two dramas, *The History of Cardenio* and *The Two Noble Kinsmen*. The first is lost, the other is still vigorously alive.

The reader who comes upon *The Two Noble Kinsmen* for the first time has a great pleasure in store. The pleasure lies in hearing Shakespeare loud and clear as he deftly tells a familiar tale from Chaucer. We hear the music we know well: the surge and the thunder. Once again we recognize Shakespeare's familiar play with images as he runs one image into another until they fuse into a third image, which then goes in search of a fourth, and often these images turn back to their first anchorage. Here, too, we enter the Shakespearean landscape: the crags, the mists, the full light of summer, and the brightly colored people moving about with an effortless assurance, carrying their doom like prizes. Thomas De Quincey thought this play was "the most superb work in the English language" and had not the slightest doubt that it came from the loom of Shakespeare. Academic critics still quarrel about Shakespeare's and Fletcher's share in its composition, but to no purpose. The ordinary reader finds himself being carried away in Shakespeare's full tide.

The play begins with a flourish of trumpets. The reader of the prologue, who is likely to have been Shakespeare himself, strides onto the stage and delivers himself of an amused salute to new plays, maidenheads, and Chaucer:

New plays and maidenheads are near akin,
Much followed both, for both much money gain
If they stand sound and well: and a good play
(Whose modest scenes blush on his marriage day
And shakes to loose his honour) is like her
That after holy tie and first night's stir

Yet still is modesty and still retains
More of the maid to sight than husband's pains.
We pray our play may be so, for I am sure
It has a noble breeder, and a pure,
A learned, and a poet never went
More famous yet twixt Po and silver Trent.
Chaucer (of all admired) the story gives
There constant to eternity it lives.
If we let fall the nobleness of this,
And the first sound this child hear be a hiss,
How will it shake the bones of that good man
And make him cry from underground. O fan
From me the witless chaff of such a wrighter
That blasts my bays, and my famed works makes lighter
Than Robin Hood? This is the fear we bring,
For to say truth it were an endless thing,
And too ambitious to aspire to him,
Weak as we are, and almost breathless swim
In this deep water. Do but you hold out
Your helping hands, and we shall take about
And something do to save us. You shall hear
Scenes though below his art may yet appear
Worth two hours travail. To his bones, sweet sleep.
Content to you. If this play do not keep
A little dull time from us, we perceive
Our losses fall so thick, we must needs leave.

It is a wonderful prologue, full of kindly mockery and self-mockery. It was clearly delivered for a first-night audience: the young wife's "first night stir" is likened to the play about to be performed. The well-loved Chaucer is in his grave, and at this point Shakespeare jerks his thumb downward toward the trapdoor to indicate that he lies beneath the boards and will soon be resurrected. Chaucer's *The Knight's Tale* will be performed with some admirable changes. It will be told in Shakespeare's words, and Shakespeare will interpret it as he pleases, with Chaucer's tale open on the table in front of him. He says: "Weak as we are, and almost breathless swim in this deep water." But this is a manner of speaking. He was saying: "We are fairly satisfied with this play and thoroughly commend ourselves to you." There follows another flourish of the silver trumpets. Then, without further warning, we find ourselves in the familiar territory of *A Midsummer Night's Dream*, for *The Two Noble Kinsmen* begins where the dream left off—with the marriage of Theseus and Hippolita.

First comes the wedding. A boy dressed in white enters, strewing flowers; then comes Hymen with his burning torch; then a nymph "encompast in her Tresses." They are followed by Theseus, resplendent in his kingly robes, attended by two nymphs with wheaten chaplets on their heads, who are followed by Hippolita and another nymph who holds a garland over her head. Emilia, the sister of Theseus and most beautiful of women, holds up the train of Hippolita.

All this would suggest we are about to see a masque, but the masque consists of a single song followed by a kind of formal dance as three queens, crowned and wearing black veils, kneel and plead to be allowed to bury the bodies of their husbands killed by Creon, the tyrannical and cruel King of Thebes. They address themselves to Theseus, Hippolita, and Emilia in turn. They do this while the lingering notes of one of Shakespeare's most magical songs still hang in the air.

> Roses, their sharp spines being gone,
> Not royal in their smells alone,
>   But in their hue;
> Maiden pinks, of odour faint,
> Daisies smell-less, yet most quaint,
>   And sweet thyme true.
>
> Primrose, firstborn child of Ver,
> Merry springtime's harbinger
>   With her bells dim;
> Oxlips in their cradles growing,
> Marigolds on death-beds blowing,
>   Larks'-heels trim:
>
> All dear Nature's sweet
> Lie 'fore bride and bridegroom's feet,
>   Blessing their sense,

Not an angel in the air,
Bird melodious or bird fair,
  Be absent hence.

The crow, the slanderous cuckoo, nor
The boding raven, nor chough hoar,
  Nor chattering pie,
May on our bride-house perch or sing,
Or with them any discord bring,
  But from it fly.

When the dark pageant of the mourning queens is over, the story
begins to move toward its main theme, which is the love of the
knights Palamon and Arcite for the divinely beautiful Emilia, the
sister of Theseus. Palamon and Arcite are the two noble kinsmen,
nephews of King Creon of Thebes, and their rivalry for Emilia's
affection begins at the moment when, being imprisoned after the
capture of Thebes by Theseus, they look through the prison windows and see her walking in the garden among the flowers. And
since they have both caught fire and are madly in love with her, they
quarrel bitterly and hurl abuse at one another. They are shackled in
the same cell, and each dreams of the day when he will escape and
marry Emilia, having performed feats of great daring to be worthy
of her hand.

We have entered the dreamlike world of fairy tale, where nothing
happens according to rule, where madness lurks in every dark corner,
and insignificant events acquire astonishing importance. Arcite is set
free, banished from the kingdom. Palamon is thrown into a darker
dungeon and can no longer gaze out of the window at Emilia among
the flowers. These misfortunes only make them more determined than
ever to pursue Emilia. Banishment and the deep dungeon work their
miracles. The banished Arcite learns that the country people will soon
be performing the May Day games before Theseus and no doubt
Emilia will be in attendance, and the imprisoned Palamon is set free by
the jailer's daughter who has fallen in love with him. Theseus is so
impressed by Arcite's performance at the May Day games that he
presents him to Emilia, whose servant he becomes. About the same
time the jailer's daughter learns that because she has freed Palamon
from his dungeon, her father will be hanged.

This might be the scenario for a nineteenth-century opera performed to a full orchestra. The verses have their own music. Here, for example, Arcite invokes the person of Emilia in the innocent days before he learns that Palamon has escaped from prison:

> O Queen Emilia,
> Fresher than May, sweeter
> Than her gold buttons on the boughs, or all
> Th' enamelled knacks of the mead and garden, yea
> We challenge too the bank of any nymph
> That makes the stream seem flowers: thou a jewel
> O' the wood, o' the world . . .

When Palamon surprises his cousin in the simplest possible way—by leaping out at him from behind a bush—Arcite is still so enthralled by his love for Emilia that he forgets the deadly feud between them. Palamon remembers. He would like to fight to the death. Arcite reminds him that he is in no shape to fight, needing food in order to regain his strength, new clothes, and "perfumes to kill the smell o' th' prison." The good Arcite brings venison and tries to take Palamon's mind off this feud that threatens to destroy them. But Palamon is determined that there should be a duel to the death and he exacts from Arcite the promise that he will bring swords and shields for the battle.

Emilia, of course, knows nothing about their intentions. They are caught up in the mythology that decrees that since they are the most handsome and valiant men in the world, she will choose one of them. Even Arcite, while dubious of the upshot, is curiously attracted to the proposition that one of them must die so that the other may marry Emilia:

> When we are armed
> And both upon our guards, then let our fury
> Like meeting of two tides, fly strongly from us.
> And then to whom the birthright of this beauty
> Truly pertains (without abraidings, scorns,
> Despisings of our persons, and such pouting
> Fitter for girls and schoolboys) will be seen

And quickly, yours or mine: wilt please you arm, sir,
Or if you feel yourself not fitting yet
And furnished with your old strength, I'll stay, cousin
And every day discourse you into health.
As I am spared, your person I am friends with,
And I could wish I had not said I loved her,
Though I had died.

They are about to fight when they hear the horns announcing
that King Theseus is approaching with his hunting party. It occurs
to Arcite that Theseus will be enraged when he discovers that
Palamon has escaped from prison and equally enraged when he
learns that Arcite, instead of serving Emilia, is engaged in an absurd
duel with a man who should be in prison. Theseus acts according to
his sovereign character, condemns them both to death, and permits
Emilia and Hippolita to plead for their lives. They may live but
must be punished. Emilia says they should be banished to two
different places, but the cousins plead with her that they be allowed
to fight to the death. Theseus reluctantly agrees to permit them to
fight for the hand of Emilia in a month's time, the loser to be
executed. The cousins are overjoyed at the prospect of the duel.

Meanwhile the jailer's daughter has gone mad and wanders
disconsolately in search of Palamon, whom she loves to distraction.
She knows her father will be hanged. She is a lost soul in the
ultimate extremity of doubt and fear, having no reason to live, no
cause to die for. She does not know that Palamon has interceded for
her with Theseus and in addition given her a sum of money for her
marriage, and her life has been saved without her knowing it. Many
years before, as a boy in Stratford, Shakespeare had acted the role of
Ariadne abandoned by Theseus, and the jailer's daughter echoes
Ariadne's lamentations. A wandering scholar who encounters her in
her wanderings says kindly: "Are you mad, good woman?" She
answers: "I would be sorry else." Like Ophelia she sings snatches of
obscene songs. While she is still mad, a Wooer appears and speaks
to the jailer, now free from prison, and as he speaks he has the
power to re-create the girl in her madness, to bring us into her
presence, so that we are mysteriously close to her. It is the jailer's
daughter seen in the visionary light of the poetic imagination, and

there are only a few other passages in Shakespeare's works that can be compared with it. The passage is very long but must be quoted in full.

Jailer.   Why all this haste, sir?

Wooer.   I'll tell you quickly. As I late was angling
In the great lake that lies behind the palace,
From the far shore, thick set with reeds and sedges,
As patiently I was attending sport,
I heard a voice, a shrill one; and attentive
I gave my ear; when I might well perceive
'Twas one that sung, and by the smallness of it,
A boy or woman. I then left my angle
To his own skill, came near, but yet perceiv'd not
Who made the sound, the rushes and the reeds
Had so encompass'd it. I laid me down
And listen'd to the words she sang; for then,
Through a small glade cut by the fishermen,
I saw it was your daughter.

Jailer.   Pray go on, sir.

Wooer.   She sang much, but no sense; only
                   I heard her
Repeat this often, Palamon is gone,
Is gone to th' wood to gather mulberries
I'll find him out tomorrow.

First Friend.   Pretty soul!

Wooer.   His shackles will betray him, he'll be taken;
And what shall I do then? I'll bring a bevy,
A hundred black-eyed maids that love as I do,
With chaplets on their heads of daffadillies,
With cherry lips and cheeks of damask roses,
And all we'll dance an antic 'fore the Duke
And beg his pardon. Then she talk'd of you, sir—
That you must lose your head tomorrow morning,
And she must gather flowers to bury you
And see the house made handsome. Then she sang
Nothing but 'willow, willow, willow'; and between

Ever was 'Palamon, fair Palamon'
And 'Palamon was a tall young man.' The place
Was kneedeep where she sat; her careless tresses
A wreath of bulrush rounded; about her stuck
Thousand fresh water-flowers of several colours
That methought she appear'd like the fair nymph
That feeds the lake with waters, or as Iris
Newly dropp'd down from heaven. Rings she made
Of rushes that grew by, and to 'em spoke
The prettiest posies—'Thus our true love's tied,'
'This you may lose, not me,' and many a one;
And the she wept, and sang again, and sigh'd,
And with the same breath smil'd and kiss'd
                    her hand.
Second Friend.   Alas, what pity it is!
Wooer.   I made in to her.
She saw me and straight sought the flood.
                    I sav'd her
And set her safe to land; when presently
She slipped away, and to the city made
With such a cry and swiftness that, believe me,
She left me far behind her. Three or four
I saw from far off cross her—one of 'em
I knew to be your brother; where she stay'd,
And fell, scarce to be got away. I left them with her
And hither came to tell you . . .

The Wooer's speech is spoken with the whole breath in uninter-
rupted flow. The furious pace explains the fact that the most
dramatic moment is quickly passed over—the Wooer's rescue of the
girl is related in a single sentence. "I sav'd her and set her safe to
land." But there is a psychological rightness in this brief dismissal.
The Wooer is in earnest. He has fallen in love with the jailer's
daughter, and he is not concerned with himself.

The rest of the complicated story may be quickly told. Emilia
confronts the portraits of the two cousins in fear and trembling; she
can no more choose between them than she can choose between the

sun and the moon. Emilia refuses to watch the duel. Like the jailer's daughter, she is in torment. A doctor suggests to the Wooer that there is a simple way for him to win the jailer's daughter's heart; he has only to disguise himself as Palamon. The cousins fight their duel; Arcite wins; Palamon is led out to be executed, according to the agreement, and he is about to lay his head on the block when a messenger arrives to say that Arcite's black horse has been frightened by a spark, has thrown him and trampled him to death. The victor has become the loser. Arcite with his dying breath praises the valor of Palamon, King Theseus pronounces the benediction as Palamon is assured that Emilia belongs to him, and the play ends.

Shakespeare is an uneven playwright and *The Two Noble Kinsmen* is a play so uneven that it appears to have been written at different times in different moods, rather carelessly, in fits and starts. Fletcher certainly had a hand in it, and it is likely that the play was written in such close collaboration that even the authors might have wondered sometimes who wrote the individual lines. Fletcher may have written lines that sound most authentically Shakespearean, offering his friend that tribute of imitation, and Shakespeare out of affection for Fletcher may have written lines which sounded like Fletcher. A line like "The blissful dew of heaven does arouse you" could be written by either of them. It is possible that Fletcher could have written:

Were I at liberty, I would do things
Of such a virtuous greatness, that this Lady,
This blushing virgin, should take manhood to her
And seek to ravish me.

The words are spoken by Palamon while he awaits the return of Arcite; there is a harsh edge to them, and Shakespeare demonstrated in *Hamlet* that the harsh edge of ravishment was not foreign to him, that he could say singularly unpleasant things with ease, and that he enjoyed writing them. Fletcher could also on occasion write with a hard vulgarity. He has Shakespeare's gift of writing effortlessly, but he lacks the power to command the full orchestra and the massed choir of exaltation:

Thou mighty one, that with thy power hast turned
Green Neptune into purple; whose approach
Comets prewarn; whose havoc in vast field
Unearthed skulls proclaim; whose breath blows down
The teeming Ceres foison; who dost pluck
With hand armipotent from forth blue clouds
The mason'd turrets; that both mak'st and break'st
The stony girths of cities; me thy pupil,
Youngest follower of thy Drom, instruct this day
With military skill, that to thy laud
I may advance my streamer, and by thee
Be styled the Lord o' th' day.

In this way Arcite appeals to Mars to assist him in victory, the thunder of his voice imitating the thunder of Mars. Indeed the words must be spoken thunderously, for there is a stage direction that reads: "There is heard clanging of armor, with a short thunder as the burst of a battle, whereupon they all rise and bow to the altar."

Palamon also makes his appeal to Heaven, choosing Venus as his protectress. But while Arcite invokes Mars with a fierce fervor, praising him for the destruction he creates—laying low the walls of cities and the summer harvest, turning the seas purple, and leaving, "unearthed skulls" on battlefields—Palamon speaks to Venus on more intimate terms, for after praising her, he chides her, argues with her, engages in a kind of battle with her, defends himself against her claims upon him, and recites some of his adventures and encounters, and he is especially concerned with the fate of old men who fall under the spell of Venus.

Little known, this long passage with its sudden discoveries and sudden changes of direction must be included among the most wonderful creations of Shakespeare. It is the last of Shakespeare's long speeches that have come down to us. Here for the last time he asserts his quarrel with love in an argument that mingles despair with the wildest hope:

Hail sovereign Queen of secrets, who hast power
To call the fiercest tyrant from his rage;
And weep unto a girl; that hast the might

Even with an eye-glance to choke Mars's Drom
And turn the alarm to whispers, that canst make
A cripple flourish with his crutch, and cure him
Before Apollo; that mayest force the King
To be his subject's vassal, and induce
Stale gravity to dance, the pouled bachelor
Whose youth like wanton boys through bonfires
Have skipped thy flame, at seventy, thou canst catch
And make him to the scorn of his hoarse throat
Abuse young lays of love. What godlike power
Hast thou not power upon? To Phoebus thou
Add'st flames, hotter than his the heavenly fires
Did scorch his mortal Son, thine him: the huntress
All moist and cold, some say began to throw
Her bow away, and sigh: take to thy grace
Me the vowed soldier, who do bear thy yoke
As 't were a wreath of roses, yet is heavier
Than lead itself, stings more than nettles;
I have never been foul-mouthed against thy law,
Never revealed secret, for I knew none; would not
Had I kenned all that were; I never practiced
Upon man's wife, nor would be libels read
Of liberal wits: I never at great feasts
Sought to betray a beauty but have blushed
At simpering sirs that did: I have been harsh
To large confessors, and have hotly asked them
If they had mothers. I had one, a woman,
And women 't were they wronged, I knew a man
Of eighty winters, this I told them, who
A lass of fourteen brided, 't was thy power
To put life into dust, the aged cramp
Had screwed his square foot round,
The gout had knit his fingers into knots,
Torturing convulsions from his globy eyes
Had almost drawn their spheres, that what was life
In him seemed torture: this anatomy
Had by his young fair fere* a boy, and I

*Wife.

Believed it was his, for she swore it was,
And who would not believe her? Brief I am
To those who prate and have done; no companion
To those that boast and have not; a defier
To those that would and cannot; a rejoicer.
Yea, him I do not love that tells close offices
The foulest way, nor names concealments in
The boldest language. Such a one I am,
And vow that lover never yet made sigh
Truer than I. O then most soft sweet goddess,
Give me the victory of this question, which
Is true love's merit, and bless me with a sign
Of thy great pleasure.

Palamon's speech to Venus, with the memorable portrait of the
old man married to the fourteen-year-old girl, has all the marks of
being written in a single sitting, the pen scarcely rising from the
paper. Chaucer in *The Knight's Tale* had placed in the lips of
Palamon one of those high-minded speeches which praise Venus for
her virtues, saying nothing about her aberrations; it was the safer
way. The authors of *The Two Noble Kinsmen*, living in a different
age and speaking in a different idiom, could speak more boldly.
Who wrote this passage? Shakespeare under the influence of
Fletcher? Fletcher under the influence of Shakespeare? Almost it is
a stream of consciousness, or rather two streams meeting and
commingling. Shakespeare and Fletcher were the two noble kinsmen who never needed to engage in a duel for they wrote together in
a great calm, like brothers.

Unless *Cardenio* came later, *The Two Noble Kinsmen* was the
last triumphant flare of Shakespeare's spirit. Afterward there was
only silence.

The Death
of the
Poet

THE WINTER OF 1615-16 was strangely mild and warm, but what made it remarkable was that it rained nearly every day, the streets became quagmires, and the low-lying fields were flooded. A contemporary chronicler spoke of "perpetual weeping weather, foul ways and great floods." The wind came from the west and southwest, with the result that ships in the English Channel were unable to sail into the Atlantic. We hear of East Indian ships anchored for ten weeks off the Downs because not a breath of wind caught their sails. The spring came too early; in London the black-birds hatched out their young in February. Doctors observed that pestilential vapors were abroad, and there was fear that the plague might come back again. Indeed, there had never been such a bad season since 1605, when it seemed that nearly everyone suffered from fevers.

In January, feeling ill or with a presentiment of coming illness, Shakespeare summoned his lawyer, Francis Collins, a member of Clement's Inn, to attend to the writing of his will. Collins was a mild-mannered elderly man who would be elected town clerk of

Stratford in the following year and die three months later. Shakespeare was friendly with him and had done some business with him in the past. The will was drawn up on good foreign-made paper, on three large sheets each measuring twelve by fifteen inches, and on these immense pages Collins or his clerk wrote out in a cramped secretary's hand Shakespeare's careful and exact bequests to his family and friends. He possessed a considerable estate and so his will included more bequests than are generally found in the wills of this period.

The thrust of the will was very clear: the greater part of the estate would go to his daughter Susanna, his favorite, who had married Dr. John Hall in 1607. A lesser portion went to his daughter Judith, who was still unmarried when he dictated the will. From a canceled passage we learn that he had intended to settle a marriage portion on Elizabeth, Susanna's only child, who was then eight years old, but thought better of it when it occurred to him that the Halls might have more children. He therefore left it to the Halls to make whatever settlements they wished, having full confidence in their wisdom. Although the will is usually regarded as a rather dull document full of dry legalistic phraseology, it conceals a passionate desire for male descendants. Since he had no living son, he had no hope that there would be any descendants bearing his name. He hoped that Susanna and Judith would both bear sons. In fact, the three sons later born to Judith would all die without issue and Elizabeth Hall had no children.

Just two weeks after drawing up the will, on February 10, 1616, on the feast day of Scholastica Virgin, Shakespeare gave Judith away in marriage at Holy Trinity Church. Judith was now a spinster of thirty-one, and in Jacobean England it was rare for a woman to marry so late. Susanna had the good fortune to marry a well-regarded doctor, capable, intelligent, and strong-willed, with a large practice and influential friends in high places. Judith married Thomas Quiney, a wine seller and tavern keeper, something of a tippler, with a weak character and without any trace of distinction. He was a member of the large Quiney family, who had always been close friends with the Shakespeares, but he was the least important of them. He was four years younger than Judith. It was the kind of marriage that had obviously been arranged at a family conference, and there is the suggestion that they were two rather feckless people who might improve if they were made to share the same bed.

Certainly Thomas Quiney needed improving. The rumor was already spreading through Stratford that he had got a young woman with child. The rumor was true. The woman was Margaret Wheeler and she was in the last stages of pregnancy when Thomas Quiney married Judith. It was a good marriage for Quiney, for Judith had great expectations as an heiress of one of Stratford's richest landowners. For Margaret Wheeler it was a disaster. Three days after the marriage she died giving birth to Quiney's child, who also died, and both mother and child were buried in the graveyard of Holy Trinity Church on March 15, 1616.

The death of Margaret Wheeler caused a furor: the death coming so soon after the marriage was more than a coincidence. In a small town, where everyone knew everyone else, such matters were endlessly debated. It was remembered that the marriage of Judith and Thomas was somewhat irregular, for they had failed to secure a license from the consistory court at Worcester Cathedral. Summoned before the court, they failed to appear and were promptly excommunicated. Quiney was also summoned before the church court at Stratford, where he was charged with carnal knowledge of Margaret Wheeler, now dead. He admitted the crime and submitted himself for punishment. It was decreed that he should be punished by making a public penance clothed in a white sheet on three Sundays at Holy Trinity. He argued in favor of a smaller punishment and offered five shillings in the poor box for the remission of his punishment. This was accepted. Instead of standing in his white sheet on a bench just below the pulpit through a whole morning and making a public confession of his sins, he was permitted to pay a small fine. Others who committed the same crime were less fortunate. The standing of the Quineys and the Shakespeares in the community must have had a great deal to do with the ease with which he avoided punishment.

Shakespeare, in the last weeks of his life, was having a long hard look at Thomas Quiney, and what he saw was not at all comforting. The church court met on March 26. On the previous day Shakespeare summoned his lawyer and revised his will, tearing out the first of the three sheets and substituting another. Judith was very much on his mind, but Thomas Quiney is not mentioned. John Hall is mentioned approvingly together with his daughter Elizabeth, who in the Elizabethan fashion is described as his "niece." Shakespeare is aware that Judith has married, but will not permit himself to refer to her husband. After the first page Judith is not mentioned again except toward the end when he remembers to give her "my broad silver gilt bowl." The dictating of the will appears to have exhausted him, for he meanders a little, repeats himself, goes off at tangents, and comes to rest on a legalistic point. As we read the document, we are aware of a sick man's weary voice and of long pauses while he gathers up the energy to resume dictating, the lawyer sitting by his side to supply the proper legal terms.

The will preserved in the museum of the Public Record Office in London is worth studying as much for what is omitted as for what it contains. He lists all the properties he possesses and names the inheritors. His career as an actor and playwright is not forgotten, for he remembers to give to John Heminge, Richard Burbage, and Henry Condell each twenty-six shillings and eightpence to buy mourning rings, and the same sum went to William Reynolds, gentleman, who had farmed Shakespeare's tithes, for the same purpose. Reynolds was a well-to-do man of middle age, a Catholic who had spent some time in Warwick jail for recusancy, and thereafter returned to Stratford to become a thorn in the side of the Corporation. He lived in Chapel Street, only a few steps from New Place, in a large house, where he concealed a resident priest. He kept twenty-two servants and lived in considerable state. Everyone knew he was a Papist, but he was in no danger of arrest: his wealth kept his enemies at bay.

There are times when the will becomes an exercise in fantasy. Shakespeare, determined to have grandsons, concentrates his attention on the nonexistent sons of Susanna, counting them one by one, demanding that if the first should die, the second shall obtain the inheritance, and if the second dies—and so on to the seventh son. There follows an extraordinary passage, where the legal language assumes something of the character of an incantation. After saying that all his barns, stables, orchards, gardens, lands, tenements, hereditaments, and all their appurtenances shall go to Susanna Hall for and during the term of her natural life, he continues:

& after her decease to the first son of her body lawfully
issuing
& to the heirs male of the body of the said first son lawfully
issuing
& to the heirs male of the body of the said second son
lawfully issuing
& for default of such issue to the second son of her body
lawfully issuing
& to the heirs male of the said second son lawfully issuing
& for default of such heirs to the third son of the body of
the said Susanna lawfully issuing
& of the heirs male of the body of the said third son
lawfully issuing
& for default of such issue the same so to be
& remain to the fourth fifth sixth & seventh sons of her
body lawfully issuing one after another
& to the heirs male of the bodies of the said fourth fifth
sixth & seventh sons lawfully issuing in such manner as it
is before limited to be
& remain to the first second and third sons of her body and
to their heirs male . . .

And clearly, in this incantatory language, he is imagining a
quiverful of grandsons, and he also imagines that they might die one
after another until only the seventh remains alive. What if there
were eight sons? What if there were seven daughters? He goes on to
contemplate the possibility that only his granddaughter Elizabeth
Hall will survive. If she has no issue the entire estate reverts to his
daughter Judith and the heirs male of her body lawfully issuing.
And if Judith has no heirs the estate goes "to the right heirs of me
the said William Shakespeare for ever." Here he comes to a dead
end, for he does not know who they could be.

There follows the famous words: "Item I give unto my wife my
second best bed with the furniture."

These words have caused more comment than they deserve.
They have been regarded as a kind of repudiation of his wife, a cold
and uncharitable rebuke to a woman he no longer loved. If in the
context of the will they come with surprising force—she is not

otherwise mentioned—they cannot be made to serve the myth of Shakespeare's unhappy marriage. We know nothing about the state of the marriage, but we know that it continued. He may have given her the second best bed because the best was in the guest room, or because this was the bed they slept in when they were first married, or for many other reasons. It was not unusual for a will to mention a second best bed. William Bracey of Snitterfield wrote his will in 1557: "My wife Margery shall have to her use all my household stuff except one bed, the second best, the which I give and bequeath to John my son with three pair of sheets."

At the conclusion of the will are the words: "In witness whereof I have hereunto put my seal the day and year first above written." Shakespeare struck out the word "seal" and wrote above it the word "hand." Then he wrote: "By me William Shakespeare." It was as though he had no faith in seals, the hot wax stamped with the impress of his signet ring, but he had faith in the written word.

A month after signing his will Shakespeare died, probably of typhoid fever. He must have been attended by Dr. John Hall during his illness. The Reverend John Ward, of Stratford, is our only source for the story that "Shakespeare, Drayton and Ben Jonson had a merry meeting, and it seems drank too hard, for Shakespeare died of a fever there contracted." It is a good story. We know that the poet Michael Drayton, a Warwickshire man, often stayed at nearby Clifford Chambers, in the large manor house owned by Lady Rainsford. The house was two miles south of Stratford. The meeting could have taken place at New Place or at Clifford Chambers or anywhere at all, at Christmas or to celebrate Judith's marriage or at any other time. Ward does not say where it took place, and he may not have known. He was an intelligent man, who took his degree at Oxford when he was nineteen, studied divinity, went on to study Hebrew, Arabic, and Anglo-Saxon, and was deeply interested in medicine. He became a soldier and fought on the King's side at the battle of Naseby and was captured by the Cromwellians. He came to Stratford in 1662, forty-six years after Shakespeare's death, when there were still people who remembered Shakespeare. Elizabeth Hall died in 1649, but his sister Judith Hart was alive, and so were some of the Hart children, and there were townspeople with long memories. Ward wrote in his notebook: "I have heard that Mr. Shakespeare was a natural wit, without any art at all; he frequented the plays all his younger time, but in his older days lived at Stratford: and supplied the stage with 2 plays every year, and for it had an allowance so large that he spent at the rate of £1,000 a year, as I have heard." The last statement is a little surprising, for £1,000 a year would mean that he was living in splendor. It was an enormous sum in those days. On the evidence available to us, he was in fact living at the rate of about £300 a year, enough for him to live like a member of the minor nobility.

The Reverend Richard Davies, vicar of Sapperton in Gloucestershire, wrote about 1681 that Shakespeare "died a papist." There are many reasons for doubting this statement, the most powerful being that there is nothing in Shakespeare's poems and plays to suggest that he had any deep feeling for the Catholic Church. Yet a man can be a Protestant all his life and feel the need for a Catholic priest at his death. There was nothing to prevent William Reynolds from sending over his private chaplain to administer the last sacraments at Shakespeare's deathbed. It could be done quietly, even secretly, and very few people may have been aware of it. The Combe and Reynolds families were very close to Shakespeare, and both were Catholics.

The funeral took place on April 25, 1616. According to the Stratford custom, the body was placed in an elm coffin. There was a large cortege, for all the family servants, farmhands, and stable boys, and all the relatives from Snitterfield and Wilmcote attended, together with the high bailiff and aldermen of the town. Dr. John Hall, Susanna Hall, and their daughter Elizabeth; Thomas Quiney and his bride Judith; the widow, Anne Shakespeare, now nearly sixty years old and still robust, with seven more years ahead of her. The passing bell was tolled in the Gild Chapel by Thomas Miller, the weaver, and the church bells rang out from the Church of the Holy Trinity. July Shaw was the high bailiff, and he would have stood very close to Anne during the long ceremony, which followed the Book of Common Prayer. It was a rainy April, with the smell of damp soil in the church, for the grave had been dug below the chancel rail. Many years later it would be said that the grave was dug seventeen feet deep, so anxious was Shakespeare to avoid having his bones placed in the charnel house.

Full fathom five thy father lies:
Of his bones are coral made.

And there were, of course, other ways to prevent the removal of his bones. He could, and did, lay a curse on the sexton and everyone else who might be tempted to throw them in the bone house that lay on the other side of the chancel wall. He ordered that the curse should be inscribed on his stone:

Good friend for Jesus' sake forbear
To dig the dust enclosed here:
Blest be the man that spares these stones,
And curst be he that moves my bones.

He could write doggerel as well as the next man, and there is no doubt that he wrote these lines.

From time to time men have dreamed of opening his grave, hoping to find his skull or the manuscripts that were supposed to lie in a bronze casket beneath his head. Those who had brought themselves to believe that Shakespeare was Sir Francis Bacon or Lord Oxford or Queen Elizabeth hoped to find in the coffin the demonstrable proof that the strolling player of Stratford was incapable of writing the plays, and those who believed he had written the plays wanted to see him face to face, even if it was only to peer at the empty sockets of his eyes. But if we dug down seventeen feet, we would find only a few shreds of the coffin. The Avon has overflowed its banks innumerable times, and like the body of a pirate washed by the tides, he has melted into the river Avon and become water. Nothing remains of him.

His monument was erected on the north wall of the chancel. Shakespeare had been a lay rector of the Church of the Holy Trinity; his son-in-law Dr. John Hall was also a lay rector; the monument was therefore given a prominent position. It consisted of a bust with suitable ornaments; delicate columns, heraldic arms, verses composed in his honor, angels, a skull, and those intricate devices that serve to dignify architectural compositions. The bust would be painted, and he would be shown gazing down at his own grave. Gheerart Janssen, a young Dutch sculptor who had a studio in Southwark not far from the Globe Theatre, made the bust. His father had emigrated from Holland in 1567, and he was sometimes known as Gerard Johnson. He may have met Shakespeare. The poet's wife and daughters and Dr. Hall would have seen to it that the sculptor was provided with paintings or drawings. Life masks and death masks were rarely made in those days except for royalty. Gerard Johnson appears to have worked from two drawings: one in profile, the other full face. He produced a sculpture which is completely credible though curiously unsatisfying. The life, the energy, can only be guessed at. We see a portly Shakespeare wearing the robes of a scholar, a pen in one hand while the other rests on a sheet of paper, and there is about his expression the blandness of a man who has totted up the figures in his account books and is supremely satisfied. It is a surprising, even alarming portrait, for we do not normally regard self-satisfaction as one of his traits.

The portrait is authoritative; we cannot argue with it. There must have been moments in his later life when Shakespeare looked like this or was remembered to look like this. When we look closer, we are surprised to discover how carefully he dresses his hair: the moustache follows the line of the upper lip and then turns upward, balancing the thick tuft of beard on his chin. Nearly bald, he wears his remaining hair in coiling curls about his ears. But the most remarkable thing of all is the gap of flesh between the nose and the moustache, an effect that can only be achieved by a very careful use of the razor. He has studied his face; he knows exactly how to show his features to their best advantage and to achieve an aristocratic appearance, for only the minor aristocracy wore their moustaches and beards in this way.

John Aubrey in his *Brief Lives* has a description of Shakespeare which had been handed down from William Beeston, who was a fellow of Shakespeare in the Chamberlain's Company. "He was a handsome well-shaped man: very good company, and of a very ready and pleasant smooth wit." Gerard Johnson's bust suggests that even when he was grown to fat, and was prematurely bald and jowly, he took immense pains to cultivate a precise image of himself. He was vain of his appearance when it was almost too late for vanity.

The bust is set in a niche ornamented with gleaming black marble columns topped with gilded Corinthian capitals, and it is therefore difficult to see him in profile. Photographs of a plaster cast made in the present century show a profile that is far more appealing and much closer to the image we have formed of him. The nose is strong and well shaped, the upper lip protrudes slightly over the lower, the high forehead and the bald dome are finely made and large enough to contain the teeming worlds of his imagination. From seeing him in profile it is possible to imagine the youthful Shakespeare before he put on flesh and prosperity. Full face, he is about fifty, while in profile he is about fifteen years younger. Some of the ambiguities of the bust may be because Gerard Johnson worked with portraits made at different times.

Shakespeare's family paid for the bust and was evidently satisfied with it. Carried out in the prevailing ornate Jacobean style, the heavy frame dominating the bust and the heraldic emblems confusing the design, the monument is nevertheless curiously appealing. Shakespeare's free spirit is here caged, polished, decorated beyond reasonableness. He is given his full escutcheon including the helmet with the open visor, signifying the military traditions of his father's family. The naked *putti* sit incongruously among the emblems of their trade: one holds a spade, signifying Labor; the other touches a skull with one hand and holds an extinguished torch upside down with the other, signifying Death, and above the monument there is an especially ugly and shapeless skull to emphasize that Death rules over all things. The *putti* have been carved awkwardly and might be taken for naked old men.

On a panel below the bust of Shakespeare there are two inscriptions, one in Latin, the other in English:

Judicio Pylium, genio Socratem, arte Maronem,
Terra tegit, populus maeret, Olympus habet.

which may be translated: "With the judgment of Nestor, the genius of Socrates, the art of Vergil, earth covers him, the people mourn him, Olympus has him." The Latin lines appear to have been written by a local Latinist, perhaps Dr. John Hall. Nestor, King of Pylus, was the type of the elder statesman, the sweet-tempered and indulgent prince. *Judicio Pylium* therefore refers to Shakespeare's wise and gentle character. *Genio Socratem* refers to his wit and profoundly philosophical character. *Arte Maronem* to his greatness as a poet, comparable with Vergil.

The second inscription is more puzzling because it appears to have been written for a monumental tomb with the body of Shakespeare inside it:

Stay passenger, why goest thou by so fast?
Read, if thou canst, whom envious death hath plac'd
Within this monument: Shakespeare with whom
Quick nature died; whose name doth deck the tomb
Far more than cost; sith all that he hath writ
Leaves living art but page to serve his wit.

This inscription, painfully carved into the marble, and painfully composed, remains vapid and obscure. It can be argued that nature did not die with Shakespeare and that living art must be more than a page boy serving his wit. "Far more than cost" raises many questions. The cost of what? The cost to whom? It is odd that Shakespeare's monument should be so unpoetical.

He had lived for poetry, fantastically extended its bounds, ruled as emperor over the peoples and landscapes of his imagination, charged them with such energy that they would continue to haunt men's dreams for centuries. He helped to shape the character of an age, so that today we speak of the "Shakespearean Age" as often as we speak of "the Age of Elizabeth." He was the Renaissance in England incarnate. He explored unknown regions of the human spirit, as Drake and Raleigh explored the unknown oceans. He wrote from the heart to the heart, with more power and passion than any English poet before or after him. He was rewarded with a rather shabby monument inscribed with muddy verses.

His Rage
and Influence

WHEN WILLIAM SHAKESPEARE DIED, there happened
what nearly always happens at the death of an author.
After the last eulogy is pronounced at the graveside, he is put safely
away and forgotten or half forgotten. His plays continued to be
performed by the King's Men, but it was as though they existed
independent of him. They were the property of the King's Men, not
of Shakespeare, who had abandoned them. They were part of the
repertory, no better and no worse than other parts of the repertory.
He was not regarded as the luminary of his age, but as just another
dramatist. In his lifetime he had achieved some fame, but very few
imagined that his works would be read and performed for centuries.
They regarded him simply as a popular dramatist, with more
gentleness and wit than most, with a gift for sudden dramatic effects
and for some fine soliloquies, but otherwise not to be distinguished
from his contemporaries. He was one among many.

So Thomas Heywood in *The Hierarchie of the Blessed Angels*,
published in 1635, mentions Shakespeare in the same breath as
Nashe, Beaumont, Jonson, Fletcher, Decker, Webster, Middleton,

and Ford. He is not above them, not set on a pinnacle; and he is Will Shakespeare, as Benjamin Jonson was Ben Jonson and John Ford was Jack Ford. Shakespeare was still common clay and had not yet risen to the ranks of the immortals.

The processes of posthumous fame appear to follow known laws. First the reputation plummets and there follows a long silence, almost an indifference. In the darkness of limbo the reputation ripens or decays, and the works themselves seem to change their form, to reach out to one another, the strong supporting the weak, while all acquire the patina of age. The works are no longer seen as they appeared to contemporaries; time and darkness test their power of endurance. When they reemerge at last, it is as though great pressure had accumulated beneath them and shot them out into the daylight. The new fame acquired by these long-buried works of art may have little enough to do with the artist's achievements. "Fame," wrote the poet Rainer Maria Rilke, "is merely the sum of misunderstandings."

In our own time we have been able to watch these processes at work with D. H. Lawrence and Joseph Conrad, with T. E. Lawrence and Gerard Manley Hopkins, and many others. Their posthumous fame is out of all proportion to the fame they enjoyed when alive, and of a different quality. They would not recognize the images we have created of them. Their works, as they wrote them, are not the works we read. They wrote in and for their times, with the beliefs and predilections of their times, in an intimacy with their times, which are no longer ours. At our own distance from Shakespeare we can scarcely hope to know exactly what his words meant to his contemporaries.

If Shakespeare at his death had left only his published works behind—the poems he saw through the press, the pirated sonnets, and the eighteen pirated plays published in his lifetime in good and bad quartos—we would have only a small understanding of his range. There would be only a ruined and mutilated torso. We would have no *Tempest,* no *Antony and Cleopatra,* no *Macbeth,* no *Julius Caesar,* no *Twelfth Night,* no *Winter's Tale,* no *Coriolanus,* no *Timon of Athens,* no *Comedy of Errors,* no *As You Like It,* no *All's Well That Ends Well,* no *Third Part of Henry VI,* no *Henry VIII,* no *Two Gentlemen of Verona,* no *Cymbeline,* no *Measure for*

Measure, no *King John,* no *Taming of the Shrew,* no *Pericles. Lear, Hamlet,* and *Romeo and Juliet* had appeared in defective editions, and thus he was assured of being remembered. *Titus Andronicus* and *The Merchant of Venice,* those two plays in which he was least deeply engaged, had also appeared in quartos, and so had *Othello* and *Richard III,* in which he was engaged to the uttermost. The quartos had appeared by the accidents of thieving publishers hoping to meet a popular demand. Only people with long memories could appreciate the prodigality of his works for the theatre, which were in the keeping of the King's Men, sometimes in the form of original manuscripts and sometimes in actor's copies. Bundled up, stored in bins, never properly put in order, without careful records of the dates of their first performances, at the mercy of hungry silver fish and rats, they survived by a series of miracles. Actors are notoriously inefficient. Sometimes only a single mutilated copy survived, and there was the danger that unless a tribe of scriveners were employed to make fair copies of the surviving manuscripts, they would all be lost.

John Heminge and Henry Condell, fellow actors and sharers in the company, and Shakespeare's neighbors when he lived in Cripplegate, came to the rescue just in time. It is significant that they were both deeply religious men and like Ben Jonson worshiped Shakespeare "this side of idolatry." They had some difficulty finding manuscripts: *Troilus and Cressida,* for example, was lost for many years, turning up at the last minute when the complete works were already in the press. Their task was to finance the production of the book, to collect and edit the texts, to set them in a suitable order, and to arrange that the book be published under the proper auspices. Only once before had there been any comparable book. This was *The Workes of Benjamin Jonson,* published in 1616, shortly after Shakespeare's death. Jonson edited and supervised the production of his works and thus produced an authoritative text. Heminge and Condell deliberately avoided the word "works" in order to spell out the range of his achievement, and they chose for their book the title:

Mr. WILLIAM
SHAKESPEARE'S
COMEDIES,
HISTORIES, &
TRAGEDIES.

Published according to the True Originall Copies

"Mr." should be read as "Master," and implied profound respect. By "True Originall Copies" they meant, and could only mean, "the original manuscripts."

From the beginning they were faced with difficulties. There were the difficulties of financing the work, of which we know nothing, for all the documents have vanished. Probably the Earls of Pembroke and Montgomery, to whom the book was dedicated, were induced to contribute to the expenses. The publication involved an outlay of about £1,000, for it would finally become a long book of 908 pages of double columns within printer's rules. The page is rather ugly and crowded, and the fact that the rules are rarely completely straight adds to its somewhat disorganized appearance. Ben Jonson's *Workes* were printed in a larger and better type on a more spacious page. Heminge and Condell had to skimp on the printing costs and evidently employed the cheapest printer available. Yet the finished book by its very size acquires a monumental appearance.

Neither Heminge nor Condell were rich men, and they knew nothing about the editing of manuscripts. Their poverty explains why the book took so long to produce, and their inexperience as editors explains why the text is so often corrupt. They were busy men as actors and managers, they both had large families—Condell had nine children, and Heminge had fourteen—and although Heminge had a head for finance, since his name appears as receiver of payments to the company for performances at court, they both may have felt that they were caught up in a discouraging situation. They needed help and this was given to them by Ben Jonson.

Jonson's relations with Shakespeare took the form of running battles interrupted by occasional embraces. They quarreled like lovers and made up like lovers. Shakespeare acted in Jonson's plays and Jonson must therefore have returned the compliment by acting in Shakespeare's. Their characters were diametrically opposed: Shakespeare the rapier, Jonson the two-handed sword and the cudgel. Drummond said of Jonson that "he was passionately kind and angry," and there were occasions when he was very angry indeed with Shakespeare, as when he described *Pericles* as a moldy tale and refused to consider the possibility that Bohemia might have a seacoast for the purposes of a play. Jonson's conversations with Drummond of Hawthornden were delivered by a man who became grandiloquent in his cups and are not to be taken literally. He had no modesty. He enjoyed flaring up in indignation. He enjoyed acting the role of the Great Panjandrum, a role which it is impossible to imagine Shakespeare playing. He loved Shakespeare more than he despised his lack of learning, and he was perfectly prepared to become the editor of the plays.

Jonson was then at the height of his power and prestige. He was the dominant man of letters in England, on excellent terms with King James and the members of his court, and the accepted arbiter of poetic excellence. His help therefore was crucial, and the preliminary pages of the folio testify to the careful way he set about the arrangement of the book. He was probably responsible for choosing the young Flemish engraver Martin Droeshout to engrave the portrait of Shakespeare; he may have been responsible for the choice of words on the title page; he wrote the verses which simultaneously applaud Shakespeare and the engraving, and went on to write a magnificent eighty-line panegyric "To the memory of my beloved, the Author Mr. William Shakespeare: And what he hath left us"; he wrote or rewrote from an original draft by Heminge and Condell the dedication to the Earls of Pembroke and Montgomery, and did the same for *The Epistle to the great Variety of Readers,* written in a style which was inimitably his own. But all this was only the beginning of his assistance to the project. Ben Jonson was responsible for the arrangement of the plays, placing *The Tempest* first even though it was among the last to be written, because poetically this is where it belonged. He had once condemned Shakespeare for writing "tales, tempests and such like drolleries," but now thought better of the play. He was also responsible for dividing the plays into acts and scenes, until he grew weary of it, with the result that while eighteen plays have the divisions in full, eleven plays are divided into acts without scenes, and *Hamlet* has divisions as far as Act Two, Scene Two, and there are no more. Jonson must also have been responsible for putting *Cymbeline* at the last, for essentially it is a fairytale fading into quietness, a sunset to *The Tempest's* dawn. Lord Tennyson, who was reading *Cymbeline* as he lay dying, regarded this play in spite of its improbabilities and absurdities as the greatest of them all.

We do not know how much of the text was edited by Ben Jonson. Shakespeare acted one of the leading roles in Jonson's *Sejanus* in 1603. He appears to have rewritten his own part and many other parts, and this so incensed Jonson that when he printed it, he added a note to the reader explaining that he had expunged these illegitimate lines and replaced them with the lines of his own. He wrote in exasperation:

> I would inform you that this book, in all numbers, is not
> the same with that which was acted on the public stage;
> wherein a second pen had good share: in place of which I
> have rather chosen to put weaker, and, no doubt, less
> pleasing, of mine own, than to defraud so happy a genius of
> his right by my loathed usurpation.

There can be no doubt whatsoever that Shakespeare was "the second pen" and the "so happy a genius" who had the audacity to interfere with his text. Only Shakespeare, as one of the sharers of the King's Men, and the only one of them who could write dramatic verse, would possess the authority to do it. The play was a failure and hissed off the stage. Shakespeare had done his best to save it, and failed.

When Jonson came to edit the works of Shakespeare, he must have felt an overwhelming need to correct Shakespeare's text where he was wrong and to ensure that the finished book, while not as magnificently produced as his own *Workes,* was eminently presentable to the public. His own honor was involved in it, for he was the one who came forward in the introductory pages to introduce and recommend the book. There was, however, one play to which he took violent exception. This was *Macbeth,* the only play on a Scottish subject. Jonson, a Scot, had many reasons for disliking it.

According to John Dryden, he especially hated what he called "bombast." "In reading some bombast speeches of *Macbeth*, Ben Jonson used to say that it was horror, and I am much afraid that this is so." And if Jonson thought it was horror, what more likely than that he would expunge those passages that seemed most horrible? The text of *Macbeth* in the Folio is the shortest of all the great tragedies, covering only twenty-one pages. *Lear* is twenty-seven pages, *Hamlet* thirty-one. It is possible that whole scenes have been omitted from *Macbeth* and that Jonson deliberately omitted them.

The Folio, then, came out under Jonson's protection and with his auspices, prefaced with altogether ninety lines of Jonson's verses, under his overall editorship. Except for the commendatory poems, which he signed, he made no claims for himself, and this too was in character. We know that he contributed an account of the revolt of the Carthaginian mercenaries to Sir Walter Raleigh's *The History of the World*, which was written in the Tower. Jonson's name was not mentioned, nor did he want it mentioned. He was content with the knowledge that he had been of assistance to someone he admired. So with all the work he accomplished for the Folio: he was not hiding his light. This was how he wanted it.

Jonson's verses "To the memory of my beloved" are not, like so many commendatory verses, inspired by piety. They are inspired by deep affection and knowledge, and they are the fruit of many arguments, quarrels, intoxications. Jonson is attempting among many other things to discover exactly what was Shakespeare's place in English poetry. He pulls out the organ stops when it is required, drops into whispered incantations, amuses himself with simple melodies, soars again with the sound of trumpets, composing what is in effect a symphony in honor of Shakespeare. It is one of his most accomplished performances.

> Soul of the Age!
> The applause! delight! the wonder of our Stage!
> My Shakespeare, rise; I will not lodge thee by
> Chaucer, or Spenser, or let Beaumont lie
> A little further, to make thee a room:
> Thou art a monument without a tomb,
> And art still alive, while thy Book doth live,

And we have wits to read, and praise to give.
That I not mix thee so, my brain excuses;
I mean with great but disproportion'd Muses:
For, if I thought my judgment were of years,
I should commit thee surely with thy peers,
And tell how far thou didst our Lily outshine
Or sporting Kyd or Marlowe's mighty line.
And though thou hadst small Latin and less Greek,
From thence to honour thee I would not seek
For names, but call forth thundering Aeschylus,
Euripides, and Sophocles to us,
Paccuvius, Accius, him of Cordova dead,
To life again to hear thy buskin tread
And shake a stage. Or when thy socks were on,
Leave thee alone, for the comparison
Of all that insolent Greece or haughty Rome
Sent forth, or since did from their ashes come.
Triumph, my Britain, thou hast one to show
To whom all scenes of Europe homage owe.
He was not of an age, but for all time!
And all the Muses still were in their prime,
When like Apollo he came forth to warm
Our ears, or like a Mercury to charm!
Nature herself was proud of his designs
And joy'd to wear the dressing of his lines!
Which were so richly spun, and woven so fit,
As since she will vouchsafe no other wit.
The merry Greek, tart Aristophanes,
Neat Terence, witty Plautus, now not please;
But antiquated and deserted lie
As they were not of Nature's family.
Yet must I not give Nature all: Thy art,
My gentle Shakespeare, must enjoy a part.
For though the Poets matter, Nature be,
His art doth give the fashion. And that he
Who casts to writing a living line must sweat
(Such as thine are) and strike the second heat
Upon the Muse's anvil: turn the same

(And himself with it) that he thinks to frame;
Or for the laurel he may gain a scorn,
And such wert thou. Look how the father's face
Lives on his issue, even so the race
Of Shakespeare's mind and manners brightly shines
In his well turned and true filed lines;
In each of which he seems to shake a lance
As brandished at the eyes of ignorance.
Sweet Swan of Avon! what a sight it were
To see thee in our waters yet appear,
And make those flights upon the banks of Thames
That so did take Eliza and our James!
But stay, I see thee in the Hemisphere
Advanced, and made a Constellation there!
Shine forth, thou Star of Poets, and with rage
Or influence chide or cheer the drooping stage,
Which, since thy flight from hence, hath mourned like
        night,
And despair's day, but for thy volumes light.

The well-known poem is far more than a conventional tribute
from one poet to another. It comes like a funeral oration spoken in
sight of Shakespeare's mortal remains. Nor was the imagery conventional: Jonson was using his intellectual and poetic muscles in an
attempt to explain the miracle of Shakespeare. The turning of the
iron in the fire, the striking of the second heat upon the Muse's
anvil, was an image more appropriate to Shakespeare than to any
other poet of his time. Shakespeare's rage and influence—by influence Jonson meant his stream of poetic power—were properly
left to the last. Jonson paid tribute to Shakespeare as an actor as
well as a playwright, and he was concerned to justify a comparison
with the greatest dramatist of the past. In Jonson's eyes Shakespeare was "the soul of the age" and "for all ages." Immortality had
fallen upon him, and he was like a fixed star in the heavens.

Jonson's verdict was not shared by his contemporaries. Only
Heminge and Condell in a passage in *The Epistle to the great
Variety of Readers,* printed among the introductory pages of the
First Folio, using words which have clearly been revised and rewrit-

ten by Jonson, speak of him with a grave deference while claiming for him only that he was "a happy imitator of nature" and "a most gentle expresser of it." Heminge and Condell had worked beside Shakespeare for twenty years and probably knew him better than any of his friends, and they wrote about him with a suitable modesty and decorum. They labored to provide a perfect text, and it may not be their fault that the hurried printer provided future generations with a text which is astonishingly imperfect. They claimed that "we have scarce received from him a blot in his papers," thus suggesting that the entire First Folio was printed from Shakespeare's manuscripts. No doubt many were so printed, but there are printers' errors on every page, lines are jumped or run together, letters are dropped, there are whole sentences which make no sense at all. They claimed that they were offering to public view Shakespeare's plays "cured, and perfect of their limbs; and all the rest, absolute in their numbers, as he conceived them," and unfortunately it was not true. The faulty text has provided scholars with entertaining games of guesswork for generations and some of their wildest guesses are now regarded as Shakespeare's own words.

Shakespeare's reputation ebbed and flowed like the tides. A new edition came out nine years late. James I had died, Charles I was on the throne, and the Cavalier poets were in the ascendant. Charles I possessed a copy of Shakespeare's works and appears to have enjoyed them without any great enthusiasm: Shakespeare was gradually being forgotten. When Oliver Cromwell proclaimed the Republic of England and ruled as the Lord Protector, the Puritans took care to abolish the theatre, and no new edition of Shakespeare's plays was published under the Protectorate. In 1663, three years after Charles II ascended the throne and reopened the theatres, the third edition was published. The volume is very rare, for many unsold copies went up in flames during the Fire of London in 1666. A fourth edition appeared in 1685, and this magnificently clumsy edition was largely responsible for the revival of interest in Shakespeare; and when Nicholas Rowe, the first editor of Shakespeare, set to work to study the text, he labored over this fourth edition, paying no attention to the First Folio or the Quartos. He was a scrupulous and intelligent scholar to whom we are indebted for the first brief life of Shakespeare. His edition of the works appeared in 1709.

Then the flood began. At intervals of about ten years new editions of Shakespeare appeared under capable and sometimes brilliant editors. Nicholas Rowe was followed by Alexander Pope, Lewis Theobald, Thomas Hanmer, William Warburton, Samuel Johnson, Edward Capell, George Stevens, and Edward Malone, whose ten-volume edition appeared in 1790. Towering above them all, Malone, an Irishman, possessing an abundance of wit and imagination, succeeded in presenting an edition that is thoroughly satisfying. He wrote an invaluable *Attempt to ascertain the Order in which the Plays of Shakespeare were written* and a *History of the Stage.* There is a sense in which Malone was the first and last of the great Shakespearean scholars. The garden was surveyed, the overgrowth was cut away, the flowers were given their proper names; it remained for future scholars to trim and prune, to nip off a leaf there and to remove the creeping vines.

Shakespeare himself would have been puzzled by the huge edifice of Shakespearean scholarship, which weighs so heavily on his work. The weight is stifling; he is continually struggling to go free. He is safer in the hands of actors than of scholars, who rarely understand actors. He had no liking for scholars and indeed he appears to have had a loathing for them, and there is some irony in the fact that the scholars have appropriated him. Schoolboys who have to learn his plays by heart have reason to complain; so have the Ph.D. candidates who annually clutter the shelves with their bound typewritten manuscripts. The modern editors of his works would be well advised to leave them alone, for they cannot improve on the First Folio and the best Quartos. What is important is the urgent life flowing through the plays, the colors of his imagination, his rage and influence.

Rubens said of Leonardo da Vinci that he gave every object he painted "its most appropriate and most living aspect, and exalted majesty to the point where it became divine." The same may be said of Shakespeare, who exalted the majesty of the human creature and gave dignity to mankind.

Appendixes

The Testament

of

John Shakespeare

THE TESTAMENT found by Joseph Moseley was published by Edmond Malone in his ten-volume edition of Shakespeare's works. It is here printed exactly as it appears in the second volume of that work.

I,

" In the name of God, the father, fonne, and holy ghoft, the moft holy and bleffed Virgin Mary, mother of God, the holy hoft of archangels, angels, patriarchs, prophets, evangelifts, apoftles, faints, martyrs, and all the celeftial court and company of heaven, I John Shakfpear, an unworthy member of the holy Catholick religion, being at this my prefent writing in perfect health of body, and found mind, memory, and underftanding, but calling to mind the uncertainty of life and certainty of death, and that I may be poffibly cut off in the bloffome of my fins, and called to render an account of all my tranfgreffions externally and internally, and that I may be unprepared for the dreadful trial either by facrament, pennance, fafting, or prayer, or any other purgation whatever, do in the holy prefence above fpecified, of my own free and voluntary accord, make and ordaine this my laft fpiritual will, teftament, confeffion, proteftation, and confeffion of faith, hopinge hereby to receive pardon for all my finnes and offences, and thereby to be made partaker of life everlafting, through the only merits of Jefus Chrift my faviour and redeemer, who took upon himfelf the likeness of man, fuffered death, and was crucified upon the croffe, for the redemption of finners.

II.

" *Item* I John Shakfpear doe by this prefent proteft, acknowledge, and confefs, that in my paft life I have been a moft abominable and grievous finner, and therefore unworthy to be forgiven without a true and fincere repentance for the fame. But trufting in the manifold mercies of my bleffed Saviour and Redeemer, I am encouraged by relying on his facred word, to hope for falvation and be made partaker of his heavenly kingdom, as a member of the celeftial company of angels, faints and martyrs, there to refide for ever and ever in the court of my God.

III.

" *Item*, I John Shakfpear doe by this prefent proteft and declare, that as I am certain that I muft paffe out of this tranfitory life into another that will laft to eternity, I do hereby moft humbly implore and intreat my good and guardian angell to inftruct me in this my folemn preparation, proteftation, and confeffion of faith, at leaft fpiritually, in will adoring and moft humbly befeeching my faviour, that he will be pleafed to affift me in fo dangerous a voyage, to defend me from the fnares and deceites of my infernall enemies, and to conduct me to the fecure haven of his eternal bliffe.

IV.

" *Item* I John Shakfpear doe proteft that I will alfo paffe out of this life, armed with the laft sacrament of extreme unction: the which if through any let or hindrance I fhould not then be able to have, I doe now alfo for that time demand and crave the fame; befeeching his divine majefty that he will be pleafed to anoynt my fenfes both internall and externall with the facred oyle of his infinite mercy, and to pardon me all my fins committed by feeing, fpeaking, feeling, fmelling, hearing, touching, or by any other way whatfoever.

V.

" *Item*, I John Shakfpear doe by this prefent proteft that I will never through any temptation whatfoever defpaire of the divine goodnefs, for the multitude and greatnefs of my finnes; for which although I confeffe that I have deferved hell, yet will I ftedfaftly hope in gods infinite mercy, knowing that he hath heretofore pardoned many as great finners as my felf, whereof I have good warrant fealed with his facred mouth, in holy writ, whereby he pronounceth that he is not come to call the juft, but finners.

VI.

" *Item*, I John Shakfpear do proteft that I do not know that I have ever done any good worke meritorious of life everlafting: and if I have done any, I do acknowledge that I have done it with a great deal of negligence and imperfection; neither fhould I have been able to have done the leaft without the affiftance of his divine grace. Wherefore let the devill remain confounded; for I doe in no wife prefume to merit heaven by fuch good workes alone, but through the merits and bloud of my lord and faviour, jefus, fhed upon the crofe for me moft miferable finner.

VII,

" *Item*, I John Shakfpear do proteft by this prefent writing, that I will patiently endure and fuffer all kind of infirmity, ficknefs, yea and the paine of death it felf: wherein if it fhould happen, which god forbid, that through violence of paine and agony, or by fubtility of the devill, I fhould fall into any impatience of temptation of blafphemy, or murmuration againft god, or the catholike faith, or give any figne of bad example, I do henceforth, and for that prefent, repent me, and am moft heartily forry for the fame: and I do renounce all the evill whatfoever, which I might have then done or faid; befeeching his divine clemency that he will not forfake me in that grievous and paignefull agony.

VIII.

" *Item*, I John Shakfpear, by virtue of this prefent teftament, I do pardon all the injuries and offences that any one hath ever done unto me, either in my reputation, life, goods, or any other way whatfoever; befeeching fweet jefus to pardon them for the fame: and I do defire, that they will doe the like by me, whome I have offended or injured in any fort howfoever.

IX.

" *Item*, I John Shakfpear do heere proteft that I do render infinite thanks to his divine majefty for all the benefits that I have received as well fecret as manifeft, & in particular, for the benefit of my Creation, Redemption, Sanctification, Confervation, and Vocation to the holy knowledge of him & his true Catholike faith: but above all, for his fo great expectation of me to pennance, when he might moft juftly have taken me out of this life, when I leaft thought of it, yea even then, when I was plunged in the durty puddle of my finnes. Bleffed be therefore and praifed, for ever and ever, his infinite patience and charity.

X.

" *Item*, I John Shakfpear do proteft, that I am willing, yea, I doe infinitely defire and humbly crave, that of this my laft will and teftament the glorious and ever Virgin mary, mother of god, refuge and advocate of finners, (whom I honour fpecially above all other faints,) may be the chiefe Executreffe, togeather with thefe other faints, my patrons, (faint Winefride) all whome I invocke and befeech to be prefent at the hour of my death, that fhe and they may comfort me with their defired prefence, and crave of fweet Jefus that he will receive my foul into peace.

XI.

" *Item*, In virtue of this prefent writing, I John Shakfpear do likewife moft willingly and with all humility conftitute and ordaine my good Angel, for Defender and Protectour of my foul in the dreadfull day of Judgement, when the finall fentance of eternall life or death fhall be difcuffed and given; befeeching him, that, as my foule was appointed to his cuftody and protection when I lived, even fo he will vouchfafe to defend the fame at that houre, and conduct it to eternall blifs.

XII.

" *Item*, I John Shakfpear do in like manner pray and befeech all my dear friends, parents, and kinsfolks, by the bowels of our Saviour jefus Chrift, that fince it is uncertain what lot will befall me, for fear notwithftanding leaft by reafon of my finnes I be to pafs and ftay a long while in purgatory, they will vouchfafe to affift and fuccour me with their holy prayers and fatiffactory workes, efpecially with the holy facrifice of the maffe, as being the moft effectuall meanes to deliver foules from their torments and paines; from the which, if I fhall by gods gracious goodneffe and by their vertuous workes be delivered, I do promife that I will not be ungrateful unto them, for fo great a benefitt.

XIII.

" *Item*, I John Shakfpear doe by this my laft will and teftament bequeath my foul, as foon as it fhall be delivered and loofened from the prifon of this my body, to be entombed in the fweet and amorous coffin of the fide of jefus Chrift; and that in this life-giveing fepulcher it may reft and live, perpetually inclofed in that eternall habitation of repofe, there to bleffe for ever and ever that direfull iron of the launce, which, like a charge in a cenfore, formes fo fweet and pleafant a monument within the facred breaft of my lord and faviour.

XIV.

" *Item*, laftly I John Shakfpear doe proteft, that I will willingly accept of death in what manner foever it may befall me, conforming my will unto the will of god; accepting of the fame in fatisfaction for my finnes, and giveing thanks unto his divine majefty for the life he hath beftowed upon me. And if it pleafe him to prolong or fhorten the fame, bleffed be he alfo a thoufand thoufand times; into whofe moft holy hands I commend my foul and body, my life and death: and I befeech him above all things, that he never permit any change to be made by me John Shakfpear of this my aforefaid will and teftament. Amen.

"I John Shakfpear have made this prefent writing of proteftation, confeffion, and charter, in prefence of the bleffed virgin mary, my Angell guardian, and all the Celeftiall Court, as witneffes hereunto: the which my meaning is, that it be of full value now prefently and for ever, with the force and vertue of testament, codicill, and donation in caufe of death; confirming it anew, being in perfect health of foul and body, and figned with mine own hand; carrying alfo the fame about me; and for the better declaration hereof, my will and intention is that it be finally buried with me after my death.

"Pater nofter, Ave maria, Credo.
"jefu, fon of David, have mercy on me.

Amen."

Chronology

1551	April 29	John Shakespeare of Snitterfield appears on Stratford records as a householder on Henley Street.
1556	November 24	Robert Arden leaves all his land at Wilmcote to his youngest daughter Mary.
1557		John Shakespeare marries Mary Arden.
1558	September 15	Joan, their first daughter, is baptized. She dies in infancy.
1558	November 17	Queen Elizabeth ascends the throne.
1562	December 2	Margareta, their second daughter, is baptized.
1563	April 30	Margareta Shakespeare is buried.
1564	April 26	William, their first son, is baptized.
1564	Summer	Plague strikes Stratford.
1566	July 4	John Shakespeare is elected Alderman.
1566	October 13	Gilbert Shakespeare, their second son, is baptized.
1568	September 4	John Shakespeare elected high bailiff of Stratford.

1569	April 15	Joan Shakespeare, their fifth child, is baptized.
1571	September 28	Anne Shakespeare, their sixth child, is baptized.
1575	July	Queen Elizabeth visits Kenilworth.
1576	April 13	James Burbage leases from Giles Alleyn land in Shoreditch and sets about building the Theatre. In the following year he builds another theatre called the Curtain nearby.
1579	April 4	Anne Shakespeare is buried.
1579	December 17	Katherine Hamlet is drowned in the Avon.
1580	May 1	Edmund Shakespeare is baptized.
1581		William Shakespeare, at seventeen, probably begins to write *A Lover's Complaint*.
1582	November 27	Marriage license issued by the office of the Bishop of Worcester to William Shakespeare and Anne Whateley (Hathaway).
1583	May 26	Susanna, first child of William and Anne Shakespeare, is baptized.
1583	December	John Somerville and Edward Arden executed for an attempt to assassinate Queen Elizabeth.
1583 or early 1584		William Shakespeare presumably sets out for London and is apprenticed to the Theatre in Shoreditch.
1585	February 2	The twins, Hamnet and Judith Shakespeare, are baptized.

1586-7		Shakespeare probably wrote *War Hath Made All Friends*, which introduces his ancestor Turchill de Eaderne.
1588-9		Shakespeare probably wrote *The Reign of King Edward the Third*.
1590-1		Shakespeare probably wrote *Titus Andronicus*.
1592	September 20	In Robert Greene's pamphlet *Groats-worth of Wit* Shakespeare is described as an "upstart crow."
1592	September 25	John Shakespeare listed as a recusant.
1593	April 18	*Venus and Adonis* entered in Stationers' Register by Richard Field.
1593	May 30	Christopher Marlowe killed.
1594	May 9	*The Ravishment of Lucrece* entered in Stationers' Register.
1594	September 22	Part of Stratford destroyed by fire.
1595	September	Another fire in Stratford.
1596	August 11	Hamnet Shakespeare, eleven years old, is buried at Stratford.
1596	October 20	Grant of arms made to John Shakespeare.
1596	November 29	William Wayte secures writ against Francis Langley, William Shakespeare, Dorothy Soer and Anne Lee.
1597	May 4	Shakespeare buys New Place in Stratford from William Underhill for £60.
1598	January 24	Shakespeare is approached by the

		Quineys about buying land near Shottery.
1598	September 7	Francis Mere's *Palladis Tamia* entered in Stationers' Register. He lists twelve plays by Shakespeare including *Romeo and Juliet, Midsummer Night's Dream, The Merchant of Venice,* and *Richard III.*
1598	December	The Theatre at Shoreditch is torn down and the timbers carted to Bankside.
1599	October 6	Shakespeare's name appears as delinquent in his tax payments in the parish of St. Helen's, Bishopsgate. He was probably living at Bankside.
1600	October 6	Shakespeare's name appears as delinquent in tax payments in the county of Surrey. He may be already living with the Mountjoys.
1601	February 6	*Richard II* performed for friends of the Earl of Essex.
1601	February 8	Earl of Essex leads unsuccessful revolt.
1601	February 25	Earl of Essex is beheaded.
1601	September 8	John Shakespeare is buried in Stratford.
1603	March 14	Queen Elizabeth dies.
1603	April 7	King James arrives in London.
1603	May 19	The Chamberlain's Men are renamed the King's Men. Shakespeare is prominently mentioned in the patent.

1603	Winter	Shakespeare acts in Ben Jonson's *Sejanus*.
1604	August 9-17	Shakespeare and eleven other members of the King's Men are in attendance at Somerset House during visit of the Spanish ambassador.
1604	November 1	*Othello* first performed at the Palace of Westminster.
1605	May 4	Augustine Phillips wills Shakespeare thirty shillings in gold.
1606	December 16	*King Lear* performed by King's Men before King James at Whitehall.
1607	June 5	Susanna Shakespeare marries Dr. John Hall at Stratford.
1607	July-November	The Plague: theatres closed.
1607	August 12	Register of St. Giles Church, Cripplegate, records burial of Edward, son of Edward Shakespeare.
1607	December 31	Edmund Shakespeare, a player, buried at St. Saviour's Church in Southwark.
1608	February 21	Elizabeth, daughter of Susanna and John Hall, baptized.
1608	September 7	Mary Shakespeare, mother of the poet, is buried at Stratford.
1609	May 10	Shakespeare's *Sonnets* entered at Stationer's Hall by Thomas Thorpe.
1611	April 20	Simon Forman sees *Macbeth* at the Globe.
1612	May 11	Shakespeare signs deposition

concerning Bellott's suit against Christopher Mountjoy.

1612	October 16	Frederick, Elector Palatine, arrives in England to marry Princess Elizabeth.
1612	November 6	Prince Henry dies.
1613	March 10	Shakespeare buys the Blackfriars Gatehouse in London.
1613	March 31	Shakespeare and Richard Burbage are paid for an impresa for the Earl of Rutland.
1613	June 8	*Cardenio*, the lost play, acted by King's Men for the ambassador of Savoy.
1613	June 19	Globe Theatre burns during first performance of *Henry VIII*.
1613	July 15	Susanna Hall sues John Lane for defamation.
1614	June	Globe Theatre reopens.
1616	about January 15	Shakespeare dictates his will to Francis Collins.
1616	February 10	Judith Shakespeare marries Thomas Quiney.
1616	March 15	Margaret Wheeler buried at Holy Trinity Church with her dead son.
1616	March 25	Shakespeare rewrites his will.
1616	March 26	Thomas Quiney in court to answer charges.
1616	April 25	Shakespeare buried in Holy Trinity Church.
1623	November 8	The First Folio is entered at Stationers' Register.

1649   July 11   Lady Elizabeth Barnard,
                             Shakespeare's grandchild, dies
                             without issue. Shakespeare's line
                             dies with her.

Select
Bibliography

I HAD THE GOOD LUCK, while writing this book, to be within easy reach of original editions of most of the Elizabethan and Jacobean authors I was interested in. Sir Walter Raleigh's *History of the World* stood beside Shakespeare's Fourth Folio and Ben Jonson's *Workes*. I had Foxe's *Acts and Monuments of the Martyrs*, John Calvin's *Institutions*, and the Great Bible of 1539 in magnificent black letters. There was the Geneva Bible, Raphael Holinshed's *Chronicles*, John Stow's *Annales* and also his *Survey of London*, which permits you to wander around Elizabethan London at your pleasure. And there was Edmund Malone's *Plays and Poems of William Shakespeare in Ten Volumes*, published in 1790, with his voluminous essays on Shakespeare and the stage. After Shakespeare, Malone was my closest companion, for he is by far the most admirable of Shakespearean critics. I have included here about a hundred books of more recent times that I found useful, and I have marked with an asterisk those that seemed to me to have major importance.

Adams, Joseph Quincy. *A Life of William Shakespeare.* Boston: Houghton Mifflin, 1923.

Akrigg, G. P. V. *Jacobean Pageant.* Cambridge, Mass.: Harvard University Press, 1962.

——————. *Shakespeare and the Earl of Southampton.* London: Hamish Hamilton, 1968.

Aldington, Richard, ed. *A Book of Characters.* New York: E. P. Dutton, n.d.

Alexander, Peter. *Shakespeare's Life and Art.* New York: New York University Press, 1967.

Allen, Thomas. *The History and Antiquities of London.* London: Cowie & Strange, 1827.

*Baldwin, Maxwell. *Studies in Shakespeare Apocrypha.* New York: Columbia University Press, 1956.

Baldwin, Thomas Whitfield. *The Organization and Personnel of the Shakespearean Company.* Princeton: Princeton University Press, 1927.

——————. *William Shakespeare's Small Latine & Lesse Greeke.* Urbana: University of Illinois Press, 1944.

Bellew, J.C.M. *Shakespeare's Home at New Place.* London: Virtue Brothers, 1863.

Bentley, Gerard Eades. *Shakespeare: A Bibliographical Handbook.* New Haven: Yale University Press, 1961.

——————. *Shakespeare and Jonson: Their Reputation in the Seventeenth Century Compared.* Chicago: University of Chicago Press, 1945.

*Bertram, Paul. *Shakespeare and the Two Noble Kinsmen.* New Brunswick, N.J.: Rutgers University Press, 1965.

The Bible (Geneva Version). London: The Deputies of Christopher Barker, 1589.

Brandes, George. *William Shakespeare.* New York: Macmillan Co., 1927.

Brassington, W. Salt. *Shakespeare's Homeland.* London: J. M. Dent, 1903.

Bridenbaugh, Carl. *Vexed and Troubled Englishmen 1590-1642.* New York: Oxford University Press, 1968.

Brinkworth, E. R. C. *Shakespeare and the Bawdy Court of Stratford.* London: Phillimore, 1972.

Brooke, C. F. Tucker. *The Shakespeare Apocrypha.* Oxford: Clarendon Press, 1929.

*Buxton, John. *Elizabethan Taste.* New York: St. Martin's Press, 1964.

——————. *Sir Philip Sidney and the English Renaissance.* London: Macmillan & Co., 1954.

Calvin, John. *The Institutions of Christian Religion.* London: Thomas Norton, 1574.

Carter, T. *Shakespeare: Puritan and Recusant.* Edinburgh: Oliphant, Anderson & Ferrier, 1897.

Cavendish, George. *The Life and Death of Cardinal Wolsey.* Boston: Houghton Mifflin, 1905.

Certaine Sermons of Homilies Appointed to be Read in Churches. London: John Bill, 1625.

*Chambers, E. K. *The Elizabethan Stage.* Oxford: Clarendon Press, 1967.

——————. *Shakespeare: A Survey.* New York: Hill & Wang, 1962.

——————*. *William Shakespeare: A Study of Facts and Problems.* Oxford: Clarendon Press, 1963.

Chambers, R. W. *England Before the Norman Conquest.* London: Longmans Green, 1928.

Colman, E. A. M. *The Dramatic Use of Bawdy in Shakespeare.* London: Longmans, 1974.

Crane, Milton. *Shakespeare's Prose.* Chicago: University of Chicago Press, 1952.

Cunngingham, J. V., ed. *In Shakespeare's Day.* Greenwich, Conn.: Fawcett Publications, 1970.

Davis, William Stearns. *Life in Elizabethan Days.* New York, Harper & Brothers, 1930.

Dick, Oliver Lawson, ed. *Aubrey's Brief Lives.* Ann Arbor: University of Michigan Press, 1957.

Dowden, Edward. *Shakespeare: His Mind and Art.* New York: Capricorn Books, 1962.

Eccles, Mark. *Shakespeare's Warwickshire.* Madison: University of Wisconsin Press, 1963.

Eliot, T. S. *Essays in Elizabethan Drama.* New York: Harcourt, Brace & World, 1960.

Elton, Charles Isaac. *William Shakespeare: His Family and Friends.* New York: E. P. Dutton, 1904.

*Everitt, E. B. *Six Early Plays Related to the Shakespeare Canon.* Copenhagen: Rosenkilde & Bagger, 1965.

_____*. *The Young Shakespeare: Studies in Documentary Evidence.* Copenhagen: Rosenkilde & Bagger, 1954.

Foxe, John. *The Ecclesiastical History, Containing the Acts and Monuments of the Martyrs.* London: Peter Short, 1596.

*Fripp, Edgar I. *Shakespeare: Man and Artist.* London: Oxford Univeristy Press, 1938.

*Furness, Horace Howard. *A New Variorum Edition of Shakespeare.* New York: Dover Publications, 1963.

Furnivall, Frederick J., ed. *Harrison's Description of England in Shakespeare's Youth.* London: The New Shakespeare Society, 1877.

Granville-Barker, H., and Harrison, G. B. *A Companion to Shakespeare Studies.* Garden City, N.Y.: Doubleday, 1960.

The Great Bible. London: Edward Whitechurch, 1539.

Halliday, F. E. *The Life of Shakespeare.* Baltimore: Penguin Books, 1961.

_____. *Shakespeare: A Pictorial Biography.* New York: Thomas Y. Crowell, 1958.

_____. *A Shakespeare Companion.* New York: Funk & Wagnalls, 1952.

_____. *Shakespeare and His Critics.* London, Gerald Duckworth, 1950.

*Halliwell-Phillipps, J. O. *Outlines of the Life of Shakespeare.* London: Longmans, Green & Co., 1889.

Harbage, Alfred. *Shakespeare's Audience.* New York: Columbia University Press, 1958.

_____. *Shakespeare's Songs.* Philadelphia: Macrae Smith, 1970.

Harris, Benard. *A Portrait of a Moor.* In *Shakespeare Survey* 11. Cambridge: Cambridge University Press, 1958.

Harrison, G. B. *Introducing Shakespeare.* New York: New American Library, 1953.

_____*. *A Last Elizabethan Journal.* London: Constable & Co., 1933.

_____*. *Shakespeare at Work 1592-1603.* Ann Arbor: University of Michigan Press, 1950.

_____*. *Shakespeare Under Elizabeth.* New York, Henry Holt, 1933.

Heywood, Thomas. *The Hierarchie of the Blessed Angells.* London: Adam Islip, 1635.

*Hodges, C. Walter, *The Globe Restored*. New York: Coward McCann, 1954.

—————*. *Shakespeare's Second Globe: The Missing Monument*. London: Oxford University Press, 1973.

*Holinshed, Raphael. *Chronicles of England, Scotland and Ireland*. London: At the Signe of the Starre, 1587.

Hotson, Leslie . *I, William Shakespeare*. London: Jonathan Cape, 1937.

—————. *Mr. W. H.* New York: Alfred A. Knopf, 1965.

—————. *Shakespeare's Motley*. New York: Haskell, 1971.

—————. *Shakespeare's Sonnets Dated*. Oxford: Oxford University Press, 1949.

—————.* *Shakespeare Versus Shallow*. Boston: Little, Brown & Co., 1931.

Ingleby, C. M., ed *The Shakespeare Allusion Book*. New York: Duffield & Co., 1909.

Jonson, Benjamin. *Selected Works*. Edited by David McPherson. New York: Holt, Rinehart & Winston. 1972.

—————. *The Workes of Benjamin Jonson*. London: Richard Bishop, 1640.

Laneham, Robert. *A Letter: Whearin, part of the entertainment unto the Queens Majestie at Killingworth Castle in Warwick Sheer*. London, n.d.

Langbaine, Gerard. *Momus Triumphans*. London: Nicholas Cox, 1688.

Lee, Sir Sidney. *A Life of William Shakespeare*. New York: Dover Publications, 1968.

Lewis, B. Roland. *The Shakespeare Documents*. Stanford: Standford University Press, 1940.

*Malone, Edmund. *The Plays and Poems of William Shakespeare in Ten Volumes. London: H. Baldwin, 1790.*

Marlowe, Christopher. *Hero and Leander*. London: Haslewood Reprints, 1924.

*Muir, Kenneth. *Shakespeare as Collaborator*. London: Methuen, 1960.

Murry, John Middleton. *Shakespeare*. London: Jonathan Cape, 1961.

Mutschmann, H., and Wentersdorf, K. *Shakespeare and Catholicism*. New York: Sheed & Ward, 1952.

*Nagler, A. M. *Shakespeare's Stage*. New Haven: Yale University Press, 1973.

Neale, J. E. *Queen Elizabeth I*. Harmondsworth: Penguin Books, 1960.

Onions, C. T. *A Shakespeare Glossary*. Oxford: Clarendon Press, 1975.

Parker. M. D. H. *The Slave of Life: A Study of Shakespeare and the Idea of Justice*. London: Chatto & Windus, 1955.

Parrott, Thomas Marc. *William Shakespeare: A Handbook*. New York: Charles Scribner's Sons, 1934.

Partridge, Eric. *Shakespeare's Bawdy*. New York: E. P. Dutton, 1948.

Pitcher, Seymour M. *The Case for Shakespeare's Authorship of the Famous Victories*. London: Alvin Redman, 1962.

Prior, Roger. *The Life of George Wilkins. In Shakespeare Survey 25*. Cambridge University Press, 1972.

Rabelais, François. *The Complete Works*. New York: The Modern Library, n.d.

Reese, M. M. *Shakespeare: His World and His Work*. London: Edward Arnold, 1958.

*Rowse, A. L. *Sex and Society in Shakespeare's Age*. New York: Charles Scribner's Sons, 1974.

Schoenbaum, S. *Shakespeare's Lives.* Oxford: Clarendon Press, 1970.

_____*. William Shakespeare: A Compact Documentary Life.* New York: Oxford University Press, 1977.

Scott-Giles, C. W. *Shakespeare's Heraldry.* New York: E. P. Dutton, 1950.

Shakespeare, William, *The Complete Works.* Edited by Herbert Farjeon. London: Nonesuch Press, 1953.

*Smart, John S. *Shakespeare: Truth and Tradition.* Oxford: Clarendon Press, 1966.

Smith, Irwin. *Shakespeare's Globe Playhouse.* New York: Charles Scribner's Sons, 1956.

Smith. Logan Pearsall. *On Reading Shakespeare.* New York: Harcourt, Brace & Co., 1933.

Smith, Lucy Baldwin. *The Elizabethan World.* Boston: Houghton Mifflin, 1972.

Spencer, Hazelton. *The Art and Life of William Shakespeare.* New York: Harcourt, Brace & Co., 1940.

Spencer, T. J. B. *Shakespeare: A Celebration.* Baltimore: Penguin Books, 1964.

Spurgeon, Caroline F. E. *Shakespeare's Imagery.* Boston: Beacon Books, 1960.

*Stopes, C. C. *Shakespeare's Family.* London: George Bell & Sons, 1901.

_____*. Shakespeare's Industry.* London: George Bell & Sons. 1916.

*Stow, John. *Annales, or a Generall Chronicle of England.* London: Edmund Howes, 1631.

_____. *A Survey of London.* London: Elizabeth Purslow, 1633.

Strachey, Lytton. *Elizabeth and Essex.* New York: Harcourt, Brace & Co., 1928.

Thorndike, Ashley H. *Shakespeare's Theater.* New York: Macmillan Co., 1961.

Traversi, Derek, *An Approach to Shakespeare.* Garden City, N.Y.: Doubleday, 1956.

_____. *Shakespeare: The Last Phase.* New York: Harcourt, Brace & Co., 1955.

Van Doren, Mark. *Shakespeare.* Garden City, N.Y.: Doubleday, 1953.

*Wallace, Charles William. *The First London Theatre.* New York: Benjamin Blom, 1969.

_____. *New Shakespeare Discoveries.* In *Harper's Monthly Magazine*, March 1910.

*Williams, Charles. *The English Poetic Mind.* Oxford: Clarendon Press, 1932.

Williams, Frayne. *Mr. Shakespeare of the Globe.* New York: E. P. Dutton, 1941.

Williams, Neville. *The Life and Times of Elizabeth I.* Garden City, N.Y.: Doubleday, 1972.

Wilson, John Dover. *The Essential Shakespeare.* Cambridge University Press, 1962.

_____. *Life in Shakespeare's England.* Baltimore: Penguin Books, 1964.

Wright, Louis B. *A Voyage to Virginia in 1609.* Charlottesville: University Press of Virginia, 1967.

Chapter Notes

THE NOTES are given in an abbreviated form. Thus, E. K. Chambers, *William Shakespeare*, is referred to as Chambers; while J. O. Halliwell-Phillips, *Outlines of the Life of Shakespeare*, is referred to as H-P. Similarly Edgar I. Fripp, *Shakespeare: Man and Artist*, is referred to as Fripp; and John Stow, *Annales, or a Generall Chronicle of England*, is referred to as Stow.

Page

8. He was a glover's son . . . Chambers, II, 247.
13. Canute the King greeteth . . . R. W. Chambers, *England Before the Norman Conquest*, p. 281.
15. All my land in Wilmcote . . . Fripp, 31.
19. In the name of God, the father . . . Malone, II, 330.
23. In the City of Gloucester . . . Malone, II, 21; H-P, I, 41.
25. MORE I Prithee, tell me . . . Brooke, *The Shakespeare Apocrypha*, 403.
28. If you would have your kennel . . . Markham, *Discourse*, xvii.
28. matched in mouth like bells . . . *Midsummer Night's Dream*, IV, 1.
28. durable, well-mouthed, cold-nosed . . . Markham, *Discourse*, 3.
29. The Gentry and the Citizens . . . Aubrey, *Lives*, xxxii.
32. At Pentecost . . . *Two Gentlemen of Verona*, IV, 4.
33. These trumpeters, being six in number . . . Laneham, *A Letter*, p. 10.
34. Then rememb'rest . . . *Midsummer Night's Dream*, II, 1.
35. He exercised his father's trade . . . Chambers, II, 253.
36. Much given to all unluckiness . . . Chambers, II, 257.
37. the deceased was going with a milk pail . . . Fripp, 146.
38. There is a willow . . . *Hamlet* IV, 7.
44. From off a hill . . . Lover . . . *A Lover's Complaint*, stanza 1.
45. Upon her head a plaited hive . . . *A Lover's Complaint*, stanza 2.
46. A thousand favors . . . *A Lover's Complaint*, stanzas 6, 7.
47. But woe is me . . . *A Lover's Complaint*, stanza 12.
48. So on the tip of his subduing tongue . . . *A Lover's Complaint*, stanza 18.
48. Oh father, what a hell of witchcraft . . . *A Lover's Complaint*, stanza 42.
49. In this beautiful poem . . . Malone, X, 371.

49. It is silly sooth . . . *Twelfth Night*, II, 4.
51. First, I bequeath . . . H-P, II, 53.
52. Unless you can make . . . Fripp, 195.
53. A dreadful example . . . Holinshed, 1356.
58. I went down to the nut garden . . . The Great Bible, fol. xli.
62. Comedians and stage players . . . Stow, 698.
63. The father of us was the first . . . H-P, I, 317.
67. I tell thee, Viceroy . . . Kyd, *The Spanish Tragedy*, V, 3.
68. Stand still, you ever-moving spheres . . . Marlowe, *Doctor Faustus*, V, 2.
68. Now walk the angels . . . *Tamburlaine Part Two*, II, 4.
71. In this office he became . . . Chambers, II, 287.
73. the more to be admired . . . Chambers, II, 252.
73. He lives in Shoreditch . . . Chambers II, 252.
74. The execution is mentioned by Stow, 751.
75. The City is a map of vanities . . . *Scialetheia*, 10.
76. received into the Company . . . Chambers, II, 263.
77. His leaves are fatter . . . H-P, I, 89.
85. LEOFRIC   We two trusty subjects . . . Everitt, *Six Early Plays*, 111.
87. CANUTUS   A traitor may be likened to a tree . . . Everitt, *Six Early Plays*, 117.
88. Go tell your master . . . Everitt, *Six Early Plays*, 121.
89. You are the sun, my lord . . . Everitt, *Six Early Plays*, 124.
91. Methought that I had broken . . . *Richard III*, I, 4.
92. Rather like an angel . . . Stow, 269.
93. The love you offer me . . . Everitt, *Six Early Plays*, 211.
94. I am not Warwick . . . Everitt, *Six Early Plays*, 213.
94. COUNTESS   O perjured beauty . . . Everitt, *Six Early Plays*, 217.
96. Audeley, the arms of death . . . Everitt, *Six Early Plays*, 229.
96. Good friend, convey me . . . Everitt, *Six Early Plays*, 234.
97. If Shakespeare had no hand . . . Kenneth Muir, *Shakespeare as Collaborator*, 30.
102. My lovely Aaron . . . *Titus Andronicus*, II, 3.
103. For now I stand . . . *Titus Andronicus*, III, 1.
104. TITUS   What dost thou strike at . . . *Titus Andronicus*, III, 2.
106. As he was small and little . . . Holinshed, 760.
107. Grief fills the room . . . *King John*, III, 3.
108. Death, death . . . *King John*, III, 4.
108. O death, made proud . . . *King John*, IV, 3.
108. 'Tis strange that death . . . *King John*, V, 7.
108. Gaunt am I . . . *Richard II*, II, 1.
108. Even through the hollow . . . *Richard II*, II, 1.
109. Come Lammas-eve . . . *Romeo and Juliet*, I, 3.
110. She is the fairy's midwife . . . *Romeo and Juliet*, I, 4.
113. At Sestos, Hero dwelt . . . Marlowe, "Hero and Leander," first sestiad.
115. "Fondling," she said . . . "Venus and Adonis," stanza 39.
115. Like a dive-dapper . . . "Venus and Adonis," stanza 86.
115. Or as the snail . . . "Venus and Adonis," stanza 163.
116. Round-hoof'd, short-jointed . . . "Venus and Adonis," stanza 50-52.
117. TO THE RIGHT HONORABLE . . . "Venus and Adonis," Dedication.

118. "Thou art," quoth she . . . "Rape of Lucrece," 1.652.
111. Be it known that . . . Hotson, *Shakespeare versus Shallow*, 9, 20.
118. But she hath lost . . . "Rape of Lucrece," 1.687.
119. The love I dedicate . . . "Rape of Lucrece," Dedication.
119. My Lord Southampton . . . Chambers, II, 266.
121. Like as the waves . . . Sonnet 60.
122. ceaseless lackey to eternity . . . "Rape of Lucrece," 1.967.
122. Devouring time . . . Sonnet 19.
123. When in disgrace . . . Sonnet 29.
123. When to the sessions . . . Sonnet 30.
123. Full many a glorious morning . . . Sonnet 33.
123. The expense of spirit . . . Sonnet 129.
124. To the Most Noble . . . Ben Jonson, *Volpone*, Dedication.
125. TO THE ONLIE BEGETTER . . . Sonnets, Dedication.
126. TO THE RIGHT WORSHIPFUL . . . Lee, *Life of William Shakespeare*, 682.
133. Men of all sorts . . . *2 Henry IV*, I, 2.
134. THIEF Here is a good fellow . . . Pitcher, *The Case for Shakespeare's Authorship of the Famous Victories*, 19.
135. Tut, tut . . . *1 Henry IV*, IV, 2.
136. I have a whole school . . . *2 Henry IV*, IV, 3.
136. SHALLOW O, Sir John . . . *2 Henry IV*, III, 2.
138. FALSTAFF Lord, Lord . . . *2 Henry IV*, III, 2.
139. FALSTAFF A good sherris-sack . . . *2 Henry IV*, IV, 3.
140. Falstaff, the old white-bearded Satan . . . *1 Henry IV*, II, 4.
140. FALSTAFF *That he is old* . . . *1 Henry IV*, II, 4.
141. FALSTAFF That thou art my son . . . *1 Henry IV*, II, 8.
142. FALSTAFF Can honor set a leg? . . . *1 Henry IV*, V, 1.
143. FALSTAFF Go thy ways . . . *1 Henry IV*, II, 4.
145. You have played your roles very well . . . Rabelais, *Gargantua and Pantagruel*, p. 541.
146. And quick comedians . . . *Antony and Cleopatra*, V, 2.
147. Sirrah, go you . . . *Taming of the Shrew*, Induction, scene 1.
149. But there be some of them . . . Jonson, *The Devil Is an Ass*, II, 8.
152. In the place between . . . Harrison, *A Last Elizabethan Journal*, 130.
152. Weep with me . . . Jonson, *Poems*, 60.
153. Moved the audience to tears . . . G. Tillotson, "Othello and the Alchemist at Oxford in 1610," *Times Literary Supplement*, July 20, 1933.
153. As for the actors . . . F. Williams, *Mr. Shakespeare of the Globe*, 299.
154. The boys are daily wearing out . . . H-P, I, 317.
156. Among the Arabians . . . *Certaine Sermons or Homilies*, 87.
156. What patrimony . . . *Certaine Sermons or Homilies*, 83.
158. You must borrow me . . . *As You Like It*, II, 2.
159. The codpiece that will house . . . *King Lear*, III, 2.
159. HAMLET Lady, shall I lie . . . *Hamlet*, III, 2.
160. This is the monstruosity . . . *Troilus and Cressida*, III, 2.
160. I stalk about her door . . . *Troilus and Cressida*, III, 2.
160. I am giddy . . . *Troilus and Cressida*, III, 2.
161. FALSTAFF Welcome, Ancient Pistol . . . *2 Henry IV*, II, 4.

161. *Enter Falstaff...2 Henry IV*, II, 4.
162. MERCUTIO   Now will he sit ... *Romeo and Juliet*, II, 2.
163. FALSTAFF   The Windsor bell ... *Merry Wives of Windsor*, V, 5.
163. PAROLLES   Are you meditating ... *All's Well That Ends Well*, I, 1.
167. And so to Tyburn ... Stow, 768.
168. I have discovered ... Neale, *Queen Elizabeth I*, 340.
170. Some there be ... *Merchant of Venice*, II, 9.
170. LORENZO   The moon shines bright ... *Merchant of Venice*, V, 1.
171. SHYLOCK   I pray you ... *Merchant of Venice*, IV, 1.
172. The quality of mercy ... *Merchant of Venice*, IV, 1.
173. How sweet the moonlight ... *Merchant of Venice*, V, 1.
177. This John showeth ... Chambers, II, 20.
178. To all and singular ... Chambers, II, 18.
180. Justice, verity, temperance ... *Macbeth*, IV, 3.
182. In a field of gold ... Scott-Giles, *Shakespeare's Heraldry*, 37.
183. To my loving good friend ... Chambers, II, 102.
184. he hoped within a week ... Fripp, 497.
186. SOGLIARDO   Nay, I will have him ... Jonson, *Every Man Out of His Humor*, III, 4.
187. CARLO   Now look you, sir ... Jonson, *Every Man Out of His Humor*, III, 4.
192. The said Cuthbert Burbage ... Wallace, *The First London Theatre*, 278.
195. Tomorrow being Thursday ... Halliday, *A Shakespeare Companion*, 58.
197. He rather prays you will ... Jonson, *Every Man in His Humor*, Prologue.
198. FLUELLEN   All the water ... *Henry V*, IV, 7.
199. PISTOL   News have I ... *Henry V*, V, 1.
199. Even as men wracked ... *Henry V*, IV, 1.
200. A good leg will fall ... *Henry V*, V, 2.
200. Why, man, he doth bestride ... *Julius Caesar*, I, 2.
201. I have not slept ... *Julius Caesar*, II, 1.
202. After dinner on the 21 September ... Halliday, *A Shakespeare Companion*, 487.
203. Now the melancholy god ... *Twelfth Night*, II, 4.
203. If music be the food of love ... *Twelfth Night*, I, 1.
208. Yet I ... *Hamlet*, II, 2.
209. Blest are those ... *Hamlet*, II, 2.
210. The satirical rogue ... *Hamlet*, II, 2.
210. There's rosemary ... *Hamlet*, IV, 5.
212. O what a noble mind ... *Hamlet*, III, 1.
212. *Enter Ophelia* ... *Hamlet*, II, 1.
214. Nay, then, let the devil ... *Hamlet*, III, 2.
215. OPHELIA   You are a good chorus ... *Hamlet*, III, 2.
215. Let the blunt King ... *Hamlet*, III, 4.
216. HAMLET   A man may fish ... *Hamlet*, IV, 3.
216. Alas, poor Yorick ... *Hamlet*, V, 1.
220. Look on beauty ... *Merchant of Venice*, V, 3.
221. whether the love she bears ... Rowse, *Sex and Society*, 98.
227. William Shakespeare of Stratford ... Chambers, II, 91.
234. They are despisers of God ... Calvin, *Institutions*, 89.

235. Rebels are the cause . . . *Certaine Sermons or Homilies*, 293.
239. But now behold . . . *Henry V*, V, Prologue.
243. MORE   Grant them removed . . . Sir Thomas More, II, 4, in Brooke, *Shakespeare Apocrypha*, 394.
249. I am Richard II . . . Halliday, *A Shakespeare Companion*, 349.
249. Beauty, truth and rarity . . . Threnos of "The Phoenix and Turtle."
254. I tell you my seat . . . Williams, *Elizabeth*, 215.
254. Who but our cousin of Scotland . . . William, *Elizabeth*, 215.
255. Nor doth the silver-tongued Melicert . . . Henry Chettle, *England's Mourning Garment*.
256. James, by the Grace of God . . . Malone, II, 40.
260. I would inform you that this book . . . Jonson, *Sejanus*, Induction.
260. I remember the players . . . Ben Jonson, *Selected Works*, 384.
262. There entered dancing . . . Bentley, *Shakespeare and Jonson*, 23.
265. Notwithstanding all that kindness . . . Stow, 791.
267. Set you down this . . . *Othello*, V, 2.
267. I spoke of most disastrous chances . . . *Othello*, I, 3.
273. It is the cause . . . *Othello*, V, 2.
274. Cytherea, How bravely . . . *Cymbeline*, II, 2.
275. I lay with Cassio . . . *Othello*, III, 3.
276. O ill-starred wench . . . *Othello*, V, 2.
279. My mother had a maid . . . *Othello*, IV, 3.
280. RODERIGO   It is silliness . . . *Othello*, I, 3.
280. Come, be a man! . . . *Othello*, I, 3.
281. In Macbeth at the Globe . . . Chambers, II, 337.
285. Fear not, Macbeth . . . *Macbeth*, V, 3.
285. A soldier, and afeard? . . . *Macbeth*, V, 1.
286. There lay Duncan . . . *Macbeth*, II, 3.
287. And pity, like a naked . . . *Macbeth*, I, 7.
288. LADY MACBETH   Out damned spot! . . . *Macbeth*, V, 1.
289. Come, seeling night . . . *Macbeth*, III, 3.
292. LEAR   Howl, howl, howl . . . *Lear*, V, 3.
294. KENT   Is this the promis'd end . . . *Lear*, V, 3.
294. O let this vile world end . . . *2 Henry VI*, V, 2.
296. I will have such revenges . . . *Lear*, II, 4.
296. EDGAR   Come on, sir . . . *Lear*, IV, 5.
298. CORDELIA   How does my royal lord . . . *Lear*, IV, 7.
299. I am bound . . . *Lear*, IV, 7.
300. LEAR   And my poor fool is hanged . . . *Lear*, V, 3.
301. We two alone . . . *Lear*, V, 3.
304. Edmund Shakespeare A Player . . . Chambers, II, 18.
305. PAINTER   You are rapt . . . *Timon of Athens*, I, 1.
305. I scorn thy meat . . . *Timon of Athens*, I, 2.
306. What a coil's here . . . *Timon of Athens*, I, 2.
306. Maid, to thy master's bed . . . *Timon of Athens*, IV, 1.
307. This yellow slave . . . *Timon of Athens*, IV, 3.
308. Common mother, thou . . . *Timon of Athens*, IV, 3.
308. The sun's a thief . . . *Timon of Athens*, IV, 3.
309. Say to Athens . . . *Timon of Athens*, IV, 1.

310. They are dissolved . . . *Coriolanus*, I, 1.
311. CITIZEN   You have deserved . . . *Coriolanus*, II, 3.
314. ENOBARBUS   The barge she sat on . . . *Antony and Cleopatra*, II, 2.
317. CLEOPATRA   His face was as the heavens . . . *Antony and Cleopatra*, V, 2.
318. CLEOPATRA   How heavy weighs my lord . . . *Antony and Cleopatra*, IV, 15.
318. CLEOPATRA   Give me my robe . . . *Antony and Cleopatra*, V, 2.
320. as it determines, so . . . *Antony and Cleopatra*, III, 13.
332. You meaner beauties . . . Sir Henry Wotton, *Reliquiae Wottonianae*.
334. Strike up, my masters . . . Bertram, *Shakespeare and the Two Noble Kinsmen*, 195.
337. O wonder! . . . *Tempest*, V, 1.
339. Did you not name . . . *Pericles*, V, 3.
339. The God of this great vast . . . *Pericles*, III, 1.
340. A terrible child-bed . . . *Pericles*, III, 2.
341. I will rob Tellus . . . *Pericles*, IV, 1.
342. I am a maid, my lord . . . *Pericles*, V, 1.
343. PERICLES   I embrace you . . . *Pericles*, V, 1.
343. You gods . . . *Pericles*, V, 3.
344. False to his bed! . . . *Cymbeline*, III, 4.
345. What should we speak of . . . *Cymbeline*, III, 3.
345. With fairest flowers . . . *Cymbeline*, IV, 2.
346. Fear no more . . . *Cymbeline*, IV, 2.
347. These flowers are like . . . *Cymbeline*, IV, 2.
348. FIRST GAOLER   A heavy reckoning . . . *Cymbeline*, V, 4.
349. Hang there like fruit . . . *Cymbeline*, V, 5.
349. Remember also the story . . . Chambers, II, 338.
350. Where then? . . . *Cymbeline*, III, 4.
352. Here's flowers for you . . . *The Winter's Tale*, IV, 4.
355. CLEOMENES   The climate's delicate . . . *The Winter's Tale*, III, 1.
355. Come, poor babe . . . *The Winter's Tale*, III, 3.
358. SHEPHERD   Here's a sight . . . *The Winter's Tale*, III, 3.
362. a little round light . . . Wright, *A Voyage to Virginia*, 12.
364. Over hill, over dale . . . *Midsummer Night's Dream*, II, 1.
365. OBERON   My gentle Puck . . . *Midsummer Night's Dream*, II, 1.
367. All torment, trouble, wonder . . . *Tempest*, V, 1.
367. ADRIAN   The air breathes . . . *Tempest*, II, 1.
369. The island's mine . . . *Tempest*, I, 2.
371. Ariel's Song . . . *Tempest*, I, 2.
372. Upon a rock . . . Marlowe, "Hero and Leander," first sestiad.
373. Leander strived . . . Marlowe, "Hero and Leander," second sestiad.
373. Ariel's Song . . . *Tempest*, I, 2.
374. Our revels now are ended . . . *Tempest*, IV, 1.
378. I am the most unhappy . . . *Henry VIII*, III, 1.
378. O Cromwell . . . *Henry VIII*, IV, 1.
379. Now to matters . . . Fripp, 781.
380. It was a great marvel . . . F. Williams, *Mr. Shakespeare at the Globe*, 373.
380. A Sonnet on the Pitiful Burning . . . H-P, I, 310.

383. Here is the end and fall . . . Cavendish, *Life and Death of Cardinal Wolsey*, 185.
383. Farewell? A long farewell . . . *Henry VIII*, III, 2.
384. I have ventured . . . *Henry VIII*, III, 2.
384. PORTER'S MAN   I missed the meteor . . . *Henry VIII*, V, 4.
384. For Goodness sake . . . *Henry VIII*, Prologue.
388. The force of the fire . . . Eccles, *Shakespeare's Warwickshire*, 135.
390. My cousin Shakespeare . . . Chambers, II, 142.
391. I also writ . . . Chambers, II, 143.
392. Master Shakespeare telling J Greene . . . Chambers, II, 143.
392. had the running of the reins . . . Chambers, II, 12.
395. They lived together on the Bankside . . . Aubrey, *Lives*, 21.
395. You are much mistaken, wench . . . Fletcher, *The Maid's Tragedy*, II, 2.
396. What a wild beast . . . Fletcher, *The Maid's Tragedy*, IV, 2.
396. PHILASTER   Oh, but thou dost not know . . . Fletcher, *Philaster*, III, 1.
397. New plays and maidenheads . . . *The Two Noble Kinsmen*, Prologue.
398. Roses, their sharp spines . . . *The Two Noble Kinsmen*, I, 1.
401. O Queen Emilia . . . *The Two Noble Kinsmen*, III, 1.
401. When we are armed . . . *The Two Noble Kinsmen*, III, 6.
403. GAOLER   Why all this haste, sir? . . . *The Two Noble Kinsmen*, IV, 2.
406. Thou mighty one . . . *The Two Noble Kinsmen*, V, 1.
406. Hail sovereign Queen of secrets . . . *The Two Noble Kinsmen*, V, 1.
414. My wife Margery . . . Fripp, II, 827.
414. Shakespeare, Drayton and Ben Jonson . . . Chambers, II, 250.
415. I have heard that Mr. Shakespeare . . . Chambers, II, 249.
425. I would inform you that this book . . . J. Q. Adams, *A Life of William Shakespeare*, 360.
426. In reading some bombast speeches . . . Ingleby, *Shakespeare Allusion Book*, II, 175.

Index of Plays and Characters

General Index